Public-Private Partnerships for Sustainable Development

Public-Private Partnerships for Sustainable Development

Special Issue Editor

Axel Marx

MDPI • Basel • Beijing • Wuhan • Barcelona • Belgrade

Special Issue Editor
Axel Marx
University of Leuven
Belgium

Editorial Office
MDPI
St. Alban-Anlage 66
4052 Basel, Switzerland

This is a reprint of articles from the Special Issue published online in the open access journal *Sustainability* (ISSN 2071-1050) from 2018 to 2019 (available at: https://www.mdpi.com/journal/ sustainability/special_issues/Public_Private_Partnerships)

For citation purposes, cite each article independently as indicated on the article page online and as indicated below:

LastName, A.A.; LastName, B.B.; LastName, C.C. Article Title. *Journal Name* **Year**, *Article Number*, Page Range.

ISBN 978-3-03897-832-9 (Pbk)
ISBN 978-3-03897-833-6 (PDF)

Cover image courtesy of pexels.com user pixabay.com.

Contents

About the Special Issue Editor

Axel Marx is Deputy Director of the Leuven Centre for Global Governance Studies, University of Leuven. He studied in Leuven, Hull, and Cambridge. He has managed over 40 funded research projects including multi-team and international FP7 and Horizon 2020 projects and acted as a consultant to several national and international organizations including the European Parliament, the European Commission, the Committee of the Regions, International Labour Organization, United Nations Industrial Development Organization, the OECD, IDEA, World Bank, the Belgian, Dutch, and German Governments. His academic publications (100+) have appeared in four dozen leading international peer-reviewed journals and six different languages (English, French, Spanish, German, Dutch, and Chinese). He has edited more than ten books and Special Issues. As a guest lecturer Axel Marx has thought inter alia at European University Institute and China University of Political Science and Law. His research interests include voluntary sustainability standards, human rights, global governance, governance through trade, EU trade policy, and comparative case methods.

Editorial

Public-Private Partnerships for Sustainable Development: Exploring Their Design and Its Impact on Effectiveness

Axel Marx

Leuven Centre for Global Governance Studies, University of Leuven, 3000 Leuven, Belgium; axel.marx@kuleuven.be

Received: 14 February 2019; Accepted: 18 February 2019; Published: 19 February 2019

Public-private partnerships for sustainable development have been in operation for several decades from the local to the international level. On the one hand they are a result of a changing nature of public policy-making. This is captured by the so-called shift from 'government' to 'governance', signaling that governments are no longer the only providers of public policy but increasingly engage private actors [1]. In this type of public-private partnerships private actors are involved in one or more of the different steps or parts of policy-making: agenda-setting, negotiation, resource provision implementation, monitoring, and/or enforcement. In this type of public-private partnerships a key policy function is delegated to private actors. One could argue that this form of public-private partnerships is still hierarchical and dominated by public policy-makers. Private actors perform functions which public actors cannot do or which private actors perform more efficiently. This form of public private partnerships complements more traditional forms of command and control policies. On the other hand, one observes the emergence of a new type of public-private partnerships in which autonomous public or private policy instruments are combined in new governance structures and arrangements. This is more a collaborative form of governance which is less structured and steered and in which autonomous policy-actors combine forces on all components of the policy-process [2–4]. This goes beyond the typical service provision private actors perform in the first type of public policy-making.

With the adoption of the 2030 Agenda for Sustainable Development and the Sustainable Development Goals (SDGs) public-private partnerships have become even more prominent. The UN agenda is a plan of action for 'people, planet, and prosperity'. The 17 Goals cover all crucial policy areas to secure a sustainable future including education, health, economic development, social protection, environmental protection, and natural resources governance. The 17 goals are operationalized in 169 targets which need to be reached by 2030 or earlier. The SDGs build on the Millennium Development Goals and aim to complete what these Millennium Development Goals did not achieve. A crucial difference between the Millennium Development Goals and Sustainable Development Goals is that the former were mainly targeted to governments while the latter target many different stakeholders including the private sector. Indeed, a shift in approach between the Millennium Development Goals and the Sustainable Development Goals is the recognition that policy objectives are best achieved by involving and integrating private actors in the policy process.

Private actors may contribute significantly towards achieving the SDGs by providing resources, expertise and knowledge, implementation and enforcement capacity, and legitimacy [5]. The United Nations and the international community recognize explicitly that achieving sustainable development will not be possible without the involvement of private sector and public-private partnerships. Currently more than 4000 partnerships are recognized and linked to one SDG or more SDGs. The effectiveness of these public-private partnerships will be crucial to achieve the SDGs. One factor which determines the effectiveness of public-private partnerships is the institutional design of these partnerships. Institutional design is defined as the rules establishing and governing an interaction between actors in a collaborative setting to achieve a specific policy goal. Significant research focuses on the design of how policy objectives are determined (agenda-setting and negotiation, monitored, implemented, and enforced) [5–7].

Another aspect of institutional design which is especially relevant for public-private partnerships focuses on how the partnerships themselves are designed. Several researchers have made databases on public-private partnerships and provided an aggregate picture of the different types of partnerships, the issues on which they focus, and the partners involved [8,9]. Less attention has focused on the different design components which are relevant in the context of a specific partnership or set of partnerships. Which actors are involved, do private actors contribute significantly to policy outcomes, does the integration of private actors in the policy process possibly create unintended effects, how are relationships between actors in a public-private partnership governed, etc. are all questions which are open to investigation and debate.

This special issue aims to identify some key insights into these questions and in how public-private collaboration for sustainability operates across the globe. The response to the call for papers resulted in a diverse set of papers which capture different ways in which public and private actors interact and how the partnerships are designed. It is interesting to observe that there seems to be distinct approaches towards public private partnerships in Europe and Asia. Four contributions focus on public-private partnerships in Asia and mainly in China. In these public-private partnerships the design is very much driven by government which integrates private components to implement policies or provide resources. In this approach private actors are brought in the policy-making process for cost-efficiency reasons or for effectiveness reasons. The papers which discuss European examples of public-private partnerships focus more on the discrete contribution private actors can make, in complementarity with public actors, to pursue sustainable development. Here, private actors might engage public actors to achieve their results.

A common thread through all contributions is that they focus on the design of the public-private partnerships and how that might relate to their performance and effectiveness. Effectiveness in this context can be operationalized on multiple dimensions. Effectiveness can refer to impact on the ground of certain projects and initiatives to reach specific policy goals (goal-attainment effectiveness, i.e. contributions by Yang; Zheng et al.; Franssen et al., and Ingram et al. this volume), lead to increased adoption of private governance mechanisms scaling up their potential impact (process-effectiveness, Marx this volume) or contribute to an increase in recognition of certain public-private initiatives as the most appropriate governance approach to address certain policy issues (constitutive effectiveness, i.e., Tellbro et al., Martens et al.; Moratis; Schouten, and Hospes this volume).

This focus on institutional design and its relationship to effectiveness builds on a longstanding stream of research which was pioneered by Elinor Ostrom [10] and further developed by 'institutional scholars'. In this volume, we focus on different aspects of design, both in terms of substance as well as procedures. In terms of substance the focus is on the degree to which public-private initiatives really take sustainability concerns, in all their dimensions, into consideration. In procedural terms, the focus is on which rules govern the design of public-private partnerships in order to make them more effective. Most contributions in the special issue focus on these procedural aspects in order to identify what works or not. Taken together, the different contributions identify several key-factors which contribute to the potential of public-private partnerships to address sustainability challenges.

A first important issue in the design of public-private partnerships is the degree to which they integrate sustainability concerns in their operations. For several initiatives this sustainability focus is the core reason for their existence and hence in these cases this is not much of an issue since their establishment is enshrined in the idea of sustainability. However, in several cases existing public-private partnerships have increasingly had to integrate sustainability concerns. If they do this insufficiently it is difficult to achieve sustainability results in the first place. This issue is explored in the paper by Cheng Chen, Dan Li and Caixia Man (*Toward Sustainable Development? A*

Bibliometric Analysis of PPP-Related Policies in China between 1980 and 2017). They provide a quantitative bibliometric analysis of 299 PPP-related policy documents issued by the Chinese central government between 1980 and 2017. They develop a framework to analyze the sustainability components of these policy documents. Sustainability is operationalized along the three traditional dimensions of ecological sustainability, social sustainability, and financial sustainability. The bibliometric analysis is conducted on policy documents which contained information about the date, title, policymaking departments, content, and effective status of the policies at issue. The paper identifies three distinct historical phases in PPP development and the role of sustainable development therein: Phase I (1980–1997), the encouragement of foreign investment in the public infrastructure, Phase II (1998–2008), the encouragement of the marketization of the urban public utilities, and Phase III (2009–2017), the intensive institutionalization and extensive application of PPPs for solving the local debt problem. Corresponding to the abovementioned policy priorities, this article finds that the pattern of PPP-related policies has shifted from the total absence of sustainable development policies in Phase I, to a few sustainable development policy attempts in Phase II, and finally, to a tendency toward policies favoring sustainable development in Phase III. It emerges that the principles of sustainable development, rather than being treated as the ultimate goals, are the side products of PPP-related policies that are aimed to achieve economic development and public financial problem-solving. Therefore, it is suggested that, in terms of establishing sustainable development as the core value of PPPs, a fundamental change in the understanding of PPPs as governance scheme rather than a pragmatic economic tool is required.

A second design factor concerns who is involved in public-private partnerships. A first question to address is whether it is always advisable to include private actors in the design of policy instruments to achieve sustainability goals. Two papers generate insights on this question. The paper by Chia-Lee Yang, Ming-Chang Shieh, Chi-Yo Huang, and Ching-Pin Tung, (*A Derivation of Factors Influencing the Successful Integration of Corporate Volunteers into Public Flood Disaster Inquiry and Notification Systems*) aims to identify the factors enabling corporate volunteers to respond to inquiries and notify the public disaster management system of flood disasters, which represent an important issue for sustainable development and require current and accurate information. This paper investigates whether systems which use private actors in monitoring and implementation perform better than systems which do not include private actors. The authors add the private and public-private dimension, defined as the collaboration between a public sector entity and a private sector entity to achieve a specific goal or set of objectives, as one of the influencing dimensions. The paper uses a number of data sources and data collection techniques and applies their framework to flood disaster notification systems in Taiwan. Experts were asked to identify possible factors enabling corporate volunteers to provide information to the flood disaster inquiry and notification system and the validity of the results were further confirmed by summarizing opinions provided by other experts. It emerged that systems which included private actors did not perform better and the integration of private actors in the design of policies only ranked low as a key component for performance. Also the systems which integrated private actors required more resources and hence were not more cost-efficient. This contribution shows that linking private and public actors is not always the most cost-efficient or effective way to achieve policy objectives.

A second paper on the integration of private actors in public policies is provided by Axel Marx on *Integrating Voluntary Sustainability Standards in Trade Policy: The Case of the European Union's GSP Scheme*. He investigates whether private governance instruments can play a role in addressing compliance gaps in public policy-making by focusing on a specific case study in EU trade policy. Trade policy is increasingly being used as a policy instrument to pursue non-trade objectives, such as environmental protection or the protection of labor rights. The paper investigates the potential role that Voluntary Sustainability Standards (VSS) can play in addressing current compliance gaps in the European Union's Generalized Scheme of Preferences (GSP). GSP is a preferential trade arrangement by which the EU grants unilateral and non-reciprocal preferential market access to goods originating in developing countries. VSS could be integrated in GSP in two ways. The first option is to allow access to the European market if products comply with VSS standards. The second option is to give tariff preferences (lower tariffs or elimination of tariffs) to VSS certified products. The overall conclusion of the paper is that it might be difficult to integrate the VSS in EU trade policy. The integration of the VSS in EU trade policy might negatively affect the utilization rate of GSP, which would result in a lesser use of GSP, and hence defeat the objectives on which GSP is built. This analysis shows that integrating private actors in public policy might create trade-offs. It might result in the fact that the private governance instruments are more adopted, but it might defeat the objectives of public trade policy due to a lower use of a specific trade instrument. This paper illustrates some of the limitations of integrating private mechanisms in public policies in the case of trade policy.

Also linked to the debate on the integration of private actors in public-private partnerships is the question of how inclusive public-private partnerships are in relation to the private actors who are involved in the partnerships. This issue is addressed in the paper by Deborah Martens, Annelien Gansemans, Jan Orbie, and Marijke D'Haess (*Trade Unions in Multi-Stakeholder Initiatives: What Shapes Their Participation?*). They examine the determinants that enable and constrain trade union participation in multi-stakeholder initiatives (MSIs) designed to improve social and environmental sustainability in global supply chains. For this purpose, the authors develop an analytical framework that takes into account both the structure of the MSI as well as the agency of the participant. Based on interviews, focus groups, observations, and document analysis the authors determine local trade union participation in three MSIs, operating at company, national, and transnational level respectively, in the Costa Rican pineapple industry. The interdisciplinary research presented in this paper is based on 37 semi-structured interviews with various actors from different stakeholder categories, three focus groups with trade union members, eight non-participant observations missions, and document analysis. Extensive field research was conducted in Costa Rica (2015–2016) with Costa Rican representatives and in Belgium (2015–2017) with EU representatives. These two rounds of data collection were followed-up by interviews in 2018 to collect additional information on the concerned multi-stakeholder initiatives for this case study. The findings endorse the concern that MSIs are not as inclusive as they aspire or pretend to be. Physical attendance does not necessarily imply participants will be heard. To achieve a better quality of participation and deliberation, power inequalities among its participants should be addressed by improving MSI design. First, the selection criteria for participation to the MSI should be clearly predefined and ensure the representativeness of the participants. Stakeholders should be identified together with a mapping of potential conflicts, expectations, and their power resources. Second, regarding procedural fairness, clear goals and rules of decision-making should be set from the start and agreed by all stakeholders, stronger and weaker stakeholders alike. Third, concerning the consensual orientation in MSIs, the authors see that building trust between actors with divergent positions is challenging. Therefore, the format of MSIs should recognize existing power differences and facilitate a rapprochement between business and unions, for example through small working groups and capacity-building events. The analysis also indicates that the design of an MSI is not all-decisive as insights on trade union power resources also helped to explain their participation. Also strong network embeddedness and improved infrastructural resources enhanced trade union participation, whereas the lack of internal solidarity and unfavorable narrative resources had a negative effect on their participation. This implies for practitioners involved in MSIs that improving the design of MSIs is necessary but not sufficient to enhance trade union participation. Unions need to mobilize their resources and the willingness and commitment of all participants in the MSI to meaningfully engage in deliberation. The authors call for a continuous evaluation of MSI participatory processes (regarding representativeness, procedural fairness, and consensual orientation) and strengthening of union power resources (internal solidarity, network embeddedness, narrative and infrastructural resources). From an institutional design perspective this paper clearly shows how design is influenced by dynamics in the partnership as well as dynamics within one partner in the partnership. In order to achieve inclusiveness, partnerships have to develop a clear strategy which also provides incentives for specific actors to join in.

The latter, the incentives and motivational aspects of private actors to engage in public private partnerships is further explored by Shengqin Zheng, Ke Xu, Qing He, Shaoze Fang, and Lin Zhang (*Investigating the Sustainability Performance of PPP-Type Infrastructure Projects: A Case of China*). They focus on the proliferation of public-private partnership (PPP) in China. Their focus is less on the implementation part of policies and more on agenda-setting and revenue-generation to facilitate policy-making. PPPs, as an innovative procurement mode, have been playing a vital role in developing public infrastructures in China. The demand for public infrastructure is continuously increasing due to the acceleration of urbanization and the rapid growth of the economy. Faced with the shortage of funds, governments are compelled to seek cooperation from private sectors who can provide a large number of funds, to participate in public infrastructure construction. As a result, PPP has experienced a rapid expansion and a boom period for the last five years in China. However, the authors argue that a series of social issues arise when an increasing number of PPPs are applied in infrastructure development due to profit-seeking behavior of private actors. As a result the paper aims to understand whether and how behaviors of private actors in PPPs influence the execution of the project with specific attention towards sustainability concerns. They show that there might be serious sustainability concerns in the current PPPs approach in infrastructure development and provide a series of suggestions, both to governments and private actors, on how to address them.

Besides the issue of which actors are involved in the public-private partnership, their interrelation is also important, and constitutes a third design component. By engaging in public-private partnerships actors develop relations which will influence the outcome of their collaboration. Several papers engage on this issue.

First, there is the issue of how the partnership is governed and who takes the lead. Camilla Thellbro, Therese Bjärstig, and Katarina Eckerberg (*Drivers for Public-Private Partnerships in Sustainable Natural Resource Management—Lessons from the Swedish Mountain Region*) focus on environmental partnerships which aim to improve the environmental quality or natural resource utilization. They are especially interested in factors contributing to the success of PPPs with a specific focus on leadership, incentives, and previous projects. The authors examine the shaping of participation, leadership, and the implementation of partnering processes on natural resource management of environmental PPPs in the Swedish mountain region. This study builds upon 38 semi-structured interviews with representatives from environmental PPPs in the Swedish mountain region randomly selected from a database of 245 public-private collaborative projects. The interviews were compiled according to contextual variables and four essential drivers: leadership, consequential incentives, interdependence, and uncertainty. Leadership refers to a present and identified leader who holds a position that allows him/her to initiate and aid in securing resources and support for a collaborative arrangement; consequential incentives are positive or negative incentives that make leaders and participants engage collectively; interdependence is the driver when individuals and organizations cannot achieve their objectives on their own; uncertainty can drive parties to collaborate in order to reduce, spread, and share risk(s). This case study of the Swedish mountain region shows that the mountain municipalities have an important facilitating role with regard to the leadership driver. Furthermore, the authors identified consequential incentives as being a major driver for most of the PPPs, where funding, a previous successful collaboration, and the presence of an issue/area that otherwise would not be handled stood out as the main reasons. Shared engagement and responsibility were also put forward by the respondents to some extent, suggesting that interdependence and uncertainty are indeed important drivers, but often function as intermediate drivers and/or in combination with the two main drivers: leadership and consequential incentives.

Second, there is the issue of the nature of the relationship between the actors and how that influences the performance of public-private partnerships. The paper by Xiaodan Zheng, Jingfeng Yuan, Jiyue Guo, Mirosław J. Skibniewski, and Sujun Zhao (*Influence of Relational Norms on User Interests in PPP Projects: Mediating Effect of Project Performance*) focuses on how mutual relations relate to performance and effectiveness. Using a sample of 109 questionnaires from Chinese project professionals who had experience with public-private partnership projects, this paper examines the relationships between the public and private actors, the norms shaping this relation (flexibility, information exchange and solidarity) their impact on project performance and how they shape the interests of different users of public-private partnership projects. The results show that relational norms between the public and private sectors had a positive relationship with project performance, and project performance could facilitate the protection of the interests of different users. The different dimensions of the relational norms between actors all contribute towards improving project performance. This is because the public and private sectors can flexibly adjust to changing environmental conditions, can share information to reduce mutual suspicion and conflicts, and can make decisions based on project interests rather than self-interest. As a result, good relational norms between private and public actors can have a direct positive effect on user interests through improving project performance. The argument is further substantiated by a specific case study which focuses on the Hong Kong Western Harbor Tunnel PPP project.

This focus on trust underlying actor relationship has been long established in the literature on inter-organizational cooperation [11]. This is a very important aspect of relationships in public-private partnerships since partners are of a very different nature. Continued support by public actors might make the public-private partnership more effective. Greetje Schouten and Otto Hospes (*Public and Private Governance in Interaction: Changing Interpretations of Sovereignty in the Field of Sustainable Palm Oil*) analyze how states that are connected to different positions of a global value chain interpret sovereignty over a longer period of time in their interactions with transnational private governance. The paper focuses on the interactions of Indonesian and Dutch state actors with the Roundtable on Sustainable Palm Oil (RSPO), which is a global private governance initiative that developed sustainability standards for the palm oil industry. Indonesia was selected as it is the biggest palm oil producer in the world, and the Netherlands, as the biggest importer of palm oil in Europe. Schouten and Hospes identify two distinctive episodes in which the type of interactions taking place between the Indonesian or Dutch state actors and the RSPO shifted significantly. The first episode took place during the rule formation process of the RSPO (2003–2009). During this time, the Indonesian government was willing to share the control of cross-border flows of palm oil with a private regulatory arrangement and implicitly practiced a notion of interdependence sovereignty, in which state and non-state actors shared control over cross-border flows of goods. In this first time lapse also the Dutch government used and interpreted sovereignty in the same ways as the Indonesian one and the RSPO was seen as sovereign over the global palm oil value chain. The second episode started with the announcement and development of a national Indonesian standard: the Indonesian Sustainable Palm Oil (ISPO) standard (2010–2017). The Indonesian government explicitly distanced itself from the RSPO and established a competing sustainability standard. The changing nature of the interactions indicates that the notions of interdependence sovereignty have faded, and have been replaced by notions of domestic and Westphalian sovereignty: the Indonesian government no longer wants to share sovereignty over the sustainability of palm oil that is produced on its territory. To the contrary, the Dutch government maintained its collaborative and supportive attitude toward the RSPO, assuming that a sustainable palm oil supply chain for the world can only be achieved if all of the public and private stakeholders work together in a coherent way according to each role and responsibility. The paper shows that sovereignty is not a static concept; instead, it is used strategically by different state actors and its use changes over time. When the Indonesian government realized that the RSPO might actually hamper the economic interests of Indonesian producers, they began to interact differently with the RSPO and started to develop a national standard. The development of rival standards by producing countries may create a further differentiation and fragmentation of the governance of sustainable agricultural commodities, especially when consuming states focus solely on promoting private voluntary standards. Aligning the public strategies of different countries and private strategies with one another might increase regulatory coherence to increase sustainable practices in global value chains.

This 'relational' component of institutional design focuses on the relationship between actors 'within' a partnership. There is a third component of the institutional design which looks at how the partnership interacts with other actors, mainly the object or target of their initiative. In regulatory governance this is often referred to as the rule-taker. Different types of relationships can unfold between the partnership and the rule-taker depending on the perceived effectiveness of the partnership. This is explored in two papers, which provide for a rule-takers perspective. In a first paper, Lars Moratis (*Signalling Responsibility? Applying Signalling Theory to the ISO 26000 Standard for Social Responsibility*) starts from the observation that voluntary standards involving governments, non-governmental organizations, and companies have gained much traction in recent years and from a firm perspective, sustainability standards can be a way to demonstrate that they engage in corporate social responsibility (CSR) in a credible way. To capitalize on their CSR activities, firms need to ensure their stakeholders are able to recognize and assess their CSR quality. However, because the relative observability of CSR is low and since CSR is a contested concept, information asymmetries in a firm-stakeholder relationship arise. Adopting CSR standards and using these as signaling devices is a strategy for firms to reduce these information asymmetries, by revealing their true CSR quality. This paper investigates the voluntary ISO 26000 standard for social responsibility as a form of public-private governance and contends that, despite its objectives, this standard suffers from severe signaling problems. By applying signaling theory to the ISO 26000 standard, this article takes a critical stance towards this standard and argues that firms adhering to this standard may actually emit signals that compromise rather than enhance stakeholders' ability to identify and interpret firms' underlying CSR quality. Moratis concludes that firms, their stakeholders, governments, and organizations involved in the standardization of business conduct should be aware of the signals firms emit by ISO 26000 in order to not let the standard become part of the problems it set out to solve and exacerbate rather than reduce problems in public-private governance.

The second paper by Verina Ingram, Fedes van Rijn, Yuca Waarts, and Henk Gilhuis (*The Impacts of Cocoa Sustainability Initiatives in West Africa*) looks at the social, economic, and environmental effects of public-private-civil society partnerships of stakeholders, which try to implement voluntary sustainability standards and corporate initiatives in the cocoa sector. They focus on the 'rule-takers' in the cocoa sector. The paper is based on empirical evidence from large-scale, mixed-method studies using a suite of socioeconomic, agronomic, and environmental indicators to compare the situation of UTZ certified with non-certified farmers in 2012 and 2015 in Ghana, and 2013 and 2017 in Ivory Coast. The UTZ standard focuses on mainstreaming sustainability in farming practices, promoting the improvement of farmer's agricultural and management practices, with a chain of custody approaches, traceability, and transparency reflecting concerns by consumers and NGOs about chain governance. Seven of the main trader-exporters and processors in West Africa have adopted UTZ and, often, a second certification scheme. The study uses a large sample of stakeholders in the two largest cocoa producing countries, rigorous quantitative and qualitative methods to investigate the impacts of voluntary certification, and the related package of services, to understand what has been the impact of sustainability-focused interventions on cocoa farmers in West Africa. To analyze the contribution of sustainability initiatives to farmer livelihoods, panel data were collected from over 778 cocoa farming households in Ghana and the Ivory Coast between 2012 and 2017 and 18 focus group interviews with farmers, and 22 interviews with other stakeholders in the value chain were conducted. Two rounds of farmer household surveys were implemented in each country among UTZ and non-certified farmers. The results show that, on average, outcomes are mixed and generally modest. However, significant cocoa productivity and income increases were experienced by certified farmers receiving a full package of services. However, the type and intensity of services have changed over time, decreasing for half of the farmers, and productivity and income increases are leveling off. These findings suggest that whilst partnerships have created new governance arrangements with an increased focus on sustainable value chains, initiatives which result in a living income and optimize productivity, whilst limiting environmental impacts, require sectoral transformation, continued partnerships, plus a range of other policy instruments to address the persistent problems in cocoa production.

Finally, on the topic of inter-organizational relations between public and private actors it is also interesting to analyze how they interact on a more aggregate level, i.e. in a more wide and complex network of international actors which aim to address global public policy objectives such as environmental protection. This is precisely the focus of the paper by Luc Fransen, Jelmer Schalk, Marcel Kok, Vivek Voora, Jason Potts, Max Joosten, Philip Schleifer, and Graeme Auld on (*Biodiversity Protection through Networks of Voluntary Sustainability Standard Organizations*). They investigate the degree to which Voluntary Sustainability Standard (VSS–private actors) policies can contribute positively to biodiversity protection. It examines the degree to which VSS organizations' current connections with one another, with other non-governmental parties, and with intergovernmental treaties, laws, and organizations allow for collectively advancing biodiversity goals. The study first draws from datasets from Fransen, which focused on VSS organizations governing global agro-commodity chains, such as coffee, tea, cocoa, sugar, palm oil, cotton, soy, and flowers. Information from this dataset is complemented with data on these commodities from the International Institute for Sustainable Development Sustainability Standards Initiative report on standards and biodiversity, the International Trade Centre's Standards Map data, and the study by Tayleur et al. [12] on the location of agriculture-focused VSS organization standard-compliant areas. Combining these four data sources allowed the authors to analyze 11 relevant VSS focused on agro-commodities and how they interact with other actors, most notably public organizations. To gauge their significance, authors rank VSS organizations according to three criteria: the amount of hectares covered by a VSS in terms of standard-compliant areas; the proximity of standard-compliant areas to so-called biodiversity hotspots, i.e., regions with significant biodiversity under threat of destruction; and the stringency of biodiversity criteria in the implementation of a given VSS. They conclude that only a few VSS organizations are in a promising position to potentially contribute through their policy-making to biodiversity protection goals. At the same time, based on the analysis of network positions, VSS organizational links to relevant biodiversity actors and institutions are still quite scarce, signaling that their ability to engage in collaborative policy-making and policy exchange with relevant biodiversity policymakers is, at present, limited. Currently, most of these VSS organizations have relatively few ties with the relevant governmental and intergovernmental biodiversity policymakers. At present, their policy networks, in terms of actors, reflect an orientation towards nongovernmental rather than governmental organizations, and, substantively, an orientation towards developmental rather than environmental protection issues.

Taken together these contributions provide insights into the different aspects of the design of public-private partnerships and how their effectiveness might be affected. First, there is a question as to what degree partnerships internalize and operationalize norms and standards in relation to the sustainability which they want to pursue. Second, there is an important component of public-private partnerships which addresses who is involved in a public-private partnership, how they are governed, and which inter-organizational relationships are established. Third, public-private partnerships interact with other parties, rule-takers or rule-targets. This can have different forms and different outcomes. Finally, public-private partnerships operate in a broader context of inter-organizational relations within a specific policy-field. How they operate in a complex web of policy-actors will also determine their effectiveness.

Funding: Work on this special issue was made possible by funding from the Belgian Ministry of Foreign Affairs—Directorate-General for Development Cooperation and VLIR (Flemish Inter-university Council) under the KLIMOS Project.

Conflicts of Interest: The author declares no conflict of interest.

Sustainability **2019**, *11*, 1087

References

1. Rosenau, J.R. Governance in the Twenty-first Century. *Glob. Gov.* **1995**, *1*, 13–43.
2. Lambin, E.F.; Meyfroidt, P.; Rueda, X.; Blackman, A.; Börner, J.; Cerutti, P.O.; Dietsch, T.; Jungmann, L.; Lamarque, P.; Lister, J.; et al. Effectiveness and Synergies of Policy Instruments for Land Use Governance in Tropical Regions. *Glob. Environ. Chang.* **2014**, *28*, 129–140. [CrossRef]
3. Lambin, E.; Thorlakson, T. Sustainability Standards: Interactions between private actors, civil society and governments. *Annu. Rev. Environ. Resour.* **2018**, *43*, 369–393. [CrossRef]
4. Eberlein, B.; Abbott, K.; Black, J.; Meidinger, E.; Wood, S. Transnational Business Governance Interactions: conceptualization and framework for analysis. *Regul. Gov.* **2014**, *8*, 1–21. [CrossRef]
5. Abbott, K.W.; Levi-faur, D.; Snidal, D. Theorizing Regulatory Intermediaries. *Ann. Am. Acad. Political Soc. Sci.* **2017**, *670*, 14–35. [CrossRef]
6. Marx, A.; Wouters, J. Redesigning enforcement in private labor regulation. Will it work? *Int. Labor Rev.* **2016**, *155*, 435–459. [CrossRef]
7. Marx, A. Varieties of Legitimacy: A Configurational Institutional Design Analysis of Eco-labels. *Innov. Eur. J. Soc. Sci. Res.* **2013**, *26*, 268–287. [CrossRef]
8. Mert, A. Sustainable Development Partnerships in the UN System. In *Networks for Prosperity: Advancing Sustainability through Partnerships*; UNIDO/University of Leuven: Leuven, Belgium, 2015; pp. 55–67.
9. Pattberg, P.; Chan, M.; Mert, A.; Biermann, F. *Public-private Partnerships for Sustainable Development: Emergence, Influence and Legitimacy*; Edward Elgar: Cheltenham, UK, 2012.
10. Ostrom, E. *Governing the Commons*; Cambridge University Press: Cambridge, UK, 1990.
11. Uzzi, B. The Sources and Consequences of Embeddedness for the Economic Performance of Organizations: The Network Effect. *Am. Sociol. Rev.* **1996**, *61*, 674–698. [CrossRef]
12. Tayleur, C.; Balmford, A.; Buchanan, G.M.; Butchart, S.H.; Walker, C.C.; Ducharme, H.; Tracewski, L. Where are commodity crops certified, and what does it mean for conservation and poverty alleviation? *Boil. Conserv.* **2018**, *217*, 36–46. [CrossRef]

Article

Toward Sustainable Development? A Bibliometric Analysis of PPP-Related Policies in China between 1980 and 2017

Cheng Chen [1], Dan Li [2,*] and Caixia Man [3]

[1] Center for Chinese Public Administration Research, Sun Yat-sen University, Guangzhou 510275, China; chench92@mail.sysu.edu.cn
[2] School of Public Administration, South China University of Technology, Guangzhou 510641, China
[3] School of Public Administration and Policy, Renmin University of China, Beijing 100872, China; mancx@ruc.edu.cn
* Correspondence: lidanlily@126.com; Tel.: +86-020-8711-2562

Received: 26 November 2018; Accepted: 22 December 2018; Published: 28 December 2018

Abstract: This article aims to fill the void in the literature regarding the sustainable development of public–private partnerships (PPPs) by answering the following research questions: (1) Between 1980 and 2017, what were the PPP-related policy priorities in the three different historical phases of the Chinese national agenda that we have identified herein? (2) Have the PPP-related policies shown a pattern of moving toward sustainable development, and if so, to what extent? Against a criteria framework of evaluating how PPP-related policies could contribute to sustainable development, this article conducted a quantitative bibliometric analysis of 299 PPP-related policy documents issued by the Chinese central government between 1980 and 2017. By visualizing the networks of policy keywords and policy-issuing departments, this article identified the PPP-related policy priorities in the following three distinct historical phases: Phase I (1980–1997), the encouragement of foreign investment in the public infrastructure; Phase II (1998–2008), the encouragement of the marketization of the urban public utilities; and Phase III (2009–2017), the intensive institutionalization and extensive application of PPPs for solving the local debt problem. Corresponding to the abovementioned policy priorities, this article found that the pattern of PPP-related policies has shifted from the total absence of sustainable development policies in Phase I, to a few sustainable development policy attempts in Phase II, and finally, to a tendency toward policies favoring sustainable development in Phase III.

Keywords: bibliometric analysis; China; PPPs; policy changes; sustainable development

1. Introduction

Public–private partnerships (PPPs) can be defined as "agreements where public sector bodies enter into long-term contractual agreements in which private parties participate in, or provide support for the provision of infrastructure and public service" [1]. Since the 1980s, China has adopted PPPs in the public service sector, particularly in the area of public infrastructure. Correspondingly, the Chinese central government has issued PPP-related policies since 1980. Based on a collection of 299 PPP-related policy documents from 1980 to 2017, this article aims to explore two specific research questions as follows: (1) Between 1980 and 2017, what were the PPP-related policy priorities in the different historical phases of the Chinese national agenda? (2) Have the PPP-related policies shown a pattern of moving toward sustainable development, and if so, to what extent?

By answering these two research questions, this article has two research objectives.

One research objective is to respond to the concerns about how to assess the extent to which PPP-related policies have contributed to sustainable development in China.

PPPs have been recognized internationally as an important tool of achieving sustainable development. The United Nations (UN), one of the most important international organizations to promote worldwide sustainability, called for the use and improvement of PPPs for sustainable development with UN Sustainable Development Goals (SDGs) and the 2030 Agenda for Sustainable Development [2]. In 2017, the UN Economic Commission for Europe (UNECE) published a conference room paper, which served as a draft of the guiding principles on people-first PPPs in connection to the UN SDGs; this conference room paper provided eight specific principles regarding PPPs for the purposes of working toward sustainable development [3].

China has actively responded to the advocacies of the UN. The first call for sustainable development in China was in the Chinese National Agenda 21 of 1994, which clearly raised the specific objectives of achieving sustainable development in China and echoed the principles of the UN Agenda 21 [4]. In 2016, responding to the UN's 2030 Agenda for Sustainable Development, China published the "National Plan on Implementation of the 2030 Agenda for Sustainable Development" [5]. This national plan stated for the first time that China will actively promote PPPs to facilitate the development of social resources for sustainable development. The political rhetoric above has raised concerns about how to assess whether the formal regulations and policies regarding PPPs have provided sufficient guidance for PPPs to influence sustainable development in China. This article aims to address this concern.

The second research objective is to fill in the research gap of PPPs, in the following two aspects.

Firstly, while there has existed a relatively well-developed body of research regarding PPPs, the perspective of sustainable development has not obtained enough attention in the current state of knowledge. In the last two decades, the extant literatures of PPPs have covered various aspects. Based on a bibliometric analysis of PPPs and PFI literature, de Castro e Silva Neto et al. figured out a list of research topics that covered the majority of the present PPPs' themes from 1990 to 2014, sequencing as contract performance, qualitative costs and benefits, contract design and risk sharing, PPP/PFI political and institutional issues, value for money (VFM, see Appendix A 1) test, stakeholder management, contract management, accountability, financing PPP/PFIs projects, procurement model, renegotiation and dispute resolution, literature review, environmental issues, and contract termination [6]. In the literature review of PPPs from public management perspective, Wang et al. identified the research focuses on PPPs concept, risk sharing amongst PPPs participants, the drivers of PPPs adoption and PPPs performance [7]. In the latest review of PPPs for the last two decades, Hodge and Greve concluded the following aspects of PPPs literatures: economics of PPPs; project finance and management of PPPs, which mainly look at the risk management, financial and economic visibility in the project level; and political, public management and social aspects of PPPs, mainly raised the issues about accountability, governance of PPPs. As shown in the above literature reviews, the perspective of sustainable development is not yet at the core of current research; however, it deserves much more attention in future research agendas. As Hodge and Greve pointed out that, the research ideas of PPPs have evolved from early technical issues and narrow disciplinary lenses towards far broader sets of concerns [8]. Obviously, as a cross-disciplinary governance issue, PPPs for sustainable development is one of these concerns. This article, by distinguishing "PPPs for sustainable development" and "PPPs via a sustainable approach" and connecting these two aspects to ecological, social and financial sustainability, aims to fill in this research gap.

Secondly, in the existing research regarding PPPs and sustainable development [9,10], there is little work exploring the institutional arrangements of PPPs, mainly consisting of policies and regulations, from the perspective of sustainability. The current relevant research has tended to focus on developing indicators from the concept of sustainability and applying them onto the evaluation of PPPs performance [10–12]; providing empirical assessment about whether and how PPPs lead to sustainable development [13–15]; and debating the role of PPPs in sustainable development [16–18]. While the above extant research has provided insightful thoughts on PPPs and sustainable development, an important aspect of understanding PPPs—policies and regulations for PPPs—has not obtained more attention in the research agenda. As Koppenjan and Enserink argued, the contribution of PPPs to sustainability depends on the quality of the policies and regulations by which the private contributions are regulated and the extent to which regulation issues are recognized and acted on [16]. Hodge and Greve also argued that the attention of researchers ought to be turning to 'politics of PPPs'—in which political governance and formal institutional arrangement to steer and regulate PPPs deserve future attention [19]. This article, with the focuses on PPP-related policies and sustainable development, aims to provide the first bibliometric analysis of PPP-related policies to explore whether and to what extent the institutional arrangements of PPPs have shown a pattern of moving toward sustainable development.

The article is structured as follows. In the next section, we design a criteria framework by which to evaluate the extent to which PPP-related policies move toward sustainable development. In Section 3, the research methods are presented. The findings are presented in Section 4, followed by our conclusions and discussions in Section 5.

2. PPP-Related Policies and Sustainable Development

In order to evaluate whether the policies have shown the pattern of moving toward sustainable development, this section aims to establish a criteria framework for determining what criteria could be developed to evaluate PPP-related policies for sustainable development in China. It is important to set up this framework, because although the role of PPPs for sustainable development has been justified in extant literature, how and in what way PPPs and PPP-related policies could contribute to sustainable development are still hard to identify due to the lack of a concrete criteria framework.

This framework firstly developed the concept of sustainability into ecological sustainability, social sustainability and financial sustainability [20]. Then these three aspects of sustainability are integrated into two dimensions. The dimension of "PPPs for sustainable development" refers to whether the PPP-related policies encourage PPPs to be used for ecological and social sustainable development. The dimension of "PPPs via a sustainable approach" refers to whether the PPP-related policies encourage PPPs to be used via ecologically, socially, and financially sustainable approaches. Therefore, five criteria are developed in this framework (see Table 1). PPPs for financial sustainability are not applicable here, as financial sustainability is a concept regarding the approach rather than the sector. We discuss these five criteria below, drawing on the extant literature regarding the benefits and limitations of PPPs, and the management of PPPs in various countries in achieving sustainable development.

Table 1. Criteria framework for identifying and categorizing PPP-related policies moving toward sustainable development.

Sustainability	PPPs for Sustainable Development	PPPs via a Sustainable Approach
Ecological sustainability	Policies that encourage PPPs to be used for ecological/environmental protection projects.	Policies that demand that PPPs be used via an environmentally friendly approach, such as the innovative use of a resource or environmentally friendly technologies.
Social sustainability	Policies that encourage PPPs to be used for social infrastructure and service projects.	Policies that demand that PPPs be used via a transparent and due process approach.
Financial sustainability	Not applicable.	Policies that demand that PPPs be used via a financially sustainable approach, such as the VFM test and the financial affordability test and forbidding government guarantees

2.1. PPPs for Sustainable Development

The dimension of "PPPs for sustainable development" contains two criteria, examining whether PPP-related policies have encouraged PPPs to be applied to 1) ecological infrastructure and services, which refer to projects and services for protecting the natural environment; 2) social infrastructure and services, which refer to projects and services for households, intending to improve the quality of life and welfare in a community, such as schools, hospitals, and health services.

These criteria are inspired by the increasing trend of using PPPs in social and ecological sector in various countries. With the rise of the concern regarding sustainable development and the benefits and advantages of PPPs in ecological and social infrastructure and services provision [21], the practices of PPPs in various countries have increasingly moved from the traditional economic sector to the provision of ecological and social infrastructure and services [17,21]. For example, the European Union (EU) countries and the United States of American (USA) have promoted PPPs as an approach to environmental protection and poverty eradication [22]. Australia is one of the most advanced countries in adopting PPPs to deliver social services, covering health, education, social housing, correction, and justice [23,24]. In Canada, the Ministry of Finance carried out a 10-year investment plan for social infrastructure starting from 2016, including affordable housing, early learning and childcare, cultural and recreational infrastructure, and safe public health care facilities. For developing countries, although economic infrastructure is still the priority of PPPs, the social and environmental sectors were gradually considered into plans. In Chile, there are three phases of the PPPs concessions development. From 1991 to 1994 Chile focused on expanding its highway networks. From 1995 to 2002, Chile's government focused on the construction of urban highways and airports. From 2003 to 2010, Chile's government started to pay attention on building social infrastructure such as hospitals, prisons, and public buildings [23]. In India, so far, although private investment has been confined to economic infrastructure with high value, governments have started to include social and environmental sectors such as water and wastewater services into PPP plans to attract the attention of private capital [25,26].

2.2. PPPs via Sustainable Approach

Although the benefits claimed above, a significant number of studies have raised concerns over the limitations and problems of PPPs, such as the ambiguous outcome, high transaction costs between stakeholders or the cost compared to government borrowing [18,27,28]. Such mixed evidence shows that the benefits of PPPs in environmental and social infrastructure and services do not automatically contribute to sustainable development, unless the limitations and problems occurred in the design and management of PPPs can be mitigated, in other words, unless the management of PPPs itself is sustainable. This is where the dimension of 'PPPs via a sustainable approach' is derived from.

PPPs via an ecologically sustainable approach evaluates whether the policies have encouraged environmentally friendly technologies such as the innovative use of natural resources or environmentally friendly technologies in the process of implementing a PPPs project. This criterion is derived from the experience from various countries. For example, the United Kingdom (UK) published "green public–private partnerships" outlining steps that can be taken within a PPPs or PFI project, to incorporate environmental considerations. These steps in incorporating green issues, such as reducing the use of energy, water and other resources, minimizing waste and controlling pollution and other quality objectives, are required to be instigated at the specification stage, and selecting bidders and awarding contracts stage [29]. Also, in USA, Canada, Europe, Japan, and South Korea, incentives such as certification payment, tax reduction, financial support for green component technologies, and interest rate reduction have been incorporated into policies [30].

PPPs via a socially sustainable approach evaluates whether the policies have guaranteed the transparency and due process that ensure equal and effective collaboration among the stakeholders, that are, the public sector, the private partners, and citizens. PPPs are complex organizational structures embedded in the intensive tension among stakeholders with different knowledge, divergent goals and values, and stark differences in organizational experience [31]. Either the public sector or the private sector has the tendency to show opportunistic behavior owing to information asymmetry [32,33]. Furthermore, "in the absence of the information, the political purchase of huge infrastructure projects will continue to leave citizens open to political and commercial trade off. If the price is higher than it needs to be, citizens inevitably pay" [34]. Echoing on the above reflection, many countries have realized the necessity of setting up a clear and transparent process for procurement and implementation of PPPs projects. Australia sets up a clear and transparent procurement process for large-scale social infrastructure projects with well-understood procurement policy methodologies and guidelines [35]. Chile establishes a concession process in order to remain clear, transparent and fair so that the private sector can know the criteria in the evaluation of the offer and contracts that are open for the public access [23]. The India government has specifically emphasized the need for promoting sustainable and inclusive growth and mandated the need to involve people in PPPs projects, and proposed the need to structure an innovative procurement model in the form of PPPP (People Public–Private Partnership) [10,36].

PPPs via financially sustainable approach evaluates whether the policies have required the VFM test, long-term financial affordability test in project design and forbidding government guarantees on private returns at the cost of the financial interests of future generations. This approach draws on the discussion about the project finance of PPPs, which is one of the critical issues in PPPs literatures [8]. Originating in the UK, VFM test has become a common method to justify PPPs approach in international experience [37–39]. Also in the UK, before any VFM tests are performed, a long-term affordability test is required to detect whether the government has the ability to keep its responsibilities without jeopardizing the economic sustainability of the system [40]. In Australia, Canada, Ireland, and the Netherlands, the VFM, which requires time and cost efficiency, great assurance of income, innovation, and the effort to release public sector resources, has become one of the key factors for government adopting the PPPs model [23,41–45]. In South Africa, a VFM test is mandatory before bids are presented [40]. In India, the decision to opt for PPPs as the preferred route is primarily based on the outcome of VFM test [10]. Furthermore, the criterion of forbidding government guarantees is derived from the review of the overuse of guarantees at the price of future finance interests in many countries, such as water projects in Bolivia, Chile, Argentina, and Hungary, Sydney Airlink BOOT project in Australia, and Channel Tunnel project in the UK and France [46–50].

3. Methodology

This article collected 299 PPP-related policies and regulations promulgated by the Chinese State Council and its affiliated departments between 1980 and 2017 as the sample for this research. The policy documents between 1980 and 2012 were mainly collected from the Law-lib Database (see Appendix A 2) and supplemented by resources collected from the official websites of various ministries and departments. The major collection of PPP-related policies since 2013 were mainly from the website of China Public–Private Partnerships Center (CPPPC) under the Ministry of Finance (MoF) (see Appendix A 3) and the website of PPPs Column under the National Development and Reform Commission (NRDC) (see Appendix A 4).

We selected these policies and regulations based on three criteria that policies can fall into. (1) Specific policies that directly guide or restrict PPPs introduction, employment and operation, such as the policy entitled "Notice on Attracting Foreign Investment via Build-Operate-Transfer (BOT)" issued by the Ministry of Foreign Trade and Economic Cooperation (MFTEC) in 1995 and the policy in name of "Notice on Promoting Public–Private Partnership Model" issued by the MoF in 2014 which offer guidance for the operation of PPP projects. (2) Macro financial regulation policies that generally facilitate PPPs development through investment, fiscal and financial system reform, such as the policy entitled "Notice on the Issuance of a Recent Plan of Investment Management System Reform" in 1988 and the policy of "Notice on Strengthening Local Government Financing Vehicles (LGFVs) Management" (see Appendix A 5) issued by the State Council in 2010 which paved the way for further PPPs development. (3) Specific local government debts regulation policies, calling for PPPs as a substitution to local government debt in providing financial resources, such as the policy of "Notice on Strengthening LGFVs Management" issued by the State Council in 2010, the policy of "Advice on Strengthening Management of Local Government Debts" released by the State Council in 2014, and the policy of "Notice on Budgetary Controlling and Cleaning Up the Stock of Local Government Debts" put forward by the MoF in 2014.

For the interest of the research questions, this article conducted a bibliometric analysis on these policy documents. These 299 policy documents contained information about the date, title, policymaking department(s), content, and effective status of the policies at issue. Therefore, the patterns of PPP-related policies in each phase were mapped out by social network analysis (SNA) through visualizing the co-keyword network of the policy contents and the interdepartmental cooperation network of the policies.

To present the co-keyword network of the policy contents, we started by labeling no more than three keywords for each policy. The keywords were mainly extracted from the titles and inferred from the policy contents, particularly the paragraphs of introduction, which clearly convey policy intention. For those keywords conveyed the same meaning but were expressed in different ways, we assigned them the same name. For the other keywords abstracted, we just left them as same as expressed in the original policies. The keywords were selected and crosschecked by the authors after several rounds of discussion and screening. We used SATI 3.2 (see Appendix A 6) to construct a co-occurrence matrix of keywords and then imported the matrix into UCINET 6 (see Appendix A 7) to visualize the co-occurrence network of the keywords, in which the different subgroups were clustered. Within these networks, the nodes represented the keywords, and the links represented the co-occurrence among the keywords. These nodes were sized by their degree centrality, which was viewed as an important index of the central position in the network. The degree centrality measures the frequency of a given keyword's co-occurrence with other keywords [51,52]. The bigger the size of the nodes, the higher the degree centrality of the keywords, which meant that these keywords had more co-appearance with other keywords in different policy documents and received more attention by the policymakers. Furthermore, we conducted cluster analysis based on Girvan–Newman's algorithm (see Appendix A 8) in UCINET 6, to cluster these connected keywords into different subgroups, marked with different colors. The cluster analysis was derived from the concept of betweenness centrality, which measured the time a node represented as an intermediary pathway between two other nodes. This meant that the keywords that were more connected to other keywords had a higher probability of staying in one subgroup [53,54]. As a result, these visualized clusters helped us easily identify the various focuses of the policies in the whole network. By analyzing the changes of the keywords with high degree centrality and the changes of the clusters between different phases, the researchers could observe the shifts of the policy priorities throughout these years.

To display the interdepartmental cooperation network, we used SATI 3.2 to calculate frequency statistics and construct a co-occurrence matrix of the policymaking departments. The co-occurrence matrix was then imported into UCINET 6 to visualize the interdepartmental policy-issuing network. The nodes in the network represented the departments, and the links represented the joint issuance of policies (see Appendix A 9). These nodes were sized by the number of policies issued by the department. The larger the size of a node, the more policies the department had issued individually or jointly and the more active and dominant the role the department(s) had played in certain phases. With further analysis of the functions of these active departments, this visualization contributed to identifying the policy priorities of each phase and the changes in priorities between different phases.

We used SNA methods rather than descriptive statistic in our bibliometric analysis for three reasons. (1) Although the descriptive statistics can illustrate the emergence and proliferation of keywords, co-word analysis of SNA has the advantage of measuring relationship between keywords in the documents, and then locating the cluster of keywords according to different level of relationship. The higher the degree centrality of the keyword, the more important the keyword in policies. The more connections between certain keywords, the more obvious the policy priority is emerged in certain period. Therefore, the pattern of policies can be identified [55,56]. (2) SNA has the advantage of presenting the power network between policy issuing departments in China [54,56,57]. Policies and regulations in China are individually or jointly issued by several departments, which implies a power network between departments: the more the policies and regulations issued or leading issued by certain department, the more significant power certain department possessed in this policy area. Furthermore, the rank of jointly issuing departments implies the connection between departments. The more co-presence in the policies, the stronger connections are between certain departments in the policy area. Therefore, different clusters of departments can be identified through mapping out the connections. (3) SNA has the function of visualization for identifying and comparing the different clusters, which is the advantage that the descriptive statistics does not have. This is why co-word analysis and cluster analysis of SNA are commonly used in mapping out research topics or tracing policy patterns [55,56,58–60].

In order to provide a comprehensive picture of the policy priorities, we provided in-depth qualitative analyses of certain important policies and historical events in each phase to supplement the quantitative analysis above. Furthermore, applying the criteria framework above, this article further identified the pattern of the policies to explore whether and to what extent such policies have contributed to sustainable development.

4. Findings

Figure 1 and Table 2 illustrate the annual number of PPP-related policies released in China between 1980 and 2017. These policies can be divided into three phases, considering the annual distribution of the policies and some specific historical events. Phase I lasted from 1980 to 1997, beginning with the era of China's economic reform and opening to foreign investors and ending with the Asian financial crisis of 1997 (see Appendix A 10). In this phase, the number of new policies released annually varied from one to three, with a few, very small fluctuations. Phase II extended from 1998 to 2008, starting with the campaign to 'clean up' illegal foreign-invested BOT projects and the rapid development of China's urbanization and ending with the global financial crisis of 2008. This period saw an obvious wave of policymaking, peaking in 2002 and falling until 2008. Phase III covered the period from 2009 to 2017, with the rise of policies aiming to relieve the local government debts that stemmed from LGFVs and promoting PPPs development. This period was characterized by the explosion of PPP-related policies, with a sudden rise from 2014 to 2017, which has not yet slowed down. The number of PPP-related policies promulgated during these four years accounted for as much as 78% of the total 299 PPP-related policies released in the past 36 years. The following sections provide the findings and discussion based on the presentation of the co-keyword networks, the networks of the policy-issuing departments, and the rankings of the policy-issuing departments by the number of policies promulgated in these three historical phases, respectively.

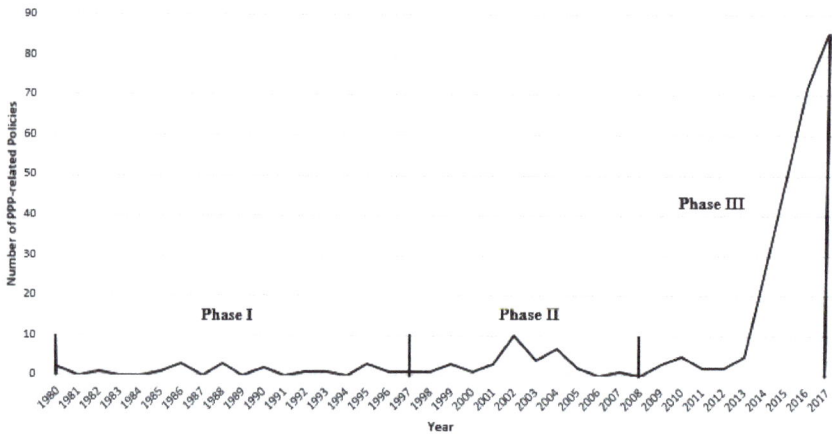

Figure 1. Annual number of released PPP-related policies in China, 1980–2017.

Table 2. Number of PPP-related policies in China from 1980 to 2017.

Phase I: 1980–1997		Phase II: 1998–2008		Phase III: 2009–2017	
Year	Number	Year	Number	Year	Number
1980	2	1998	1	2009	3
1982	1	1999	3	2010	5
1985	1	2000	1	2011	2
1986	3	2001	3	2012	2
1988	3	2002	10	2013	5
1990	2	2003	4	2014	26
1992	1	2004	7	2015	48
1993	1	2005	2	2016	72
1995	3	2007	1	2017	85
1996	1				
1997	1				
18 Years	19	11 Years	32	9 Years	248

Note: The data for the PPP-related policies database from 1980 to 2017 was self-collected. There were no PPP-related policies released in 1981, 1983,1984, 1987,1989, 1991, 1994, 2006 and 2008, so these years are not listed in the table.

4.1. Phase I, 1980–1997: Encouragement of Foreign Investment and No Relevance to Sustainable Development

As indicated in Figure 1 and Table 2, there were only 19 PPP-related policies that were issued during this period. The result of the bibliometric analysis for these 19 policies, provided below, shows that Phase I presented a policy priority of encouraging foreign investment in the public infrastructure, accompanied by fiscal and investment system reforms. These policy features were not relevant to the concept of sustainable development.

This policy priority was identified through the keyword clusters, which consisted of two subgroups (see Figure 2): (1) The major subgroup of keywords, which is shown in red in Figure 2, related to encouraging foreign investment. This subgroup reveals how the policies encouraged the influx of foreign and overseas capital—particularly from Hong Kong, Macao, and Taiwan—by giving preferential treatment to foreign investors, promoting cooperation approaches (BOT, joint ventures, and franchised projects), stipulating that certain industries receive or restrict foreign investment (e.g., infrastructure is allowed while utility network is forbidden), and reforming supportive procedures (administrative approval and open bidding). The keywords 'encourage' and 'foreign investment' had the highest degree centrality among the keywords, implying that "encouraging foreign investment" was the core value of Phase I. (2) A subgroup of keywords about investment system reform and economic development, as shown in blue in Figure 2, also emerged. This subgroup revealed that, in the pursuit of economic development, during the transition from a state-planning economy to a market economy, the Chinese central government turned to investment system reform, creating a fiscal-contracting system and a tax distribution system related to revenue sharing between the central and local governments, which incentivized the local governments to employ PPPs for local infrastructure development.

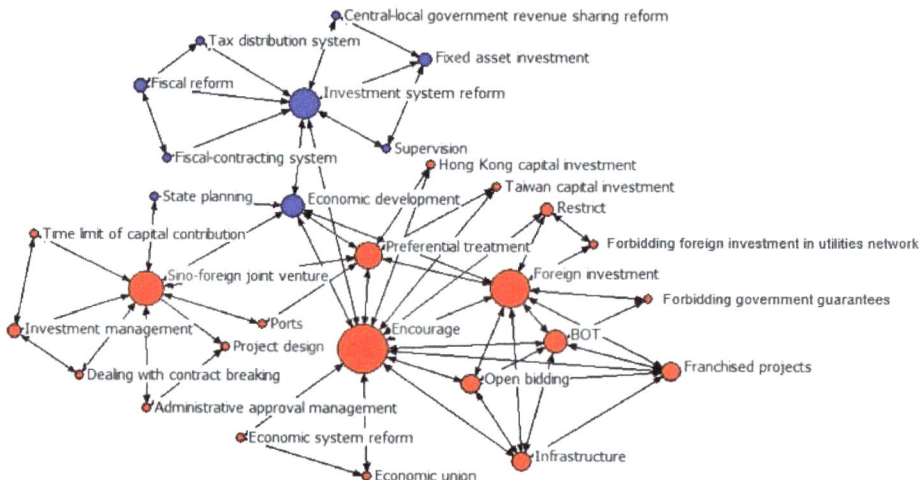

Figure 2. Co-keyword analysis and cluster analysis in Phase I.

The network analysis and the number of policies issued by the policymaking departments (see Figure 3 and Table 3) provided further evidences for this finding. Following the State Council, the MFTEC, which is responsible for regulating foreign investments, took second place by issuing six PPP-related policies. The State Development Planning Commission (SDPC) ranked third, having issued four PPP-related policies, supported by the Ministry of Transport and the Ministry of Electric Power. The functions of these departments reflect the policy priority of encouraging foreign investment in the public infrastructure areas.

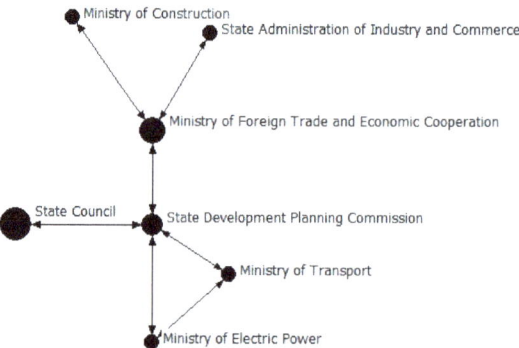

Figure 3. Network of the PPP-related policymaking departments in Phase I.

Table 3. Number of PPP-related policies issued by each department in Phase I.

Department	Number
State Council	11
Ministry of Foreign Trade and Economic Cooperation	6
State Development Planning Commission	4
State Administration of Industry and Commerce	1
Ministry of Construction	1
Ministry of Electric Power	1
Ministry of Transport	1

The policy network above reveals that foreign investors (investors from Hong Kong, Taiwan, Macao and overseas) were the major resource of the private actor in this phase (see subgroup in red). This finding was supported by the understanding of the specific historical changes in this phase. Since 1978, supported by the economic reform and opening-up policies and the central–local fiscal contracting reform, the Chinese local governments have been extraordinarily eager for foreign investments to solve the problems presented by the public infrastructure needs and the local public finance shortages. The PPP-related policies encouraging foreign investment and employing BOT in the public infrastructure areas were evoked by the abovementioned need. In 1986, the State Council published the policy of "Decision on Encouraging Foreign Investment". In 1988 and 1990, the State Council specifically issued policies to open market for foreign investors from Taiwan, Hongkong and Macao. As a result, the first booming phase of private participation in infrastructure development in China began in the 1990s, and foreign investors were the major players [61]. In this phase, foreign investors mainly played the role of capital and technology provider in BOT infrastructures particular in toll roads, energy and water supply areas, such as the Laibin B power plant, Chengdu no. 6 water supply BOT plant and the Changsha Wangcheng power BOT plant [62]. On the other hand, the local government's unprincipled guarantees of a fixed or even minimum return to foreign partners also led to severe financial risks at local level, and resulted in policy restriction in the end of 1990s. For example, the MFTEC came up with a series of policies forbidding government guarantees in BOT, such as the policy entitled "Notice on Attracting Foreign Investment via BOT" of 1995. Affected by this top-down policy restriction and by the Asian financial crisis of 1997, foreign private actors gradually exited PPPs market in China [61].

Having identified the policy priority of encouraging foreign investment in the public infrastructure, we argue that the policies in this phase neither promoted PPPs for sustainable development nor provided sustainable approaches for PPPs. With respect to ecological sustainability, all the 19 PPP-related policies were aimed at areas of economic infrastructure rather than environmental protection projects, and no ecologically sustainable approach was mentioned in any of the policies. In terms of social sustainability, there were no social infrastructure projects or services encouraged by these policies. Although the quality of life of the public could be improved through economic infrastructure, this was not the intent of the policies; instead, the main goal was economic development. This was identified through the frequent connection between the keywords about economic development and the keyword "PPP". For example, in the "Notice Regarding the Permission of Trail Foreign Investment Concession" issued by the SDPC, the Ministry of Electricity, and the Ministry of Transport, it was clearly stated that, for a long time, transportation, energy, and other infrastructures have been the bottleneck of China's national economy. Foreign investment was to be facilitated to develop these infrastructure areas. Also, there were few socially sustainable approaches mentioned, except the keyword "open bidding", which represented the socially advantageous concept of transparency. Furthermore, concerning financial sustainability, there was only one keyword referring to financial affordability, "forbidding government guarantees", which only appeared in one policy at the end of Phase I to prohibit serious government borrowing with a guaranteed return. This policy was "Notice on Attracting Foreign Investment via BOT", issued by the MFTEC in 1995.

Two factors have contributed to our understanding of the complete lack of connection between PPPs and sustainable development in Phase I. One is that Phase I was embedded in the period of China's economic take-off. This explains why keywords such as "economic development" and economic system reform obtained high degree centrality in the network. In other words, the PPP-related policies in Phase I were created for economic development rather than for other reasons. Furthermore, since the concept of sustainable development was not introduced in China until the Agenda 21 by 1994, it would have been impossible to see any policies intending to promote PPPs based on the concept of sustainable development.

4.2. Phase II, 1998–2008: Promoting the Marketization of the Municipal Public Utilities and a Few Attempts to Encourage Sustainable Development

From Figure 1 and Table 2, we can see that there were 32 PPP-related policies issued during this period, which peaked in 2002 with an obvious wave of policymaking. This phase was characterized by the promotion of the marketization of the municipal public utilities, which resulted in some attempts to encourage sustainable development.

The cluster analysis of the keywords (see Figure 4) consisted of three subgroups, marked with different colors: (1) The largest subgroup regarding the marketization of the municipal public utilities is marked in blue. These keywords and their degree centrality in the network demonstrate the main policy focus on the marketization of the municipal public utilities. In contrast to Phase I, which had BOT as the only keyword representing PPPs, Phase II showed the keywords "marketization" and "concession", which referred to PPPs. The keyword "marketization" had a high degree centrality and mainly connected to the keywords about the municipal public utilities, such as "water supply", "waste treatment", "urban rail", "pipeline gas", and so on. (2) The second biggest subgroup included those keywords encouraging domestic private investment and regulating foreign investment, as shown in red in Figure 4. This subgroup shows that, on the one hand, domestic private investment was permitted with loosened administrative approval, preferential treatment, and more financing approaches; however, on the other hand, foreign investment was, for the first time, allowed in the utilities network, but it faced stricter regulations in participating in the construction industry, construction engineering services, and urban planning services. (3) There was a smaller subgroup of keywords forbidding guarantees by the local governments, which aimed to alleviate local financial risks by forbidding government guaranteed return on investment (ROI) and disguised borrowing, as shown in yellow in Figure 4.

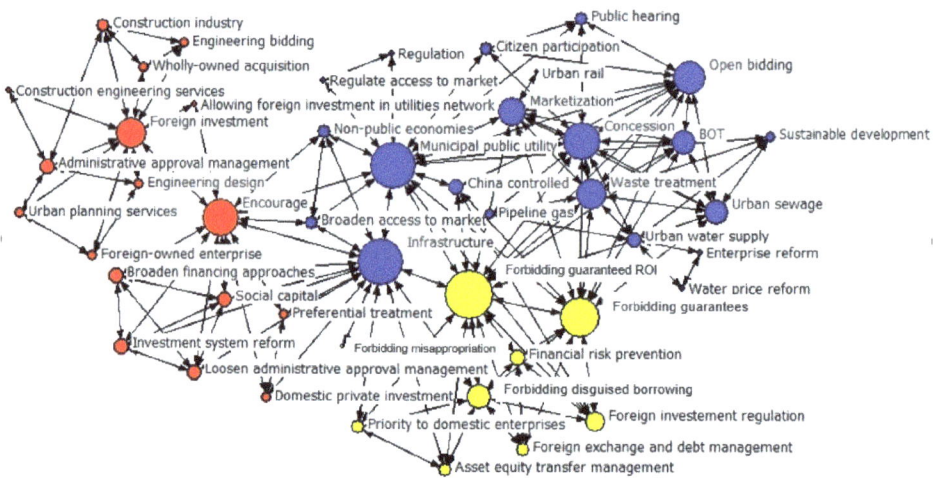

Figure 4. Co-keyword analysis and cluster analysis in Phase II.

The network analysis and the number of PPP-related policies issued by the policymaking departments (see Figure 5 and Table 4) echoed these findings, with the obvious increase in the number of policymaking departments with urban development and regulation functions. The Ministry of Construction replaced the State Council and became the leading policy-issuing department, promulgating 14 PPP-related policies aimed at promoting the marketization of the urban public utilities. The Ministry of Commerce (for which the MFTEC was the precursor) issued 11 PPP-related policies, ranking as the second most prolific department. The State Council fell to third place, with nine self-issued PPP-related policies used to control local government debts, regulate foreign investment, and encourage the growth of the domestic private sector. As the major department for macro-regulation, the NRDC (for which the SDPC was the precursor) occupied an important connecting position by coordinating the MoF, the Ministry of Water Resources, the Ministry of Construction, and the State Environmental Protection Administration (SEPA) to propel the marketization of the urban sewage and waste disposal industry and by organizing the Ministry of Commerce and the State Economic and Trade Commission to facilitate the access to the market by foreign investors.

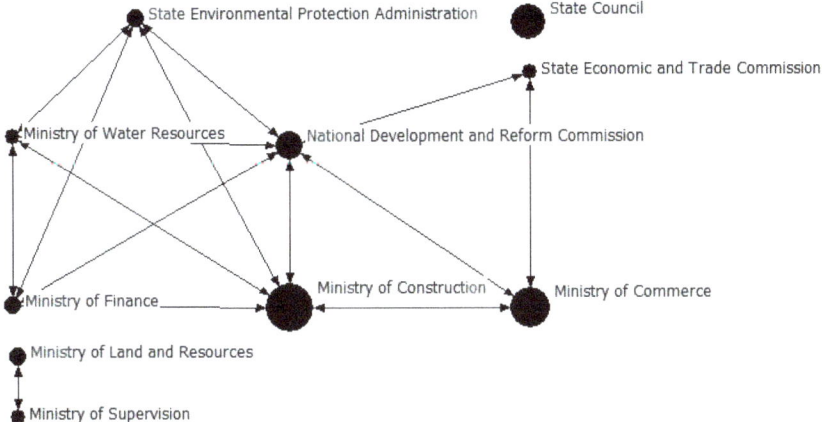

Figure 5. Network of the PPP-related policymaking departments in Phase II.

Table 4. Number of PPP-related policies issued by each department in Phase II.

Department	Number
Ministry of Construction	14
Ministry of Commerce	11
State Council	9
National Development and Reform Commission	6
State Environmental Protection Administration	2
Ministry of Land and Resources	2
Ministry of Finance	2
State Economic and Trade Commission	1
Ministry of Water Resources	1
Ministry of Supervision	1

The policy network of Phase II also exposed the change of government's attitude toward private investors, that is, encouraging domestic investors and strengthening regulations on foreign investors (see subgroup in red). These policies took effect in practice: Phase II witnessed the exit of foreign investors and the growth of domestic private investors. On one hand, numerous foreign companies have been either reducing their business or have retreated from the market [63]. On the other hand, domestic private enterprises started to play an increasing important role of urban developers and competed with foreign investors for PPPs projects in municipal infrastructure areas [64]. until 2007, the provision of public infrastructure and services had been steadily moving away from the realm of government to that of domestic private sector through PPPs [65].

Two significant historical events accounted for this change in Phase II. The first was a continuous campaign launched by the central government to "clean up" local BOT projects with guaranteed repurchase or payment contracts, which expelled the majority of foreign investors [66]. This campaign, aiming to mitigate the financial risks of such guarantees, led to the explosion of a series of PPP-related policies forbidding government guarantees, as shown in yellow in Figure 4. One of the most powerful examples was the policy entitled "On Properly Dealing with BOT Projects that Promise Guaranteed

Return of Investments for Foreign Capital", issued by the State Council in 2002. Together with the Asian financial crisis in 1997, this campaign expelled the majority of the foreign capital, originating from Hong Kong, Macao, and Taiwan, out of the mainland market and affected the activity of foreign investment in China.

The second event was the rapid urbanization in China that has been occurring since the end of the 1990s, which intensified the serious public financial shortage problem and facilitated the policies of encouraging the partnerships with domestic private actors [67,68]. A series of PPP-related policies on the marketization of the municipal public utilities through domestic private investment, as we identified in blue in Figure 4, were issued. For example, in 2001, the SDPC issued a policy entitled "On Promoting Domestic Private Investment", encouraging domestic private actors participate in urban public utilities. With the withdrawn of foreign investors, the domestic private actors became the major partners in PPPs projects.

Considering the prominence of the policies encouraging the marketization of the municipal public utilities and domestic investment, it is argued here that the policies in this phase made only a few attempts toward achieving sustainable development.

Regarding ecological sustainability, keywords such as "waste treatment", "urban sewage", and "urban water supply" were found to have high degree centrality, connecting with the keyword "marketization". This implies that these policies encouraged PPPs to be employed in areas critical for environmentally sustainable development. The typical example is "Notice on Accelerating the Industrialization of Urban Sewerage and Waste Treatment". This policy acknowledged the negative impact of rapid urbanization on environmental protection. Therefore, the encouragement of private participation in the urban sewage and waste treatment was one of the main approaches to solve such environmental protection problems. This policy was jointly issued by the NRDC, the Ministry of Construction, and the SEPA, the last of which appeared in the network for the first time during this phase. However, there were no keywords mentioning ecologically sustainable approaches, such as environmentally friendly technologies or the innovative use of natural resources to implement PPPs.

With respect to social sustainability, the policies in this phase mainly took effect in the area of municipal public utilities, which have a direct impact on the quality of life of urban citizens. In contrast with Phase I, these policies showed the intention to meet citizens' needs, although economic development was still the priority. For example, in "Opinion about Accelerating Marketization of Public Utilities" issued by the Ministry of Construction, it was stated that, "urban public utilities are the carrier of urban economic and social development, it is directly related to the public interest, the citizens' quality of life, and the sustainable development of urban economy and society". On the other hand, the policies in Phase II provided socially sustainable approaches to implementing PPPs, by asking for open bidding, citizen participation, and public hearings to ensure the fair completion and social supervision of the PPPs process. Keywords such as "citizen participation" and "public hearing" appeared in the network for the first time during Phase II. Furthermore, the policies in this phase started to encourage domestic private investment, which can be regarded as a socially sustainable approach to PPPs, because they provided equal treatment for domestic investors, who had suffered from policy discrimination for a long time.

In Phase II, the policies made attempts to provide financially sustainable approaches, consisting of foreign exchange and debt management, asset equity transfer management, financial risk prevention, and foreign investment regulation. Furthermore, the high degree centrality of keywords such as "forbidding guaranteed ROI", "forbidding guarantees", and "forbidding disguised borrowing", illustrated the government's reaction against the problem of using PPPs without considering the long-term financial affordability of such actions. Moreover, it is interesting to note that this is the first time that the MoF, as a critical department for PPPs development, appeared in the network, although it only issued one PPP-related policy. The policy was entitled "Notice on Further Promoting Reform of Urban Water Supply Price" and jointly issued by the NRDC, the MoF, the Ministry of Construction, the Ministry of Water Resources, and the SEPA in 2002.

4.3. Phase III, 2009–2017: The Institutionalization of PPPs and an Obvious Tendency toward Sustainable Development

As showed in Figure 1 and Table 2, the number of PPP-related policies during this period increased dramatically with a total of 248 policies issued, accounting for nearly 83% of total amount of PPP-related policies. This phase presented the policy priority of the intensive institutionalization and extensive application of PPPs, bearing an obvious tendency toward sustainable development.

As with Phases I and II, the cluster analysis of keywords (see Figure 6) helped identify the policy priority of this phase via the visualization of subgroups with different colors:

(1) The largest subgroup of keywords were those promoting PPPs and encouraging 'social capital' (see Appendix A 11) in multiple infrastructure and public service areas, as shown in red in Figure 6. This cluster presents not only the traditional economic infrastructure areas in which PPPs would continue to be employed, such as toll roads and transportation energy, but also multiple novel environmental and social infrastructure and services consisting of elderly care, tourism, education, healthcare, culture, sports, environmental protection, and so on, which were connected with the keywords "promote PPP". Compared with Phases I and II, these environmental and social areas were presented in the network extensively for the first time, implying that there was a shift in PPP-related policies from those supporting traditional economic infrastructure to those introducing more ecological and social infrastructure and services. Furthermore, in contrast with Phases I and II, the keywords "encourage social capital to participate" occupied the central position for the first time, indicating a stronger policy emphasis on mobilizing private funds in this phase.

(2) The second largest subgroup, as shown in blue in Figure 6, included keywords regarding the institutionalization of PPPs through due process. The keyword "PPP" in English, was centered in the subgroup and surrounded by keywords representing due process, such as "government procurement", "PPP project assessment", "VFM" and "financial affordability assessment", "example PPP cases", and "contract management", which were absent in the previous phases. Moreover, compared with Phase I, in which the keyword "BOT" was used to refer to PPPs, and Phase II, in which the keywords "marketization", "BOT", and "concession" were used, Phase III was the first time that the English expression of PPP appeared in the network, showing an effort to institutionalize the concept of PPPs by transferring standardized international concepts and procedures [69].

(3) The third largest subgroup of keywords relating to PPPs information disclosure is shown in green in Figure 6. This subgroup was centered on the keyword "information disclosure" and was connected to other high degree centrality keywords, such as the "National PPP Integrated Information Platform", "fair competition", "social supervision", "information resource sharing", and so on.

(4) The minor subgroup of keywords regarding the cleaning-up of local debts, as shown in yellow in Figure 6, centered on the keyword "local government debt" and was connected with other high degree centrality keywords, such as "local government financing vehicles", "forbidding illegal financing", and "forbidding illegal guarantees", which illustrated an obvious aim in this phase to use PPPs to relieve the increasing financial pressure especially associated with local government debts [70].

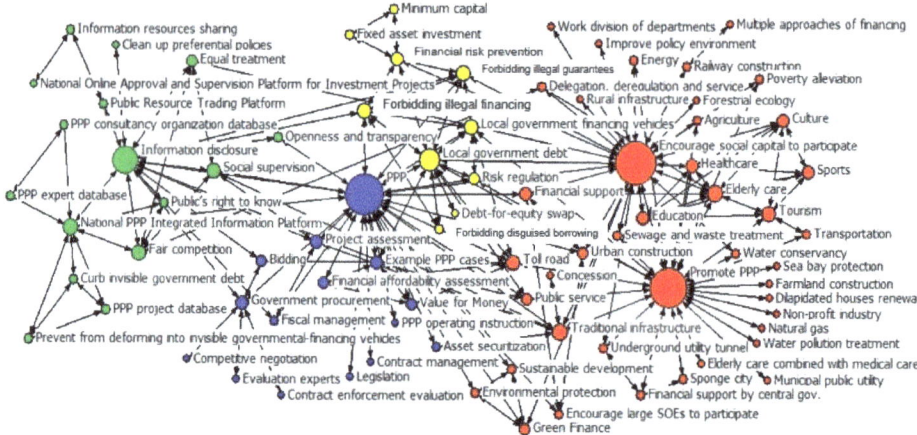

Figure 6. Co-keyword analysis and cluster analysis in Phase III.

The network analysis and the number of PPP-related policies issued by the policymaking departments (see Figure 7 and Table 5) furtherly confirmed the policy priorities shown above. The MoF and the NRDC were situated at the center of the policy-issuing department network, issuing 106 and 73 policies, respectively. This signifies that PPPs had been institutionalized as a major tool of public finance and social economic management.

Furthermore, compared with the seven policymaking departments identified in Phase I and the 10 policymaking departments in Phase II, there were as many as 57 policymaking departments involved in Phase III, covering extensive governmental functions. The newly added departments were social infrastructure and service providers, such as the Ministry of Civil Affairs, the Ministry of Education, and so on, signifying that PPPs were no longer limited to the area of economic infrastructure, as they had been in Phases I and II. Other newly added departments were regulatory institutions, such as the China Banking Regulatory Commission (CBRC), the China Insurance Regulatory Commission (CIRC), the Supreme People's Court, the China Securities Regulatory Commission (CSRC), and so on, signifying the stricter regulations that had been implemented throughout the process of PPPs institutionalization.

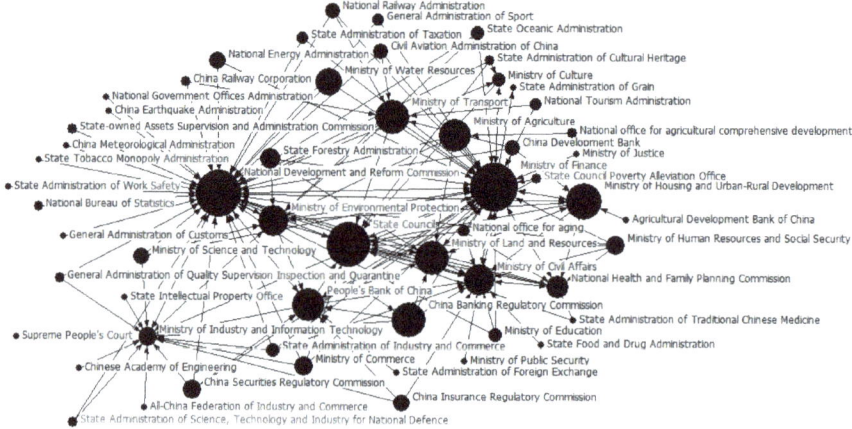

Figure 7. Network of PPP policymaking departments in Phase III.

Table 5. Number of PPP-related policies issued by each department in Phase III.

Department	Number
Ministry of Finance	106
National Development and Reform Commission	73
State Council	68
Ministry of Housing and Urban–Rural Development	34
China Banking Regulatory Commission	20
Ministry of Land and Resources	19
Ministry of Transport	17
People's Bank of China	16
Ministry of Agriculture	16
Ministry of Environmental Protection	14
Ministry of Water Resources	12
National Health and Family Planning Commission	9
State Forestry Administration	8
Ministry of Human Resources and Social Security, Ministry of Industry and Information Technology, Ministry of Commerce, China Securities Regulatory Commission	7
China Insurance Regulatory Commission, National Energy Administration, Ministry of Science and Technology	6
National Railway Administration, Civil Aviation Administration of China, China Development Bank	5
Ministry of Culture, State Administration of Industry and Commerce, Ministry of Education, State Oceanic Administration	4
National office for aging, General Administration of Sport, State Administration of Taxation, National Tourism Administration	3

Note: For departments that issued only one or two PPP-related policies, see Appendix A 12.

The policy network above revealed a new change regarding the resource and role of private actor in Phase III. Compared with the policy priority on foreign investors in Phase I and priority on domestic investors in Phase II, policies in Phase III released the signal of welcoming any capitals, including foreign capital, domestic private capital and even capitals from state-owned enterprises (SOEs) to join in PPPs. In Phase III, the keyword with highest degree centrality is "social capital" in subgroup in red, which refers to the "private" of PPPs, and was defined as the enterprises duly organized, validly existing, and in good standing as a legal person under the law of the People's Republic of China (P.R.C.), consisting of domestic private enterprises, foreign enterprises and even SOEs. In other words, the "private" of the PPPs in this phase includes not only private enterprises but also SOEs. The inclusion of SOEs in the resource of private actor in this phase resulted in debates on whether there are 'public–public partnerships' or 'public–private partnerships', when the second "P" is from SOEs. Although subsequent policies restricted the participation of SOEs capitals by forbidding SOEs participate in PPPs projects launched by the local governments that the SOEs belonged to, the data so far has shown that the SOEs were still the major players and have the largest market share in most of infrastructure sectors, while domestic private enterprises and foreign investors were only active in several sectors and with smaller market share [71].

In Phase III, the major role of 'private' actors is to relieve the long term accumulated local government debts through injecting capitals into the partnership projects. The evidence could be found from the keyword subgroup in yellow, visualizing the central government's motivation of using PPPs to solve local government debts (see Appendix A 13). The local government debts were derived from the local government's overinvestment in infrastructure areas since 2008, under the incentive of "4 Trillion Investment Plan" designed by central government to deal with the global financial crisis in 2008 [70]. As a result, the solution was to use PPPs to replace the traditional governmental investment, and swap the government debt for equity in PPPs projects.

Having identified the primary policy priority of the institutionalization of PPPs, it is argued here that the PPP-related policies in Phase III have shown an obvious tendency toward sustainability in both aspects of sustainable development and sustainable approach. This argument is strongly supported by China's promotion of "New Urbanization". In 2014, the Communist Party of China (CPC) and the State Council officially issued the "National Plan on New Urbanization (2014–2020)", attaching more importance to the sustainable development of urban areas, especially to sustainable basic public service systems and sustainable urbanization financing approaches.

Regarding ecologically sustainable development, we identified policies promoting PPPs in environmental protection areas, from the traditional environmental projects including sewage and waste treatment and water pollution treatment, to newly emerging projects, such as sea and bay protection and "sponge city" (see Appendix A 14) projects [72]. Keywords such as "environmental protection" and "forestry ecology" appeared in the network. Although ecologically sustainable approaches were still rare in the network, keywords such as "green finance" had at least been given some policy attention in this phase. In 2016, the People's Bank of China, the MoF, the NRDC, the Ministry of Environmental Protection (for which the SEPA was the precursor), the CBRC, the CSRC, and the CIRC jointly launched a policy known as "Guidance on Constructing Green Finance System" under the context of promoting an ecological civilization. The term "green finance" refers to the financial services, consisting of project financing and operation and risk management provided for projects in areas such as environmental protection, energy saving, clean energy, green building, and so on.

Furthermore, the emergence of multiple environment-related government departments was the more evidence of the tendency to promote sustainable development. Phase III was the first time that the environmental protection departments, such as the Ministry of Water Resources, the National Energy Administration, the State Oceanic Administration, the Chinese Earthquake Administration, and the China Meteorological Administration, had a major presence in the network; however, the presence of such departments was nonexistent in Phase I and relatively rare in Phase II.

Concerning social sustainability, PPPs were strongly advocated in the social infrastructure and service areas, which are vital to improve the quality of life. The keywords regarding "elderly care", "tourism", "education", "healthcare, "culture", and "sports" were highly connected with the keyword "PPP". Departments functioning in social service areas were also more frequently shown in the network, such as the Ministry of Civil Affairs, the National Health and Family Planning Commission, the Ministry of Human Resources and Social Security, the Ministry of Culture, the Ministry of Education, and the National Office for Aging, to name a few. There was also an obvious advancement regarding the prevalence of socially sustainable approaches, as shown in the subgroup of keywords regarding PPPs information disclosure and the subgroup of keywords involving the institutionalization of PPPs through due process, such as "fair competition", "social supervision", "equal treatment", and "project assessment". Compared with Phases I and II, in which only a few such relevant keywords were shown in the network, Phase III formed two subgroups relevant to social sustainability, reflecting a strong policy tendency to utilize socially sustainable approaches in PPPs.

Phase III, in particular, witnessed the growth of a tendency toward using PPPs via financially sustainable approaches. The process of using PPPs was regulated by a more structured and deliberate financially sustainable approach, as shown by the appearance of keywords such as "VFM", "financial affordability assessment", "debt-for-equity swap", "asset securitization", "forbidding illegal guarantees", "forbidding illegal financing", and, especially, "financial risk prevention". More strong evidence was reflected in the dominance of the MoF in the policy-issuing department network. Shifting from its total absence in Phase I and a supporting role in Phase II, the MoF assumed the most dominant role in directing PPPs toward financial sustainability in Phase III.

5. Conclusions and Discussion

This article aims to answer two specific research questions: (1) Between 1980 and 2017, what were the PPP-related policy priorities in the different historical phases of the Chinese national agenda? (2) Have the PPP-related policies in China shown a pattern of moving toward sustainable development, and if so, to what extent? As revealed in the analysis above, PPP-related policy development in China has gone through three historical phases: in the early 1980s, PPPs were used to develop public/economic infrastructure; in the late 1990s, PPPs were used to encourage the marketization of the urban public utilities; and then, in recent years, there has been intensive institutionalization and extensive application of PPPs in public services.

The policy priorities in each phase also shaped the resource and the role of private actors, and how they evolved over time. In Phase I, with the policy priority of encouraging foreign investment for public infrastructure, foreign investors were the main resource of private actor in PPPs, and played the role of providing capitals and technologies. In Phase II, due to gradual exit of foreign investors and the urgent need of urban development, domestic private sector became a new resource of private actors in PPPs, and played the role of urban public utility developers. In Phase III, with the aim of intensive promoting PPPs to relief local government debts, policies in this phase released the signal of welcoming any capitals, either from foreign investors, domestic investors or even from SOEs to join the PPPs. In this phase, "private" actors played the role of relieving local government debts.

Corresponding with the policy priority changes, there was also a trajectory showing how PPP-related policies gradually began to comply with the principles of sustainable development: in Phase I, there was a total absence of any commitment to the concept of sustainability; in Phase II, there were only a few policy attempts to pursue sustainable development; and in Phase III, there developed an obvious pattern of encouraging the use of PPPs for sustainable development and implementing PPPs via sustainable approaches.

Furthermore, the policy priorities identified by our analysis clearly show that PPPs have been utilized by policymakers as pragmatic financial tools, either for economic development in Phase I, for urban development in Phase II, or for solving urgent local debt problems in Phase III. Although the keywords relevant to ecological, social, and financial sustainability have gradually begun to increase, they have never been the top keywords in any of the three phases. Also, the role of private actors in each phase played as the finance provider, revealed the government's pragmatic attitude toward PPPs. This means that the principles of sustainable development, rather than being treated as the ultimate goals, are the side products of PPP-related policies that were aimed to achieve economic development and public financial problem-solving.

This could be explained from the common features that China shared with other countries in PPPs development, and the specific institutional features that China possessed.

It is a common feature in various countries that, PPPs were used as a pragmatic financial tool for solving public finance problems before it was understood as the governance scheme in which the sustainable development is considered. For most countries we reviewed above, developed countries such as the UK, USA, and European countries have more initiative to apply PPPs in environmental and social sectors, and implement PPPs via sustainable approaches, while they have passed through the stage in which PPPs were taken as the financial tool [73]. However, for developing countries, such as Chile and India, economic development is still the priority for which PPPs were the approach to invite private capitals, and the concept of sustainability is gradually taken into policies. Therefore, China is not a unique case for its PPP-related policies development toward sustainable development.

On the other hand, China has its context-specific institutional obstacles against PPPs achieving sustainable development. As revealed by the policymaking department network above, while the increasingly complicated keywords network and policy-issuing departments network that have evolved in Phase III have shown the growing attention of the government on PPPs, they have also exposed the fragmented, authoritarian policymaking system that exists in China. These 299 policy documents were mainly issued or joint-issued by the State Council and its tens of affiliated ministries and departments. As the highest administrative authority, the State Council leads the all administrative ministries and organizations and takes charge of national planning, leading and managing infrastructure construction and public service supply, and allocating functions, tasks and resources to local governments [74]. Promoting and regulating PPPs development is one of its tasks. Under the State Council, various ministries and departments play crucial roles, such as the Ministry of Construction, the Ministry of Commerce, the NRDC, the MoF, etc. Such diversity of the policy issuing authorities reflects the China's context-specific fragmented bureaucratic structure, which, although policy making power related to consensus building is concentrated in central government, it is actually fragmented among the State Council and its affiliated departments, resulting into a policy process that is protracted, disjointed, and incremental [68]. Situated in Chinese political context and institutional arrangements, China's PPPs development in past nearly four decades is also sensitive to various, changing, and even conflicting PPP-related policies and regulations [74]. For example, the frequent policies issued by the MoF and the NRDC, respectively, have exposed the conflict of interest between them and their fight for dominance in the field of PPPs development and regulation, and have resulted in the aimless local implementation of PPPs.

Therefore, it is suggested here that, in terms of establishing sustainable development as the core value of PPPs, a fundamental change in the understanding of PPPs as governance scheme rather than a pragmatic economic tool is required [8]. In such a governance system, a broader criterion of sustainability should be raised as the fundamental measure of the success of PPPs. This means that ecological, social, and financial sustainability would be stated by all PPP-related policies as the primary goal of the PPPs and that governmental support, departmental integration, and public accountability would be the focus of such PPP-related policies.

By providing the findings and discussions above, this article aims to provide theoretical contributions to the current state of knowledge regarding PPPs and sustainable development. This article is the first to establish a criteria framework of evaluating the sustainability of PPP-related policies, and the first to conduct bibliometric analysis of PPP-related policies in China. As China is a country ruled by department-made policies and regulations, by identifying the priorities of the policies and their changes over time, a bibliometric analysis of the policy documents could help to discern the unspoken intention and rhetoric of the policymakers, which were usually a "black box" to the public. Moreover, by revealing the China's context-specific institutional features in PPPs policy making, this article aims to add value to the research concern of the politics and institutional arrangements of PPPs, which have not been paid much attention in extant PPPs literatures.

Considering the contributions above, the article has some limitations which will serve as the stimulus for future work. The first limitation is that, the application of criteria framework to other countries requires further observation and adjustment. For example, this article adopted "whether policies encouraged VFM test and long-term financial affordability test" as the criterion of financial sustainability. This is derived from the reflection on the lack of financial evaluation in Chinese PPP-related decisions. However, the VFM test has been debated in scholarship regarding its purpose and technical complexity, and whether government could perform rigorous VFM test [75–77]. These insightful thoughts should be brought into the future evaluation. The second limitation is that, although the issue of private actor is important in PPPs studies, this article could only explore the policy contents regarding the issue of private actor, as it is constrained by the unit of analysis and research method. A comprehensive analysis of private actors requires further empirical research in the future.

Furthermore, it must be acknowledged that, because actual PPPs practices usually fall short of what is mandated by formal institutions, the evaluation of the central policies by this article has offered an upper boundary of the estimation of the existence of PPPs that contribute to sustainable development in China. This means that further empirical research about the implementation of PPPs for sustainable development will be necessary in the future.

Author Contributions: C.C. developed the theoretical model; D.L. and C.X. collected the data; C.X. and D.L. processed the data; C.C. and D.L. analyzed the data and wrote the paper.

Funding: This research was funded by the National Social Science Foundation of China (grant no.16BGL157).

Conflicts of Interest: The authors declare no conflict of interest.

Appendix A

1. The VFM test is a two-fold analysis conducted prior to the PPPs implementation. First, the calculation of the benchmark cost of providing the specified service under traditional procurement and, second, a comparison of this benchmark cost with the cost of providing the specific service under a PPPs scheme. More details see Grimsey, D.; Lewis, M. Are public private partnerships value for money? Evaluating alternative approaches and comparing academic and practitioner views. *Accounting Forum.* 2005, 29(4), 345-378.

2. Law-lib Database is an influential Chinese database of laws and regulations, recording all the policies, laws, and regulations since 1949. It is available at the following link: http://www.law-lib.com/law/bbdw-zy.htm.

3. The CPPPC was established by the MoF in December 2014. It is responsible for policy research, consulting training, information statistics, and the international cooperation of PPPs. The PPPs project database, expert database, consultancy organization database, and policy database are available at this official website: http://www.cpppc.org/zh/pppzczd/index.jhtml.

4. The PPPs column is a special column built by the NRDC. A second source of PPPs projects, example PPP cases, and PPP-related policies are available at this official website: http://tzs.ndrc.gov.cn/zttp/PPPxmk/.

5. LGFVs is short for local government financing vehicles. As quasi-government entities, LGFVs are used by local governments to borrow from banks or issue bonds, while the money collected is used in urban infrastructure areas. For more details, see [70].

6. SATI 3.2 is a domestic tool designed by researchers of Zhejiang University, China for bibliographic statistical analysis. More details see Liu, Q.; Ye, Y. A Study on Mining Bibliographic Records by Designed Software SATI: Case Study on Library and Information Science. *Journal of Information Resources Management.* 2012, 1, 50–58. (In Chinese)

7. A UCINET 6 tutorial by Bob Hanneman and Mark Riddle is available at the following link: http://faculty.ucr.edu/~{}hanneman/nettext/. More details see Borgatti, S.P., Everett, M.G. and Freeman, L.C. *Ucinet for Windows: Software for Social Network Analysis.* Harvard, MA: Analytic Technologies. 2002.

8. The Girvan–Newman's algorithm detects communities by progressively removing edges from the original graph. The algorithm removes the "most valuable" edge, traditionally the edge with the highest betweenness centrality, at each step. As the graph breaks down into pieces, the tightly knit community structure is exposed and the result can be depicted as a dendrogram. More details are available at the following link: https://networkx.github.io/documentation/latest/reference/algorithms/community.html.

9. In Phase III, several PPPs policies were jointly issued by more than 10 departments. For the better effect of visualization, for each policy, we only presented the connection between the leading policy-issuing department and the other non-leading departments, and did not present the connection amongst the other non-leading departments.

10. We selected 1980 as the starting year for analysis, as it was at that time that China started to engage in PPPs development under the reform and opening-up policies.

11. In 2014, the MoF created a policy entitled "Guidance on Regulating PPPs Contract Management" and defined the concept of 'social capital' (she hui zi ben) in detail. Social capital refers to enterprises duly organized, validly existing, and in good standing as a legal person under the law of the People's Republic of China (P.R.C.), consisting of domestic private enterprises, SOEs,

and foreign enterprises. However, LGFVs affiliated with native local governments and other SOEs controlled by native local governments are not allowed to act as the social capital to participate in PPP projects launched by native local governments. For example, regarding the SOEs controlled by the Beijing municipal government. This company cannot take part in PPPs projects launched by the Beijing municipal government, for it is not 'social capital' relative to the Beijing municipal government. However, it can participate in PPPs projects launched by the Shanghai municipal government, because the company is not affiliated to or controlled by the Shanghai municipal government.

12. Considering the length of the paper, the policymaking departments that issued only one or two PPP-related policies during Phase III are not listed in the Table. The details are as follows. (1) The policymaking departments that issued two PPP-related policies during Phase III consisted of the National Office for Agricultural Comprehensive Development, the State-Owned Assets Supervision and Administration Commission, the China Railway Corporation, the National Bureau of Statistics, the State Administration of Science, Technology, and Industry for National Defense, the State Council Poverty Alleviation Office, the General Administration of Quality Supervision Inspection and Quarantine, and the State Administration of Cultural Heritage. (2) The policymaking departments that issued only one PPP-related policy during Phase III consisted of the National Government Offices Administration, the Supreme People's Court, the Chinese Academy of Engineering, the State Administration of Work Safety, the State Administration of Foreign Exchange, the Ministry of Justice, the State Tobacco Monopoly Administration, the China Earthquake Administration, the State Administration of Grain, the General Administration of Customs, the State Intellectual Property Office, the State Food and Drug Administration, the All-China Federation of Industry and Commerce, the Agricultural Development Bank of China, the State Administration of Traditional Chinese Medicine, the Ministry of Public Security, and the China Meteorological Administration.

13. Some examples can be seen in the policy of "Notice on Strengthening LGFVs Management" issued by the State Council in 2010, the policy of "Advice on Strengthening Management of Local Government Debts" issued by the State Council in 2014, and the policy of "Notice on Budgetary Controlling and Cleaning up the Stock of Local Government Debt" issued by the MoF in 2014. The policy of "Notice on Strengthening LGFVs Management", issued by the State Council in 2010, clearly required using PPPs for solving local government debt problems. The policy of "Notice on Promoting Debt for Equity swap by Using Governmental Funds", issued by Commission of National Development and Reform, raised the guidance to swap local government debt into equity in PPPs.

14. In 2015, the State Council issued a policy entitled "Guidance on Promoting Sponge City Construction" to minimize the side effects of urban construction on the ecological condition and to accelerate the absorption and use of rainfall. The term 'sponge city' refers to cities that can adapt flexibly, similar to sponges, to changes in the environment, such that they absorb, store, permeate, and purify rainwater and are able to make use of stored water when needed.

References

1. Grimsey, D.; Lewis, M. Accounting for public private partnerships. *Account. Forum* **2002**, *26*, 245–270. [CrossRef]
2. United Nations. Transforming Our World: The 2030 Agenda for Sustainable Development. 2015. Available online: https://sustainabledevelopment.un.org/post2015/transformingourworld (accessed on 13 September 2018).
3. Economic Commission for Europe. Draft Guiding Principles on People-First Public-Private Partnerships for the United Nations Sustainable Development Goals, Conference Room Paper Submitted by the Secretariat. November 2017. Available online: http://www.unece.org/ppp/wppppl.html (accessed on 13 September 2018).

4. United Nations. Agenda 21. United Nations Conference on Environment & Development. Rio de Janerio, Brazil, 3 to 14 June 1992. Available online: https://sustainabledevelopment.un.org/content/documents/Agenda21.pdf (accessed on 12 November 2018).

5. Ministry of Foreign Affairs of the People's Republic of China. China's National Plan on Implementation of the 2030 Agenda for Sustainable Development. 2016. Available online: https://www.fmprc.gov.cn/web/ziliao_674904/zt_674979/dnzt_674981/qtzt/2030kcxfzyc_686343/ (accessed on 15 September 2018).

6. de Castro e Silva Neto, D.; Cruz, C.O.; Rodrigues, F.; Silva, P. Bibliometric analysis of PPP and PFI literature: Overview of 25 years of research. *J. Constr. Eng. Manag.* **2016**, *142*, 06016002. [CrossRef]

7. Wang, H.; Xiong, W.; Wu, G.; Zhu, D. Public–private partnership in Public Administration discipline: A literature review. *Public Manag. Rev.* **2018**, *20*, 293–316. [CrossRef]

8. Hodge, G.; Greve, C. Contemporary public–private partnership: Towards a global research agenda. *Financ. Account. Manag.* **2018**, *34*, 3–16. [CrossRef]

9. Du, J.; Wu, H.Y.; Zhao, X.B. Critical factors on the capital structure of public-private partnerships projects: A sustainability perspective. *Sustainability* **2018**, *10*, 2066. [CrossRef]

10. Patil, N.A.; Tharun, D.; Laishram, B. Infrastructure development through PPPs in India: Criteria for sustainability assessment. *J. Environ. Plan. Manag.* **2016**, *59*, 708–729. [CrossRef]

11. Dasgupta, S.; Tam, E.K. Indicators and framework for assessing sustainable infrastructure. *Can. J. Civ. Eng.* **2005**, *32*, 30–44. [CrossRef]

12. Ugwu, O.O. A service-oriented framework for sustainability appraisal and knowledge management. *J. Inf. Technol. Constr. (ITcon)* **2005**, *10*, 245–263.

13. Hueskes, M.; Verhoest, K.; Block, T. Governing public-private partnerships for sustainability: An analysis of procurement and governance practices of PPP infrastructure projects. *Int. J. Proj. Manag.* **2017**, *35*, 1184–1195. [CrossRef]

14. Bjärstig, T. Does Collaboration Lead to Sustainability? A Study of Public–Private Partnerships in the Swedish Mountains. *Sustainability* **2017**, *9*, 1685. [CrossRef]

15. Shen, L.; Tam, V.W.; Gan, L.; Ye, K.; Zhao, Z. Improving sustainability performance for public-private-partnership (PPP) projects. *Sustainability* **2016**, *8*, 289. [CrossRef]

16. Koppenjan, J.F.; Enserink, B. Public–private partnerships in urban infrastructures: Reconciling private sector participation and sustainability. *Public Adm. Rev.* **2009**, *69*, 284–296. [CrossRef]

17. Colverson, S.; Perera, O. *Sustainable Development: Is There a Role for Public–private Partnerships?* International Institute for Sustainable Development (IISD): Winnipeg, MB, Canada, 2011; Available online: https://www.iisd.org/library/sustainable-development-there-role-public-private-partnerships-summary-iisd-preliminary (accessed on 19 October 2018).

18. Powell, J. PPPs and the SDGs: Don't Believe the Hype. University of Greenwich Working Paper. , 2016. Available online: http://gala.gre.ac.uk/16843/ (accessed on 19 October 2018).

19. Hodge, G.A.; Greve, C. PPPs: The passage of time permits a sober reflection. *Econ. Aff.* **2009**, *29*, 33–39. [CrossRef]

20. Watson, R.T.; Hamburg, S.P.A.; Janetos, A.C.A.; Moss, R.H.A.; Dixon, J.A.A. *Protecting Our Planet, Securing Our Future: Linkages among Global Environmental Issues and Human Needs*; United Nations Environment Programme: Nairobi, Kenya; National Aeronautics and Space Administration: Washington, DC, USA, 1998.

21. Barlow, J.; Roehrich, J.; Wright, S. Europe sees mixed results from public-private partnerships for building and managing health care facilities and services. *Health Aff.* **2013**, *32*, 146–154. [CrossRef] [PubMed]

22. Stigson, B. Paper on Partnerships Involving the Private Sector. OECD and WBCSD. Conference of EECCA Environment Ministers and their partners. October 2004. Available online: https://www.oecd.org/environment/outreach/33811690.pdf (accessed on 24 November 2018).

23. Oktavianus, A.; Mahani, I. A Global Review of Public Private Partnerships Trends and Challenges for Social Infrastructure. In MATEC Web of Conferences (Volume 147, p. 06001). EDP Sciences, 2018. Available online: https://www.matec-conferences.org/articles/matecconf/abs/2018/06/matecconf_sibe2018_06001/matecconf_sibe2018_06001.html (accessed on 25 November 2018).

24. Infrastructure Partnership Australia. *Australian Infrastructure Investment Report 2015*. Perpetual: Sydney, Australia, 2015. Available online: http://www.urbanaffairs.com.au/downloads/2015-10-29-2.pdf (accessed on 27 December 2018).

25. Planning Commission. Annual Report (2007–08). Government of India. Available online: http:// planningcommission.nic.in/reports/genrep/ar_0708E.pdf (accessed on 23 November 2018).
26. Planning Commission. Annual Report (2008–09). Government of India. Available online: http:// planningcommission.nic.in/reports/genrep/ar0809eng.pdf (accessed on 23 November 2018).
27. Liebe, M.; Pollock, A. The experience of the private finance initiative in the UK's National Health Service. University of Edinburgh, Centre for International Public Health Policy: Edinburgh, UK, August 2009. Available online: https://www.allysonpollock.com/wp-content/uploads/2013/04/CIPHP_2009_Liebe_NHSPFI.pdf (accessed on 25 November 2018).
28. Roehrich, J.K.; Lewis, M.A.; George, G. Are public–private partnerships a healthy option? A systematic literature review. *Soc. Sci. Med.* **2014**, *113*, 110–119. [CrossRef]
29. Ryan, B. Public Private Partnerships and Sustainability Principles Guiding Legislation and Current Practice. Dublin Institute of Technology, 2004. Available online: https://arrow.dit.ie/cgi/viewcontent.cgi?article=1007&context=futuresacrep (accessed on 25 November 2018).
30. Global Green Growth Institute. Green Public-private Partnerships for Public Infrastructure in Mongolia: PPP Model and Technical Guidelines for Green Education Buildings. 2016. Available online: http://gggi.org/site/assets/uploads/2017/02/2016-Green-Public-Private-Partnerships-for-Public-Infrastructure-in-Mongolia-1.pdf (accessed on 25 November 2018).
31. Caldwell, N.D.; Roehrich, J.K.; George, G. Social value creation and relational coordination in public-private collaborations. *J. Manag. Stud.* **2017**, *54*, 906–928. [CrossRef]
32. Lonsdale, C. Post-contractual lock-in and the UK private finance initiative (PFI): The cases of National Savings and Investments and the Lord Chancellor's Department. *Public Adm.* **2005**, *83*, 67–88. [CrossRef]
33. Kivleniece, I.; Quelin, B.V. Creating and capturing value in public-private ties: A private actor's perspective. *Acad. Manag. Rev.* **2012**, *37*, 272–299. [CrossRef]
34. Hodge, G.A. The risky business of public–private partnerships. *Aust. J. Public Adm.* **2004**, *63*, 37–49. [CrossRef]
35. JETRO. Public Private Partnerships in Australia and Japan: Facilitating Private Sector Participation. Japan External Trade Organization, Asia and Oceania Division, Overseas Research Department, August 2010. Available online: https://www.jetro.go.jp/ext_images/en/reports/survey/pdf/2010_01_other.pdf (accessed on 25 November 2018).
36. Planning Commission, India. Faster, Sustainable and More Inclusive Growth: An Approach to the Twelfth Five Year Plan. Working Papers, id: 4452, eSocialSciences. New Delhi: Planning Commission, Government of India; 2011. Available online: https://ideas.repec.org/p/ess/wpaper/id4452.html (accessed on 25 November 2018).
37. Grimsey, D.; Lewis, M. Public private partnerships and public procurement. *Agenda J. Policy Anal. Reform* **2007**, *14*, 171–188.
38. HM Treasury. *PFI, Meeting the Investment Challenge*; The Stationery Office: London, UK, 2003.
39. HM Treasury. *Draft Value for Money Appraisal Guide*; The Stationery Office: London, UK, 2004.
40. Cruz, C.O.; Marques, R.C. *Infrastructure Public-Private Partnerships*; Springer: Berlin/Heidelberg, Germany, 2013; p. 33.
41. Partnerships Victoria. *Guidance Material: Practitioners' Guide*; Department of Treasury and Finance: Melbourne, Australia, 2001.
42. Partnerships Victoria. *Guidance Material: Public Sector Comparator, Supplementary Technical Note*; Department of Treasury and Finance: Melbourne, Australia, 2003.
43. British Columbia Ministry of Finance. *Capital Asset Management Framework: Guidelines*; British Columbia Ministry of Finance: Victoria, UK, 2002.
44. Department of the Environment and Local Government. *Public-Private Partnership Assessment Guidance Note Four*; Department of the Environment and Local Government: Dublin, Ireland, 2000.
45. Netherlands Ministry of Finance. *PPP and Public Procurement*; PPP Knowledge Centre: The Hague, The Netherlands, 2001.
46. Xu, Y.; Yeung, J.F.; Jiang, S. Determining appropriate government guarantees for concession contract: Lessons learned from 10 PPP projects in China. *Int. J. Strateg. Prop. Manag.* **2014**, *18*, 356–367. [CrossRef]
47. Lobina, E.; David, H. *Problems with Private Water Concessions: A Review of Experience*; Public Service International Research Unit: London, UK, 2003.

48. Walker, B.; Walker, B.C. *Privatisation: Sell off or Sell out? The Australian Experience*; ABC Books for the Australian Broadcasting Commission: Sydney, Australia, 2000; ISBN 0 7333 0797 3.

49. Ke, Y.; Wang, S.; Chan, A. Revelation of the Channel Tunnel's failure to risk allocation in Public-Private Partnership projects. *China Civ. Eng. J.* **2008**, *41*, 97–102. (In Chinese)

50. Cao, T. BOT Financing Research—Take ShaJiao B Power Plant as an Example. Master's Thesis, Jinan University, Jinan, China, 2006. (In Chinese)

51. Freeman, L.C. Centrality in social networks conceptual clarification. *Soc. Netw.* **1978**, *1*, 215–239. [CrossRef]

52. Yan, E.; Ding, Y. Applying centrality measures to impact analysis: A coauthorship network analysis. *J. Am. Soc. Inf. Sci. Technol.* **2009**, *60*, 2107–2118. [CrossRef]

53. Himelboim, I.; Smith, M.; Shneiderman, B. Tweeting apart: Applying network analysis to detect selective exposure clusters in Twitter. *Commun. Methods Meas.* **2013**, *7*, 195–223. [CrossRef]

54. Zhang, Q.; Lu, Q.B.; Zhong, D.P.; Ye, X.T. The pattern of policy change on disaster management in China: A bibliometric analysis of policy documents, 1949–2016. *Int. J. Disaster Risk Sci.* **2018**, *9*, 55–73. [CrossRef]

55. Callon, M.; Courtial, J.P.; Laville, F. Co-word analysis as a tool for describing the network of interactions between basic and technological research: The case of polymer chemistry. *Scientometrics* **1991**, *22*, 155–205. [CrossRef]

56. Huang, C.; Su, J.; Xie, X.; Ye, X.; Li, Z.; Porter, A.; Li, J. A bibliometric study of China's science and technology policies: 1949–2010. *Scientometrics* **2015**, *102*, 1521–1539. [CrossRef]

57. Tang, Y.; Ma, Y.; Wong, C.W.; Miao, X. Evolution of government policies on guiding corporate social responsibility in China. *Sustainability* **2018**, *10*, 741. [CrossRef]

58. Courtial, J. A coword analysis of scientometrics. *Scientometrics* **1994**, *31*, 251–260. [CrossRef]

59. Coulter, N.; Monarch, I.; Konda, S. Software engineering as seen through its research literature: A study in co-word analysis. *J. Am. Soc. Inf. Sci.* **1998**, *49*, 1206–1223. [CrossRef]

60. Ding, Y.; Chowdhury, G.G.; Foo, S. Bibliometric cartography of information retrieval research by using co-word analysis. *Inf. Process. Manag.* **2001**, *37*, 817–842. [CrossRef]

61. Wang, S.; Ke, Y.J.; Xie, J. *Public-private Partnership Implementation in China. Taking Stock of PPP and PFI around the World*; Certified Accountants Educational Trust: London, UK, 2012; pp. 29–36. Available online: https://study.sagepub.com/sites/default/files/ACCA%20on%20PPPs%20around%20the%20world.pdf (accessed on 25 November 2018).

62. Chen, C.; Doloi, H. BOT application in China: Driving and impeding factors. *Int. J. Proj. Manag.* **2008**, *26*, 388–398. [CrossRef]

63. Choi, J.; Chung, J.; Lee, D. Risk perception analysis: Participation in China's water PPP market. *Int. J. Proj. Manag.* **2010**, 580–592. [CrossRef]

64. Jin, Y.X. Five periods of PPPs development in China. *Water Ind. Mark.* **2014**, *7*, 55–58. (In Chinese)

65. Mu, R.; De Jong, M.; Koppenjan, J. The rise and fall of Public–Private Partnerships in China: A path-dependent approach. *J. Transp. Geogr.* **2011**, *19*, 794–806. [CrossRef]

66. Shen, J.Y.; Wang, S.Q.; Qiang, M.S. Political risks and sovereign risks in Chinese BOT/PPP projects: Case studies. *Chin. Bus. Invest. Financ.* **2005**, *1*, 50–53. (In Chinese)

67. Wu, Q.L. Issues and solutions of financing urban infrastructure projects. *Urban Manag. Sci. Technol.* **2007**, *2*, 34–37. (In Chinese)

68. Lieberthal, K.; Oksenberg, M. *Policy Making in China: Leaders, Structures, and Processes*; Princeton University Press: Princeton, NJ, USA, 1990.

69. Chen, C.; Li, D. Policy change and policy learning in China's public-private partnership: Content analysis of PPP policies between 1980 and 2015. *Chin. Public Adm.* **2017**, 102–107. (In Chinese)

70. Zhao, Z.R.; Su, G.C.; Li, D. The rise of public-private partnerships in China. *J. Chin. Gov.* **2018**, *3*, 158–176. [CrossRef]

71. China Public Private Partnerships Center. Quarterly Report of National PPPs Projects Development. 26 October 2018. Available online: http://www.cpppc.org/zh/pppjb/7450.jhtml (accessed on 25 November 2018).

72. Shao, W.W.; Zhang, H.X.; Liu, J.H.; Yang, G.Y.; Chen, X.D.; Yang, Z.Y.; Huang, H. Data integration and its application in the sponge city construction of China. *Procedia Eng.* **2016**, 779–786. [CrossRef]

73. Grimsey, D.; Lewis, M.K. The Governance of Contractual Relationships in Public-Private Partnerships. *J. Corp. Citizensh.* **2004**, 91–109. [CrossRef]

74. Zhang, S.; Gao, Y.; Feng, Z.; Sun, W. PPP application in infrastructure development in China: Institutional analysis and implications. *Int. J. Proj. Manag.* **2015**, *33*, 497–509. [CrossRef]

75. Boardman, A.E.; Vining, A.R. Assessing the economic worth of public–private partnerships. In *International Handbook on Public–Private Partnerships*; Hodge, G.A., Greve, C., Boardman, A.E., Eds.; Edward Elgar Publishing: Cheltenham, UK, 2010; Chapter 8.

76. Hodge, G. *Public-Private Partnership: Ambiguous, Complex, Evolving and Successful: Keynote Address to Global Challenges in PPP: Cross-Sectoral and cross-Disciplinary Solutions?* Universiteit Antwerpen: Antwerpen, Belgium, 2013.

77. Yescombe, E.R. PPPs and project finance. In *The Routledge Companion to Public-private Partnerships*, 1st ed.; De Vries, P., Etienne, B.Y., Eds.; Routledge: London, UK, 2013; pp. 227–246.

 *sustainability*

Article

A Derivation of Factors Influencing the Successful Integration of Corporate Volunteers into Public Flood Disaster Inquiry and Notification Systems

Chia-Lee Yang [1], Ming-Chang Shieh [2,3], Chi-Yo Huang [4,*] and Ching-Pin Tung [3]

[1]   National Center for High-Performance Computing, Hsinchu 300, Taiwan; joy.yang@nchc.narl.org.tw
[2]   10th River Management Office, Water Resources Agency, Ministry of Economic Affairs, Taipei 106, Taiwan;
       mcshieh59@gmail.com
[3]   Department of Bioenvironmental Systems Engineering, National Taiwan University, Taipei 106, Taiwan;
       cptung@ntu.edu.tw
[4]   Department of Industrial Education, National Taiwan Normal University, Taipei 106, Taiwan
*   Correspondence: georgeh168@gmail.com; Tel.: +886-2-7734-3357

Received: 15 May 2018; Accepted: 4 June 2018; Published: 12 June 2018

Abstract: Flood hazards have become increasingly common and serious over the last few centuries. Volunteers can observe instant flood information in their local environment, which presents a great opportunity to gather flood information. The information provided by individual volunteers is too much for them to truly understand. Corporate volunteers can offer more accurate and truthful information due to their understanding of the roles and requirements of specific tasks. Past studies of factors influencing the success of corporate volunteers in flood disaster are limited. Thus, this research aims to derive the factors that enable corporate volunteers to successfully integrate the flood information to help reduce the number of injuries and deaths being caused by flood disasters. This research used the information success model and the Public-Private Partnership (PPP) model to develop an analytic framework. The nature of flood disaster management problems is inherently complex, time-bound, and multifaceted. Therefore, we proposed a novel hybrid multi-criteria decision-making (MCDM) model to address the key influence factors and the cause-effect relationships between factors. An empirical study in Taiwanese public flood disaster inquiry and notification systems was used to verify the effectiveness of the proposed methodology. The research results can serve as guidelines for improving the government's policies and the public sector in the context of corporate volunteer involvement in flood disaster inquiry and notification and in relation to other natural and manmade disasters.

Keywords: public-private partnership (PPP); disaster notification system; flood disaster; information system success model; multiple criteria decision making (MCDM)

---

1. Introduction

The flood hazard is the most frequent natural hazard, which accounts for nearly half of all natural disasters worldwide [1]. Since the dawn of human history, destructive floods have jeopardized settlements near rivers. In the past two decades, flood hazards have become even more destructive and dangerous due to climate change, population growth, and greenhouse gas concentrations [2–4]. Now, the global flood losses have increased worldwide, causing billions of US dollars in damages per year [5]. According to recent statistics by the United Nations [6], 157,000 people died as a result of floods from 1995 to 2015. In the same period, 2.3 billion people were affected by floods, accounting for 56% of all those affected by weather-related disasters [6]. Flood damage in the world's major coastal cities may top $1 trillion a year by 2050 due to rising seas and subsiding land [7]. Apparently, the flood hazard is more dangerous compared to any other type of weather-related disasters [8].

Sustainable development can be defined as that which helps to fulfill the present needs of the world's poor without compromising the capability of future generations [9]. The societal goal of sustainable development is converted into a set of objectives—objectives for the safety and objectives for the preservation of natural functions [10]. Therefore, devastating floods, which have brought more death and suffering to humans and other living things than any other types of weather-related disasters, could be viewed as enemies of sustainable development; accordingly, systems of flood protection and management are being increasingly considered in the context of sustainable development [8].

Traditionally, flood hazard mitigation has focused on engineering methods such as construction of dikes to prevent damages and losses from flood. However, engineering methods can be extremely costly and involve construction work. Further, increasingly more flood hazard events have started to occur in urban areas due to continuous urban development in headwater regions, as well as climate change effects on river discharges and flood probabilities [11,12]. It is hard to find suitable areas that are available for dikes construction. Therefore, the paradigm of flood hazard mitigation has shifted to sustainable flood management [13], which emphasizes efficiently minimizing flood influences together with stakeholders, while considering economy, society, and environment both from short-term and long-term perspectives [14].

Sustainable flood management is a continuous process that aims to avoid or reduce the effect of flood hazards. All phases of flood management require current and accurate information. The flood disaster inquiry and notification system involves selecting, receiving, processing, and transmitting current disaster information immediately. Existing flood disaster inquiry and notification systems monitor flood hazards using sensor technologies. The collected flood hazard information varies in nature due to the adoption of different sensing technologies, for example, water gauges, seismometers, aerial sensors, satellite remote sensing technology, and others. Eye witness reports by professional staff are another traditional and still very valuable flood monitoring method for situational awareness in recent flood disasters [15]. The eye witnesses by volunteers (also called volunteered information (VI)) are playing increasingly critical roles in flood monitoring. For example, from December 2010 to February 2011, the State of Queensland in Australia experienced a series of damaging floods that led to the loss of more than 20 lives and several billion-dollar properties. The Queensland's government used VI, such as the photographs and videos provided by volunteers, to assist the mapping of the flood geographic information map. Apparently, the integration of VI with existing flood disaster inquiry and notification systems can provide valuable real-time flood information for disaster management during floods. The real-time flood information from VI can also improve hydrological modeling to help with future flood disaster management and prevention [16]. However, various challenges must be resolved before VI can be considered as a useful information source. Usually, volunteers can be divided into two categories: individuals and corporate volunteers. Individual volunteers are usually recruited from social networks or public media, where there are serious overloads and impure information [17]. In contrast, corporate volunteers may offer more accurate and timely information for flood emergency decision-making [18], but corporate volunteers are involved in volunteer activities during working hours and have the responsibility to provide quality flood information.

Corporate volunteers can offer a great opportunity to play a more dominant role by collaborating to enhance the response effectiveness of flood disasters for the community. The study of corporate volunteers has grown quickly in the last decade, especially in Europe and North America [18]. While the literature provides valuable insights into how corporate volunteers contribute to disaster relief, there is a need for a more comprehensive understanding of how to build long-term partnerships with the public sector, corporations, and information technology providers [19]. Most existing research has focused on the effectiveness of individual volunteers recruited from social networks or the development of sensor technology for flood disasters. Very limited prior works have tried to analyze possibilities or factors influencing the integration of corporate volunteers into the public disaster management system from the aspects of corporate volunteers and flood disasters. Thus, the analysis of factor dimensions influencing the integration of corporate volunteers into a disaster management system is very important. The identified factors can be used to evaluate and select strategies to improve corporate volunteers' effectiveness and efficiency in the inquiry and notification of flood disasters.

This research aims to identify the factors enabling corporate volunteers to respond to inquiries and notify the public disaster management system of flood disasters. Because flood disaster management problems are inherently complex, time-bound, and multi-faceted, involving many decision-makers, high decision stakes, limited technical information, and difficult tradeoffs, the problem involves multiple-criteria decision making. To identify the relevant factors, this research introduces a novel hybrid multi-criteria decision-making (MCDM) framework based on the Information System Success Model and the model of Public-Private Partnership (PPP) to solve the complex problem of decision-making. The Decision Making Trial and Evaluation Laboratory (DEMATEL) is used to construct the influence relation map (IRM) between factors [20]. Then, the Analytical Network Process (ANP) is used to derive the weights versus the dimensions and criteria based on the concept of the Markov chain. An effective analytic framework for integrating corporate volunteers in the public disaster management system can then be defined. An empirical study based on the integration of corporate volunteers into the public flood disaster inquiry and notification system in Taiwan is used to verify the feasibility of the proposed framework. The survey experts included water resource agency officers, information system service providers, managers from the 7-Eleven Corporation, and flood disaster notification researchers in Taiwan.

The analytic results can serve as a foundation for increasing the participation of corporate volunteers in the disaster inquiry and notification systems. The satisfaction and benefits of such systems can then be increased; thus, the costs of collecting flood information can be greatly reduced. The proposed multi-criteria decision support framework can also be used to enhance communications among various stakeholders, including the public sector, and corporate and information system providers. The analytic results can also be used to improve public-private partnerships in the field of disaster management.

The rest of this paper is organized as follows. Section 2 presents a review of flood hazards, flood disaster inquiry and notification systems, the PPP model, and the information system success model. The research methods and the MCDM framework are presented in Section 3. The empirical study on the integration of corporate volunteers into the Taiwanese public flood disaster inquiry and the notification system is presented in Section 4. Section 5 discusses advances in management practices and compares the empirical study results with past research. Finally, Section 6 concludes the paper with major research findings, contributions, and future research possibilities. The proposed decision framework has important implications for both academics and practitioners in gaining a better understanding of the factors influencing the integration of corporate volunteers into public disaster inquiry and notification systems.

2. Conceptual Framework

To review the current involvement of corporate volunteers in public flood disaster inquiry and notification systems and to construct an analytic framework, a conceptual framework is reviewed and summarized below. We focus on flood hazard management, disaster inquiry, and notification systems, as well as the public-private partnership and information success model.

2.1. Flood Hazard Mitigation

Flood hazard mitigation is a concept complicated by the social, economic, and political aspects of our environment [21]. Since flood hazards are becoming increasingly dangerous, flood hazard mitigation has become dramatically more important in recent years. To manage flood damage and risk, various flood hazard mitigation strategies have been studied. The most widely adopted strategies of flood hazard mitigation are structural and non-structural. The structural strategy comprises general structural engineering methods in civil engineering. Such methods are introduced to resist and mitigate the effects of floods by constructing dikes and dams, among others. In contrast, non-structural methods aim to adjust human activities and communities to mitigate flood damages through land-utilization plans, decree norms, flood warning systems, and public education for disaster preparedness [22]. Typically, non-structural flood hazard mitigation strategies are knowledge, practices, or agreement-based approaches to reduce risks and effects of flood; such strategies do not involve physical constructions [23]. Since studies based on past floods have shown that structural engineering-based strategies are not able to completely overcome flood hazards, adequate non-structural strategies can be considered to decrease the costs of flood mitigations and to further reduce the loss of life and properties [11]. Therefore, in many cases, both structural and non-structural mitigation strategies are used within a single jurisdictional flood program.

Given that non-structural flood mitigation strategies, such as risk management, are playing dominant roles, interest in non-structural flood mitigation strategies in general and flood risk management in particular is increasing [24]. Traditionally, the government plays a key role in structural flood hazard mitigation strategies [12]. Since non-structural mitigation strategies are playing a critical role in flood mitigation, the private sector can play a more dominant role by adopting more flood mitigation measures, such as the use of flood protection devices, adapted building use, or flood insurance [3].

2.2. Flood Disaster Inquiry and Notification System

The terms disaster, crisis, catastrophe, and emergency are used almost synonymously by scholars. A disaster is defined by the United Nations as a serious disruption of the functioning of a society, and catastrophe refers to disasters that cause widespread human, material, or environment losses [23]. Therefore, disaster management problems are inherently complex, time-bound, and multi-faceted. Such problems involve many decision-makers, high stakes, limited technical information, and difficult tradeoffs [2,25], in which information systems that use information and communication technologies are becoming increasingly important as ways to coordinate and support emergency management. Four phases can be identified in the emergency management process: preparedness, mitigation, response, and recovery. Emergency management information systems (EMIS) play a critical role in the disaster response phase, because the EMIS can collect and coordinate distributed information and support the personnel involved so that immediate actions can be taken during and after the disaster [26]. Numerous EMISs already exist. Current literature on EMIS can be placed into three categories: system frameworks, design requirements and approaches, and critical factors and applications, based on different perspectives (e.g., emergency response, e-government, IT service management, and decision support systems) [27].

Disaster inquiry and notification systems are parts of EMIS; such systems provide information for disaster managers, local authorities, and emergency services. This information is subsequently disseminated to the public to provide sufficient time for effective mitigative actions before the disaster arrives [28]. Disaster inquiry and notification systems are critical when flooding is imminent. The flood inquiry and notification systems can be placed into two categories: sensor-based and human eye-witness-based. A sensor-based flood monitoring and detection system uses a rainfall recorder and a water level recorder to collect the data to predict water level. Nowadays, most flood detection systems utilize a wireless sensor network (WSN) [29], which consists of numerous sensors with the capabilities to monitor environmental conditions through wireless communications and computations. The disaster inquiry and notification system then passes the detected and recorded data through the internet to an emergency center for further analysis and decision making [30].

2.3. Volunteer Information and Disaster Inquiry and Notification System

Flood inquiry and notification by human eye-witnesses has been in use for many years. Such human-based notifications have their own benefits and risks. In most developed countries, flood inquiry and notification management rely largely on a workforce of professionals and trained volunteers who are affiliated with official agencies due to their high specialization [31].

These professionals and trained volunteers can provide the precise information required for flood emergency decision-making. However, given the increasing frequency of flood disasters worldwide due to population growth, urban development, and climate change, professionals and trained volunteers are not sufficient for monitoring flood disasters and damages in the field during a disaster, and they often remain long after official services have ended [32]. Ordinary citizens provide much of the additional surge capacity required to respond to more frequent emergencies and disasters in the future [32]. Various scholars have argued about the value of ordinary citizens and their participation in disaster notification systems. For example, Shan et al. [27] argued that disaster notification systems should involve both government departments and the public in collecting emergency information, responding to feedback, connecting to external information, and providing emergency rescue proposals. Palen et al. [33] believed that better emergency management should include activities and information from the public; such activities and information rely on the integration of multiple subfields of computer science and a commitment to understanding the domain applications. Jaeger et al. [34] explored the viability of facilitating resident-to-resident assistance to coordinate community responses to disasters.

Recent studies have shown that implementations of flood inquiry and notification by ordinary citizens including the household and individual citizen levels are adequate [35–37]. However, empirical literature on inquiries and notification by corporate volunteers is still scarce, specifically about how corporate volunteers' capabilities can be integrated into public flood-management systems. Further studies on corporate volunteers can be very useful.

2.4. Public-Private Partnership (PPP)

The public-private partnership (PPP) concept is often used as "the collaboration between a public sector (government) entity and a private sector (for-profit) entity to achieve a specific goal or set of objectives" [38]. According to the categorization of PPPs being adopted by the European Union [39] and many other countries, there are two types of PPPs: the contractual PPPs and the institutionalized PPPs, according to the legal status and governance model. Contractual PPP refers to the relationship between public and private sectors based on the formal contact, which is typically structured with a special juridical and economic purpose. In the contractual PPPs, the private partners are solely responsible for providing services based on a rigid written contract. Instead, the institutionalized PPPs join the public and private partners together in a single PPP to manage and deliver the services. Institutionalized PPPs mix public and private firms included in joint-ventures between public sector entities and private investors [40,41]. The low-cost airport of Charleroi in Belgium is an example of institutionalized PPP. The shareholders' structure of Charleroi airport has diversity investors: the Regional Authorities (28%), Sowaer (49%), venture capital firm—Sambrinvest (19%), private construction company—Sabca (1%), and Sonaca (aerospace industry) 1%. However, the influence of the public authority in airport management is larger than the one provided by its shares, because the Regional Authority also owns 100% of Sowaer and 50% of Sambrinvest [42].

The primary characteristics of PPPs are that added value can be achieved from greater co-operation between public and private actors [43]. None of the definitions have specified that remuneration to the private sector of PPP will necessarily be through user charges [44]. Thus, the governments worldwide agree that PPP should be considered in further disaster management. Increasingly, countries are adopting policies that emphasize the importance of PPPs in disaster resilience. These PPP-related policies recognize that preventing breakdowns of critical infrastructures during disasters cannot be assured even with investment levels exceeding the capacity of most economies; hence, they focus on risk reduction via co-operation between public and private actors rather than risk prevention [45].

Numerous PPP studies have been conducted since the late 1990s, focusing mostly on the success factors of PPP [46]. For example, Osei-Kyei et al. [46] reviewed the studies of the critical success factors for PPP and then identified that risk allocation and sharing, strong private consortium, political support, community/public support, and transparent procurement are critical success factors. Other research areas, such as project management [47], disaster management [48], and corporate social responsibility [49], have also been explored and investigated. The PPP has become a topic of increasing interest to national governments, universities, and scholars around the world. However, most studies have focused on general or institutionalized PPPs. The contractual PPPs were less studied, and still need more attention. The factors that can enable future implementation(s) of contractual PPP projects, and thus, reduce costs, as well as add value, to public interests, should be explored. Therefore, this paper aims to explore further contractual PPPs, downplay conflicts of interest, and achieve win-win outcomes in partnerships in the disaster management area.

2.5. Information System Success Model

Information systems are used to communicate, coordinate, and support disaster inquiry, as well as notify and mitigate emergency events. Many competing theoretical models, such as classic Technology Acceptance Model, Decomposed Theory of Planned Behavior (DTPB), and diffusion of innovations (IDT), coexist in the information system acceptance and adoption literature, each with a different focus and each tested in different contexts. In the field of information system evaluations, DeLone and McLean [50] conducted a landmark study. After reviewing more than 180 papers researching the factors affecting information technology investment, DeLone and McLean developed the information system success model, which is comprised six factors, system quality, information quality, user satisfaction, system use, individual impact, and organizational impact. In 2003, as the service concept was added to information technology along with the use of the Internet, DeLone and McLean [51] further improved the model by adding "service quality" as one of the information system success factors and analyzed the interdependence and correlation of these seven factors (refer to Figure 1). Their proposed information system success model has been widely accepted for the evaluation of information systems in various applications.

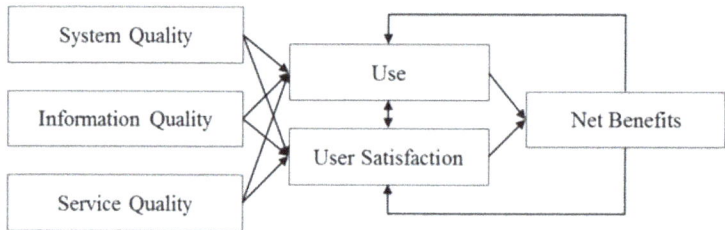

Figure 1. DeLone and McLean information system success model [51].

Many researchers have constructed research frameworks based on the information system success model. For example, Chen [52] evaluated success factors for emergency management engineering information system (EMEIS) based on the information system success model and found that five critical success factors are significantly related: internal organization management, quality of product and technology of suppliers, external technical environment, external policy environment, and coordination and supportive ability of the information center. Lee et al. [53] examined the information systems success model in disaster management of public safety, finding that information quality and system quality are major barriers to efficient and effective multi-agency decision-making, and are critical antecedents to information systems success for efficient and effective disaster management.

2.6. The Analytic Framework

The framework of this study—the success factors of corporate volunteer participation in public flood disaster inquiry and notification systems—is based on the information system success model developed by DeLone and McLean. The assessment system uses five dimensions of DeLone and McLean's model: system quality, information quality, service quality, user satisfaction, and benefits. In DeLone and McLean's [50] original model, information system success was measured at both individual and organizational levels and is determined by systems use and user satisfaction. Because the stakeholders of flood disaster inquiry and notification systems are from multiple agencies—corporate volunteers, public flood disaster management sectors, and information system service providers—information system success is not used to support multi-agency DM operations [53]. We changed user satisfaction to system satisfaction to include all stakeholders. Additionally, we added PPP as one of the influencing dimensions through the Modified Delphi method. The description of five dimensions of DeLone and McLean's model in corporate volunteers into the flood disaster inquiry and notification system application as Table 1.

Table 1. Five dimensions of DeLone and McLean's model in corporate volunteers into the flood disaster inquiry and notification system application.

Dimensions	Description
System Quality	System quality is defined as the degree to which system users believe that a system is easy to use, user-friendly, easy to learn, easy to connect to, and enjoyable to use [54,55]. The quality of an information system concerns the whole process, from the methodology used for IS development to the process of transferring a completed system [56]. System quality concerns the performance characteristics of the information systems measured in terms of ease of use, being easy to learn, response time, and flexibility [53]. Therefore, system quality can be a measure of the functionality of the information system itself, including performance characteristics, such as contents of the database, data accuracy and reliability, response time, and ease of use [57], and thus technical success [50]. The measurement of quality of information system can help ascertain the "fitness for use" of the information system and identify benefits in terms of usage and improvements in productivity [58]. In the context of flood disaster inquiry and notification, system quality is used to evaluate the response time being generated by the output. From the aspect of corporate volunteers, being easy to learn, and ease of use are the two most dominant measures. From the organizational aspect, the system response time and fast integration into public flood-management system during disaster are more important measures, since the corporate volunteers are one of the flood disaster inquiry and notification sources, and the available time for flood disaster inquiry and notification is very limited in floods.
Information Quality	Information quality is the desirable characteristics of the system outputs, i.e., management reports and Web pages [59], and it can be defined as the degree to which system users think that online learning information is up-to-date, accurate, relevant, comprehensive, and organized [55,60]. According to the definition by Eppler [61], information quality is composed of the characteristics of an information product (e.g., a set of information bundled for a specific purpose) that is of high value to its users and meets or exceeds the requirements of all its stakeholders [62]. Information quality measures the quality of the output produced by the information system, including such items as output timeliness, reliability, completeness, and appearance [57], which are the values being perceived by a customer of the output produced by information [63,64]. The mitigation operations of disasters (including floods) are information-intensive processes [53]. The effectiveness of such operations depends largely on the availability of necessary information. The attributes of information quality included in this study include accuracy, completeness, usefulness, and timeliness.

Table 1. *Cont.*

Service Quality	Service quality is the quality of the support that system users receive from the information systems organization and IT support personnel [59]. According to Delone and Mclean [51], service quality of an information system is concerned with information technology organizations, and measuring and comparing user expectations and their perceptions of the effectiveness of the information technology organization [51]. Service quality signifies overall customer evaluations and judgements about the quality of service delivery by an information system [64]. Service quality can be evaluated using attributes, which include tangible, reliability, responsiveness, assurance, functionality, interactivity, and empathy [51,55,65,66]. In the context of flood disaster inquiry and notification, the attributes include individual services, empathy, incentives, procedure consistency, and information feedback. The flood disaster inquiry and notification require skills in geographic information systems (GIS) and reports. Corporate volunteers may not receive training in advance. They may want to do something to help but may not know how or who to contact. System service may offer individual services, specific training, or incentives to engage volunteers. In addition, Rogstadius, Jakob, et al. [67] highlighted that new tools may be a mismatch between system functionality and decision-makers' needs because of the suitable procedures for volunteer management. Thus, the attributes of service quality include procedure consistently and information feedback.
System Satisfaction	User satisfaction is the recipient's response to the use of the outcomes of an information system [51]. Lin and Wang [68] defined user satisfaction as system user's satisfaction with system speed, number of functions, quality, and format. User satisfaction is considered one of the main indicators when assessing the success of new system adoption, and it has been widely used as a measure in the field of IS [59]. According to Hu [69], user satisfaction refers to the extent to which a user perceives a system to be useful and wants to use it again. Attitudes toward the flood disaster inquiry and notification system have been measured by achievement, constant improvement, and volunteer number growth rate.
Benefits	Benefit is the extent to which information systems contribute to the success of individuals, groups, organizations, industries, and nations [70]. Benefits have been suggested to range from efficiency gains to public disaster management sector and corporate volunteers [71]. The attitudes of the flood disaster inquiry and notification system include cost reduction, quality of decision, economic benefits to corporate volunteers, non-economic benefits to corporate volunteers, and the corporate–government trust relationship.
Public-Private Partnership	A Public Private Partnership is generally a medium- to long-term relationship between the public and private sectors (including the voluntary and community sector) involving the sharing of risks and rewards and the utilization of multi-sectoral skills, expertise, and finance to deliver desired policy outcomes that are in the public interest [72]. A public-private partnership is a contractual agreement formed between public and private sector partners that allows more private sector participation rather than traditional participation [73]. The public private partnership is a (relatively) long-term collaboration as a part of an objective to provide a public service as defined by public authority [74]. The measures for evaluating the public-private partnership between a corporate volunteer and the flood disaster inquiry and notification system include regulations, social responsibilities, contract relationship, and partner relationship.

3. Methodology

Flood disaster management problems are inherently complex and multi-faceted, involving many decision-makers, high decision-stakes, limited technical information, and difficult tradeoffs [2]. The MCDM method can model multi-faceted complex systems because of its simplicity and generality. Thus, we employed both qualitative and quantitative methods in the study. We used the qualitative approach of focus group discussion to establish a research framework comprising a set of determinants in the context of formation system success model. Then, the Modified Delphi method was introduced to confirm the dimensions and factors. A hybrid MCDM framework consisting of DEMATEL and ANP was developed for flood disaster inquiry and notification system evaluation in this study. DEMATEL [20] was used to construct an IRM and derive the interrelations between factors. Based on the IRM, the ANP being proposed by Saaty [75] was used to derive the weights. The analytic framework allows us to establish a decision-making framework for a flood disaster inquiry and notification system evaluation (refer to Figure 2).

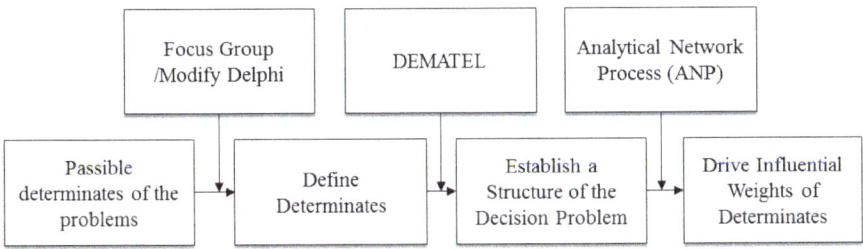

Figure 2. Research Flow of decision-making framework.

Various MCDM approaches such as the ANP, ELECTRE, the Weighted Sum Model (WSM), the Technique for Order of Preference by Similarity to Ideal Solution (TOPSIS), and the Preference Ranking Organization Method for Enrichment Evaluation (PROMETHEE), etc., can be considered while selecting appropriate methods for solving a decision making problem. However, assumptions, weakness or limitations associated with some methods limit the applications of such methods in this work. For example, the weighted sum model (WSM) is the simplest and the most commonly used aggregation operator in MCDM [76]. The TOPSIS method determines a solution with the shortest distance to the ideal solution and the greatest distance from the negative-ideal solution, but it does not consider the relative importance of these distances [77]. The ELECTRE and the PROMETHEE were proposed for ranking alternatives. However, the ELECTRE is weak regarding provisions of ranking scores and intransitivity [78]. The definitions of proper preference functions being required by PROMETHEE are not easy. The Analytic Hierarchical Process (AHP) is one of the traditional methods for deriving weights being associated with each aspect and criteria. A common problem for the above-mentioned MCDM methods is the assumption of independence among criteria, which is unrealistic for decision problems in the real world. Since aspects and criteria inside real-world decision making problems always influence other, an analytic framework consisting of the DEMATEL and the ANP is very suitable. The influence of relationships between the aspects and criteria can be constructed by using the Decision Making and Trial and Evaluation Laboratory (DEMATEL). The ANP can be used to derive the weights associated with each aspect and criterion when considering the influence relationships, and thus the dependences between these aspects and criterion. Therefore, a combination of the DEMATEL and the ANP is very reasonable and suitable for the derivation of factors influencing the successful integration of corporate volunteers into public flood disaster inquiry and notification systems, since dependences between aspects and criteria exist in such problem(s) and should be considered.

3.1. Modified Delphi Method

The Delphi method, designed by Dalkey and Helmer [79], is a method for structuring a group communication process to facilitate group problem-solving and to structure models. The method can be applied to problems that do not lend themselves to precise analytical techniques but rather to those that could benefit from the subjective judgments of individuals on a collective basis and that focus their collective human intelligence on the problem at hand [80]. In other words, when the knowledge of a problem or phenomenon is insufficient, the Delphi method can be used as a quantitative technique.

The Delphi method is a mature and very adaptable research method used in many information systems and IT research arenas [81].

Murry and Hammons [82] modified the traditional Delphi technique by replacing the first round of a survey with the conventionally adopted open style survey. The modified Delphi technique is similar to the full Delphi in terms of procedure and intent. The advantages of the modified Delphi method include time savings and a focus on research themes, eliminating the need for speculation on the open questionnaire and improving the response to the main topic [83]. Accordingly, in this investigation, we developed a quality evaluation criterion to evaluate the factors enabling corporate volunteers to monitor flood disasters by combining the modified Delphi method with interviews of anonymous experts.

3.2. DEMATEL Method

The Geneva Research Centre of the Battelle Memorial Institute developed the DEMATEL method to convert complex systems into a clear causal structure that simplifies interrelationships among consideration factors [20]. The aim of the DEMATEL method is to identify direct and indirect causes and the strength of influence of considered factors by applying matrix computations. Unlike the classical approach of structural equation modeling (SEM), which requires a large sample size to derive causal relationships among variables, the expert opinion-driven DEMATEL method can yield good results from a relatively small sample size [84] and assess the associated cause and effect relationships [85].

The DEMATEL technique has been frequently applied in many situations, such as identifying the key successful factors in emergency management [86], flood mitigation [87], and risk factors of IT outsourcing [88]. Because the current study concentrates on the adoption of corporate volunteers into the public flood information system, survey respondents need to possess both a good understanding of flood emergency management and a background in information systems. The available sample size of those with such qualifications was understandably limited. As such, we employed the DEMATEL method to identify the causation and the strengths of influence of the considered factors. The method can be summarized based on the earlier works by Tzeng and Huang [89], as well as Yang et al. [90]. Please refer to Appendix A for the detail procedures.

3.3. ANP Method

AHP and ANP are two popular MCDM methods that aid decision-makers to derive weights for evaluating and select the best choice in situations characterized by more than one criterion. AHP, introduced by Saaty [75], is a useful approach for resolving complex decision-making problems with some impact factors through the process of analyzing, estimating, and synthesizing. ANP extended the AHP to address restrictions of the hierarchical structure in which criteria are independent from each other. ANP can systematically overcome all types of dependencies by allowing interaction and feedback both within criteria (inner dependence) and between clusters (outer dependence). In fact, ANP uses a network without needing to designate levels, as in a hierarchy. A network of ANP can build a control hierarchy or network of criteria and sub-criteria that controls the interactions and then identifies influences and weights among the components and their clusters [90]. The method can be summarized based on the earlier works by Saaty [75] and Yang et al. [91]. Please refer to Appendix B for the detail procedures.

4. Empirical Study

In this section, an empirical study is discussed to illustrate the application of the proposed model for evaluating flood disaster inquiry and notification systems in Taiwan. First, the background and nature of the empirical study case in Taiwan are introduced. Then, we describe a group discussion meeting we held for the study. We used modified Delphi methods to construct the decision-making framework by inviting domain experts from the water resource agency in Taiwan.

Subsequently, we designed questionnaires in compliance with DEMATEL and ANP format to derive the relationships among factors.

4.1. Flood Disaster Inquiry and Notification System in Taiwan

Taiwan is an island highly vulnerable to natural disasters. The five major natural hazards confronting Taiwan include typhoons, earthquakes, landslides, floods, and debris flow [92,93]. In Taiwan, 73% of the land and population are exposed to three or more types of natural hazards, and 90% of the land and population are exposed to two types of hazards. Since Taiwan is located on the western edge of the Pacific Ocean and in a typhoon-prone area, typhoons bring heavy rainfall in July and August of each year. With an average of 3.6 typhoons per year, flood hazards have significantly affected the lives of Taiwan residents and have caused severe property loss. For example, in 2009, one of the deadliest typhoons, Morakot, dumped heavy rain on Taiwan and caused one of the most severe natural disasters. Typhoon Morakot destroyed 61,163 houses completely or partially, which accounted for $5 billion losses [94] and resulted in 643 fatalities. After Typhoon Morakot, the Taiwanese Water Resources Agency (WRA) of Ministry of Economic Affairs in Taiwan reconfigured the national disaster notification system. In the past, the Water Resource Agency monitored flood disasters by passively receiving information from the public and the media. However, since 2010, the WRA changed the attitude and started to monitor the disaster information proactively. The WRA recruited and trained volunteers every year to monitor the current conditions of flood disaster because of limited labor to perform extensive flood inspections. To become a qualified monitor, volunteers must attend training sessions held by the WRA. In 2011, the WRA reconfigured flood volunteers by engaging corporate volunteers in the original public flood notification systems. To get effective and timely flood information form volunteers, WRA operates a platform flood disaster inquiry and notification system built by Chunghwa telecom in Taiwan. The flood disaster inquiry and notification system is a part of "Disaster Prevention Information Service Network" (Website: http://579.wra.gov.tw/dn/). The public flood control volunteers and corporate volunteers may report the current flood status using the flood disaster inquiry and notification system.

Corporate volunteers who are involved in flood monitoring include clerks of the largest 24-h convenient store system, the 7-Eleven Corporation, the Taiwan Sugar Corporation (Taisugar), and the employees of the leading all-day operated gas station chains, the Chinese Petroleum Corporation (CPC). Since the corporate volunteers are from the largest 24-h shop chains, the notification system can operate 24 h a day, 365 days per year, and in most urban areas of Taiwan. Included in this system are 7027 notification sites. At least one site can be found in each town and village. To monitor the flood disasters, the system automatically informs the clerks of the 7-Elevens and the employees of the gas stations using auto dial and automatic speech recognition systems about whether a flood is happening and whether the flood level is more than 30 cm or less. The clerks or the employees can reply easily by pressing buttons to send a message to the Water Resource Agency in about three minutes. Comprehensive information on the flood can be completely collected by the system in 30 min. Such corporate volunteers can serve as a reference for resource allocation and rescue-team dispatches. The system also provides flood disaster notification information to the 7-Eleven post and display system.

4.2. Decision-Making Framework Construction

To identify the factors influencing the integration of corporate volunteers into public flood disaster inquiry and notification systems, this study used the information systems success model and the PPP model to define the decision-making framework based on experts' opinions summarized by Delphi. Five domain experts were heavily involved in the focus group meetings. They were asked to identify possible factors enabling corporate volunteers to provide information to the flood disaster inquiry and notification system. The rigor and validity of the results were further confirmed by the modified Delphi method by summarizing opinions provided by 18 experts. The experts included water resource agency officers, information system service providers, managers from the 7-Eleven Corporation, and flood disaster notification researchers. All experts had more than five years of work experience related to flood disasters. As a result, 24 factors belonging to 6 dimensions were summarized. After confirming the possible criteria using the Modified Delphi method, an evaluation framework for investigating the factors influencing the integration of corporate volunteers into the flood disaster inquiry and notification system evaluation model was constructed (Table 2).

4.3. Results

To assess the effects among the various criteria and then derive the weights being associated with the criteria, the causal structures were developed first by using the DEMATEL method. Then, the weights being associated with each criterion were derived using the ANP methods. Experts' opinions regarding the influence of one factor on another were assessed using the DEMATEL method; subsequently, using Equations (A1)–(A3), we derived the total influence among the six dimensions defined in Table 2. The total relation matrices of factors belonging to each dimension were also derived and demonstrated in Equations (A9)–(A15). Using Equations (A4) and (A5), the causal diagram was constructed based on the r_i and c_i values (refer to Table A1) derived from the total relationships among the dimensions and among the factors within their respective dimensions. The causal diagrams are demonstrated in Figure 3. In this research, the threshold value was set as the average value (μ) plus 1/2 times the standard deviation (σ) of all the items in the total relationship matrix T. Accordingly, the structure of the decision problem can be defined based on the influence of the relationships or the IRM derived using DEMATEL. The IRM can serve as the basis for the ANP, which can be used to derive relative importance of each factor based on the opinions provided by the 16 experts. Based on the pairwise comparison of the factors obtained from the ANP questionnaire, the unweighted supermatrix W_c and limited supermatrix were calculated using Equations (A6)–(A8) according to the Super Decisions. The results are demonstrated in Equations (A16) and (A17). The weights corresponding to each dimension and criteria were thus obtained based on the weighted supermatrix. The results are summarized in Table 3.

The results of DEMATEL methods are illustrated in Figure 3. The axes represent the degree of influence of one dimension on another dimension, or those of one criterion on another criterion, in which the criteria belong to the same dimension. Apparently, system quality(A) dominates and influences all the other dimensions. The research results indicated that system quality (A), information quality (B), and service quality (C) influence corporate volunteers, encouraging them to engage more aggressively in disaster response during flooding. User dimensions, such as system satisfaction (D), benefit (E), and public-private partnership (PPP) (F), are dimensions that are mainly influenced by other dimensions.

According to Table 3, the importance of dimensions can be prioritized as (1) System Quality (A), (2) System Satisfaction (D), (3) Benefits (E), (4) Information Quality (B), (5) Public-Private Partnership (F), and (6) Service Quality (C). Furthermore, the local weights are transformed into global weights, which allow us to compare the importance of factors across six dimensions. The top-ranking factors with the highest weights included (1) being easy to use (a_1), (2) results being achieved (d_3), (3) partner relationship (f_3), and (4) regulations/social responsibilities (f_1). Those criteria are the most important ones for integrating corporate volunteers into the public flood disaster inquiry and notification system.

Table 2. Possible dimensions and criteria for deriving the factors influencing the integration of corporate volunteers into the flood disaster inquiry and notification system.

Dimensions	Factors	Descriptions
System Quality (A)	Easy to use (a_1)	Information system is easy to use
	Easy to learn (a_2)	Information system is easy to learn.
	Response time (a_3)	Information system communicates information quickly to the emergency responders.
	Interoperability (a_4)	Information system integrates various corporate and public inquiry and response operations.
Information Quality (B)	Accuracy (b_1)	The flood information is accurate.
	Completeness (b_2)	The coverage rate of the area is high.
	Usefulness (b_3)	The information is useful from the dimension of emergency support and recovery.
	Timely updating of information (b_4)	The system can update information in a timely manner.
Service Quality (C)	Individual services (c_1)	The system provides services to individual users (e.g., actual personnel repartee).
	Empathy (c_2)	The system offers users specific training needs (e.g., online tutorials on YouTube, face-to-face training).
	Incentives (c_3)	The system provides incentives to corporate volunteers so that the firms are willing to cooperate.
	Procedure consistently (c_4)	The system is consistently courteous with users business processing and decreases interference.
	Information feedback (c_5)	The system provides users' statistics of disaster response rates to companies for improvement.
System Satisfaction (D)	Results being achieved (d_1)	The system achieves expected results of original floods investigations.
	Constantly improves (d_2)	The system can be improved constantly.
	Volunteer number growth rate (d_3)	More firms can be recruited to increase the total number of corporate volunteers.
Benefits (E)	Cost reduction (e_1)	The cost of flood data collection can significantly be reduced.
	Quality of Decision (e_2)	The quality of decision can be significantly enhanced.
	Economic benefits to Corporate Volunteers (e_3)	The system can bring benefits to the corporate volunteers (e.g., mitigate flood damages and enhance customers' purchase intensions).
	Non-economic benefits to Corporate Volunteers (e_4)	The system has potential benefits for corporations (e.g., public interests and the coherence of staff).
	Corporate–government trust relationship (e_5)	The collaboration may enhance trust between the government and corporations.
Public-Private Partnership (F)	Regulations/social responsibilities (f_1)	Regulations and social responsibility can encourage corporates to serve as volunteers.
	Contract relationship (f_2)	The government should contract with the corporations (e.g., defining obligations and responsibilities).
	Partner relationship (f_3)	The government establishes partnerships with firms to become corporate volunteers (non-contracted relationship).

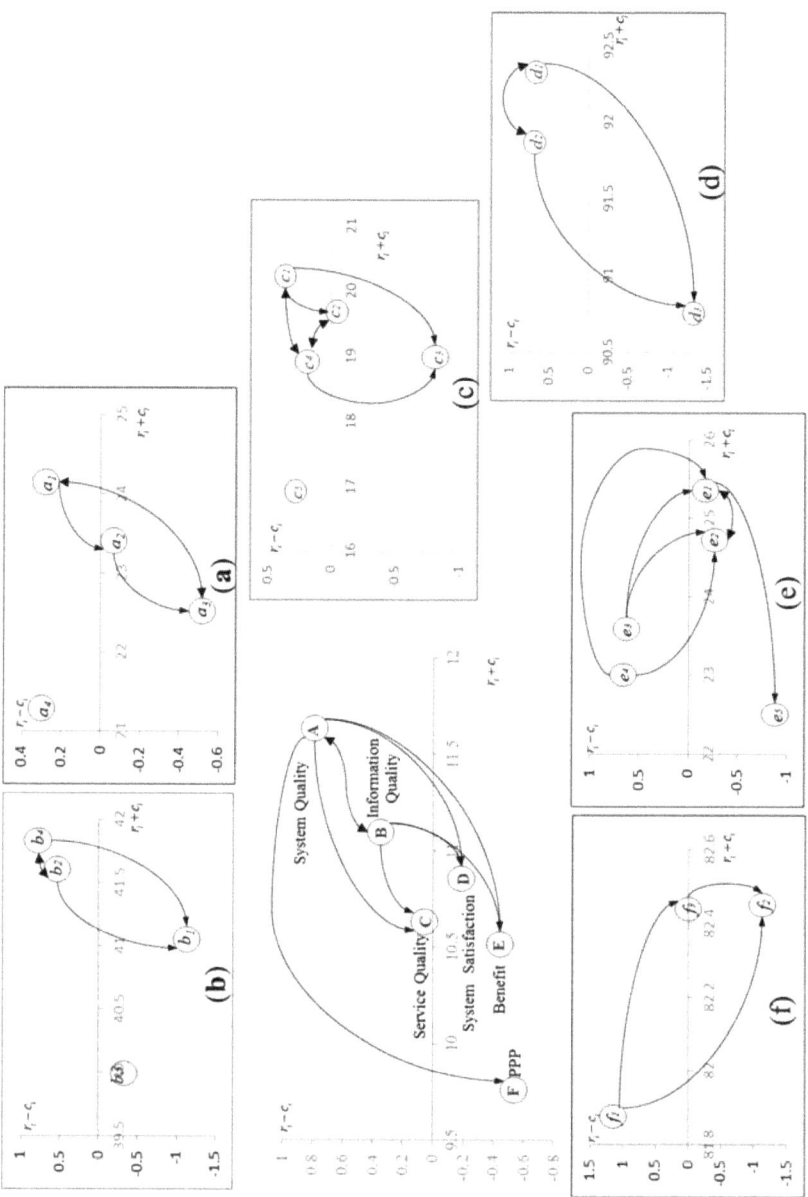

Figure 3. Causal diagram of total relationship. Note: The threshold is set at $\mu + (1/2)\sigma$ of the total relationships.

Table 3. Weights for evaluating Flood Disaster Inquiry and Notification System.

Dimension	Weight	Factors	Local Weight	Global Weight	Rank
System Quality (A)	0.171 (1)	Easy to use (a_1)	0.385	0.066	1
		Easy to learn (a_2)	0.294	0.050	8
		Response time (a_3)	0.295	0.051	2
		Interoperability (a_4)	0.026	0.004	24
Information Quality (B)	0.167 (4)	Accuracy (b_1)	0.297	0.050	10
		Completeness (b_2)	0.280	0.047	12
		Usefulness (b_3)	0.136	0.023	22
		Timely updating of information (b_4)	0.288	0.048	11
Service Quality (C)	0.157 (6)	Individual services (c_1)	0.222	0.035	17
		Empathy (c_2)	0.197	0.031	20
		Incentives (c_3)	0.238	0.037	15
		Procedure consistently (c_4)	0.260	0.041	13
		Information feedback (c_5)	0.083	0.013	23
System Satisfaction (D)	0.170 (2)	Results being achieved (d_1)	0.366	0.062	2
		Constantly improvements (d_2)	0.295	0.050	9
		Volunteer Number Growth Rate (d_3)	0.339	0.058	4
System Benefit (E)	0.168 (3)	Cost reduction (e_1)	0.234	0.039	14
		Quality of Decision (e_2)	0.215	0.036	16
		Economic Benefits to Corporate Volunteers (e_3)	0.189	0.032	18
		Non-economic benefits to Corporate Volunteers (e_4)	0.176	0.030	21
		Corporate–government trust relationship (e_5)	0.186	0.031	19
Public-Private Partnership (F)	0.167 (5)	Regulations/social responsibilities (f_1)	0.345	0.058	5
		Contract relationship (f_2)	0.303	0.051	6
		Partner relationship (f_3)	0.352	0.059	3
	1.000		6.000	1.000	

5. Discussion

The goal of this study was to assess the determinants of influencing integration of Corporate Volunteers into Public Flood Disaster Inquiry and Notification Systems and their relationships to integrate corporate volunteers into public flood inquiry and notification systems through integrating information success model and the PPP model. To this end, we constructed a two-level research framework: a high level consisting of six dimensions and a detail level consisting of 24 factors. After the DEMATEL analysis and further weight analysis using the ANP method, the research results indicated that the importance and causal effects of the determinants at these two levels differed.

5.1. Managerial Implications from the Dimensions Level

This study intended to provide an in-depth understanding of the factors enabling the integration of corporate volunteers into the public flood inquiry and notification system. Thus, the public sector can initiate more effective strategies with very limited budgets to achieve the effectiveness, efficiency, and transparency of decisions. Based on the results of DEMATEL (refer to Figure 3), system quality (A) and information quality (B) are the causal dimensions that influence system satisfaction (D), service quality (C), and benefit (E). The improvements in the system quality (A) and information quality (B) can lead to improvements in other dimensions and criteria as well. This finding is consistent with the information system success model proposed by DeLone and Mclean [50]. According to

DeLone and Mclean [50], information quality (A) and system quality (B) are the key elements for information system success that can also increase user satisfaction. Bharosa et al. [95] further confirmed that information quality and system quality are the key drivers of effective multi-agency disaster management in technical-social contexts (refer to Figure 3).

The system quality (A) with the highest prominence value plays a central role in the result of the DEMATEL, indicating this dimension's highest degree of influence in the total relations. The system quality (A) dimension is also the most critical dimension of the flood disaster inquiry and notification system based on the analytic results being derived by the ANP. The system quality (A) is regarded as a technical or engineering concept, whereas information quality (B) is a pervasive social concept. The reason of system quality (A) with the highest prominence value is that the flood disaster inquiry and notification system involves multiple stakeholders, including the Water Resources Agency, corporate volunteers, and information service providers. Ensuring high information quality among multiple disaster stakeholders is difficult due to the complexity, dynamics, and uncertainty of disaster management. Emphasizing the efforts into ensuring system quality may reduce the communication barriers among multiple stakeholders. Because the interaction between systems usually occurs within an organizational context, larger problems can always be found in the organizational architecture and can support via technical architecture. Besides, flood disaster information quality depends largely on the effectiveness of information system operations to collect for disaster information. This phenomenon is consistent with previous studies. According to Bharosa et al. [95], the mono-disciplinary system can be joined relatively easily; however, many technical and organizational problems exist among the different parties involved. Although system architects consider the information quality to be a larger concern compared to the system quality, they currently put most of their efforts into ensuring system quality rather than information quality. Further, previous research has also suggested that system quality (A) influences information quality (B). Since information depends largely on system operations and the effectiveness of information collection for disaster management, information quality is most closely related to the output of system quality [96]. Our research results demonstrated the mutual interaction between system quality and information quality.

In addition to the information quality (A) and system quality (B), the results of the DEMATEL revealed that the service quality (C) is also a cause dimension, although it ranked as the least important dimension according to the ANP results. This analytic result is not consistent with the information system success model [51]. According to Delone and McLean [51], service quality directly affects usage intentions and user satisfaction with the system, as well as the net benefits produced by the system. As the information system becomes more complicated and harder to use, users need more service support. However, people in emergencies have very limited time to deal with service issues unrelated to the emergency. Since the public flood disaster response system is designed to facilitate public administrators' decisions and is not for profit, the government decision-makers focus more on flood disaster information. In the empirical study case in Taiwan, there only two questions for corporate volunteer to respond to: whether a flood is happening, and whether the flood level is more than 30 cm or less. The system is designed to be easy to reply to and is service-free. Thus, service quality was not ranked as dominant according to the ANP result, which is also consistent with prior works.

The PPP (F) dimension ranked lower in priority compared to the system quality (A), information quality (B), and service quality (C) dimensions from the results of ANP. This research finding concurs with the recent study by Auzzir et al. [48]. Auzzir et al. [48] argued that the governments of developing countries are less attractive to actors from private sectors who usually do not actively participate in disaster management. This phenomenon is inconsistent with that observed in developed countries, where disasters are often managed strategically through public and private collaborations. In developing countries, the public sectors are the sole or major accountable institutions for disaster management because public institutes do not have sufficient resources in integrating flood information effectively. Traditionally, accurate flood information should be received on time at the earliest possibility. Inaccurate information should be detected and verified. Otherwise, the transmission or information failure will be notified. This problem is especially significant nowadays, since disaster information is provided by private sectors for disaster management, which could contribute to information overload, lack of trustworthiness, lack of reliable access, and decreased privacy protection of users [97]. In general, public sectors prefer to focus on improving the quality of information, as well as the system, so as to get real-time and accurate information. Acquiring information from the PPPs is not the major focus of these sectors.

In terms of the relationship among the dimensions, Figure 3 reveals that that the PPP (F) dimension is the effect dimension influenced by the system quality (A) dimension. This result is consistent with prior studies on PPP in disaster management, arguing that the efforts should be the core concern of corporate officials [38]. The PPP allows for a better sharing of costs and benefits between private and public sectors [98]. When a government regards one private sector as a full partner that can mitigate, prepare for, respond to, and recover from disasters by its own efforts, the private sector is expected to account for some responsibilities before, during, and after emergencies. Thus, the public and private sector actors need to define their roles in the partnership. However, in the empirical case, no contract or agreement between the public sector(s) and corporate volunteer(s) is available. Unless the responsibilities of public volunteers are clearly defined in advance, i.e., the system quality (A) can be assured, nothing can be expected from the partnership (i.e., PPP, or the dimension F). Such phenomenon can eventually erode the effectiveness of the partnership; even worse, the partnership can be abandoned [38]. This result is consistent with earlier works by Steijn et al. [43], who argued that when projects become more complex, the degree of PPP increases. Simple system quality does not need to address PPP but use of less complex arrangements. Our research provides the evidence of the influence of the relationships of system quality (A) and PPP (F).

5.2. Criteria in the System Quality (A) Dimension

Among the factors of the system quality (A) dimension, easy to use (a_1) the flood information system is the most important criterion, with a weight of 0.358. The ease of use (a_1) dimension influences easy to learn (a_2) and response time (a_3). This analytic result is consistent with earlier works by McDougall [16]. Ease of use (a_1) is a critical quality requirement for the system, because volunteers with various backgrounds are untrained and are often unable to observe flood conditions immediately. The difficulty of usage of information system should especially be reduced because there is not much or no time for corporate volunteers to learn how the system can be operated during a disaster [95]. The scenario is fully applicable to the empirical study case here, as corporate volunteers, including clerks of convenient stores (i.e., 7–11 here) or managers of gas stations, can be get very busy during a disaster. To encourage corporate volunteers to respond to flood conditions immediately (i.e., within 2 min), only 2 questions designed measured using nominal scales are provided: (1) Is it flooding or not? (2) Is the flood depth over 0.3 cm? The flood inquiry and notification system uses a telephone-based automatic audience survey system instead of web or mobile applications, which can hinder the usage of system by convenient store clerks or oil station managers. For decision-makers, traditionally, flood disaster management involves local and federal governments, which include county commissions, zoning boards, mayors, planning departments, and other local government entities [22]. Nowadays, flood control and avoidance is no longer the sole role of federal or local governments. Decision-makers also bear responsibility for collecting overall flood information from corporate volunteers within 30 min and distribute disaster information to all flood management stakeholders. Thus, according to the relationships of the system quality dimension (A) being demonstrated in the upper right-hand side of Figure 2, easy to use (a_1) and easy to learn (a_2) influence the response time (a_3).

5.3. Criteria in the Information Quality (B) Dimension

The analytic result demonstrates that accuracy (b_1) is the most important criterion in the information quality dimension. Information accuracy can greatly be improved by incorporating volunteers' into the public flood disaster inquiry and notification systems. Further, numerous mechanisms have been developed to improve the information accuracy. For example, information provided by corporate volunteers can be double-checked through other sources, such as sensors or professionally trained staffs. Therefore, corporate volunteers can become another dominant source of flood information. The value of corporate volunteers is undeniable, due to the immediate provisions of flood information. In this regard, timely updating of information (b_4) influences accuracy (b_1), as shown in Figure 3.

5.4. Managerial Implications from the Corporate Volunteer Perspective

In contrast to individual volunteers, there are two advantages to using corporate volunteers in monitoring flood hazards. (1) Corporate volunteers provide continuous and concurrent real-time observations of the flood status over a wide area. The monitoring of flood hazards requires continuous and concurrent real-time observations from several monitoring points or stations distributed in a wide geographic area. Such observations cannot be achieved easily by individual volunteers or nonprofit organizations due to the scale and scope of the required observations. As corporate volunteers persist over time, they can earn trust of the key stakeholders. Such trust enables further cooperation and thus more meaningful contributions [99]. (2) Additionally, corporate volunteers provide specific domain knowledge, skills, and resources for flood monitoring. Specific knowledge and skills are required to monitor flood hazards. Firms that are willing to provide resources to support corporate volunteers are more likely to provide resources, such as time, money, and manpower, which are necessary when training employees. In general, three implications can be drawn accordingly: (1) corporate volunteers are much more efficient from the aspect of information sharing; (2) corporate volunteers are more knowledgeable and trained about flood hazard; and (3) the self-reinforcing mechanism underlying the relation between system quality and information quality further enhances the efficiency of corporate volunteers.

5.4.1. Corporate Volunteers Are Much More Efficient from the Aspect of Information Sharing

According to the traditional definition by Grant [100], corporate volunteers offer their time, knowledge, or skills to the company as a part of a community service, outreach, or social responsibility activity without additional compensation or direct personal remuneration. Very few, if any, prior studies have discussed corporate volunteers who provide their time, knowledge, and skills with the aids of IT competencies, which means resources and capabilities obtained from the local firms. In our empirical study case, the corporate volunteers provided their services with the aid of IT competences belonging to the focal firms, making them more efficient compared to the individual volunteers. This phenomenon is consistent with the reviewed literature. The causal relationships derived in the empirical case further demonstrate this rationale.

Becta [101] described an information system as "a system consisting of the network of all communication channels used within an organization". Such communication channels include face-to-face, broadcast media, mobile communication, electronic channel, written messages, and other channels [102]. Some of the firm-level communication channels (e.g., the broadband network) and the disaster recovery mechanism (e.g., Telecommunication Infrastructure, as well as carrier and support introduced by Yang et al. [91]) are not easily available to individual volunteers. Such firm-level communication channels and information systems can enable faster completion of tasks and activities, accelerate data preparation and transmission times, increase reaction speed, and support decision-making processes-enhancing efficiency [103]; thus, they can guarantee successful flood hazard information delivery even in the event of disasters. In general, the flood disaster inquiry and notification system enables volunteers to communicate by using an information system belonging to the focal firms in a timely manner to ensure successful information delivery.

From the aspects of system response time (a_3), timely updating of information (b_5), and timely information feedback (c_5), firms can assure the above-mentioned factors through the appropriate management of information systems. In contrast, individual volunteers can assure such factors using the information-sharing mechanism, which is not as developed as a specific information system or management mechanism (refer Figure 3). According to Lin et al. [104], system response time and output information accuracy belong to the criteria for evaluating the efficiency of an information system. Based on the IRM illustrated in Figure 3, the response time (a_3) criteria in system quality aspect (A) influence the timely updating of information (b_5) in information quality aspect (B). Both the response time (a_3) and the timely updating of information (b_5) can influence information feedback (c_5) of service quality aspect (C). The Flood Disaster Inquiry and Notification System can assure efficiency of an information system from the aspects of the system response time from the system quality aspect (A) and the information quality aspect (B). The positive feedback and relationships of influence further enhance efficiency. Therefore, corporate volunteers, using the information system provided by the focal firms, can deliver information more efficiently compared to individual volunteers via information sharing.

5.4.2. Corporate Volunteers Are More Knowledgeable and Trained about Flood Hazard

In Section 4.1, the authors mentioned that since 2010, the WRA has been recruiting and training volunteers every year to help monitor the current conditions of flood disaster because of limited manpower to perform extensive inspections of flooding. To become qualified, monitor volunteers must attend training sessions held by the WRA. Therefore, these corporate volunteers are more knowledgeable and trained about flood hazards.

5.4.3. The Self-Reinforcing Mechanism of the Relation between System Quality and Information Quality Further Enhances the Efficiency of Corporate Volunteers

From the relationships of influence demonstrated in Figure 3, only system quality (A) forms a self-reinforcing mechanism with the information quality (B) aspect, in which the total influence values from system quality aspect to the information quality is 1.073 and the influence from information quality to system quality is 1.001, as shown in Table 3. The corporate volunteers can also access the Flood Disaster Inquiry and Notification System introduced in the empirical study case in Section 4.1. For private individuals, since there is no such feedback regarding the relationships between system quality and information quality, the information gathered will not be strengthen.

5.5. Contribution of This Research to Extant Literature and Future Research Possibilities

Regarding to the contribution, corporate volunteer partnerships with non-profit organizations have progressively developed in real world over the last ten years. The corporate volunteer programs have been described as one of the fastest-growing areas of voluntary activity, with North America as the market leader and with a rising interest in Western European countries. Over 90 percent of Fortune 500 companies run employee volunteer programs, formally sponsoring and subsidizing employees' efforts to perform community service and outreach activities on company time [105]. However, this field is still in its infancy and limited in magnitude. Most literatures are in the disciplines of business, management, and ethics. Researchers have emphasized a strong employee-centered and business focus and a narrow geographic spread [105]. This study focused on a developing country in Asia, because the public sector's resources are limited, and most firms are small-to-medium enterprises. Compared to the focus on financial services from Fortune 500 companies in North America and Western Europe, this study demonstrated an alternative viewpoint regarding the feasibility of integration of the corporate volunteers, as well as the firm's IT resources.

Besides, literature has strongly advised nonprofits developing strategies for successful cooperation with companies [106]. The management tools used by corporate volunteers could increase professionalism of nonprofits; thus far, the nonprofits studied have hardly developed any strategies for corporate volunteers [107]. The Public Flood Disaster Inquiry and Notification System is a useful communication tool between corporate volunteers and public sectors. The analysis of key influence factors based on successful information model may offer nonprofits effective communication strategies for coping with corporate volunteers.

Most of the past works have focused on the roles of corporate volunteers in corporate social responsibility. Future research possibilities include comparing the flood data collected by corporate volunteers and individual volunteers. Furthermore, evaluations of motivations and the quality of the data collected by corporate volunteers and individual volunteers might enable a continuous optimization of all projects and of a corporate volunteer strategy.

6. Concluding Remarks

The definition, configuration, and reconfiguration of flood disaster inquiry and notification systems are critical, attracting tremendous interest from policy-makers and researchers. In this study, we developed a decision support system to enable the integration of corporate volunteers into flood disaster inquiry and notification systems. The decision framework has further been verified as feasible based on the opinions provided by Taiwanese experts. The combination of theoretical and practical considerations in the proposed decision framework has important implications for both academics and practitioners in gaining a better understanding of the factors influencing the integration of corporate volunteers into public disaster inquiry and notification systems.

In the past, numerous studies have been conducted in the field of flood disaster detection, inquiry, and notification systems. Although corporate volunteers can play a crucial role in enhancing the efficiency and effectiveness of delivering disaster information in various disaster management contexts, studies on corporate volunteers in disaster management systems are limited. This work is the first academic research project related to the integration of corporate volunteers into public emergency management systems through adopting the information system success model and the PPP. This research further extends the existing studies by applying social science research to natural hazard threats preventions, demonstrating the partnership between corporate volunteers and the government. With the well-verified theoretical framework, a new research field of public participation in disaster management can be created.

Practically, the key objective of government flood disaster departments is to conduct overall flood disaster assessments immediately. The integration of corporate volunteers into the public flood disaster inquiry and notification system can improve the information quality. Our research results indicated that corporate volunteers can provide timely and accurate information to fill the traditional gap in flood disaster mitigation by government institutes only. Further, the analytic results can help define strategies to enhance the participation of corporate volunteers in the disaster inquiry and mitigation system, and further enhance the system's satisfaction, reducing the cost of flood information collection and increasing decision-making effectiveness and efficiency. The experiences of the incorporations of corporate volunteers into the public flood disaster inquiry and notification systems that are emerging can also serve as the basis for other countries to incorporate corporate volunteers into the public flood disaster inquiry and notification systems.

Finally, flood disaster management problems are inherently complex, time-bound, and multi-faceted. Such problems involve many decision-makers, have high stakes and limited technical information, and result in difficult tradeoffs. The hybrid MCDM-based analytic framework can solve these problems and contribute to more effective disaster management. Since the available resources of most government flood disaster management departments are limited, the research results and prioritizing improvements in system and information quality can serve as the basis for system improvement in the future. Our results can also serve as the basis for public policy definitions. The proposed multi-criteria decision support instruments can enhance communication among stakeholders, such as the administrators from the public sector, corporate management, and information system providers. The PPPs can also be improved accordingly, though the availability of resources is very limited. In the future, the framework can help improve flood disaster information inquiry and notification performance under a limited budget, increasing decision-making effectiveness, efficiency, and transparency.

Author Contributions: M.-C.S. and C.-L.Y. conducted the observations and designed research. C.-L.Y. and C.-Y.H. performed research, analyzed the data, and wrote the paper.

Acknowledgments: We thank Taiwanese Water Resources Agency of Ministry of Economic Affairs' staff for inspiring conversations, suggestions, and feedback in preparing this article.

Conflicts of Interest: The authors declare no conflict of interest.

Appendix A. DEMATEL

The following are explanations of the DEMATEL formulas based on Tzeng and Huang [89], as well as Yang et al. [90].

Step 1: Build an initial direct-relation matrix

Experts are asked to indicate the direct influence degree between factor i and factor j, as indicated by a_{ij}, using a pair-wise comparison scale designated with five levels. The initial direct-relation matrix A is obtained by deriving the influence relationships between criteria through Equation (A1).

$$A = \begin{bmatrix} a_{11} & \cdots & a_{1j} & \cdots & a_{1n} \\ \vdots & & \vdots & & \vdots \\ a_{i1} & \cdots & a_{ij} & \cdots & a_{in} \\ \vdots & & \vdots & & \vdots \\ a_{n1} & \cdots & a_{nj} & \cdots & a_{nn} \end{bmatrix} \tag{A1}$$

a_{ij} is denoted as the degree to which the ith objective affects the jth objective.

Step 2: Normalize the direct-relation matrix

The normalized direct-relation matrix N is obtained through Equation (A2).

$$N = yA, \ y = \min \left\{ 1/\max_i \sum_{j=1}^{n} a_{ij}, 1/\max_j \sum_{i=1}^{n} a_{ij} \right\}, \ i, j \in \{1, 2, \ldots, n\}. \tag{A2}$$

Step 3: Build the total relation matrix T.

The total-relation matrix T is acquired by Equation (A3):

$$\begin{aligned} T &= N + N^2 + N^3 + \ldots + N^{\varepsilon} \\ &= N(I + N + N^2 + \ldots + N^{\varepsilon-1})(I - N)(I - N)^{-1} \\ &= N(I - N^{\varepsilon})(I - N)^{-1} \\ &= N(I - N)^{-1}, \text{ when } \varepsilon \to \infty, \ N^{\varepsilon} = [0]_{n \times n} \end{aligned} \tag{A3}$$

in which $\varepsilon \to \infty$, I is the identity matrix.

Step 4: Compute the influence strength of the factors

Aggregate the values of the rows and columns in matrix T to obtain a value r and c through the Equations (A4) and (A5), respectively. Thus, r_i presents the sum of the influences dispatching from factor i to the other factors. The c_j is the column sum of the jth column of matrix T.

$$T = [t_{ij}], \ i, j \in \{1, 2, \ldots. n\}$$

$$\mathbf{r} = [r_i]_{n \times 1} = \left(\sum_{j=1}^{n} t_{ij} \right)_{n \times 1} \tag{A4}$$

$$c = \left[c_j\right]_{n \times 1} = \left(\sum_{i=1}^{n} t_{ij}\right)'_{1 \times n} \tag{A5}$$

Step 5: Produce a causal diagram

A causal diagram can be acquired by mapping a data set $(r_i + c_i, r_i - c_i)$. The value of $r_i + c_i$ indicates the strength of influence given and received. The higher the value of $r_i + c_i$ a factor has, the more related it is to the other factors. Similarly, the value of $r_i - c_i$ indicates the causal relationship between factors. If $r_i - c_i$ is positive, then the factor is a "cause factor", dispatching influence to the others. If $r_i - c_i$ is negative, the factor is an "effect factor", receiving influence from others. The higher the value of $r_i - c_i$ a factor has, the more influence it has on the other factors, and hence this factor is presumed to have a higher priority than the others. In other words, the lower the value of $r_i - c_i$ a factor has, the greater its received influence from the other factors, and, consequently, the lower the priority it is assumed to have [89].

Step 6: Set a threshold value and obtain the Network Relation Map (NRM)

The visualization of all of the network of determinates form matrix T is too complex to extract valuable information. It is necessary to set a threshold value α for the influence level to filter out minor effects. The influence value in matrix T is higher than the threshold value that will be chosen and converted into the NRM. The threshold value can be decided by the experts. When the threshold value and the relative NRM have been decided, the NRM can be drawn accordingly.

Appendix B. Analytic Network Process (ANP)

The following are explanations of the ANP formulas based on Saaty [75] and Yang et al. [91].

Step 7: Build an unweighted supermatrix through pairwise comparisons

The original supermatrix of column eigenvectors is obtained from pairwise comparison matrices of elements. The C_h denotes the nth cluster, e_{nm} denotes the mth criterion in the nth cluster, and W_{ij} in the supermatrix is a principal eigenvector of the influence of the elements in the ith component of the network on an element in the jth component. In addition, if the jth cluster has no influence on the ith cluster, then $W_{ij} = [0]$.

$$W = \begin{array}{c} \\ C_1 \\ \\ \\ C_2 \\ \\ \\ C_2 \end{array} \begin{array}{c} e_{11} \\ e_{12} \\ \vdots \\ e_{1n_1} \\ e_{21} \\ e_{22} \\ \vdots \\ e_{2n_2} \\ \vdots \\ e_{m1} \\ e_{m2} \\ \vdots \\ e_{mn_m} \end{array} \begin{bmatrix} W_{11} & W_{12} & \cdots & W_{1m} \\ \\ W_{21} & W_{22} & \cdots & W_{2m} \\ \\ & & \ddots & \\ \\ W_{m1} & W_{m2} & \cdots & W_{mm} \end{bmatrix} \tag{A6}$$

Step 8: Obtain the weighted supermatrix by multiplying the normalized matrix

After forming the supermatrix, the weighted supermatrix is derived by transforming all columns sum to unity exactly. The weighted supermatrix is raised to limiting powers, such as Equation (A7), to get the global priority vector or called weights.

$$\lim_{\theta \to \infty} W^{\theta} \tag{A7}$$

In addition, if the supermatrix has the effect of cyclicity, the limiting supermatrix is not the only one. There are two or more limiting supermatrices in this situation, and the Cesaro sum would need to be calculated to get the priority. The Cesaro sum is formulated as follows.

$$\lim_{\psi \to \infty} \left(\frac{1}{\nu}\right) \sum_{j=1}^{\nu} W_j^{\psi} \tag{A8}$$

to calculate the average effect of the limiting supermatrix (i.e., the average priority weights) in which W_j denotes the jth limiting supermatrix.

Appendix C. The Detailed Calculation Procedures of the DEMATEL

Total relation matrix $T_{dimensions}$ of dimensions:

$$T_{dimensions} = \begin{bmatrix} 0.906 & 1.073 & 1.056 & 1.093 & 1.082 & 1.012 \\ 1.001 & 0.827 & 0.965 & 1.006 & 0.997 & 0.920 \\ 0.933 & 0.910 & 0.760 & 0.938 & 0.913 & 0.883 \\ 0.915 & 0.931 & 0.903 & 0.790 & 0.924 & 0.862 \\ 0.872 & 0.860 & 0.846 & 0.882 & 0.741 & 0.836 \\ 0.793 & 0.775 & 0.769 & 0.811 & 0.820 & 0.637 \end{bmatrix} \tag{A9}$$

Total relation matrix T_a of factors:

$$T_a = \begin{bmatrix} 2.994 & 3.228 & 3.142 & 2.844 \\ 3.136 & 2.816 & 2.991 & 2.722 \\ 2.935 & 2.877 & 2.609 & 2.596 \\ 2.862 & 2.814 & 2.784 & 2.323 \end{bmatrix} \tag{A10}$$

Total relation matrix T_b of factors:

$$T_b = \begin{bmatrix} 4.942 & 5.054 & 4.935 & 5.053 \\ 5.457 & 5.077 & 5.222 & 5.326 \\ 5.154 & 5.011 & 4.686 & 5.016 \\ 5.530 & 5.390 & 5.268 & 5.134 \end{bmatrix} \tag{A11}$$

Total relation matrix T_c of factors:

$$T_c = \begin{bmatrix} 15.279 & 15.542 & 15.682 \\ 15.535 & 15.128 & 15.609 \\ 15.012 & 14.930 & 14.759 \end{bmatrix} \tag{A12}$$

Total relation matrix T_d of factors:

$$T_d = \begin{bmatrix} 1.992 & 2.189 & 2.188 & 2.091 & 1.843 \\ 2.122 & 1.889 & 2.097 & 1.984 & 1.746 \\ 1.945 & 1.914 & 1.750 & 1.830 & 1.636 \\ 2.040 & 2.034 & 2.033 & 1.742 & 1.699 \\ 1.824 & 1.828 & 1.834 & 1.713 & 1.391 \end{bmatrix} \tag{A13}$$

Total relation matrix T_e of factors.

$$T_e = \begin{bmatrix} 2.525 & 2.704 & 2.455 & 2.395 & 2.504 \\ 2.685 & 2.406 & 2.390 & 2.330 & 2.429 \\ 2.643 & 2.573 & 2.185 & 2.300 & 2.408 \\ 2.558 & 2.509 & 2.326 & 2.080 & 2.364 \\ 2.338 & 2.293 & 2.115 & 2.066 & 1.986 \end{bmatrix} \tag{A14}$$

Total relation matrix T_f of factors.

$$T_f = \begin{bmatrix} 13.364 & 14.169 & 13.979 \\ 13.409 & 13.552 & 13.692 \\ 13.591 & 14.076 & 13.552 \end{bmatrix} \tag{A15}$$

Table A1. $r_i + c_i$ and $r_i - c_i$ values calculated from the direct/indirect matrix T.

Dimensions	A		B		C		D		E		F	
$r_i + c_i$	11.644		11.091		10.636		10.846		10.514		9.754	
$r_i - c_i$	0.802		0.341		0.036		−0.194		−0.440		−0.545	
Factors	a_1	a_2	a_3	a_4	b_1	b_2	b_3	b_4	c_1	c_2	c_3	
$r_i + c_i$	24.132	23.401	22.544	21.266	41.066	41.614	39.979	41.851	92.329	91.873	90.751	
$r_i - c_i$	0.281	−0.071	−0.509	0.299	−1.099	0.550	−0.244	0.793	0.677	0.671	−1.349	
Factors	d_1	d_2	d_3	d_4	d_5	e_1	e_2	e_3	e_4	e_5	f_1	f_2	f_3
$r_i + c_i$	20.228	19.693	18.978	18.908	16.905	25.331	24.725	23.580	23.008	22.489	81.876	82.450	82.442
$r_i - c_i$	0.379	−0.018	−0.826	0.189	0.276	−0.166	−0.244	0.638	0.665	−0.894	1.149	−1.145	−0.004

Appendix D. The Detailed Calculation Procedures of the ANP

Weighted supermatrix W_c:

$$W_c =$$

(A16)

Limited supermatrix W_c^*:

$$W_{c\_factors}^* =$$

0.0002	0.0002	0.0002	0.0002	0.0002	0.0002	0.0002	0.0002	0.0002	0.0002	0.0002	0.0002	0.0000	0.0002	0.0002	0.0002	0.0002	0.0002	0.0002	0.0002	0.0002	0.0002	0.0002	0.0002
0.0002	0.0002	0.0002	0.0002	0.0002	0.0002	0.0002	0.0002	0.0002	0.0002	0.0002	0.0002	0.0000	0.0002	0.0002	0.0002	0.0002	0.0002	0.0002	0.0002	0.0002	0.0002	0.0002	0.0002
0.0002	0.0002	0.0002	0.0002	0.0002	0.0002	0.0002	0.0002	0.0002	0.0002	0.0002	0.0002	0.0000	0.0002	0.0002	0.0002	0.0002	0.0002	0.0002	0.0002	0.0002	0.0002	0.0002	0.0002
0.0000	0.0000	0.0000	0.0000	0.0000	0.0000	0.0000	0.0000	0.0000	0.0000	0.0000	0.0000	0.0000	0.0000	0.0000	0.0000	0.0000	0.0000	0.0000	0.0000	0.0000	0.0000	0.0000	0.0000
0.0000	0.0000	0.0000	0.0000	0.0000	0.0000	0.0000	0.0000	0.0000	0.0000	0.0000	0.0000	0.0000	0.0000	0.0000	0.0000	0.0000	0.0000	0.0000	0.0000	0.0000	0.0000	0.0000	0.0000
0.0000	0.0000	0.0000	0.0000	0.0000	0.0000	0.0000	0.0000	0.0000	0.0000	0.0000	0.0000	0.0000	0.0000	0.0000	0.0000	0.0000	0.0000	0.0000	0.0000	0.0000	0.0000	0.0000	0.0000
0.0000	0.0000	0.0000	0.0000	0.0000	0.0000	0.0000	0.0000	0.0000	0.0000	0.0000	0.0000	0.0000	0.0000	0.0000	0.0000	0.0000	0.0000	0.0000	0.0000	0.0000	0.0000	0.0000	0.0000
0.0000	0.0000	0.0000	0.0000	0.0000	0.0000	0.0000	0.0000	0.0000	0.0000	0.0000	0.0000	0.0000	0.0000	0.0000	0.0000	0.0000	0.0000	0.0000	0.0000	0.0000	0.0000	0.0000	0.0000
0.0003	0.0003	0.0003	0.0003	0.0003	0.0003	0.0003	0.0003	0.0003	0.0003	0.0003	0.0003	0.0000	0.0003	0.0003	0.0003	0.0003	0.0003	0.0003	0.0003	0.0003	0.0003	0.0003	0.0003
0.0003	0.0003	0.0003	0.0003	0.0003	0.0003	0.0003	0.0003	0.0003	0.0003	0.0003	0.0003	0.0000	0.0003	0.0003	0.0003	0.0003	0.0003	0.0003	0.0003	0.0003	0.0003	0.0003	0.0003
0.0004	0.0004	0.0004	0.0004	0.0004	0.0004	0.0004	0.0004	0.0004	0.0004	0.0004	0.0004	0.0000	0.0004	0.0004	0.0004	0.0004	0.0004	0.0004	0.0004	0.0004	0.0004	0.0004	0.0004
0.0004	0.0004	0.0004	0.0004	0.0004	0.0004	0.0004	0.0004	0.0004	0.0004	0.0004	0.0004	0.0000	0.0004	0.0004	0.0004	0.0004	0.0004	0.0004	0.0004	0.0004	0.0004	0.0004	0.0004
0.0001	0.0001	0.0001	0.0001	0.0001	0.0001	0.0001	0.0001	0.0001	0.0001	0.0001	0.0001	0.0000	0.0001	0.0001	0.0001	0.0001	0.0001	0.0001	0.0001	0.0001	0.0001	0.0001	0.0001
0.1600	0.1600	0.1600	0.1600	0.1600	0.1600	0.1600	0.1600	0.1600	0.1600	0.1600	0.1600	0.0000	0.1609	0.1609	0.1609	0.1590	0.1590	0.1590	0.1590	0.1590	0.1600	0.1600	0.1600
0.1287	0.1287	0.1287	0.1287	0.1287	0.1287	0.1287	0.1287	0.1287	0.1287	0.1287	0.1287	0.0000	0.1294	0.1294	0.1294	0.1279	0.1279	0.1279	0.1279	0.1279	0.1287	0.1287	0.1287
0.1480	0.1480	0.1480	0.1480	0.1480	0.1480	0.1480	0.1480	0.1479	0.1479	0.1479	0.1479	0.0000	0.1488	0.1488	0.1488	0.1470	0.1470	0.1470	0.1470	0.1470	0.1480	0.1480	0.1480
0.0634	0.0634	0.0634	0.0634	0.0634	0.0634	0.0634	0.0634	0.0634	0.0634	0.0634	0.0634	0.0000	0.0628	0.0628	0.0628	0.0640	0.0640	0.0640	0.0640	0.0640	0.0634	0.0634	0.0634
0.0581	0.0581	0.0581	0.0581	0.0581	0.0581	0.0581	0.0581	0.0581	0.0581	0.0581	0.0581	0.0000	0.0576	0.0576	0.0576	0.0586	0.0586	0.0586	0.0586	0.0586	0.0581	0.0581	0.0581
0.0511	0.0511	0.0511	0.0511	0.0511	0.0511	0.0511	0.0511	0.0511	0.0511	0.0511	0.0511	0.0000	0.0507	0.0507	0.0507	0.0516	0.0516	0.0516	0.0516	0.0516	0.0511	0.0511	0.0511
0.0476	0.0476	0.0476	0.0476	0.0476	0.0476	0.0476	0.0476	0.0476	0.0476	0.0476	0.0476	0.0000	0.0472	0.0472	0.0472	0.0480	0.0480	0.0480	0.0480	0.0480	0.0476	0.0476	0.0476
0.0502	0.0502	0.0502	0.0502	0.0502	0.0502	0.0502	0.0502	0.0502	0.0502	0.0502	0.0502	0.0000	0.0498	0.0498	0.0498	0.0507	0.0507	0.0507	0.0507	0.0507	0.0502	0.0502	0.0502
0.0001	0.0001	0.0001	0.0001	0.0001	0.0001	0.0001	0.0001	0.0001	0.0001	0.0001	0.0001	0.0000	0.0001	0.0001	0.0001	0.0001	0.0001	0.0001	0.0001	0.0001	0.0001	0.0001	0.0001
0.0001	0.0001	0.0001	0.0001	0.0001	0.0001	0.0001	0.0001	0.0001	0.0001	0.0001	0.0001	0.0000	0.0001	0.0001	0.0001	0.0001	0.0001	0.0001	0.0001	0.0001	0.0001	0.0001	0.0001
0.0001	0.0001	0.0001	0.0001	0.0001	0.0001	0.0001	0.0001	0.0001	0.0001	0.0001	0.0001	0.0000	0.0001	0.0001	0.0001	0.0001	0.0001	0.0001	0.0001	0.0001	0.0001	0.0001	0.0001
0.0003	0.0003	0.0003	0.0003	0.0003	0.0003	0.0003	0.0003	0.0003	0.0003	0.0003	0.0003	0.0000	0.0003	0.0003	0.0003	0.0003	0.0003	0.0003	0.0003	0.0003	0.0003	0.0003	0.0003
0.0001	0.0001	0.0001	0.0001	0.0001	0.0001	0.0001	0.0001	0.0001	0.0001	0.0001	0.0001	0.0000	0.0001	0.0001	0.0001	0.0001	0.0001	0.0001	0.0001	0.0001	0.0001	0.0001	0.0001
0.0006	0.0006	0.0006	0.0006	0.0006	0.0006	0.0006	0.0006	0.0006	0.0006	0.0006	0.0006	0.0000	0.0006	0.0006	0.0006	0.0006	0.0006	0.0006	0.0006	0.0006	0.0006	0.0006	0.0006
0.1540	0.1540	0.1540	0.1540	0.1540	0.1540	0.1540	0.1540	0.1540	0.1540	0.1540	0.1540	0.0000	0.1549	0.1549	0.1549	0.1530	0.1530	0.1530	0.1530	0.1530	0.1540	0.1540	0.1540
0.1352	0.1352	0.1352	0.1352	0.1352	0.1352	0.1352	0.1352	0.1352	0.1352	0.1352	0.1352	0.0000	0.1341	0.1341	0.1341	0.1365	0.1365	0.1365	0.1365	0.1365	0.1352	0.1352	0.1352
0.0003	0.0003	0.0003	0.0003	0.0003	0.0003	0.0003	0.0003	0.0003	0.0003	0.0003	0.0003	0.0000	0.0003	0.0003	0.0003	0.0003	0.0003	0.0003	0.0003	0.0003	0.0003	0.0003	0.0003

$$(A17)$$

References

1. Sodhi, M.S.; Tang, C.S. Buttressing supply chains against floods in Asia for humanitarian relief and economic recovery. *Prod. Oper. Manag.* **2014**, *23*, 938–950. [CrossRef]
2. Levy, J.K.; Hartmann, J.; Li, K.W.; An, Y.; Asgary, A. Multi-Criteria Decision Support Systems for Flood Hazard Mitigation and Emergency Response in Urban Watersheds1. *JAWRA* **2007**, *43*, 346–358.
3. Bubeck, P.; Botzen, W.J.; Aerts, J.C. A review of risk perceptions and other factors that influence flood mitigation behavior. *Risk Anal.* **2012**, *32*, 1481–1495. [CrossRef] [PubMed]
4. Hirabayashi, Y.; Mahendran, R.; Koirala, S.; Konoshima, L.; Yamazaki, D.; Watanabe, S.; Kim, H.; Kanae, S. Global flood risk under climate change. *Nat. Clim. Chang.* **2013**, *3*, 816–821. [CrossRef]
5. Aerts, J.C.; Botzen, W.W.; Emanuel, K.; Lin, N.; de Moel, H.; Michel-Kerjan, E.O. Evaluating flood resilience strategies for coastal megacities. *Science* **2014**, *344*, 473–475. [CrossRef] [PubMed]
6. Wahlstrom, M.; Guha-Sapir, D. *The Human Cost of Weather-Related Disasters 1995–2015*; United Nations International Strategy for Disaster Reduction: Geneva, Switzerland, 2015.
7. Arkema, K.K.; Guannel, G.; Verutes, G.; Wood, S.A.; Guerry, A.; Ruckelshaus, M.; Kareiva, P.; Lacayo, M.; Silver, J.M. Coastal habitats shield people and property from sea-level rise and storms. *Nat. Clim. Chang.* **2013**, *3*, 913–918. [CrossRef]
8. Kundzewicz, Z.W. Flood protection—Sustainability issues. *Hydrol. Sci. J.* **1999**, *44*, 559–571. [CrossRef]
9. Hutton, R.B.; Cox, D.B.; Clouse, M.L.; Gaensbauer, J.; Banks, B.D. The role of sustainable development in risk assessment and management for multinational corporations. *Multinatl. Bus. Rev.* **2007**, *15*, 89–111. Available online: https://www.scheller.gatech.edu/centers-initiatives/ciber/projects/workingpaper/2007/013-07-08.pdf (accessed on 11 June 2018).
10. Plate, E.J. Flood risk and flood management. *J. Hydrol.* **2002**, *267*, 2–11. [CrossRef]
11. Poussin, J.; Bubeck, P.; Aerts, J.; Ward, P. Potential of semi-structural and non-structural adaptation strategies to reduce future flood risk: Case study for the Meuse. *Nat. Hazards Earth Syst. Sci.* **2012**, *12*, 3455–3471. [CrossRef]
12. Col, J.M. Managing disasters: The role of local government. *Public Adm. Rev.* **2007**, *67*, 114–124. [CrossRef]
13. Werritty, A. Sustainable flood management: Oxymoron or new paradigm? *Area* **2006**, *38*, 16–23. [CrossRef]
14. Ahmadisharaf, E.; Kalyanapu, A.J.; Chung, E.-S. Sustainability-Based Flood Hazard Mapping of the Swannanoa River Watershed. *Sustainability* **2017**, *9*, 1735. [CrossRef]
15. Poser, K.; Dransch, D. Volunteered geographic information for disaster management with application to rapid flood damage estimation. *Geomatica* **2010**, *64*, 89–98.
16. McDougall, K. Using volunteered information to map the Queensland floods. In Proceedings of the 2011 Surveying and Spatial Sciences Conference: Innovation in Action: Working Smarter (SSSC 2011), Wellington, New Zealand, 21–25 November 2011; pp. 13–23.
17. Ranke, U. *Natural Disaster Risk Management: Geosciences and Social Responsibility*; Springer International Publishing: New York, NY, USA, 2015.
18. Gatignon-Turnau, A.-L.; Mignonac, K. Using employee volunteering for public relations: Implications for corporate volunteers' organizational commitment. *J. Bus. Res.* **2015**, *68*, 7–18. [CrossRef]
19. Allen, K. The big tent. In *Corporate Volunteering in the Global Age*; Editorial Ariel, SA; Fundación Telefónica: Madrid, Spain, 2012.
20. Fontela, E.; Gabus, A. *The DEMATEL Observer*; Battelle Geneva Research Center: Geneva, Switzerland, 1976.
21. Division of Flood Management. *A Guide for Developing a Pre-flood Hazard Mitigation Plan for California Communities: Planning, the Key to Reducing Flood Damage*; Division of Flood Management, Federal Emergency Management Agency, U.S.: White Mountains, CA, USA, 1985.
22. Brody, S.D.; Kang, J.E.; Bernhardt, S. Identifying factors influencing flood mitigation at the local level in Texas and Florida: The role of organizational capacity. *Nat. Hazards* **2010**, *52*, 167–184. [CrossRef]
23. UNISDR. *Terminology on Disaster Risk Reduction*; UNISDR: Geneva, Switzerland, 2009.
24. Botzen, W.; Aerts, J.; Van Den Bergh, J. Dependence of flood risk perceptions on socioeconomic and objective risk factors. *Water Resour. Res.* **2009**, *45*. [CrossRef]
25. Raaijmakers, R.; Krywkow, J.; van der Veen, A. Flood risk perceptions and spatial multi-criteria analysis: An exploratory research for hazard mitigation. *Nat. Hazards* **2008**, *46*, 307–322. [CrossRef]
26. Van de Walle, B.; Turoff, M.; Hiltz, S.R. *Information Systems for Emergency Management*; Routledge: London, UK, 2014.

27. Shan, S.; Wang, L.; Li, L.; Chen, Y. An emergency response decision support system framework for application in e-government. *Inf. Technol. Manag.* **2012**, *13*, 411–427. [CrossRef]
28. Dawson, R.J.; Ball, T.; Werritty, J.; Werritty, A.; Hall, J.W.; Roche, N. Assessing the effectiveness of non-structural flood management measures in the Thames Estuary under conditions of socio-economic and environmental change. *Glob. Environ. Chang.* **2011**, *21*, 628–646. [CrossRef]
29. Dargie, W.; Poellabauer, C. *Fundamentals of Wireless Sensor Networks: Theory and Practice*; John Wiley & Sons: Hoboken, NJ, USA, 2010.
30. Akyildiz, I.F.; Vuran, M.C. *Wireless Sensor Networks*; John Wiley & Sons: Hoboken, NJ, USA, 2010; Volume 4.
31. Alexander, D. The voluntary sector in emergency response and civil protection: Review and recommendations. *Int. J. Emerg. Manag.* **2010**, *7*, 151–166. [CrossRef]
32. Whittaker, J.; McLennan, B.; Handmer, J. A review of informal volunteerism in emergencies and disasters: Definition, opportunities and challenges. *Int. J. Disaster Risk Reduct.* **2015**, *13*, 358–368. [CrossRef]
33. Palen, L.; Anderson, K.M.; Mark, G.; Martin, J.; Sicker, D.; Palmer, M.; Grunwald, D. A vision for technology-mediated support for public participation & assistance in mass emergencies & disasters. In Proceedings of the 2010 ACM-BCS Visions of Computer Science Conference, Edinburgh, UK, 13–16 April 2010; p. 8.
34. Jaeger, P.T.; Shneiderman, B.; Fleischmann, K.R.; Preece, J.; Qu, Y.; Wu, P.F. Community response grids: E-government, social networks, and effective emergency management. *Telecommun. Policy* **2007**, *31*, 592–604. [CrossRef]
35. Poussin, J.K.; Botzen, W.W.; Aerts, J.C. Factors of influence on flood damage mitigation behaviour by households. *Environ. Sci. Policy* **2014**, *40*, 69–77. [CrossRef]
36. Poussin, J.K.; Botzen, W.W.; Aerts, J.C. Effectiveness of flood damage mitigation measures: Empirical evidence from French flood disasters. *Glob. Environ. Chang.* **2015**, *31*, 74–84. [CrossRef]
37. Bubeck, P.; Botzen, W.; Kreibich, H.; Aerts, J. Detailed insights into the influence of flood-coping appraisals on mitigation behaviour. *Glob. Environ. Chang.* **2013**, *23*, 1327–1338. [CrossRef]
38. Busch, N.E.; Givens, A.D. Achieving resilience in disaster management: The role of public-private partnerships. *J. Strat. Secur.* **2013**, *6*, 1. [CrossRef]
39. European Commission. *Resource Book On PPP Case Studies*; European Commission (EC) Directorate-General Regional Policy: Brussels, Belgium, 2004.
40. Cruz, C.O.; Cruz, N. Public-Private Partnership: A Framework for Private Sector Involvement in Public Infrastructure Projects. In *The Governance of Infrastructure*; Wegrich, K., Kostka, G., Hammerschmid, G., Eds.; Oxford University Press: Oxford, UK, 2017; p. 103.
41. Cruz, N.; Marques, R. Mixed companies and local governance: No man can serve two masters. *Public Adm.* **2012**, *90*, 737–758. [CrossRef]
42. Cruz, C.O.; Marques, R.C. Contribution to the study of PPP arrangements in airport development, management and operation. *Transp. Policy* **2011**, *18*, 392–400. [CrossRef]
43. Steijn, B.; Klijn, E.H.; Edelenbos, J. Public private partnerships: Added value by organizational form or management? *Public Adm.* **2011**, *89*, 1235–1252. [CrossRef]
44. Sharma, M.; Bindal, A. Public-Private Partnership. *Int. J. Res.* **2014**, *1*, 1270–1274.
45. Chen, J.; Chen, T.H.Y.; Vertinsky, I.; Yumagulova, L.; Park, C. Public–private partnerships for the development of disaster resilient communities. *J. Conting. Crisis Manag.* **2013**, *21*, 130–143. [CrossRef]
46. Osei-Kyei, R.; Chan, A.P. Review of studies on the Critical Success Factors for Public-Private Partnership (PPP) projects from 1990 to 2013. *Int. J. Proj. Manag.* **2015**, *33*, 1335–1346. [CrossRef]
47. Hwang, B.-G.; Zhao, X.; Gay, M.J.S. Public private partnership projects in Singapore: Factors, critical risks and preferred risk allocation from the perspective of contractors. *Int. J. Proj. Manag.* **2013**, *31*, 424–433. [CrossRef]
48. Auzzir, Z.A.; Haigh, R.P.; Amaratunga, D. Public-private partnerships (PPP) in disaster management in developing countries: A conceptual framework. *Procedia Econ. Financ.* **2014**, *18*, 807–814. [CrossRef]
49. Jamali, D.; Karam, C.; Blowfield, M. *Development-Oriented Corporate Social Responsibility: Volume 1: Multinational Corporations and the Global Context*; Greenleaf Publishing: Austin, TX, USA, 2015; Volume 1.
50. DeLone, W.H.; McLean, E.R. Information systems success: The quest for the dependent variable. *Inf. Syst. Res.* **1992**, *3*, 60–95. [CrossRef]

51. Delone, W.H.; McLean, E.R. The DeLone and McLean model of information systems success: A ten-year update. *J. Manag. Inf. Syst.* **2003**, *19*, 9–30.

52. Chen, Y. The empirical analysis model on critical success factors for emergency management engineering information system. *Syst. Eng. Procedia* **2012**, *5*, 234–239. [CrossRef]

53. Lee, J.; Bharosa, N.; Yang, J.; Janssen, M.; Rao, H.R. Group value and intention to use—A study of multi-agency disaster management information systems for public safety. *Decis. Support Syst.* **2011**, *50*, 404–414. [CrossRef]

54. Petter, S.; McLean, E.R. A meta-analytic assessment of the DeLone and McLean IS success model: An examination of IS success at the individual level. *Inf. Manag.* **2009**, *46*, 159–166. [CrossRef]

55. Aldholay, A.H.; Isaac, O.; Abdullah, Z.; Ramayah, T. The role of transformational leadership as a mediating variable in DeLone and McLean information system success model: The context of online learning usage in Yemen. *Telemat. Inform.* **2018**. [CrossRef]

56. Duggan, E.W.; Reichgelt, H. The panorama of information systems quality. In *Measuring Information Systems Delivery Quality*; Idea Group Pub.: Hershey, PA, USA, 2006; pp. 1–27.

57. Garrity, E.J.; Sanders, G.L. *Information Systems Success Measurement*; Idea Group Publ.: Hershey, PA, USA, 1998.

58. Singh, S.R. *Information System Management*; APH Publishing Corporation: New Delhi, India, 2007.

59. DeLone, W.H.; McLean, E.R. Information systems success measurement. *Found. Trends Inf. Syst.* **2016**, *2*, 1–116. [CrossRef]

60. Acton, T.; Halonen, R.; Conboy, K.; Golden, W. DeLone & McLean success model as a descriptive tool in evaluating the use of a virtual learning environment. Paper Presented at International Conference on Organizational Learning, Knowledge and Capabilities (OLKC 2009), Amsterdam, The Netherlands, 26–28 April 2009; Available online: https://aran.library.nuigalway.ie/handle/10379/222 (accessed on 11 June 2018).

61. Eppler, M.J. *Managing Information Quality: Increasing the Value of Information in Knowledge-Intensive Products and Processes*; Springer Science & Business Media: Berlin, Germany, 2006.

62. Seppänen, H.; Virrantaus, K. Shared situational awareness and information quality in disaster management. *Saf. Sci.* **2015**, *77*, 112–122. [CrossRef]

63. Lin, H.-F. The impact of website quality dimensions on customer satisfaction in the B2C e-commerce context. *Total Qual. Manag. Bus. Excell.* **2007**, *18*, 363–378. [CrossRef]

64. Hsu, C.-L.; Chang, K.-C.; Chen, M.-C. The impact of website quality on customer satisfaction and purchase intention: Perceived playfulness and perceived flow as mediators. *Inf. Syst. e-Bus. Manag.* **2012**, *10*, 549–570. [CrossRef]

65. Pituch, K.A.; Lee, Y.-K. The influence of system characteristics on e learning use. *Comput. Educ.* **2006**, *47*, 222–244. [CrossRef]

66. Lin, F.; Fofanah, S.S.; Liang, D. Assessing citizen adoption of e-Government initiatives in Gambia: A validation of the technology acceptance model in information systems success. *Gov. Inf. Q.* **2011**, *28*, 271–279. [CrossRef]

67. Rogstadius, J.; Vukovic, M.; Teixeira, C.; Kostakos, V.; Karapanos, E.; Laredo, J.A. CrisisTracker: Crowdsourced social media curation for disaster awareness. *IBM J. Res. Dev.* **2013**, *57*. [CrossRef]

68. Lin, W.-S.; Wang, C.-H. Antecedences to continued intentions of adopting e-learning system in blended learning instruction: A contingency framework based on models of information system success and task-technology fit. *Comput. Educ.* **2012**, *58*, 88–99. [CrossRef]

69. Hu, X. Effectiveness of information technology in reducing corruption in China: A validation of the DeLone and McLean information systems success model. *Electron. Libr.* **2015**, *33*, 52–64.

70. Petter, S.; DeLone, W.; McLean, E. Measuring information systems success: Models, dimensions, measures, and interrelationships. *Eur. J. Inf. Syst.* **2008**, *17*, 236–263. [CrossRef]

71. Scott, M.; Golden, W. Understanding net benefits: A citizen-based perspective on e-government success. In Proceedings of the International Conference on Information Systems, ICIS 2009, Phoenix, AZ, USA, 15–18 December 2009.

72. Geddes, M. *Making Public Private Partnerships Work: Building Relationships and Understanding Cultures*; Gower: Wales, UK, 2005.

73. Buxbaum, J.N.; Ortiz, I.N.; Board, N.R.C.T.R.; Program, N.C.H.R.; Highway, A.A.O.S.; Officials, T.; Administration, U.S.F.H. *Public Sector Decision Making for Public-Private Partnerships*; Transportation Research Board: Washington, DC, USA, 2009.

74. Ministry of Economy, F.A.D. *Public Private Partnership in Burkina Faso*; Ministry of Economy, Finance and Development, Burkina Faso: Ouagadougou, Burkina Faso, 2016. Available online: http://www.pndes2020.com/pdf/03-en.pdf (accessed on 11 June 2018).

75. Saaty, T.L. Fundamentals of the analytic network process. In Proceedings of the 5th International Symposium on the Analytic Hierarchy Process, Kobe, Japan, 12–14 August 1999; pp. 12–14.

76. Triantaphyllou, E.; Baig, K. The impact of aggregating benefit and cost criteria in four MCDA methods. *IEEE Trans. Eng. Manag.* **2005**, *52*, 213–226. [CrossRef]

77. Opricovic, S.; Tzeng, G.-H. Compromise solution by MCDM methods: A comparative analysis of VIKOR and TOPSIS. *Eur. J. Oper. Res.* **2004**, *156*, 445–455. [CrossRef]

78. Figueira, J.R.; Greco, S.; Roy, B.; Słowiński, R. ELECTRE methods: Main features and recent developments. In *Handbook of Multicriteria Analysis*; Springer: New York, NY, USA, 2010; pp. 51–89.

79. Dalkey, N.; Helmer, O. An experimental application of the Delphi method to the use of experts. *Manag. Sci.* **1963**, *9*, 458–467. [CrossRef]

80. Linstone, H.A.; Turoff, M. *The Delphi Method: Techniques and Applications*; Addison-Wesley: Boston, MA, USA, 2002.

81. Gallego, D.; Bueno, S. Exploring the application of the Delphi method as a forecasting tool in Information Systems and Technologies research. *Technol. Anal. Strat. Manag.* **2014**, *26*, 987–999. [CrossRef]

82. Murry, J.W.; Hammons, J.O. Delphi: A versatile methodology for conducting qualitative research. *Rev. High. Educ.* **1995**, *18*, 423–436. [CrossRef]

83. Liao, S.; Wu, M.-J.; Huang, C.-Y.; Kao, Y.-S.; Lee, T.-H. Evaluating and enhancing three-dimensional printing service providers for rapid prototyping using the DEMATEL based network process and VIKOR. *Math. Probl. Eng.* **2014**, *2014*, 1–16. [CrossRef]

84. Hwang, B.-N.; Huang, C.-Y.; Wu, C.-H. A TOE approach to establish a green supply chain adoption decision model in the semiconductor industry. *Sustainability* **2016**, *8*, 168. [CrossRef]

85. Hwang, B.-N.; Huang, C.-Y.; Yang, C.-L. Determinants and their causal relationships affecting the adoption of cloud computing in science and technology institutions. *Innovation* **2016**, *18*, 164–190. [CrossRef]

86. Li, Y.; Hu, Y.; Zhang, X.; Deng, Y.; Mahadevan, S. An evidential DEMATEL method to identify critical success factors in emergency management. *Appl. Soft Comput.* **2014**, *22*, 504–510. [CrossRef]

87. Rahman, N.A.; Tarmudi, Z.; Rossdy, M.; Muhiddin, F.A. Flood Mitigation Measres Using Intuitionistic Fuzzy Dematel Method. *Malays. J. Geosci.* **2017**. [CrossRef]

88. Fan, Z.-P.; Suo, W.-L.; Feng, B. Identifying risk factors of IT outsourcing using interdependent information: An extended DEMATEL method. *Expert Syst. Appl.* **2012**, *39*, 3832–3840. [CrossRef]

89. Tzeng, G.-H.; Huang, C.-Y. Combined DEMATEL technique with hybrid MCDM methods for creating the aspired intelligent global manufacturing & logistics systems. *Ann. Oper. Res.* **2012**, *197*, 159–190.

90. Yang, C.-L.; Huang, C.-Y.; Kao, Y.-S.; Tasi, Y.-L. Disaster Recovery Site Evaluations and Selections for Information Systems of Academic Big Data. *Eurasia J. Math. Sci. Technol. Educ.* **2017**, *13*, 4553–4589. [CrossRef]

91. Yang, C.-L.; Yuan, B.J.; Huang, C.-Y. Key determinant derivations for information technology disaster recovery site selection by the multi-criterion decision making method. *Sustainability* **2015**, *7*, 6149–6188. [CrossRef]

92. Dilley, M. *Natural Disaster Hotspots: A Global Risk Analysis*; World Bank Publications: Washington, DC, USA, 2005; Volume 5.

93. World Bank. *Natural Disaster Hotspots: A Global Risk Analysis Synthesis Report*; The World Bank: Washington, DC, USA, 2005.

94. Tsou, C.-Y.; Feng, Z.-Y.; Chigira, M. Catastrophic landslide induced by typhoon Morakot, Shiaolin, Taiwan. *Geomorphology* **2011**, *127*, 166–178. [CrossRef]

95. Bharosa, N.; Appelman, J.; Van Zanten, B.; Zuurmond, A. Identifying and confirming information and system quality requirements for multi-agency disaster management. In Proceedings of the ISCRAM 2009 the 6th International Conference on Information Systems for Crisis Response and Management, Gothenborg, Sweden, 10–13 May 2009.

96. Nelson, R.R.; Todd, P.A.; Wixom, B.H. Antecedents of information and system quality: An empirical examination within the context of data warehousing. *J. Manag. Inf. Syst.* **2005**, *21*, 199–235. [CrossRef]

97. Hiltz, S.R.; Plotnick, L. Dealing with information overload when using social media for emergency management: Emerging solutions. In Proceedings of the 10th International ISCRAM Conference, Baden-Baden, Germany, May 2013; pp. 823–827.

98. Johannessen, Å.; Rosemarin, A.; Thomalla, F.; Swartling, Å.G.; Stenström, T.A.; Vulturius, G. Strategies for building resilience to hazards in water, sanitation and hygiene (WASH) systems: The role of public private partnerships. *Int. J. Disaster Risk Reduct.* **2014**, *10*, 102–115. [CrossRef]

99. Muthuri, J.N.; Matten, D.; Moon, J. Employee volunteering and social capital: Contributions to corporate social responsibility. *Br. J. Manag.* **2009**, *20*, 75–89. [CrossRef]

100. Grant, A.M. Giving time, time after time: Work design and sustained employee participation in corporate volunteering. *Acad. Manag. Rev.* **2012**, *37*, 589–615. [CrossRef]

101. Hunt, M.; Davies, S.; Pittard, V. *Becta Review 2006: Evidence on the Progress of ICT in Education*; British Educational Communications and Technology Agency (BECTA): Coventry, UK, 2006.

102. Williams, F.A. *Combustion Theory*; CRC Press: Boca Raton, FL, USA, 2018.

103. Jamil, G.L.; Soares, A.L.; Pessoa, C.R.M. *Handbook of Research on Information Management for Effective Logistics and Supply Chains*; IGI Global: Hershey, PA, USA, 2016.

104. Lin, Y.-H.; Tsai, K.-M.; Shiang, W.-J.; Kuo, T.-C.; Tsai, C.-H. Research on using ANP to establish a performance assessment model for business intelligence systems. *Expert Syst. Appl.* **2009**, *36*, 4135–4146. [CrossRef]

105. Dreesbach-Bundy, S.; Scheck, B. Corporate volunteering: A bibliometric analysis from 1990 to 2015. *Bus. Ethics Eur. Rev.* **2017**, *26*, 240–256. [CrossRef]

106. Hahn, T.; Pinkse, J.; Preuss, L.; Figge, F. Tensions in corporate sustainability: Towards an integrative framework. *J. Bus. Ethics* **2015**, *127*, 297–316. [CrossRef]

107. Samuel, O.; Wolf, P.; Schilling, A. Corporate volunteering: Benefits and challenges for nonprofits. *Nonprofit Manag. Leadersh.* **2013**, *24*, 163–179. [CrossRef]

Article

Integrating Voluntary Sustainability Standards in Trade Policy: The Case of the European Union's GSP Scheme

Axel Marx

Leuven Centre for Global Governance Studies, University of Leuven, 3000 Leuven, Belgium;
axel.marx@kuleuven.be

Received: 15 October 2018; Accepted: 16 November 2018; Published: 23 November 2018

Abstract: Trade policy is increasingly being used as a policy instrument to pursue non-trade objectives such as environmental protection or the protection of labour rights. A key example is the European Union's Generalised Scheme of Preferences (GSP). The current approach is being confronted with significant challenges. How these challenges can be addressed is currently subject to debate, and increased attention is turning to the role that private governance mechanisms can play in this context. This paper will look into the potential role that Voluntary Sustainability Standards (VSS) can play. The paper will analyse and assess the complementarity between VSS and EU GSP, and it contributes to the literature on interactions between private and public policy-making for sustainability. The main research question focuses on what role VSS can play in the European Union's GSP scheme. To answer the question, the paper develops two models by which VSS can be integrated in EU GSP (a mandatory and a voluntary approach). The study is based on interviews with key experts from different stakeholder groups and an analysis of the ITC standards map database. The paper shows that the integration of VSS in EU GSP, as outlined in the two models, is confronted with several challenges. These challenges are discussed, and alternatives are explored.

Keywords: voluntary sustainability standards; trade policy; European Union

---

1. Introduction

Trade policy is increasingly being used as a policy instrument to pursue non-trade objectives, such as environmental protection or the protection of labour rights. This trend is increasingly being well captured by the term governing through trade, which is actively pursued by the European Union (EU) [1,2]. This governance through trade can be executed by providing additional tariff preferences as an incentive to ratify and effectively implement a series of international human rights, labour, environmental and good governance instruments, such as in the case of the Generalised Scheme of Preferences (GSP) regulation [3]. Whether this governing through trade is effective is still an outstanding question and a report by the European Commission [4] identified several challenges in the case of GSP+. How these challenges can be addressed is currently subject to debate, and increased attention turns to the role that private governance mechanisms can play in this context [5–7]. This paper will look into the potential role that Voluntary Sustainability Standards (VSS—also known as private standards, eco-labels, and sustainability certificates) can play in this context.

The focus on VSS emerges in the context of a rapid proliferation of VSS. According to the Ecolabel Index Database, the number of VSS has grown by almost 400% between 1989 and 2016, now reaching 465 VSS operating worldwide. The ITC Standards Map, which is more restrictive in recognizing VSS, counts 210 VSS [8]. These VSS aim to govern through trade, and to pursue similar objectives as the EU concerning sustainable development. Hence, in terms of policy design, they might be complementary to the current GSP scheme, and especially GSP+. The link between VSS and the

GSP scheme lies in the list of international conventions that are included in the GSP scheme. These conventions aim to implement sustainable development commitments that one can also find in VSS (see Table 1. VSS do this through a set of procedures (monitoring, incentives and sanctioning) that implement, verify, and enforce these commitments. Furthermore, VSS and GSP+ start from a similar starting point. Both use trade (and access to trade benefits through access to markets) as a bargaining chip to foster sustainable development. VSS focus on the level of producers and production sites. GSP+ focuses on the level of government policies. The focus on integrating both instruments starts from the observation that both instruments might be complementary. This complementarity between public and private governance instruments is being increasingly recognized in the academic literature. Lambin et al. [9] explore the effectiveness and synergies between policy instruments for land use governance in tropical regions and show that VSS often offer complementarity functions to public policy in terms of monitoring, implementation, and/or policy enforcement. In a recent paper, Lambin and Thorlakson [10] show how new partnerships between governments, private companies, and nongovernmental organizations (NGOs) are reshaping global environmental governance. They focus specifically on the role of VSS in these new public-private partnerships. They argue that contrary to widely-held views, interactions between governments, NGOs, and private companies surrounding the adoption of sustainable practices are not generally antagonistic, and public and private environmental governance regimes rarely operate independently, but rather reinforce each other.

This focus feeds into a wider academic debate that focuses on experimentalist governance that combines public and private policy approaches and transnational business interactions. The conceptual focus on interactions between public and private is becoming increasingly prominent. Eberlein et al. [9] demonstrates the importance of interactions in transnational business governance. As they show, the number of schemes applying private authority to govern business conduct across borders has vastly expanded in numerous issue areas. VSS are a quintessential example of such private forms of authority. Eberlein et al. [11] argue that as these initiatives proliferate, they increasingly interact with one another and with state-based regimes. However, as Auld [12] shows, there are also trade-offs involved in these policy-interactive effects, and not all interactive designs might be as complementary as one might assume. In this paper, we investigate the complementarity between public and private forms of governance in the case of trade policy.

The paper will analyse and assess this complementarity. The main research question focuses on what role VSS can play in the European Union's GSP scheme. In this paper we assume that the integration of VSS in GSP is compatible with the law of the World Trade Organisation (WTO). It should be noted that this is highly debated. However, an assessment of WTO compatibility should be done on the basis of a detailed regulatory proposal that integrates VSS into the GSP scheme, which falls outside the scope of this paper. The study is prospective and uses the Delphi method to assess this complementarity. The different options to integrate VSS in GSP were discussed with 40 experts from different stakeholder groups. These include experts from academia and think tanks, the European Commission, government officials from departments dealing with human rights, economic affairs and development cooperation, voluntary standards organizations, business associations, civil society organisations, unions, and consumer groups. The aim of the discussions was to identify key issues that are related to the integration of VSS in the GSP scheme. The issues raised were then further elaborated on the basis of available data and literature. The Delphi method is a forecasting research methodology that is used to assess the strengths and weaknesses of possible future (policy) interventions [13]. The method uses experts, from different groups, to discuss policy options. The experts were chosen as follows. First, I mapped the relevant stakeholder groups. These included: the European Commission, government officials from departments dealing with human rights, economic affairs and development cooperation, voluntary standards organizations, business associations, civil society organisations, unions and consumer groups, and academic experts. Second, within each group, I identified organisations, business units, and persons that are most relevant. In most cases, there are only a few experts on GSP who are also knowledgeable about VSS. We contacted them via email to make an appointment to discuss the different options of integrating VSS in GSP. The experts received a briefing note of two pages outlining the different policy options of integrating VSS in GSP, and a set of questions that would guide the consultation. The questions inquired into the feasibility and desirability of integrating VSS in GSP according to the two options identified. Questions also inquired into the main advantages and disadvantages of each option. These were open questions which were probed with follow-up questions. There was also one open-ended question on possible other options or reforms (which inform the last section of the paper). At the end of the discussion I asked for the names of additional experts. I stopped consulting experts when all arguments for and against options recurred. In total, 40 experts were consulted, some in a one-to-one interview, and others in a group setting. The interviews were conducted in the period between August 2017 and January 2018. All interviews were conducted by the author. Discussions took between 40 min and 2 h. The results of the discussions with the experts are then supplemented and triangulated with existing literature and an analysis of data based on existing databases (ITC Standards Map of VSS, Eurostat database and TARIC database). The paper shows that the integration of VSS in EU GSP, as outlined in the two models, is confronted with several challenges, and constitutes an unfeasible option.

This remainder of the paper consists of three parts. Part 1 introduces EU's GSP, the challenges with which it is confronted and outlines the two options of integrating VSS in GSP. Part 2 provides an extensive assessment of the two options by which VSS can be integrated in the GSP scheme. Part 3 discusses the implications and explores possible alternatives.

2. Addressing the Compliance Gap in the EU's Current Generalised Scheme of Preferences by Integrating VSS

2.1. EU's Current Generalised Scheme of Preferences

The European Union's Generalised Scheme of Preferences (GSP) is a preferential trade arrangement by which the EU grants unilateral and non-reciprocal preferential market access to goods originating in developing countries. The preferences are given in the form of the partial or entire suspension of import tariffs. The EU has operated a scheme of generalised tariff preferences since 1971 (Regulation (EU) No 978/2013 of the European Parliament and of the Council, applying a scheme of generalised tariff preferences and repealing Council Regulation (EC) No 732/2008, recital (1)), with the objective of "assist[ing] developing countries in their efforts to reduce poverty, [and to] promote good governance and sustainable development" [4] The scheme consists of three arrangements that distinguish between developing countries on the basis of their development status and needs, thus providing for different levels of preferential market access. The three arrangements are: (1) the general arrangement (the "Standard GSP"); (2) the special incentive arrangement for sustainable development and good governance, known as the "GSP+"; and (3) the special arrangement for the least-developed countries (LDCs), known as "Everything But Arms" (EBA). Standard GSP provides tariff preferences for a number of products. GSP+ expands this to almost 90% of export products, while EBA provides zero-tariff access for all products, except for products related to arms. A country might become a GSP beneficiary if it complies with certain conditions, including the ratification and implementation of 27 international conventions concerning human and labour rights, environmental protection, and good governance (see Table 1). GSP+ aims at spreading and promoting the values and principles of human rights protection, sustainable development, and good governance. The additional preferences are intended as a form of compensation, or reward, for having signed up to, and for implementing the relevant international law. In other words, the GSP+ "fosters the achievement of its goals by offering the 'carrot' of preferences" [4].

Compliance with the abovementioned conditions is continuously monitored by the Commission, primarily by way of examining the conclusions and recommendations of the monitoring bodies established under the relevant conventions, but also on the basis of information supplied by the beneficiary countries themselves, and by reference to other sources of information, including information submitted by third parties, or by the European Parliament or the Council [3]. Where a

GSP+ beneficiary is in non-compliance with the regulation, the Commission may remove that country from the list of beneficiaries [13]. To date there was only one instance of temporary withdrawal of GSP+ preferences, namely Sri Lanka [14]. Apart from Sri Lanka, two other countries (El Salvador and Bolivia) have been investigated in the past by the Commission for failure to implement all of the conventions, but neither investigation ended with a suspension of preferences [14]. There are currently only nine GSP+ beneficiaries. Alongside the GSP+ mechanism for temporary withdrawal of preferences, the Regulation also features a common mechanism that is applicable to the other two arrangements Standard GSP and EBA. Similar to the GSP+ mechanism, preferences may be suspended temporarily with regard to Standard GSP and EBA, either for all products, or for certain covered products originating in a GSP beneficiary country. The grounds for suspensions include "serious and systematic violations of principles laid down" in certain of the 27 above- mentioned conventions (i.e., the 15 'core human and labour rights Conventions of the United Nations (UN) and International Labour Organisation (ILO)'). Aside from the withdrawal of Sri Lanka's GSP+ preferences, there have been only two other instances, in the Standard GSP, of temporary withdrawal of preferences (Myanmar and Belarus) [14].

2.2. The Compliance Gap

A debate has emerged on the effectiveness of the current GSP approach in fostering compliance with international conventions. The Commission review report on the implementation of GSP+ [15] shows improvement in the implementation of 27 conventions in the GSP+ beneficiaries, but also identifies challenges with the implementation on the ground. Also the recently published mid-term evaluation of the GSP regulation, which analysed the economic, social, human rights, and environmental impact in the GSP beneficiary countries, also finds indications of positive effects of the GSP scheme [16] The report notes that it is difficult, in general terms, to assess the impact on sustainable development. It does observe an economic impact in terms of export diversification, but this differs from country to country. The case studies (both sector case studies and country case studies) in the mid-term evaluation provide an indication that the scheme has had an overall positive impact on social development and human rights measured by different indicators but also found many instances of violations of labour and human rights (in Pakistan, Bangladesh, Bolivia, and Ethiopia). In addition, the mid-term evaluation only finds a limited impact on sustainable development and environmental protection. Several people consulted in the context of this study also indicated the presence of shortcomings in relation to the effective implementation on the ground (especially in the context of GSP+). However, for many countries, one can find several indications of violations in practice, resulting in a compliance gap. The compliance gap refers to the difference in the implementation of relevant international agreements in law, and in practice. While several respondents were positive about how GSP+ is currently operating, several recognized that there is room for improvement in the implementation of the GSP+ conventions. A recent report by the European Parliament showed many instances of non-compliance on the ground with several ILO conventions in export processing zones in selected GSP+ countries [17]. In a recent report by the Pakistan Workers Confederation [18], the compliance gap is also illustrated in reference to many ILO Conventions and their implementation in Pakistan. These observations correspond to a broader body of literature that emphasizes the difference between the formal ratification of international treaties and conventions, and their de facto implementation [19–23]. One key reason to further develop the enforcement design of the GSP-scheme would be to address this compliance gap. This compliance gap might be closed through several actions.

Especially relevant in the context of this paper are the VSS. VSS comprise a collection of organisations that certify producers and production processes, taking sustainability standards into account. The United Nations Forum on Sustainability Standards [24] defines VSS as "standards specifying requirements that producers, traders, manufacturers, retailers or service providers may be asked to meet, relating to a wide range of sustainability metrics, including respect for basic human rights, worker health and safety, the environmental impacts of production, community relations, land use planning and others." These standards are developed on the basis of general principles. These principles refer to a series of public goods, such as the protection of labour rights and biodiversity, and addressing climate change. This collection of VSS comprises many different initiatives. VSS have established themselves as significant governance mechanism to govern transnational economic activity and value chains [25]. The number of VSS has proliferated since 1990 [26]. In addition, the number of certified entities has grown rapidly in the last two decades [27]. Drivers for this growth include consumer demand and access to markets, including the requirement for some economic operators to obtain multiple certificates. This demand is driven by private actors (consumers, business to business, retailers) and public actors (through public procurement, integration of VSS in regulatory measures) [9].

2.3. Two Models to Integrate VSS in GSP

VSS organizations engage in three interrelated processes that are relevant in the context of GSP: (1) standard setting based on international conventions, (2) assuring compliance with standards, and (3) monitoring and evaluation. VSS can be regarded as instruments that implement and enforce international legal commitments on sustainability. They do this in a three-step approach. First, they explicitly link the sustainability standards that they develop to international legal commitments in their foundational principles. Many of these international legal commitments overlap with the 27 conventions identified in the GSP+ regulation, and the 15 conventions that can trigger a temporarily withdrawal in the case of 'serious and systematic violations of principles laid down" in these 15 conventions for GSP and EBA (These conventions are listed in Annex VIII:A (see Article 19.1(a) of the Regulation)). Second, they operationalise these principles into measurable indicators and actions. In a third step, they use a comprehensive set of procedures to monitor compliance with their sustainability standards, including the use of auditing and the provision of complaint systems. The first two steps relate to standard-setting activities. The third step relates to assessing conformity and monitoring and evaluation.

In this way, VSS might complement the current GSP scheme, and it could be integrated in it. VSS can be integrated in GSP/GSP+/EBA in two ways. The first option is to allow access to the European market, conditional on being certified, i.e., products need certification before they can enter the market and receive the GSP scheme preferential tariff rate. This approach would follow some regulatory approaches that the EU is currently pursuing, which provide market access only to certified products, such as in the case of the Renewable Energy Directive [28,29] and the EU Timber Regulation [30]. In this option, all, or a selected subset of, products entering the EU market will need certification before entering the EU market, in order to obtain the GSP preferential tariff. This could be seen as the 'mandatory' approach (see Figure 1). The second option is to give tariff preferences (lower tariffs or elimination of tariffs) to certified products. In this case, certified products would obtain additional tariff preferences (lower duties) compared to non-certified products. In this option, the EU needs to distinguish tariffs for certified and non-certified products. One tariff would be applied to certified products, while another tariff would be applied to non-certified products. In this scenario, all products would be allowed to enter the EU market under the GSP-scheme tariff, but certified products would get an additional financial advantage. A similar idea was proposed by the European Parliament (EP) Committee on International Trade, proposed in its opinion on the EU flagship initiative on the garment sector. (EP-INTA, 2017, §8). This could be regarded as a 'voluntary approach' (see Figure 2) The intent of these two options is not to replace the current system, but to add additional requirements that correspond closely to the commitments made by states in the GSP scheme, for economic actors exporting to Europe. Such an integration of VSS in GSP would add one additional element in the GSP procedure (the other three conditions are related to the rules of origin requirements.), namely, the verification of a recognized VSS certificate (both site-level certificates, as well as CoC certificates). The introduction of VSS would add one additional element in the GSP procedure, namely the verification of the use of a recognized VSS certificate (both site-level certificates, as well as CoC certificates). Firms exporting to the EU from GSP beneficiary countries will be required to have a recognized VSS certificate.

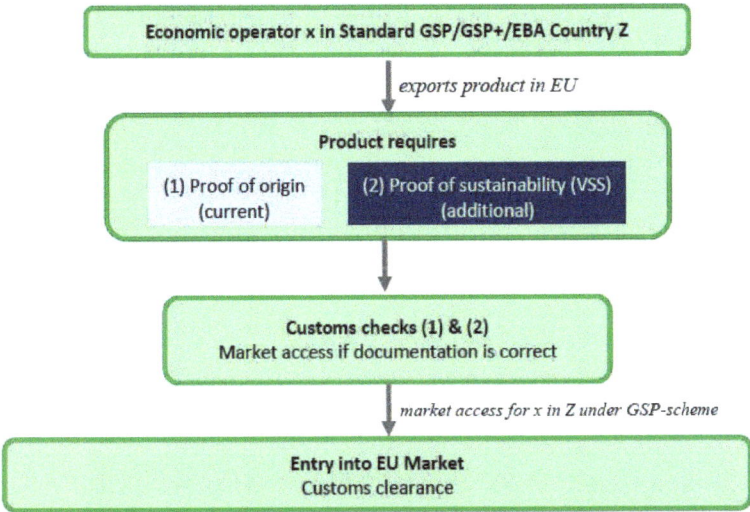

Figure 1. Integrating Voluntary Sustainability Standards (VSS) in the Generalised Scheme of Preferences (GSP) scheme as a condition for access to the EU market (option 1).

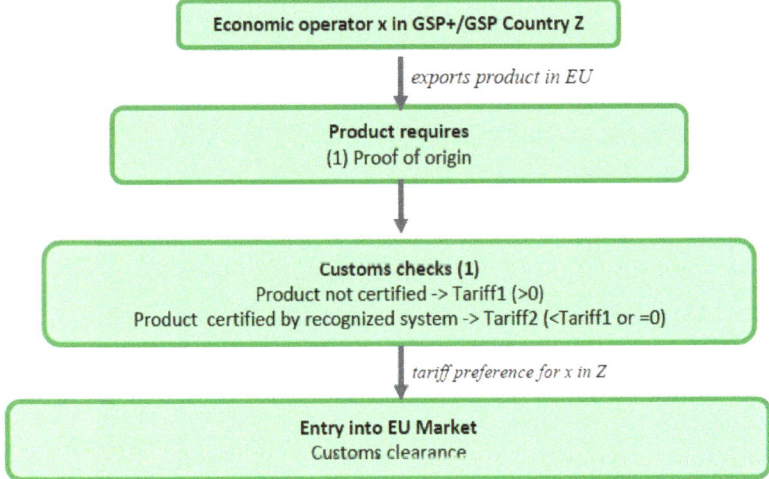

Figure 2. Integrating VSS in the GSP scheme as a condition to obtain an additional tariff preference (option 2).

3. Assessment of the Integration of VSS in the GSP Scheme

Some authors argue [6] that the integration of VSS in GSP would have several advantages, namely, lower implementation costs, since implementation and enforcement is 'outsourced' to the VSS and the ability to truly govern 'beyond EU borders'. The EU checks that quality standards are being followed in the recognition process, but itself is not required to audit businesses in non-EU countries. By relying on existing VSS, the EU does not need to develop its own certification systems, which would be time-consuming and cumbersome, and can it rely on existing VSS that have been operational for a significant amount of time. These advantages are recognized in a growing body of literature on how VSS are integrated in public policy, and how they can contribute to co-regulation [9,25,31,32]. The fact that sustainability cannot be observed in products when they cross the EU border, but are largely based on production process characteristics, means that sustainability has to be assessed at the place of production [28]. To achieve this, VSS offer some distinct advantages, since they operate in the countries in which products are made. However, there are also several challenges that are related to the idea of integrating VSS in the GSP scheme.

In this part, we summarize the key issues that were raised when discussing the integration of VSS in the GSP scheme with more than 40 experts and stakeholders. Some of the issues apply to the GSP scheme as a whole, while others are specific for Standard GSP or GSP+. The aim of the discussions with the experts were to identify key issues related to the integration of VSS in the GSP scheme. These consultations were conducted under the agreement that we would not attribute statements to specific persons or institutions. On the basis of the identification of issues, we also consulted available sources, databases, and literature to make a further assessment of the issues raised. The main issues and challenges identified are: (1) a substantive overlap of standards, (2) impacts on the nature of the GSP scheme, (3) the dynamic nature of the GSP scheme, (4) VSS as an appropriate tool (effectiveness, governance, and capacity), (5) availability of the VSS, and (6) costs related to certification.

We discuss each of them and identify the relevance for the two possible options of integrating VSS in the GSP scheme. A first option (option 1) involves creating access to the European market, conditional on being certified, i.e., products need certification before they can enter the market. This approach would follow some regulatory approaches that the EU is currently pursuing, which provide market access only to certified products. This could be seen as the 'mandatory' approach. A second option (option 2) involves giving tariff preferences (lower tariffs or elimination of tariffs) to certified products. One tariff line would be applied to certified products, while another tariff line would be applied to non-certified products. In this scenario, all products are allowed to enter the EU market, but certified products obtain a financial advantage. This could be regarded as a 'voluntary approach'. Options 1 and 2 are applicable both to the Standard GSP, as well as GSP+ and EBA. For EBA, option 2 does not apply, since (almost) all tariffs are already eliminated. For each challenge, we also identify whether the concern applies for the overall GSP scheme, or whether they are more specific to Standard GSP, GSP+, and EBA.

3.1. Overlap in Substantive Provisions

In the context of integrating VSS in the GSP scheme, an important issue concerns the implementation of and compliance with core conventions in the GSP-scheme. For the entire GSP-scheme, this refers to the first 15 conventions that which can be invoked to trigger a temporary withdrawal of the GSP scheme in the case of violations of the conventions. For GSP+ specifically, it refers to the requirement of ratifying 27 conventions in order to be eligible for GSP+. The connection between VSS and the GSP scheme lies in the fact that both base their approach towards sustainable development on a series of international commitments (see also Table 1). Hence, the reason to consider integrating VSS in the GSP scheme originates from the idea that the effectiveness of the GSP scheme in achieving its objectives could be improved by integrating VSS. However, a first critical issue which was raised concerns the substantive overlap between the conventions in the GSP, and the social and environmental standards in VSS.

Most of the well-known VSS today integrate existing international legal commitments, often developed in a multilateral context, in their standard-setting procedures. Especially relevant in the context of this paper is that the VSS, to a degree, rely on the same conventions as those that are included in the GSP scheme. In order to explore, this we analysed the ITC database, which contains some information on which conventions are covered by which VSS. Fiorini et al. [8] provide a good descriptive overview and main statistics on the VSS in the ITC database. We screened the database for a selection of VSS that could be considered in the context of the GSP scheme. We selected ISEAL-Alliance members (20 in total), since they need to comply with a series of guidelines on how to set and enforce standards. These guidelines correspond to the procedural requirements that the VSS would be expected to meet, in order to receive accreditation under a public regulatory system which would use the VSS. Table 1 reports on which international conventions are referred to by a selected number of VSS in the context of their standard-setting procedures (N = 20 VSS). Table 1 shows that these selected VSS are based on public international law, and derive their standards from international conventions, but also that they do not cover all of the conventions of the GSP scheme. This partially corresponds to the findings of a recent study on VSS that shows that VSS use or incorporate international law to varying degrees [33].

Table 1 shows that several VSS do base their standards on some of these international conventions. However, they do not cover all of the international conventions in their standard-setting process. A few aspects need to be taken into account, in this context. First, some conventions fall substantially out of the scope of issues that sustainability standards typically deal with, especially the UN Conventions on narcotic drugs and psychotropic substances. Hence, it will be difficult for VSS to cover the whole scope of conventions that are included in the GSP regulation. In addition, some of the conventions target more states than organizations or firms, such as the UN Convention against Corruption, or the Convention on the prevention and Punishment of the Crime of Genocide. Hence, these conventions are less suitable for further enforcement through VSS. Second, for those conventions falling within the scope of VSS and not covered yet within a specific VSS, it should be noted that VSS that did not yet include elements of some of the conventions can still do this. Most VSS have open and consensus-based standard-setting procedures that allow them to develop new standards in relation to other conventions. VSS are dynamic systems that align standards with changes in the regulatory environment. Hence, the integration of VSS into GSP might constitute an incentive for VSS to also include references to additional conventions in their standard-setting practices.

Table 1. Link between the GSP Conventions and the VSS.

Convention on the Prevention and Punishment of the Crime of Genocide (1948)	
International Convention on the Elimination of All Forms of Racial Discrimination (1965)	
International Covenant on Civil and Political Rights (1966)	Fairtrade Textile Standard
International Covenant on Economic Social and Cultural Rights (1966)	
Convention on the Elimination of All Forms of Discrimination against Women (1979)	
Convention Against Torture and other Cruel, Inhuman or Degrading Treatment or Punishment (1984)	Fairtrade Textile Standard
Convention on the Rights of the Child (1989)	FT Gold Standard, FT International-Small Producers Organizations, FT Textile Standard, Goodweave
Convention concerning Forced or Compulsory Labour, No 29 (1930)	ASC-Salmon-Shrimp-Pangasius, FT Standard for Hired Labour–Gold Standard-Small Producers Organizations, FT Trader, FT Textile Standard, FSC-CoC/FM, Goodweave, MSC, Responsible Jewelry Council, Roundtable on Sustainable Biomaterials, RA, Union for Ethical Biotrade
Convention concerning Freedom of Association and Protection of the Right to Organise, No 87 (1948)	ASC-Salmon-Shrimp-Pangasius, BCI, Bonsucro, FT Standard for Hired Labour, FT Gold Standard, FT-Small Producers Organizations, FT Trader, FT Textile Standard, FSC CoC/FM, Goodweave, Responsible Jewelry Council, Roundtable on Sustainable Biomaterials, RA, Union for Ethical Biotrade, UTZ, 4C-GCP

Table 1. *Cont.*

Convention concerning the Application of the Principles of the Right to Organise and to Bargain Collectively, No 98 (1949)	ASC-Salmon-Shrimp-Pangasius, BCI, Bonsucro, FT Standard for Hired Labour, FT-Gold Standard, FT Small Producers Organizations, FT Trader, FT Textile Standard, FSC CoC/FM, Goodweave, Responsible Jewelry Council, Roundtable on Sustainable Biomaterials, RA, Union for Ethical Biotrade, UTZ, 4C-GCP
Convention concerning Equal Remuneration of Men and Women Workers for Work of Equal Value, No 100 (1951)	BCI, Bonsucro, FT Standard for Hired Labour, FT-Gold Standard, FT-Small Producers Organizations, FT Trader, FT Textile Standard, FSC CoC/FM, Goodweave, Responsible Jewelry Council, Roundtable on Sustainable Biomaterials, RA, Union for Ethical Biotrade, UTZ, 4C-GCP
Convention concerning the Abolition of Forced Labour, No 105 (1957)	BCI, Bonsucro, FT Standard for Hired Labour, FT-Gold Standard, FT Small Producers Organizations, FT Trader, FT Textile Standard, FSC CoC/FM, Goodweave, Responsible Jewelry Council, Roundtable on Sustainable Biomaterials, RA, Union for Ethical Biotrade, UTZ, 4C-GCP
Convention concerning Discrimination in Respect of Employment and Occupation, No 111 (1958)	ASC-Salmon-Shrimp-Pangasius, BCI, Bonsucro, FTStandard for Hired Labour, FT Gold Standard, FT Small Producers Organizations, FT Trader, FT Textile Standard, FSC-CoC/FM, Goodweave, Responsible Jewelry Council, Roundtable on Sustainable Biomaterials, RA, Union for Ethical Biotrade, UTZ, 4C-GCP
Convention concerning Minimum Age for Admission to Employment, No 138 (1973)	ASC-Salmon-Shrimp-Pagasius, BCI, Bonsucro, FT Standard for Hired Labour, FT Gold Standard, FT Small Producers Organizations, FT Trader, FT Textile Standard, FSC CoC/FM, Goodweave, Marine Stewardship Council, Responsible Jewelry Council, Roundtable on Sustainable Biomaterials, RA, Union for Ethical Biotrade, UTZ, 4C-GCP
Convention concerning the Prohibition and Immediate Action for the Elimination of the Worst Forms of Child Labour, No 182 (1999)	ASC-Salmon-Shrimp-Pangasius, BCI, Bonsucro, FT Standard for Hired Labour, FT Gold Standard, FT Small Producers Organizations, FT Trader, FT Textile Standard, FSC CoC/FM, Goodweave, Responsible Jewelry Council, Roundtable on Sustainable Biomaterials, RA, Union for Ethical Biotrade, UTZ, 4C-GCP
Convention on International Trade in Endangered Species of Wild Fauna and Flora (1973)	ASC-Salmon-Pangasius, FSC CoC/FM, RA, Union for Ethical Biotrade, UTZ
Montreal Protocol on Substances that Deplete the Ozone Layer (1987)	Bonsucro, 4C-GCP
Basel Convention on the Control of Transboundary Movements of Hazardous Wastes and Their Disposal (1989)	Responsible Jewelry Council
Convention on Biological Diversity (1992)	FT Standard for Hired Labour, FT Gold Standard, FT Small Producers Organizations, FT Trader, Fairtrade Textile Standard, FSC CoC/FM, MSC, Roundtable on Sustainable Biomaterials, RA, Union for Ethical Biotrade
The United Nations Framework Convention on Climate Change (1992)	
Cartagena Protocol on Biosafety (2000)	
Stockholm Convention on persistent Organic Pollutants (2001)	ASC Shrimp, Bonsucro, Fairtrade Standard for Hired Labour, FT Small Producers Organizations, FT Trader, Union for Ethical Biotrade, 4C-GCP
Kyoto Protocol to the United Nations Framework Convention on Climate Change (1998)	
United Nations Single Convention on Narcotic Drugs (1961)	
United Nations Convention on Psychotropic Substances (1971)	
United Nations Convention against Illicit Traffic in Narcotic Drugs and Psychotropic Substances (1988)	
United Nations Convention against Corruption (2004)	

Source: Created by author on the basis of the ITC database.

3.2. Impact on GSP

3.2.1. Impact on the State-to-State Nature of the GSP Scheme

One of the arguments to include VSS in the GSP-scheme is that it would allow a more differentiated approach towards fostering compliance, since it would allow for a more graduated systems of incentives for firms [34]. As Schukat & Rust [6] made clear, it allows for a targeted approach towards individual firms. Under the terms of the current GSP scheme, states that violate the conventions can be confronted with a suspension of tariff preferences. Such a suspension implies punishing all companies, including those whose production systems already comply with social and environmental criteria, and with some of the relevant conventions. The VSS can directly promote the implementation of sustainability criteria, laid down in the conventions, at the level of economic operators, without either granting or withdrawing tariff preferences in a blunt fashion for all economic operators in that state. Hence, one key argument would be that by integrating VSS in the GSP scheme, not only states, but also economic operators need to comply. This is not to suggest that certified economic actors can continue to export if a beneficiary state is excluded from the GSP-scheme due to non-compliance, but that additional requirements are added, which address economic actors.

Currently, the system, in the case of non-compliance, heavily relies on either inter-state dialogue or a hard sanction tariff preferences withdrawal. The latter option is hardly used, and it is not considered to be effective by some. As a result, a recent EP report on labour rights protection in GSP+ countries [17] stresses that "finding a middle ground between 'soft' inter-state dialogue and 'hard' nation-wide sanctions is crucial to enhancing the EU's role in realizing labour rights in GSP+ beneficiaries." VSS could facilitate finding this middle ground through involving economic actors, by rewarding access to the EU market for only those economic operators that comply with the relevant requirements (option 1), or who provide additional tariff preferences to only those economic operators who comply with the relevant requirements (option 2). In this context, the introduction of VSS that which target economic actors more directly could develop a dynamic in which economic actors who need (option 1) or want (option 2) to participate in VSS push governments to pursue compliance with all economic actors. Not only might economic actors influence internal dynamics, but also influence other actors, such as non-governmental organisations. Some respondents noted that the integration of the VSS could create more space for civil society actors to become more active and contribute to creating institutional reforms within countries since several VSS engage local stakeholders in monitoring and enforcement of standards. This might in turn lead to further capacity building of civil society in countries in which VSS are active.

However, according to other respondents, integrating VSS in the GSP scheme could fundamentally change the nature of the system. The EU GSP scheme is designed as a unilateral instrument between the EU and specific developing countries, with the aim of promoting development across a variety of economic, social, and environmental domains, and based on state-to-state dialogue. The idea is to build capacity in those countries through trade. The system is built on state-to-state dialogues and cooperation. The VSS, on the other hand, focus on the level of firms, not states. Some respondents indicated that the two operate "according to different logics" and target different actors. If the VSS are incorporated as an additional compliance mechanism, not only states, but also economic operators would be responsible for achieving compliance with the GSP requirements. This might make it more challenging for the EU to hold the government accountable, since they could shift the burden of responsibility to private actors. Some respondents indicated that the integration of VSS could 'hollow up' the responsibility of the state, since the responsibility will be split between actors. This refers to a dynamic in which private regulatory action replaces public regulatory action (see also reference [9]), and which could create a dynamic in which the state capacity to deal with the issues and conventions is weakened, rather than strengthened. These arguments hold mainly when option 1 is applied (making access to the European market mandatory on being certified), and not for option 2, since in option 2, the adoption of the VSS is voluntary, and certified products get a reduced tariff. In the context of option 2, reduced tariffs for sustainable products would be an additional benefit, and they would not alter the current systems significantly. More generally, this discussion, for both options, underlines the importance that the integration of the VSS into the GSP scheme should be seen as a complementary measure, not one that would in any way substitute the current way of working, based on state-to-state dialogue.

3.2.2. Dynamic Nature of the GSP Scheme

Another identified issue concerns the dynamic nature of the GSP scheme. Countries move from one system (GSP) into another trade regime, such as a bilateral agreement or no special trade regime at all [16]. Table 2 focuses on GSP+, and shows the current and previous GSP+ beneficiary countries since January 2014.

Table 2. GSP+ beneficiary countries since January 2014.

Current	Armenia, Bolivia, Cape Verde, Mongolia, Pakistan, Paraguay, Philippines (since December 2014), Kyrgyzstan (since February 2016) and Sri Lanka (since May 2017)
Left	Costa Rica, Ecuador, El Salvador, Guatemala, Panama, Peru (exit January 2016), Georgia (exit January 2017)

Up till now, there were 16 countries that had benefitted from the GSP+ since the January 2014 reform. Seven countries left the scheme because they entered a bilateral trade agreement. If the requirements for VSS was solely required in the context of the GSP+, it might create disproportionate costs to comply, if these requirements no longer hold under other trade regimes of the EU, especially if option 1 was applied. This concern is not only valid in comparison to bilateral agreements, but also in the context of the GSP scheme. Some respondents voiced concerns that the integration of VSS in GSP+ and Standard GSP might create disadvantages for GSP+ or Standard GSP beneficiaries, compared to beneficiaries that fall under the EBA scheme. In this context, reference was made to countries such as Bangladesh, who also compete with GSP+ countries on some export commodities.

It is also important to put the GSP scheme in perspective, in terms of its overall contribution in EU's trade and imports. The importance of GSP for import in the EU market is low and decreasing [16]. In 2016, more than 82% of imports entered under WTO Most Favoured Nations arrangements, and only 4.1% under GSP. Hence, if one aims for ambitious targets to be reached in terms of sustainable products (for example in relation to sustainable textiles), a reform of the GSP scheme will only be able to contribute marginally. However, it should also be noted that for some GSP beneficiaries, their share of exports to the EU is important, and for them, the GSP scheme constitutes an important mechanism. For example, Pakistan (GSP+) and Bangladesh (EBA) gain significantly from GSP+ and EBA, respectively, as both count the EU as one of their most important trading partners. Similarly, in both countries, the textile sector constitutes a major portion of exports. The EU accounts for 43.3% of Bangladesh's exports [16]. Exports to the EU have increased by 50% since 2013, and by almost 80% since 2011. Approximately 91% of Bangladesh's exports to the EU—under the EBA, comprising of textile related products [16]. Furthermore, both countries have a high utilization ratio (see below) for the EBA and GSP+, meaning that a majority of their products that are eligible for preferential treatment utilize these benefits. The objection of the dynamic nature of the GSP scheme only applies for option 1, since economic operators would be required to obtain certification in order to access the European market. This objection does not apply for option 2, since in this case, VSS certification remains voluntary. In option 2, economic operators will make an assessment of whether it is worthwhile for them to obtain VSS certification in the context of their wider export strategy. In the case of option 2, one could contemplate also using additional preferences for sustainable products in FTAs.

3.2.3. Limitations on the Possibilities for Further Tariff Differentiation

For option 2 (tariff preferences for certified products), the issue was also raised for whether there was sufficient scope to lower tariffs, in order to make the system work. Currently, an analysis of the tariff lines used for Standard GSP, GSP+, and EBA shows that a very high percentage of tariffs under both the EBA and GSP+ arrangements have received duty-free treatment in 2014, with over 97 per cent under the GSP+ regime, leaving very few tariffs to be differentiated in terms of different tariffs for certified and non-certified products [16]. This evidence indicates that tariff differentiation (option 2) for certified products in the GSP-scheme has different implications for the different schemes. Concerning GSP+ option 2, including granting zero duty for certified products can only be applied to a small part of the export and products. If one was to consider pursuing option 2 further in GSP+, one would probably need to re-introduce tariffs. One can think of using the tariffs under the general GSP scheme and giving a zero tariff to the certified products. Theoretically, this could be done. However, on the basis of interviews conducted for this study, this option would be politically very sensitive, and some interviewees indicated that this would undo the purpose of GSP+. On the other hand, it could be argued that even if the number of products to which this could be applied is small, it still sends an important political message on the importance of sustainability. Concerning Standard GSP, the application of option 2 would hold more promise, since there is more scope for tariff differentiation, and more products could benefit from additional tariff reductions if they are certified. Option 2 would not be applicable to EBA, since there is no scope for tariff differentiation.

3.2.4. Effects on the Utilisation Rate of GSP Tariffs

The observation was also made that the application of the VSS requirement (option 1) might actually have a negative effect on the GSP scheme utilisation rate. The utilisation rate indicates preferential imports as a percentage of eligible imports under a trade agreement or the degree of usage of existing preferences [35]. Hence, it is the share of imports that are actually imported under GSP scheme preferences over all imports that are eligible in principle. Not all imports that are eligible for a preference will always be imported under a GSP scheme, because of several reasons: not all individual shipments would fulfil the rules of origin, and preference is not claimed or granted for a specific reason. Currently, utilization rates for GSP+ countries are very high. For Pakistan, Paraguay, Cape Verde, Bolivia, and Armenia, the utilization rate is above 90% [16].

High utilization rates indicate that the preferential rates are used significantly by GSP+ beneficiaries, indicating that GSP+ is reaching its objectives in terms of export support. Applying VSS according to option 1 might result in the fact that the utilization rate goes down, since economic operators may not be able to prove that they fulfil the criteria, may choose not to do so because of the costs involved in becoming certified, or they would rather pay the WTO-MFN duty rate. Especially when the costs of certification would outweigh the benefits of tariff reduction, economic operators might enter the EU market without the tariff preference. This might hollow out the purpose of GSP+. This concern applies especially for option 1 (economic operators would choose to export to Europe but not use the GSP-scheme). Similar concerns hold for Standard GSP and EBA. The utilization rates are already significantly lower and decreasing for Standard GSP beneficiaries [14]. For EBA beneficiaries, the utilization rates are currently high and increasing [16]. In both cases, the application of option 1 would in most likelihood result in a decrease of the utilization rate. For Standard GSP, the same argument holds for option 2, as is the case for GSP+, while option 2 cannot be applied to EBA countries.

3.3. VSS as an Appropriate Tool

In the interviews, several issues were raised in relation to the VSS and how they operate. Four challenges were identified concerning VSS: (1) the effectiveness of VSS, (2) the governance of VSS, and (3) the capacity of VSS and (4) the availability of VSS for export sectors.

3.3.1. Effectiveness of VSS

An argument for the integration of the VSS in the GSP scheme is that it offers an additional enforcement mechanism. The question then focuses on the effectiveness of the VSS. This issue was raised in several interviews. Some respondents questioned the effectiveness of the VSS and their potential contribution to closing the compliance gap. It is impossible to make a general assessment on the effectiveness of the VSS, since this depends on the VSS that are studied, and which parameters are analysed in the context of impact, i.e., socio-economic parameters such as poverty reduction, compliance with labour rights, etc., or environmental parameters. In this context, it is important to highlight that many studies on the impact of the VSS have been published. They provide a basis for considering the inclusion of the VSS in public policy. This is not to argue that all studies only found positive impacts. There are many critical studies on the effectiveness of the VSS as well. Throughout the literature, one can identify several different types of impacts on different levels for different VSS, and in relation to different products. Concerning agricultural commodities, several meta-studies have been published, which summarize the main results of several other studies. Two leading sources are literature reviews covering the most relevant impact studies for agriculture-related VSS across standards, commodities, and regions [36,37]. The Food Agriculture Organisation literature review [36] covers 101 studies, out of which 30 studies were deemed to be sufficiently rigorous. The ITC literature review includes 47 studies [37]. These studies focus on the impact on the ground for standard-takers on multiple dimensions of sustainability. The first dimension focuses on the level of farms and farmers, and investigates the impact on economic aspects of sustainability, such as profitability for farmers, impact on yield and quality, and market access and technology transfer. The second set of studies focuses on the social dimension of sustainability, and provides an impact assessment on parameters such as wages and assets, gender equity, health and education, and environmental sustainability. The final set of studies provides an assessment on environmental impacts covering topics such as resource management, soil conservation, biodiversity, and water quality. These studies show that on balance, certified farms perform better than non-certified farms, but that it depends on which VSS scheme is analysed, and in which country's context. Other areas in which significant impact studies have been published, also with to a certain degree of mixed results, are in the area of forest governance and forest-based products. Here also, there is evidence that certified forests (forest-management certification) and chain of custody actors perform better than non-certified entities (see [36] for an overview and discussion). The most critical studies on the effect of certification have been published in the context of the textile sector and the enforcement of labour rights; see for example [38–42]. Several respondents in the interviews pointed to the Rana Plaza disaster and the Ali Enterprises fire in Karachi to make the argument that auditing and certification by VSS is not always effective. In both disasters, companies were involved who were certified. The criticism on the effectiveness of VSS in textiles is also documented in academic research. They have been criticized on several grounds concerning their impact [42,43]. However, Locke [42] also shows that some VSS perform quite well in the context of specific countries.

In summary, there is a debate on the effectiveness of the VSS. It is clear that the VSS potentially generate positive impacts and contribute to closing the compliance gap. However, it should also be noted that not all studies univocally indicate a positive impact on the socio-economic and ecological indicators for all VSS, on all products, in all countries. How to assess this in general terms is difficult, and it is to a degree a function of the appreciation for what one can achieve with the VSS. It is safe to assume that VSS with a well-elaborated enforcement structure, and that cover a number of GSP conventions, will perform better in terms of impacts, than VSS that lack this.

3.3.2. Governance of VSS

Several respondents raised the issue and concern of the credibility and governance of the VSS, and indicated that a system should be put in place which checks the robustness and credibility of the VSS, including the process of setting standards, the assessment of the standards, and the governance of the scheme. Given the proliferation of the number of VSS, one needs to distinguish credible from non-credible systems, and assess the diversity among systems. The VSS differ significantly in how they are governed, how accountable they are, how effective they are in enforcing the standards they develop, etc. Many comparative studies have highlighted the difference between VSS [33,40,44–46] and the potential effects on effectiveness and legitimacy.

The diversity in the design of VSS [33,45] indicate that not all VSS are equal, and a recognition system to distinguish credible from non-credible VSS is necessary. This concern should be addressed in a recognition system that needs to be set up to recognize VSS in the context of a regulatory scheme and that distinguishes credible from non-credible VSS. This recognition system should be developed by the EU. Some respondents expressed the preference that the EU should build upon existing benchmarking schemes, as identified above, and support those, instead of duplicating approaches. If the EU were to recognize the VSS, it might create duplication in a context in which several actors are currently certifying or rating the 'certifiers'. On the other hand, it could also be argued that if the European Commission recognizes the VSS, this might have a strong influence and would de-facto regulate the market of VSS, and distinguish credible from non-credible VSS.

When questioning respondents on key elements of such a recognition system, several experts referred to the following requirements: a clear link to the conventions, an open and consensus-based standard-setting process that further operationalizes principles into standards, the presence of third-party auditing, the presence of public disclosure of audits (transparency), and the presence of complaint systems. Some respondents indicated that this recognition system should be very stringent, which might result in the fact that only very few VSS are recognised. For some products, no VSS might be recognised, which might influence the scope of the application of options 1 and 2.

The concern for developing a robust recognition system was also voiced in the context of not creating a race to the bottom in international standard-setting with regard to sustainability. If too many VSS were to be accredited, producers would have a choice between stringent and less stringent standards especially in a context where the business case for becoming certified still needs to be established, or even in a context where the business case for becoming certified disappears, because so many producers are certified. The later can occur when certified products are no longer be sold on the market as being certified, and hence distinctive, since many products are certified. Some noted that it will be difficult to create a level playing field among recognized VSS since there is no consensus on some of the standards.

A final governance issue that emerged in the discussions concerned the traceability through the supply chain. Some VSS have different systems to govern their supply chain [47]. Several respondents raised questions on whether it is possible to apply the VSS to the whole supply chain. Especially in relation to textiles and garments, this might be difficult. Producers in GSP/GSP+ countries source sometimes to thousands of homeworkers. Lund-Thomsen and Nadvi [48], for example, show how in the region of Sialkot in Pakistan, companies in the sportswear and apparel sector use thousands of subcontractors, who in turn outsource to a few thousand homeworkers. In addition, it should be noted that since VSS sometimes only certifies part of the supply chain, i.e., the stage at which it is produced, or converted, it does not guarantee that that the inputs to the production or conversion part of the value chain are necessarily sustainably produced. A t-shirt can be sustainably produced by labour receiving fair wages and working under safe conditions, but there is no guarantee that the cotton used in the process came from farms that similarly respected the labour laws. While these arguments have some merit, it should be noted that the proposal to integrate VSS in GSP could be limited to the trade-link between the EU and the GSP/GSP+ beneficiary country. Hence, only the economic operator in the GSP/GSP+ country should be certified, regardless of the position in the supply chain. In other words, the economic operator in the GSP/GSP+ country who exports to the EU needs to be certified. This could be a cotton farmer exporting cotton to the EU, or a sewing company making T-shirts for the EU market.

3.3.3. Capacity of VSS

An integration of the VSS in the GSP scheme might generate capacity problems with some VSS, since it will spur demand for VSS. This issue is most problematic for option 1. Although the

VSS recognize accreditation organisations, which in turn accredit certification bodies to perform the conformity assessment with standards, some VSS remain actively engaged with certified entities, in order to ensure compliance with standards, both in terms of monitoring, as well as in terms of handling complaints and disputes. This implies that some VSS can only certify a limited number of companies, and they are not necessarily interested in certifying as many as possible. An interesting example in this respect is the Dutch Fair Wear Foundation (FWF), which was created in 1999 and is a VSS that is active in the textiles and apparel sectors; for a more elaborate discussion, see [1,43]. In both the substance of its standard and its verification procedures, the FWF aims to be the "gold standard" [49]. FWF focuses on the management practices of firms, and on labour conditions in their first-tier supplier factories [50]. Firms not only sign up to the FWF Code, but they actually become "members" of the FWF, clearly committing to its values. In addition, the FWF requires members to actively engage with their suppliers (other independent firms), while taking into account that members "have influence, but not direct control, over working conditions" in supplier facilities [50]. In terms of monitoring and implementing the Code, FWF has sought to shift from factory auditing alone to a "multilevel verification process" that *utilizes inter alia* factory audits and complaints procedures. This approach exemplifies a shift from a regulatory process that involves only an independent third-party auditor, to a system involving a more complex governance structure in which several dependent and independent actors provide information, expertise, and capacity in the certification process and fostering compliance with standards [43,51,52]. This potential capacity problem is quite important in the context of integrating VSS in GSP+, since the different governance models of VSS imply the different capabilities and capacities of the VSS.

A VSS governance model that only involves independent certification bodies for granting certificates and dealing with complaints can probably quite easily deal with a significant increase in demand. However, some respondents also identified challenges for independent certification bodies if the uptake of certain VSS increases quickly and strongly. Key challenges identified were that (1) there is probably too little time to conduct a proper and correct audit, (2) the availability of qualified auditors and ensuring that auditors are competent, and (3) they might not be able to cover so many producers. Other governance models employed by the VSS, as illustrated above, will have greater difficulties in dealing with the increased demand for certificates when whole markets within one country are becoming certified. There are two issues to be considered in this context. First, the capacity problem only really emerges in option 1 which would have significant impacts on the adoption required by economic operators. In option 2, capacity issues might be addressed more gradually, following the pace of economic operators who might come to benefit from additional tariff reductions. Second, the capacity problems might, to a certain degree, be addressed using accompanying measures such as capacity-building support for VSS in GSP-beneficiary countries.

3.3.4. Availability of VSS and Applicability to Export Sectors

For both options 1 and 2, there is an issue of which products could be included in such an approach. As noted, theoretically, option 1 and 2 could be applied to one or more products, ideally to as many as possible. In order to obtain a sense of which products could be included, one needs to have a look at the major export products, and whether VSS are available for these products. In order to assess whether VSS are available for key export sectors, an analysis of the ITC Standards Map database was conducted. Table 3 provides an overview of how many VSS are available per country, per export product category. For all GSP+ countries and sectors available in the ITC database (N of VSS = 235), we calculated how many VSS certify products per sector/country that are exported to the EU. In other words, Table 3 provides an overview of how many VSS are active in a GSP+ country, and which certify export products in a specific country. Table 3 summarizes the overview. The table shows that for all sectors in the ITC database, several VSS are operational in the GSP+ countries, i.e., VSS are currently certifying products in GSP+ countries, which are exported to the EU. This indicates (1) that VSS are already operational in the GSP+ countries, and (2) that they are able to cover a wide range of products.

Sustainability **2018**, *10*, 4364

Table 3. Overview of the number of VSS per sector (ITC classification) and GSP+ country.

GSP+ Country	Agricultural Products	Cereals	Dried Fruits	Fibres	Fresh Fruits	Horticulture	Herbs and Spices	Livestock	Nuts and Oilseeds	Beverages	Fruit Juice	Construction	Electronics	Energy	Fishing	Enhanced Fishing	Wildstock	Aquarium
Armenia	20	16	15	13	18	18	16	13	16	13	13	9	11	9	14	14	11	11
Bolivia	39	27	28	25	32	31	29	23	30	23	23	14	16	18	22	22	19	18
Cape Verde	13	12	12	12	13	12	12	12	12	12	12	9	11	9	13	12	12	11
Mongolia	18	16	16	15	17	15	16	15	17	15	15	11	13	11	15	16	13	13
Pakistan	35	26	25	25	29	26	27	21	28	23	23	16	19	16	24	26	20	20
Paraguay	39	28	30	27	32	28	30	24	31	24	24	15	17	19	22	22	20	19
Philippines	19	28	28	27	31	30	29	24	30	23	23	15	18	18	23	23	20	18
Kyrgyz Rep	15	12	13	13	14	12	13	11	13	14	14	9	11	9	12	12	11	11
Sri Lanka	39	25	26	25	30	30	26	22	26	23	23	15	18	16	23	21	20	18

GSP+ Country	Fertilize	Food Products	Forestry	Timber	Non-Timber	Mining	Handicrafts	Jewellery	Natural ingredients	NI Cosmetics	NI Food Products	Services	Tourism	Textiles	Toys	Wood Products	Consumer Products
Armenia	9	16	11	10	11	12	9	10	14	11	14	11	9	11	10	9	11
Bolivia	13	27	21	20	20	18	17	14	22	18	22	16	17	17	17	16	17
Cape Verde	8	13	10	10	10	12	10	9	10	10	10	11	9	11	10	9	12
Mongolia	10	16	12	12	12	14	12	11	14	12	14	13	11	14	12	11	14
Pakistan	15	28	18	18	18	20	19	16	20	17	20	18	18	24	18	17	20
Paraguay	14	29	21	21	20	19	18	15	21	18	21	17	18	19	18	17	19
Philippines	14	28	21	21	20	19	18	15	22	18	22	17	18	23	17	9	18
Kyrgyz Rep	8	15	10	10	10	13	10	9	11	10	11	11	9	11	10	18	12
Sri Lanka	14	27	20	20	19	20	19	16	19	16	19	17	18	23	19	19	18

Source: created by authors on the basis of ITC database—note: some VSS are active in multiple sectors.

We cannot distinguish how many of these VSS would be recognized by a stringent recognition system, but there are potentially several VSS per product category that are contained in the ITC Standards Map.

For option 1, this means that there are potentially multiple VSS which could cover the main export sectors. For option 2, there is the additional question of whether for these export sectors there are still tariffs which could be lowered. We already indicated that for GSP+, most tariffs are already eliminated. If one were to consider re-introducing tariffs in order to make a differentiation in tariffs between certified products and non-certified products, one could contemplate using GSP tariff lines for non-certified (also for GSP+ countries), and zero tariffs for certified products. The availability of VSS for export products might not be an issue, and neither the identification of products to which it can applied. One can identify multiple VSS for the major export sectors/products. However, some respondents raised two concerns in this context, (1) broad-sector categories do not always accurately cover what is possible on the product level, and (2) there is the problem of 'over-certification'. Concerning the former, tea is an interesting example. There are many types of tea, and for example, Sri Lanka (a GSP+ country) is a major tea producer. However, they mainly produce specific types of tea for consumers from Russia, Turkey, the Middle East, and United Arab Emirates, which do not really demand certified tea. The type of tea demanded by the European Market is not available in Sri Lanka, due to ecological and geographical factors [53]

Concerning the latter ('over-certification'), the VSS do not necessarily have the intention of certifying as many companies or producers as possible, but rather to create 'certified markets' in which consumers demand certified products and consciously buy certified products. Hence, a key challenge for them is to have enough downstream players/buyers in consumer markets (i.e., in Europe). The option 1 proposal of integrating VSS in the GSP-scheme might lead to the situation in which producers need to be certified, and buyers need to buy certified products due to the regulations. However, not all products will be sold or marked as such on the market. It was indicated in the consultations that there is currently already an oversupply of some certified products on the market, and some certified products are being sold without certificates. A measure that would influence adoption on a large scale might defeat the purpose of some of the VSS. This problem might especially arise in option 1, which would make market access conditional on being certified. Option 2 will also create additional incentives to get certified but this—due to the voluntary nature—might generate far less market demand for certificates.

3.4. Cost Issues Related to VSS Certification

A final issue concerned the costs of the proposed change. Integrating the VSS in Standard GSP, GSP+, and EBA could imply additional costs, since the VSS aim to internalize external costs, such as the costs related to environmental and social protection. It is impossible to obtain an estimate of the additional costs involved, which would also depend on several parameters, but we can identify where additional costs might emerge. The identified additional costs are associated with the producers in the GSP/GSP+ countries, customs, and possible the VSS themselves. For economic operators, two additional costs might be involved. One cost relates to becoming certified. The other costs are related to the increased costs for production in compliance with the VSS standards. Concerning the former, becoming certified often implies additional investments, technical changes, and corrective actions, in order to be in conformity with the standards. These costs can vary significantly, depending on the steps that are still necessary in order to obtain the certificate. Some studies indicate that these costs might be very substantial. In addition, there are costs that are related to recertification, which need to be taken into account. Concerning the latter, some studies [54] show that production according to VSS is often more expensive. These additional costs might off-set any benefits such as lower tariffs, price premiums, or market access. The cost issue, especially for small exporters, was flagged by several respondents, who then also expressed the idea that governments and the EU should consider funding/financing certifications (especially for smallholders) and invest in capacity building in the area of sustainability certifications. These additional costs might not be offset by any price that premium producers might receive due to certification. In some cases, the rationale for investing in certificates is that they generate more income due to the higher prices for products. If certification becomes a requirement (option 1), this price premium might not be there. Some already doubt that there is a price premium for certified products [54]. This effect does not affect, or affects option 2 to a lesser degree.

These costs can influence the ability of producers to comply with or adopt VSS, and possibly enter certain (export) markets. This might especially be the case for LDCs. Several VSS have tried to get LDCs on board, but some evidence suggests that this is hard to do because of the costs for certification. There is no general data available on the adoption rates of VSS but Marx and Wouters [55] explored the issue for GlobalG.A.P and FSC. They found that the majority of certified entities are based in high-income economies, while hardly any are based in low-income economies. A total of 79% of GLOBALG.A.P. and 74% of FSC CoC-certified entities are based in high-income countries compared to 8% and 4% in lower-middle and low-income economies combined. For FSC FM certification, the distribution is a slightly more spread out, with the exception of 2% in low income economies. Marx and Cuypers [56] refer in this context to the 'stuck at the bottom' problem, which refers to the fact that some countries, especially LDCs, are excluded from VSS dynamics. The latter is confirmed in a paper by Tayleur et al. [57]. They focused on seven agricultural commodities (coffee, banana, cocoa, oil palm, sugarcane, soy, and tea) and received data from many leading VSS about which farms and plantations were certified, and where they were located. The paper looks into the question of where certified commodity crops are located, and whether they are located in places that are important for conserving the world's most important biodiversity, and benefiting the most vulnerable producers. The paper finds that certification appears to be concentrated in areas that are important for biodiversity conservation, but not in those areas that are most in need of poverty alleviation. They also find that global levels of certification are low, since they were able to plot the certified areas on the total area on which the specific commodities were cultivated. This analysis shows that 9% of coffee production is certified worldwide. For the other six commodities, the proportion of certification is lower (banana: 0.3%, cocoa: 2.2%, oil palm: 2.2%, sugarcane: 0.6%, soy: 0.2%, tea: 2.0%). These results indicate that it is very hard to comply for economic operators in LDCs, and hence the certification option might not be possible for EBA. The low level of participation of entities in developing countries provides support for the literature, which argues that "smallholders need to be organized in commercially viable arrangement to be able to participate in certified value chains" [53]. Even producers in those countries that are producing sustainably might not have the capacity to prove it. This generates several challenges in terms of capacity-building and facilitation of compliance with VSS standards. Especially in relation to agricultural commodities produced by smallholders in GSP+ countries, this might create problems in achieving certification. VSS systems are aware of these problems, and they are taking action that are sometimes supported by external partners, such as international donors [58].

4. Discussion

The interaction between public and private policy instruments is gaining academic attention [9,11]. Several scholars see quite some potential in these interactions in order to govern transnationally. In this paper, I investigate this potential in the context of EU trade policy. The issues identified above signal quite some challenges for integrating VSS in the GSP scheme in the two options developed. The overall conclusion is that it might be difficult, if not impossible, to integrate the VSS in EU trade policy. It might also create undesirable trade-offs in policy interaction, as identified by Auld [12]. These trade-offs can both effect EU trade policy, as well as the VSS themselves. From the perspective of EU trade policy, the analysis shows that the integration of the VSS in EU trade policy might negatively affect the utilization rate of GSP, which would result in a lesser use of GSP, and hence defeat the objectives on which GSP is built. From the perspective of VSS, the analysis shows that VSS should change in order to better fit within EU trade policy, in order to be recognized as policy instruments. The standards should better align with the conventions that are included in GSP+. Although this is possible, it also implies that VSS have to change in order to align themselves and to accommodate one specific policy instrument, which might make them less suitable for an interaction with other policy instruments. Hence, the paper clearly shows that there are trade-offs in the integration of private and public policy instruments, in the case of trade policy.

This does not imply that integrating private instruments, such as VSS, in trade policy, is not possible. During the consultations, two other suggestions were made to integrate VSS in the GSP scheme, namely (1) by using the VSS as information providers in the monitoring processes, and (2) by including the VSS as targets in roadmaps for the implementation of the conventions.

First, the VSS could act as information providers for monitoring purposes. In this context, VSS can play a meaningful role, since they have extensive monitoring requirements, including audits of firms that provide ground-level information on compliance with standards. Table 3 showed that many VSS are active in GSP+ countries. Some of them will make their audit reports publicly available following their transparency policies. GSP+ reporting could use this information of reporting purposes. Hence, instead of only relying on reports by multilateral organisations and European missions, the GSP+ monitoring team could consider the use of other information sources, including those of the VSS. The VSS could provide at least two types of information; one is based on the audit reports, and the other one is based on possible complaints against companies in the country. The audit reports could provide a good overview on what happens in the factories, or on plantations and farms. They might actually also give some sense of trends within a country, in terms of better or worse compliance. Since the European Commission is interested in these types of trends, VSS might provide longitudinal data on what happens in the factories. The complaints system of VSS might provide insights into non-compliance issues within specific firms, and how they might relate to more systemic weaknesses, for example, the absence of existing legislation, which is relevant in the context of the GSP+ conventions. Finally, actors involved in VSS certification in GSP+ countries might be included as stakeholders in stakeholder dialogues on progress, in compliance with the relevant conventions.

Second, one could further reflect on the idea of linking roadmaps to GSP implementation, and including the VSS in these roadmaps. Some respondents proposed that GSP should be reformed in such a way as to include roadmaps for the implementation of the conventions. For each beneficiary, a roadmap would be developed that would contain specific targets that are related to the conventions. These benchmarks can focus on legal reform, as well as on different mechanisms (public, public–private, private) to implement legislation and to contain specific commitments. Such roadmaps are already used in some cases, such as the EU Bangladesh Sustainability Compact. In this initiative, there is, for example, a commitment by multi-national enterprises and retailers to engage in discussion on responsible business conduct along the supply chain [4]. In such roadmaps, commitments to engage with (a selected/recognized number of) VSS could be included, and they could provide incentives for firms, mainly large firms, to engage with VSS or to have their suppliers engage with VSS. Each year, an assessment can be made on the progress towards certification, as well as an assessment to what degree this approach actually contributes to better compliance. Such an approach should not replace any state commitment to enforcing commitments to conventions, but can complement these commitments and create forms of co-enforcement [59]. This can also strengthen state–civil society–firm ties, which could further facilitate compliance with legislation and voluntary standards [60]. Such an approach would be of a very different nature, but it might support the gradual expansion of VSS in GSP+ beneficiary countries.

5. Conclusions

This study focused on the question of whether VSS can be integrated in the EU GSP scheme. VSS receive increasing attention as a complementary tool to strengthen policies that pursue sustainable development [10,61]. In this study, we explored two ways of integrating the VSS in the GSP scheme as an additional requirement. In this approach, GSP beneficiary states should still have to comply with part or all of the requirements in the GSP regulation. An additional requirement that can take the form of options 1 or 2, would apply. The first option is to make access to the European market conditional on being certified, i.e., products from GSP beneficiaries will need to be certified before they can enter the market. The second option is to give tariff preferences to certified products. In this case, certified products would receive additional tariff preferences (lower duties) or tariff elimination if they are certified. For both options, one needs an approach to recognize VSS, which would be eligible under Standard GSP, GSP+, and EBA. Such a recognition should be built on three types of requirements: substantive requirements (which make reference to the relevant GSP conventions), procedural requirements (which includes monitoring and complaint provisions) and supply chain requirements.

The assessment of these options is that they are confronted with challenges. Most of these challenges apply more to option 1 then option 2. If an integration of the VSS in the GSP-scheme according to option 1 or 2 might not be feasible, a third option of integrating the VSS in GSP might be considered. This third option, of a very different nature, would be to integrate the VSS in the reporting mechanisms of GSP, either by relying on the relevant information by the VSS, or by making an assessment of the adoption of the VSS in GSP countries part of the periodic evaluation of the GSP via a scorecard or roadmap. Such an approach has some advantages. First, it would not entail a major reform of the GSP scheme. Second, it would remain voluntary, but governments could be encouraged to promote the adoption of VSS and to provide incentives. Third, it would be a far more gradual introduction of the idea of VSS and sustainable production, which might set GSP beneficiaries further on a trajectory towards sustainable development and production.

Funding: This research was funded by a grant of the German Ministry of Development Cooperation.

Acknowledgments: The author wishes to thank Brecht Lein, Arjun Sharma and Andrei-Gavril Suse for assistance with collecting data and research support. All errors are mine.

Conflicts of Interest: The author declares no conflict of interest.

References

1. Marx, A.; Ebert, F.; Hachez, N.; Wouters, J. Dispute Settlement in the Trade and Sustainable Development Chapters of EU Trade Agreements: Report for the Dutch Ministry of Foreign Affairs. 2017. Available online: https://ghum.kuleuven.be/ggs/publications/books/final-report-9-february-def.pdf (accessed on 15 October 2018).

2. Marx, A.; Wouters, J.; Natens, B.; Geraets, D. Non-traditional Global Governance: The Case of Governing Through Trade. In *Global Governance through Trade*; Wouters, J., Marx, A., Geraets, D., Natens, B., Eds.; Edward Elgar: Cheltenham, UK, 2015.

3. REGULATION (EU) No 978/2012 OF THE EUROPEAN PARLIAMENT AND OF THE COUNCIL of 25 October 2012 Applying a Scheme of Generalised Tariff Preferences and Repealing Council Regulation (EC) No 732/2008 (GSP Regulation). Available online: https://eur-lex.europa.eu/legal-content/EN/TXT/PDF/?uri=CELEX:32012R0978&from=EN (accessed on 21 November 2018).

4. European Commission. *Report from the Commission to the European Parliament and the Council on the Generalised Scheme of Preferences covering the period 2014–2015*; COM (2016) 29 Final; European Commission: Brussels, Belgium, 2016; p. 3.

5. Marx, A.; Brando, N.; Lein, B. Strengthening Labour Rights Provisions in Bilateral Trade Agreements. The case of voluntary sustainability standards. *Glob. Policy* **2017**, *8*, 78–88. [CrossRef]

6. Schukat, P.; Rust, J. Tariff preferences for sustainable products. In *An Examination of the Potential Role of Sustainability Standards in the Generalized Preference Systems Based on the European Union Model (GSP)*; Deutsche Gesellschaft fur Internationale Zusammenarbeit (GIZ) GmbH: Bonn, Germany, 2012.

7. Schukat, P.; Rust, J.; Baumhauer, J. Tariff Preferences for Sustainable Products: A Summary. In *Voluntary Standard Systems, Natural Resource Management in Transition*; Schmitz-Hoffmann, C., Ed.; Springer: Berlin/Heidelberg, Germany, 2014; pp. 419–430.

8. Fiorini, M.; Solleder, O.; Hoekman, B.; Taimasova, R.; Jansen, M.; Wozniak, J.; Schleifer, P. *Exploring Voluntary Sustainability Standards Using ITC Standards Map: On the Accessibility of Voluntary Sustainability Standards for Suppliers*; ITC-Working Paper 04-2016; ITC: Geneva, Switzerland, 2016.

9. Lambin, E.F.; Meyfroidt, P.; Rueda, X.; Blackman, A.; Börner, J.; Cerutti, P.O.; Dietsch, T.; Jungmann, L.; Lamarque, P.; Lister, J.; et al. Effectiveness and Synergies of Policy Instruments for Land Use Governance in Tropical Regions. *Glob. Environ. Chang.* **2014**, *28*, 129–140. [CrossRef]

10. Lambin, E.; Thorlakson, T. Sustainability Standards: Interactions between private actors, civil society and governments. *Annu. Rev. Environ. Resour.* **2018**, *43*, 369–393. [CrossRef]

11. Eberlein, B.; Abbott, K.; Black, J.; Meidinger, E.; Wood, S. Transnational Business Governance Interactions: conceptualization and framework for analysis. *Regul. Gov.* **2014**, *8*, 1–21. [CrossRef]

12. Auld, G. Confronting trade-offs and interactive effects in the choice of policy focus: Specialized versus comprehensive private governance. *Regul. Gov.* **2014**, *8*, 126–148. [CrossRef]

13. Grime, M.; Wright, G. *Delphi Method*; John Wiley & Sons, Ltd.: Hoboken, NJ, USA, 2016.

14. European Parliament Research Service. *Human Rights in EU Trade Policy: Unilateral Measures*; European Parliament Research Service: Brussels, Belgium, 2017; p. 4.

15. European Commission and European External Action Service. *The EU Special Incentive Arrangement for Sustainable Development and Good Governance ('GSP+') Covering the Period 2014–2015, Joint Staff Working Document*; SWD (2016) 8 Final; European Commission: Brussels, Belgium, 2018.

16. European Commission. *Mid-Term Evaluation of the EU's Generalised Scheme of Preferences (GSP)*; European Commission: Brussels, Belgium, 2017. Available online: http://trade.ec.europa.eu/doclib/docs/2017/september/tradoc_156085.pdf (accessed on 15 October 2018).

17. Richardson, B.; Harrison, J.; Campling, L. *Labour Rights in Export Processing Zones with a Focus on GSP+ Beneficiary Countries*; European Parliament: Brussels, Belgium, 2017.

18. Pakistani Workers Confederation. *GSP Plus and Labor Standards in Pakistan: The Chasm between Conditions and Compliance*; FES: Islamabad, Pakistan, 2017.

19. Simmons, B.A. *Mobilizing for Human Rights: International Law in Domestic Politics*; Cambridge University Press: Cambridge, UK, 2009.

20. Mosley, L. *Labor Rights and Multinational Production*; Cambridge University Press: New York, NY, USA, 2011.

21. Hafner-Burton, E.M. *Making Human Rights a Reality*; Princeton University Press: Princeton, NJ, USA, 2013.

22. Marx, A.; Soares, J. Does Integrating Labour Provisions in Free Trade Agreements Make a Difference? An exploratory analysis of freedom of association and collective bargaining rights in 13 EU Trade Partners. In *Global Governance through Trade*; Wouters, J., Marx, A., Geraets, D., Natens, B., Eds.; Edward Elgar: Cheltenham, UK, 2015.

23. Marx, A.; Soares, J.; van Acker, W. The protection of the rights of freedom of association and collective bargaining. A longitudinal analysis over 30 years in 73 countries. In *Global Governance of Labour Rights*; Marx, A., Wouters, J., Beke, L., Rayp, G., Eds.; Edward Elgar: Cheltenham, UK, 2015.

24. UNFSS. *Voluntary Sustainability Standards. Today's Landscape of Issues and Initiatives to Achieve Public Policy Objectives*; United Nations Forum on Sustainability Standards: Geneva, Switzerland, 2013; p. 3.

25. Van Oorschot, M.; Kok, M.; Brons, J.; van der Esch, S.; Janse, J.; Rood, T.; Vixseboxse, E.; Wilting, H.; Vermeulen, W. *Sustainability of International Dutch Supply Chains. Progress, Effects and Perspectives*; PBL: The Hague, The Netherlands, 2014; Available online: www.pbl.nl/en (accessed on 15 October 2018).

26. Marx, A.; Wouters, J. Competition and Cooperation in the Market of Voluntary Standards. In *International standardization—Law, Economics and Politics*; Delimatsis, P., Ed.; Cambridge University Press: Cambridge, UK, 2015.

27. Potts, J.; Lynch, M.; Wilkings, A.; Huppé, G.; Cunningham, M.; Voora, V. *The State of Sustainability Initiatives Review: Standards and the Green Economy*; Joint Initiative of ENTWINED, IDH, IIED, FAST, IISD; State of Sustainability Initiatives: London, UK, 2014.

28. Ponte, S.; Daugbjerg, C. Biofuel Sustainability and the Formation of Transnational Hybrid Governance. *Environ. Politics* **2015**, *24*, 96–114. [CrossRef]

29. Schleifer, P. Orchestrating sustainability: The case of European Union biofuel governance. *Regul. Gov.* **2013**, *7*, 533–546. [CrossRef]

30. Overdevest, C.; Zeitlin, J. Assembling an experimentalist regime: Transnational governance interactions in the forest sector. *Regul. Gov.* **2014**, *8*, 22–48. [CrossRef]

31. Meliado, F. *Private Standards, Trade, and Sustainable Development: Policy Options for Collective Action*; International Centre for Trade and Sustainable Development (ICTSD): Geneva, Switzerland, 2017.

32. Ugarte, S.; Van Dam, J.; Spijkers, S.; Gaebler, M. *Recognition of Private Certification Schemes for Public Regulation. Lessons Learned from the Renewable Energy Directive*; Deutsche Gesellschaft für Internationale Zusammenarbeit (GIZ): Bonn, Germany, 2013.

33. Collins, B. *The New Regulators? Assessing the Landscape of Multi-Stakeholder Initiatives*; MSI Integrity and Kenan Institute for Ethics, Duke University: Durham, NC, USA, 2017.

34. Portela, C. *Enforcing Respect for Labour Standards with Targeted Sanctions*; Friedrich-Ebert-Stiftung: Singapore, 2018.

35. Keck, A.; Lendle, A. New evidence on preference utilization. In *Economic Research and Statistics Division*; Staff Working Paper ERSD-2012–12; World Trade Organization: Geneva, Switzerland, 2012; p. 6. Available online: https://www.wto.org/english/res_e/reser_e/ersd201212_e.pdf (accessed on 15 October 2018).

36. FAO. *Impact of International Voluntary Standards on Smallholder Market Participation in Developing Countries: A Review of Literature*; FAO: Rome, Italy, 2014.

37. International Trade Centre. The Impacts of Private Standards on Global Value Chains. In *Literature Review Series on the Impacts of Private Standards Part I*; International Trade Centre (ITC): Geneva, Switzerland, 2011.

38. Anner, M. Corporate Social Responsibility and Freedom of Association Rights the Precarious Quest for Legitimacy and Control in Global Supply Chains. *Politics Soc.* **2012**, *40*, 609–644. [CrossRef]

39. Egels-Zanden, N.; Lindholm, H. Do codes of conduct improve worker rights in supply chains? A study of Fair Wear Foundation. *J. Clean. Prod.* **2015**, *107*, 31–40. [CrossRef]

40. Fransen, L. *Corporate Social Responsibility and Global Labor Standards: Firms and Activists in the Making of Private Regulation*; Routledge: New York, NY, USA, 2012.

41. LeBaron, G.; Lister, J.; Dauvergne, P. Governing Global Supply Chain Sustainability through the Ethical Audit Regime. *Globalizations* **2017**, *14*, 958–975. [CrossRef]
42. Locke, R. *The Promise and Limits of Private Power. Promoting Labor Standards in a Global Economy*; Cambridge University Press: Cambridge, UK, 2013.
43. Marx, A.; Wouters, J. Intermediaries in Global Labour Governance. *Ann. Am. Acad. Political Soc. Sci.* **2017**, *607*, 189–206. [CrossRef]
44. Marx, A. Legitimacy, Institutional Design and Dispute Settlement: The Case of Eco-certification systems. *Globalizations* **2014**, *11*, 401–416. [CrossRef]
45. Marx, A. Varieties of Legitimacy: A Configurational Institutional Design Analysis of Eco-labels. *Innov. Eur. J. Soc. Sci. Res.* **2013**, *26*, 268–287. [CrossRef]
46. Bennett, E.A. Who Governs Socially-Oriented Standards? Not the Producers of Certified Products. *World Dev.* **2017**, *91*, 53–69. [CrossRef]
47. ISEAL Alliance. *Chain of Custody: Models and Definitions*; ISEAL Alliance: London, UK, 2016.
48. Lund-Thomsen, P.; Nadvi, K. Clusters, Chains and Compliance: Corporate Social Responsibility and Governance in Football Manufacturing in South Asia. *J. Bus. Ethics* **2010**, *93*, 201–222. [CrossRef]
49. Fair Wear Foundation (FWF). *Fear Wear Foundation Annual Report*; FWF: Amsterdam, The Netherlands, 2012.
50. Fair Wear Foundation (FWF). *Audit Manual*; FWF: Amsterdam, The Netherlands, 2012; pp. 10–11.
51. Fair Wear Foundation (FWF). *Brand Performance Check Guide for Affiliates*; FWF: Amsterdam, The Netherlands, 2014; p. 6.
52. Loconto, A. Models of assurance: Diversity and standardization of modes of intermediation. *Ann. Am. Acad.* **2017**, *670*, 112–132. [CrossRef]
53. UTZ' RESPONSE. To the report: 'External Evaluation of the UTZ tea program in Sri Lanka'. By Nucleus Foundation and Fair & Sustainable Advisory Services. Available online: https://www.utz.org/wp-content/uploads/2016/07/UTZ-Response-External-evaluation-on-the-UTZ-tea-program-in-Sri-Lanka.pdf (accessed on 21 November 2018).
54. Hidayat, N.; Offermans, A.; Glasbergen, P. On the Profitability of Sustainability Certification: An Analysis among Indonesian Palm Oil Smallholders. *J. Econ. Sustain. Dev.* **2016**, *7*, 45–62.
55. Marx, A.; Wouters, J. Is Everybody on Board? Voluntary Sustainability Standards and Green Restructuring. *Development* **2015**, *58*, 511–520. Available online: https://link.springer.com/article/10.1057/s41301-016-0051-z (accessed on 23 November 2018). [CrossRef]
56. Marx, A.; Cuypers, D. Forest Certification as a Global Environmental Governance Tool: What is the Macro-impact of the Forest Stewardship Council. *Regul. Gov.* **2010**, *4*, 304–334. [CrossRef]
57. Tayleur, C.; Balmford, A.; Buchanan, G.M.; Butchart, S.H.; Walker, C.C.; Ducharme, H.; Green, R.E.; Milder, J.C.; Sanderson, F.J.; Thomas, D.H. Where are commodity crops certified, and what does it mean for conservation and poverty alleviation? *Biol. Conserv.* **2018**, *217*, 36–46. [CrossRef]
58. Manning, S.; Von Hagen, O. Linking Local Experiments to Global Standards: How Project Networks Promote Global Institution-building. *Scand. J. Manag.* **2010**, *26*, 398–416. [CrossRef]
59. Amengual, M.; Fine, J. Co-enforcing Labour Standards: the unique contributions of state and worker organizations in Argentina and United States. *Regul. Gov.* **2016**, *11*, 129–142. [CrossRef]
60. Toffel MShort, J.; Ouellet, M. Codes in context: How states, markets, and civil society shape adherence to global labor standards. *Regul. Gov.* **2015**, *9*, 205–223. [CrossRef]
61. European Parliament Committee on the Environment, Public Health and Food Safety. *Report on Palm Oil and Deforestation of Rainforests*; European Parliament: Brussels, Belgium, 2017.

Article

Trade Unions in Multi-Stakeholder Initiatives: What Shapes Their Participation?

Deborah Martens [1,*], Annelien Gansemans [2], Jan Orbie [1] and Marijke D'Haese [2]

[1] Centre for EU-Studies, Ghent University, Universiteitstraat 8, 9000 Gent, Belgium; jan.orbie@ugent.be
[2] Department of Agricultural Economics, Ghent University, Coupure Links 653, 9000 Gent, Belgium;
   annelien.gansemans@ugent.be (A.G.); marijke.dhaese@ugent.be (M.D.)
* Correspondence: deborah.martens@ugent.be; Tel.: +32-9-264-69-50

Received: 15 October 2018; Accepted: 15 November 2018; Published: 20 November 2018

Abstract: There is a growing concern about the extent to which multi-stakeholder initiatives (MSIs), designed to improve social and environmental sustainability in global supply chains, give a meaningful voice to less powerful stakeholders. Trade unions are one particular civil society group whose participation in MSIs has received little scholarly attention so far. The objective of this paper is to examine the determinants that enable and constrain trade union participation in MSIs. Based on interviews, focus groups, observations and document analysis we determine local trade union participation in three MSIs, operating at company, national and transnational level respectively, in the Costa Rican pineapple industry. To explain the limited encountered trade union participation, an analytical framework is developed combining structural and agency dimensions, namely the MSI design and trade union's power resources. The findings show shortcomings in the representativeness, procedural fairness and consensual orientation in the design and implementation of the MSIs. These are, however, not sufficient to explain weak trade union participation as trade union power resources also have an influence. Strong network embeddedness and improved infrastructural resources had a positive effect, whereas the lack of internal solidarity and unfavourable narrative resources constrained the unions' participation.

Keywords: multi-stakeholder initiatives; participation; trade unions; power resources; Costa Rica; pineapple

1. Introduction

Multi-stakeholder initiatives (MSIs) aiming at improving environmental and social sustainability are omnipresent throughout different supply chains, from the Roundtable on Sustainable Palm Oil to the Alliance for Bangladesh Worker Safety in textiles. This form of governance is supposed to have greater legitimacy because they involve a diversity of stakeholders, including civil society, public and private actors [1–4]. Most research on MSIs has examined their functioning and legitimacy [5–7], whereas only few studies assessed the participatory aspects of MSIs [8–10]. Although MSIs aim to be inclusive and to reach the deliberative ideal where arguments overcome power dynamics, there is a considerable risk that existing power asymmetries are reproduced and that only powerful actors determine the course of action [11]. This point of critique has been raised in several studies concluding that the voices of less powerful actors, such as small farmers or local communities, are often not heard in MSIs [1,12].

Trade unions, independent workers' organisations established through the principles of Freedom of Association (see ILO Convention No. 87 (1948)), are one particular civil society group whose involvement in MSIs received little scholarly attention so far. They are, however, relevant and legitimate participants when social concerns, especially labour rights issues, are considered in the initiatives. Studies have demonstrated that certain procedures and mechanisms of MSIs can allow for more equal participation of all actors, in particular those that are traditionally less powerful [7,13,14]. For example, an impartial facilitator who keeps dominant participants in check, encourages less vocal actors to share their opinion and maintains positive group dynamics [15]. Other participatory procedures include setting clear goals and rules, providing access to information, working in small groups to build trust, using adequate materials adapted to the educational level and cultural background of (illiterate) participants, developing the technical capability of participants to meaningfully engage in the process, covering costs of participation and conducting stakeholder analysis to identify those relevant to the decision making process concerned.

The objective of this paper is to assess trade union participation in MSIs and explain the factors that enable and constrain their participation. Our contribution lies in a combination of two explanatory factors. First, the design and implementation of MSIs is analysed allowing an assessment of their deliberative potential. Second, the power resources of the relevant trade unions are described as they clarify the capacity trade unions have to participate in an MSI. By combining the importance of structure (i.e., MSI design) and agency (i.e., trade union power resources) in our analytical framework, we aim to contribute to a deeper understanding of the participatory processes of MSIs.

Trade union participation is examined through a within-case analysis of three MSIs existing in the European Union (EU)–Costa Rica pineapple supply chain. Each MSI operates at a different governance level, namely at company, national and transnational level. These are respectively the Ethical Trading Initiative (ETI), the National Platform for the responsible production and trade of pineapples (hereafter Platform) and the Civil Society Meetings (CSMs) organised within the EU–Central American Association Agreement. Based on this comprehensive overview, we found that the design and implementation of the MSIs did not enable notable substantial participation and that the union power resources also played an important role. Here, strong network embeddedness and better infrastructural resources had a positive impact, whereas fragmented internal solidarity and unfavourable narrative resources constrained trade union's participation. As such, the analysis confirms business domination and weak bargaining power of unions in the MSIs.

The paper is structured as follows. The rise of multi-stakeholderism is defined in the context of global labour governance and the basic concepts of deliberative governance are explored. Drawing on existing criteria of input legitimacy and power resource literature, an analytical framework is developed. Next, the research context, case study approach and methodology are presented before coming to the empirical findings. Here, trade union participation in the three MSIs is described and the explanatory factors—MSI design and implementation and trade union power resources—are analysed for each initiative. In the discussion and conclusion, we interpret the findings, make recommendations for improving MSIs and suggest avenues for further research.

2. Changing Labour Governance Landscape

Globalisation has brought about two trends worth considering in the light of labour rights protection.

First, a shift in global labour governance occurred in which labour rights are regulated through a combination of public (e.g., labour laws, international conventions, soft law initiatives), private (e.g., voluntary standards, codes of conducts) and hybrid (i.e., combination of both private and public initiatives) forms of governance. These new forms often seek the inclusion of non-state actors. Labour rights were historically dealt with at governmental level, as states developed labour law in the 20th century to secure justice in employment relations [16]. Through domestic labour law and the participation to dedicated international organisations such as the International Labour Organisation (ILO), states have traditionally been the drivers of labour regulation.

The expansion of supply chains around the globe beyond one state's jurisdiction gave rise to a number of governance deficits, which neither the domestic nor international institutions have been capable of governing appropriately [17]. Even though Gereffi and Mayer refer to broad societal issues, this deficit has also had an impact on the governance of labour rights. As a result, the governance landscape has been moving away from the traditional regulatory role of the state to the inclusion of non-state actors in policy processes [4,18–20]. In doing so, non-state actors were involved both to more effectively address complex cross-border issues and to increase the legitimacy of global governance. Non-state actors comprise a variety of stakeholders including private entities such as business actors, multinational corporations, non-governmental organisations (NGOs), trade unions and academia. The involvement of these actors through hybrid public–private governance is also termed multi-stakeholder governance [21]. Although there is no internationally agreed definition for multi-stakeholderism, it has been broadly conceptualised in the field of 'interactive governance' as:

> "the complex process through which a plurality of actors with diverging interests interact in order to formulate, promote and achieve common objectives by means of mobilizing, exchanging and deploying a range of ideas, rules and resources." [22]

While MSIs bring together multiple actors, they can occur in different forms and sizes such as multi-stakeholder alliances, partnerships, standards and roundtables [1,4,23]. MSIs can operate at different scales—from local to transnational—in diverse sectors, regions and topics [24]. They can follow different procedural approaches, vary in duration and can evolve over time from a dialogue platform to an independent organisation with a well-established governance structure. There is also a great diversity in the range of purposes that MSIs seek to fulfil. While some MSIs aim to solve specific problems and find a common ground, others promote learning and awareness raising, foster stakeholder dialogue or focus on standard-setting and monitoring [7,25].

Second, although "Everyone has the right to form and to join trade unions for the protection of his interests" as stipulated in the Universal Declaration of Human Rights (Article 23, paragraph 4 (1948)), many workers are not allowed to organise themselves in independent organisations, and trade unionists are persecuted or discriminated against by hostile management [26]. In general, trade union bargaining power has weakened and trade union density has declined as a result of global pressures, including increased informality and flexibilisation of labour markets [27,28]. Flexible sourcing practices of retailers and brands have increased pressures on suppliers across the globe. These demand pressures are commonly transferred onto the weakest actors at the bottom of the chain, namely the workers, who need to cope with insecure contracts, low wages and excessive overtime [29,30]. Despite these challenges to union organisation, integration into global value chains also created new opportunities for local trade unions to connect and build alliances with NGOs and international trade unions [31–33]. Through these cross-border networks, private standards and brands have been criticised in campaigns addressing violations of workers' rights at supplier sites.

These two trends, proliferation of MSIs and weak(ening) of trade unions in producing countries, are relevant when reflecting on the potential and limits of the prevailing labour governance. However, before trying to answer questions on the impact or results of MSIs one must understand the participatory processes existing within them. Therefore, this article focuses on explaining participation.

3. Deliberation and Participation

The concept of deliberative democracy is often put forward as an appropriate approach to assess new forms of governance, such as MSIs [9,34]. Deliberation—careful consideration or discussion and thoughtfully weighing options—is a central feature of MSIs since their outcome is the result of a participatory process [23,35]. Indeed, in his book 'Foundations and Frontiers of Deliberative Governance', Dryzek [36] explains how deliberative principles apply to governance networks, such as MSIs.

A first central aspect of deliberative democracy theory is the idea that deliberation promotes a kind of collective communicative power which neutralises coercive forms of power such as domination [37,38]. Common reasoning is essential in deliberative governance and deliberation is indispensable for collective decision making. Therefore, Hendricks [37] explains that deliberative procedures should be designed as such that debates are shaped by the 'force of the better argument' and not by the most powerful or dominant actor. This entails that existing power asymmetries are diminished or even neutralised during the debates and that the outcome of the deliberative process accommodates or balances the participating interests.

Evaluations on MSIs reaching this deliberative ideal vary. Positive assessments of MSIs demonstrate how powerless actors can express their voice and successfully manage to influence decision making in their favour, whereas more critical assessments point to the failure of MSIs to redress existing power imbalances, leading to uneven participation and outcomes that do not meet the needs of less powerful actors, such as small farmers and actors from the Global South [1,12,35]. In general, authors are rather critical of the optimism surrounding MSIs.

A second fundamental element of deliberative governance is participation, as it is the precondition for any other development in the process. Moreover, the involvement of all affected stakeholders in the deliberation process is considered a source of legitimacy, assuming actors can equally share their opinion, concerns, interests and knowledge [8,23]. This source of legitimacy is often referred to in terms of input legitimacy, which addresses the question of who is entitled to make decisions and who is to be represented in the decision-making process [39]. Similarly, according to Dryzek [40], the deliberative quality of MSIs depends on, among others factors, inclusiveness.

Utting [12] found that trade union involvement in MSIs varies considerably from little or no formal involvement to significant and more extensive participation. Indeed, when delving into the participation of a stakeholder, it becomes clear that physical participation does not automatically entail that the participant's interest will be taken into account or that they can contribute in a meaningful way to the process and influence the decisions made [14,20,23]. In general, two dimensions of participation reappear in multiple studies under different labels. Luttrell [41] labelled the dimensions 'nominal and meaningful participation', referring to the fact that 'physical involvement of marginalised actors and even verbal participation by them, does not guarantee their concerns will be heard'. Similarly, Fransen [4] distinguished between 'surface appearance' and 'actual involvement' of societal interest groups in decision-making. Brem-Wilson [10] talks about 'formal and substantive participation', Dingwerth [42] refers to the 'scope and quality of participation' and Reed [15] discusses different ladders of participation distinguishing degrees of engagement.

In light of deliberative democracy theory, it is necessary to understand the participatory processes in order to grasp the outcome of the process. To be able to assess the potential of MSIs for the improvement of labour rights, it is imperative to understand the participation of trade unions in these MSIs as they represent the voice of the affected stakeholders, namely the workers. The research question addressed in this paper is therefore: what shapes the participation of trade unions in MSIs? Literature on deliberative governance indicates the importance of the design of the participatory processes. In addition, when discussing the feasibility of deliberative governance, Hendrick's [37] recognises the need to look at the capacity of particular groups in civil society, especially powerless groups, to generate deliberation. Hence, these factors are integrated in the analytical framework presented in the next section.

4. Analytical Framework

This paper aims to contribute to a better understanding of the factors that enable or constrain trade union participation in MSIs. For this purpose, an analytical framework is developed that takes into account both the structure of the MSI (i.e., its design and implementation) as well as the agency of the participant (i.e., its power resources) (Figure 1). Building further on the distinctions in participation introduced above, we contrast 'procedural participation' and 'substantial participation' to describe the observed trade union participation. The former refers to the physical attendance and continuity of participation, whereas the latter specifies the actual contribution in shaping the content of the debate, such as actors expressing their opinions and negotiating between divergent interests [43].

Figure 1. Analytical framework explaining trade union participation in multi-stakeholder initiatives.

4.1. Multi-Stakeholder Initiative Design and Implementation

The design of an MSI and its implementation should be examined as it will clarify whether participation is possible, desirable and effective from the point of view of the stakeholder. If the MSI is not designed to reduce power imbalances, the power asymmetry existing outside the MSI will be reproduced which might in turn influence the possibility, interest and willingness of the weaker actor to participate and consequently also the achievement of deliberation.

Various studies have shown that the set-up of an MSI has an impact on participation, especially if it foresees power-neutralising mechanisms [23], or what Luttrell [41] calls mechanisms to 'level the playing field'. This includes power-sharing rules that allow for equal input [41], establishment of working groups and public consultation [6,9], policies to ensure balanced resourcing [44], clear selection procedures and voting systems avoiding dominance of powerful actors [5,23,41,45], an impartial facilitator [15] and providing access to information, translation services and technology [23,46].

As we will concentrate on the participatory processes within MSIs, our criteria for analysing an MSI's design are derived from existing literature on deliberative democracy and input legitimacy of transnational governance and more specifically, MSIs [2,7,34,47]. MSI design will be assessed through three criteria: representativeness, procedural fairness and consensual orientation.

First, representativeness concerns stakeholder selection and processes that guarantee the inclusion of all relevant stakeholders, namely those affected by the issue addressed by the MSI. To assess this criterion we should, therefore, look at the stakeholder selection process [44]. In addition, one should also examine whether certain groups are excluded or if the system favours a special category of stakeholders [2]. Finally, the categorisation of the stakeholders could also play a role. Bolström and Tamm Hallström [8] explained how differentiating stakeholders in separate categories could potentially constitute a principle of exclusion from crucial decision-making arenas.

Second, procedural fairness stands for measures that diminish or neutralise power differences in decision-making processes by giving each category of stakeholder an equal and valid voice [7]. This does not only involve equal voting rights, equal status as members and access to information are also part of this criterion. This is assessed by analysing the decision-making procedures, whether they be explicit formalised rules of procedure or implicit principles. In addition to decision-making, arrangements guaranteeing the feasibility for all stakeholders to use the MSI's participation potential is considered. More concretely, this means funding and capacity building for those groups that cannot afford to participate in the meetings [1,11,48,49].

Third, a consensual orientation is pursued through a culture of cooperation and reasonable disagreement [7]. According to the Habermasian ideal [50,51], consensus should be reached through open discussions, where reasoning trumps bargaining, in a non-coercive environment. However, as Mena and Palazzo [7] acknowledge, MSIs gather a multitude of actors with different backgrounds and conflicting objectives. Therefore, these authors deem consensus as highly unlikely and suggest reasonable disagreement. Similarly, Luttrell [41] suggests to acknowledge disparities of power, address sensitive issues head-on, and to discuss the extent to which participants can 'agree to disagree'.

In the context of MSI design, we will look at whether and how mutual agreement is promoted. In addition, the communication attitude of participants is considered. Are these inclined to be constructive towards other participants or rather conflictual? For multi-stakeholder processes to result in a shared initiative towards joint objectives, a constructive attitude is needed from all participants [25]. Finally, consensual orientation obviously will depend on the trust that exists between the participants. Brouwer et al. [11] found that for stakeholders to be able to address power dynamics, a basis of trust is needed. Part of the complex context of MSIs is that the weaker actors can have experienced a long history of being excluded and treated poorly, and consequently distrust the MSI if it is dominated by more powerful actors.

4.2. Union Power Resources

An underestimated and often overlooked factor in the research on participation of a weaker stakeholder in an MSI is this actor's capacity. To shed light on this aspect we rely on the theoretical notion of power resources that affect the capacity to effectively participate [8] and use the typology developed by Lévesque and Murray [27] to analyse union capacity in particular. Four trade union power resources can be distinguished: internal solidarity, network embeddedness, infrastructural resources and narrative resources.

First, internal solidarity refers to the relationship between union members, the level of engagement of members, the strategies to recruit new members, the communication methods used between union members and leaders, the leadership structure and the level of cohesion and the presence of a collective identity. Second, network embeddedness, or external solidarity, refers to the degree to which unions have horizontal and vertical links with other unions and with community groups and social movements. Trade unions act at different levels from local to global, cross borders and connect with different actors, providing different opportunities to pursue union objectives. While some unions might be isolated, others have stronger ties to (inter)national unions or other civil society actors. Such ties can be supportive [3], however, collaboration between international NGOs and trade unions can also create tensions [52]. Third, narrative resources refer to the range of values and stories about trade unions that provide shared understandings and frame the way union members think and act [27]. Brouwer et al. [11] confirm this power resource which is invisible and difficult to change. In some cases, these deeply rooted structures, culture, behaviour and norms can lead to conservative, entrenched positions. Fourth, infrastructural resources refer to the material (money, meeting rooms), human (time, expertise) and organisational resources (use of technologies, training) [27].

We expect that weak levels of these four resources will negatively affect trade union participation in MSIs.

5. Research Approach

5.1. Research Context: Labour Rights Issues in Costa Rica and Its Pineapple Industry

Costa Rica is currently the biggest exporter of fresh pineapples, exporting 90% of fresh pineapples in the world, which represents 8.4% of the country's total exports [53]. From 2000 onwards the country's pineapple industry began to expand rapidly, from 11,000 ha to more than 44,000 ha in 2018 [54]. According to the Costa Rican Chamber of Pineapple Producers (CANAPEP), the pineapple industry has generated 32,000 jobs directly and over 130,000 jobs indirectly throughout the country. However, the rapid expansion has had negative environmental and social impacts, including those upon working conditions and the protection of labour rights.

Concerning labour rights issues, Costa Rica is notorious for its anti-union culture in the private sector (see *infra*), where only 2% of the workforce is unionised. Labour struggles were most prevalent in the banana industry, where the level of unionisation dropped from 90% in 1982 to 5% in 1987 after a defamation campaign against trade unions [55]. Perhaps the most frequent obstacle to collective labour rights in this country concerns the promotion of solidarist associations (known as *solidarismo*) and, specifically, the extent to which such associations prevent the development and functioning of effective and independent workers' organisations such as trade unions [56]. These solidarist associations are partly financed by management and do not recognise the right to collective bargaining as formulated in ILO Convention No. 98 (1949) [57]. While solidarist associations are on the rise, anti-union practices such as discrimination and dismissal because of trade union membership have been repeatedly reported to the ILO Committee of Experts and are partly responsible for the weakening of trade unions across the country [58,59]. In the wake of anti-union campaigns and employers' preference for negotiating with solidarist associations, the pineapple industry is characterised by a very low unionisation rate and accordingly no collective bargaining agreement has been established in any pineapple plantation [60,61].

5.2. Case Study Selection and Description

The EU-Costa Rica pineapple supply chain is an interesting case because it demonstrates how the expansion of an export crop has affected local communities and workers and raises the issue of the effectiveness of current labour governance mechanisms. Moreover, the industry is confronted with many of the environmental and social challenges that booming export regions face around the world. During our field research, we came across three MSIs in the pineapple industry, each one operating at a different governance level (company, national, transnational). Although the MSIs' objective, scope, duration, origins and functioning differ (see Table 1), they have in common that they aim at gathering the relevant stakeholders to make businesses and trade more sustainable. Instead of a comparative case study, we opted for a comprehensive within-case analysis of three key initiatives allowing for an exhaustive examination of trade union participation in MSIs across the EU-Costa Rica pineapple supply chain, ranging from their involvement in specific company issues to broader trade-related discussions in civil society fora. By analysing three initiatives we intend to create an overall understanding of trade union participation in MSIs throughout one specific supply chain and to identify which constraining or enabling factors they have in common. In what follows, the general characteristics of the three initiatives are described.

Table 1. General characteristics of the three MSIs.

	Ethical Trading Initiative (ETI) and Fyffes	National Platform for the Responsible Production and Trade of Pineapples (Platform)	Civil Society Mechanisms within European–Central American Association Agreement (CSMs)
Governance level	Company	National	Transnational
Objective	To promote respect for workers' rights	To improve social and environmental performance	To advise and make recommendations on implementation trade and sustainable development chapter
Scope	Global value chains	Costa Rica pineapple production and trade	Trade-related aspects of sustainable development
Multi-stakeholder dimension	Business, trade unions, non-governmental organization (NGO) members	Business, civil society, academia, government	Economic, social and environmental stakeholders
Approach	Learning approach Standard setting	Project approach Formal action plan	Dialogue approach Monitoring
Duration	1998–ongoing	2011–2017	2013–ongoing
Founders	Select group of UK retailers, NGOs, trade unions and UK government	United Nations Development Programme (UNDP)	European Union (EU)
Funding	Start-up grants UK government, membership fees	UNDP, Dutch NGO, Dutch public-private partnership	Little EU funding for EU CSMs, no funding (yet) for Central American CSMs

5.2.1. The Ethical Trading Initiative and Call for Action against Fyffes

ETI is a membership-based MSI bringing together companies, trade unions and NGOs to improve working conditions in global value chains. It has been established in 1998 with the support of the UK government and has developed a Base Code for corporate members to support continuous improvement regarding decent work [62]. ETI is governed by a tripartite board (comprising trade unions, NGOs and corporate members) which reviews the performance of companies, can hold them accountable in case of complaints following disciplinary procedures, and provides remedies [63]. To examine how unions in suppliers' sites participate in the work of ETI, we do not evaluate the general functioning of ETI but single out one corporate member of ETI, namely Fyffes. This company has recently been accused of labour rights violations in its subsidiaries' pineapple (ANEXCO) and melon (Suragroh) plantations in, respectively, Costa Rica and Honduras [64,65]. Fyffes is an Irish importer and distributor of tropical produce which was sold to the Japanese conglomerate Sumitomo in 2017 [66,67]. It was mentioned in 2016 in the Make Fruit Fair awareness raising and advocacy campaign calling for "Freedom and fairness for Fyffes workers" [64]. According to the campaign, the violations concern a disregard of freedom of association, as Fyffes seems not to recognise independent trade unions. At the time of writing, Fyffes has been suspended from ETI due to a lack of progress on the accused labour right violations in Honduras [68].

5.2.2. National Platform for Responsible Pineapple Production and Trade in Costa Rica

In 2011, the Platform was established with the support of the United Nations Development Programme's (UNDP) Green Commodities Programme and coordinated by the Costa Rican Second Vice-presidency, Ministry of Agriculture and the Ministry of Energy and Environment. It received funding from a Dutch NGO, the Interchurch Organisation for Development Cooperation (ICCO), in the first phase (2011–2014) and from the Sustainable Trade Initiative (IDH), a Dutch public–private initiative, in the second phase to ensure the continuity of the process. The UNDP was the driving force behind the creation of this multi-stakeholder platform and identified a range of environmental and social challenges that should be dealt with by the Costa Rican government in collaboration with relevant stakeholders.

Over the entire period, the Platform gathered about 900 participants from more than 50 organisations from business, NGOs, communities, academia and related national government institutions to improve the sustainability performance of pineapple production through the development of a national strategy with concrete actions [69]. The Platform had to develop an action plan determining the responsibilities of the government and industry players [70]. For this purpose, it organised four annual plenary meetings, thirty thematic working groups and several panel debates. In 2016, the action plan was finalised and the Costa Rican government adopted it in decree N°39462. The Platform mechanism did not put the social dimension on equal footing with the environmental and economic considerations, nor was it able to ensure that demands of all parties were equally considered (see *infra*).

5.2.3. Civil Society Meetings of the European Union–Central America Association Agreement

The new generation EU trade agreements, starting from the EU–Korea trade agreement in 2011, contain chapters on trade and sustainable development. These chapters refer to labour and environmental standards that should be respected in the framework of the agreement. Civil society meetings (CSMs) are created to follow up on, advise and monitor the commitments made in these sustainable development chapters. Even though there is variation in the legal texts establishing these meetings [71], several foundational features reoccur. First, each party agrees to create or consult an independent domestic civil society mechanism (often called a Domestic Advisory Group (DAG)). Second, an annual transnational meeting should be organised. Here, members of the domestic mechanisms and/or other civil society actors meet. Third, some interaction is foreseen between these two meetings and the intergovernmental body (officials of the EU and its trading partner(s)) that meets annually to discuss the implementation of the trade and sustainable development chapter.

The EU and six Central American countries—Costa Rica, El Salvador, Guatemala, Honduras, Nicaragua and Panama—signed the EU–Central American Association Agreement which has been applied since 2013. Each Central American country (should have) assembled its own DAG. The Costa Rican DAG, together with that from Guatemala, is functioning relatively well in the sense that an independent DAG with civil society members actually exists, as other DAGs are characterised by governmental presence and/or a general lack of participants. In general, the meetings have, similar to those organised in the context of other EU trade agreements, experienced a slow start and have had difficulties generating an internal dynamic [72].

Following discussions on labour issues and corporate social responsibility (CSR) during the civil society and governmental meetings, two seminars, in Costa Rica (May 2017) and Guatemala (May 2018), were organised. Both events covered general CSR topics such as responsible value chains, international CSR instruments and sectoral case studies. In addition, the OECD and the ILO gave a workshop on a related issue [73,74].

5.3. Data Collection and Methodology

The interdisciplinary research presented in this paper is based on (1) 37 semi-structured interviews with various actors from different stakeholder categories, (2) three focus groups with trade union members, (3) eight nonparticipant observations during CSMs in the framework of the Association Agreement and (4) document analysis. Extensive field research was conducted in Costa Rica (2015–2016) with Costa Rican representatives and in Belgium (2015–2017) with EU representatives. These two rounds of data collection were followed-up by interviews in 2018 to collect additional information on the concerned multi-stakeholder initiatives for this case study (see Table A1 in Appendix A). To protect the identity of the respondents, we aggregated the respondents per region and type of actor. The following combination of letters and numbers were used to indicate to which group a respondent belongs (see Appendix A): Costa Rica is abbreviated by the letters CR, U refers to unions, G for government officials, and B for business representatives. The letters EU represent European officials, EUCS stands for European civil society actors and ILO officials carry the letter I.

In Costa Rica we targeted key informants, categorised in the following three groups to get a comprehensive sample of different stakeholder perspectives: business representatives (such as CANAPEP), trade unions (at national, sectoral and plantation level) and government officials (including the Ministry of External Trade, Agriculture and Labour). Through snowball sampling, we conducted face-to-face expert interviews [75] with representatives of the Costa Rican pineapple unions (6), government (8), business (5) and ILO officials (3). In addition, three focus groups (with respectively 6, 14 and 4 trade union members) were organised to become more acquainted with Costa Rican trade unionism and to gather more factual information. For the perspectives of EU civil society actors and officials involved in the CSMs, we conducted 15 expert interviews with key informants identified from the list of CSM participants as well as officials from the European Commission and the Delegation of the EU to Costa Rica.

An interview guide was developed for each group of respondents covering topics related to the perception and functioning of trade unions in Costa Rica, the challenges to improve labour rights in the pineapple industry, the existing governance mechanisms and regulatory framework, and a set of more specific questions on the MSIs discussed in this study, including the motives for participation, the design and participatory decision-making process and the results.

The document analysis concerns the content of public video footage, press releases, event reports, presentations, email correspondence, participant lists and meeting minutes of the three MSIs. In addition, one of the researchers observed two transnational meetings, two DAG-to-DAG meetings and four EU DAG meetings where she could listen to the discussions and gain insights on the participatory dynamics and methods. This qualitative data was triangulated through interviews with members of the MSIs.

The relevant parts of the interview and observation notes and transcripts were extracted in a qualitative content analysis [76,77]. A cross table was constructed for each of the three MSIs where the extracted data was summarised and reformulated in a more general language and structured according to the analytical framework (see Appendix B). Even though this analytical framework draws heavily on existing literature, it was fine-tuned in an inductive manner. This analysis was then transformed in a thick description of trade union participation and a study of the structural and agency factors determining trade union participation in MSIs.

Two important limitations of the data collection need to be acknowledged. First, the presence of the researcher in the room during the CSMs could have potentially influenced the discussions, because the participants feel they are being "watched" (i.e., observer effect [78]). Second, the subgroup of business actors was underrepresented in our sample because of the sensitivity of labour issues and their limited willingness to meet for interviews [79]. Concerning the case of Fyffes, ETI declined our interview request and only confirmed the latest status update over email to preserve the confidentiality of their members.

6. Findings

6.1. Procedural and Substantial Participation of Trade Unions

6.1.1. Participation of Trade Unions in ETI–Fyffes

"Six management assistants were assigned as facilitators [for the capacity building event]. This is worrying because they were exactly the ones behind the anti-union campaign, discrimination, persecution and dismissals. The initiative was, therefore, practically born dead for the union members. Following the pressure exercised by our members, they appointed four facilitators of the union but without adequate material and knowledge to enable facilitation. Their participation was inconstant and in some activities they could practically not participate at all. [...] They did not take union members into account in this capacity-building event, which could have served as a platform for the establishment of real social dialogue. During the capacity building, management impeded and threatened normal participation of trade union members."—Personal communication with CRU2

Procedural Participation

The participation of Costa Rican trade unions to ETI occurred indirectly through the support they received from the International Union of Food, Agricultural, Hotel, Restaurant, Catering, Tobacco and Allied Workers' Associations (IUF) and the NGO Bananalink, with whom they had long standing relationships. Bananalink is also a partner of the Make Fruit Fair campaign. Mediation attempts by ETI and the Costa Rican Ministry of Labour to bring the trade union SINTRAPEM (Sindicato Nacional de Trabajadores/as del Sector Privado Empresarial) and management of the subsidiary plantation ANEXCO together around a negotiation table in 2016 failed [80]. In response to the urgent action call, ETI conducted a field visit to investigate the allegations and produced an internal report with recommendations. One of those was a capacity-building session for unions and management which took place in November 2016 [EUCS7]. ETI financed the event and sent independent consultants to facilitate a dialogue between local management and trade union representatives to discuss the matter. The participation of most representatives was cancelled as they did not receive the permission from the management to be absent to attend the capacity-building session [CRU2].

Substantial Participation

Local unions provided evidence of violations to prepare the campaign and complaint. They determined the direction and did the legwork for the campaign whereas Bananalink supported them [EUCS7]. The NGO wrote to Fyffes Chairman in November 2016 asking him to address the issues without response; later they sent a petition letter signed by more than 40,000 people [81]. The local union was engaged and communicative, they hosted a visit that helped to gather documentation for the Fyffes campaign. The mediation by ETI allowed unions to express their concerns about the willingness of management to have dialogue and the persistent labour rights violations in the plantations. During the capacity-building event, the trade unionists' input was limited as they were in the minority. Although the local union leader denounced these practices, no further actions were taken by ETI in Costa Rica because the focus had moved to the complaint in Honduras [EUCS7].

6.1.2. Participation of Trade Unions in the Platform

"They [CANAPEP] never wanted us to be present in the Platform. We went to the launch of the platform and after a couple of months they proposed to organise working groups on soil and pesticide application among others, but none of the working groups covered labour issues. We went to the ILO to suggest a working group for the discussion of labour aspects, but CANAPEP did not want to sit together with us, they prefer to sit together with the solidarist associations only. The platform is a lie, they just waste resources."—CRU1

Procedural Participation

When assessing physical attendance over the entire period of the Platform, producers (27%) and government actors (36%) dominated the meetings while unions (1%) and NGOs (9%) were underrepresented [70]. Other smaller categories of stakeholders were buyers, international organisations, communities and academics. There was resistance from the producers' side to include trade unions upon which Bananalink pressured the Dutch NGO ICCO, which co-financed the Platform, to insist on trade union participation [EUCS7]. However, industry players refused to address any of the trade union issues and ultimately trade unions decided to withdraw their participation. Consequently, they were not involved in the final decision-making process of the action plan and were also not part of the follow-up committee monitoring its implementation [82].

Substantial Participation

Before the Platform, there was hardly space for dialogue between trade unions, business and government to find solutions for the social and environmental problems of pineapple production. Problems were mainly discussed through judicial avenues. Trade unions saw the Platform as a unique opportunity to share their viewpoint with business and government [70,83,84]. A trade union representative of SITRAP (Sindicato de Trabajadores de Plantaciones Agricolas) attempted to put freedom of association and collective bargaining on the table during the first annual meeting and drew a picture of the difficulties that they are facing. However, attempts to facilitate dialogue between government, employers and trade unions to discuss the working conditions in plantations failed because of the irreconcilable differences in opinions among the parties.

In a workshop organised to review the proposed action plan in February 2014—where unions were not present—business representatives requested the modification of the reference to worker's organisations in the action line dealing with national dialogue on labour rights [84]. In addition, CANAPEP put an ultimatum to exclude any reference to freedom of association. Industry players argued that the issue of trade unions is not unique to pineapple, and should be addressed at national level through enforcement of existing labour laws. Instead, they suggested to include in the action plan that the government should promote the international recognition of alternative labour organisations (i.e., *solidarismo*) that, according to them, represent pineapple workers in Costa Rica [83]. Consequently, promoting national dialogue on labour rights was replaced by a more general action for promoting dialogue spaces on environmental and social responsibility, omitting explicit actions related to freedom of association [70].

6.1.3. Participation of Trade Unions in Civil Society Meetings in EU–Central America Trade Agreement

"It's a new type of meeting that doesn't exist at national level. The agreement creates a space to discuss the issue of labour rights violations. But it is still a very limited and superficial dialogue. The format does not allow for an integral discussion, the debated topics are secondary, not fundamental. It is nothing more than a dialogue of the deaf. There is no interest in reaching agreement. Everyone

simply states his position. That's it. If certain sectors put their veto and don't want to discuss further, the dialogue loses its meaning."—CRU5

Procedural Participation

The official list of the members of the Costa Rican DAG contains seven trade unions. However, only two of them participate actively, namely Central del Movimiento de Trabajadores Costarricenses (CMTC) and Bloque Unitario Sindical y Social Costarricense (BUSSCO) [85] [CRU5]. All secretaries-general of the Costa Rican trade union federations were included in the list; however, most of them are not aware of their membership or even of the existence of the DAG [CRU1,CRU5]. It must be said that limited trade union participation in the DAGs is not specific to Costa Rica; in all Central American DAGs trade unions are barely represented.

Regarding trade union physical attendance during the CSR seminars, a considerable difference was noted between both seminars. Whereas this stakeholder category was barely represented during the first event in Costa Rica, there were significantly more—mainly Guatemalan—trade unionists present during the second event [EUCS5,EU3].

Substantial Participation

The limited trade union representation in the Costa Rican DAG, and Central American DAGs in general, has severe consequences on the substantive work done as little or no input is given by Central American trade unionists in the domestic meetings. During the transnational meetings Central American (and European) trade unionists have made some denunciations about labour rights violations such as the limited freedom of association or violations in specific companies (e.g., Fyffes). Nevertheless, little is done in response to these statements as the documents summarising the discussions of these meetings, which are presented to the intergovernmental board, remain general, and do not include the input [EUCS11].

In 2017, the members of the different DAGs agreed to collaborate on four themes: CSR, Decent Work, Small and Medium Enterprises and Market Access. The objective was to write a commonly agreed two-pager on each topic and to submit it to the Board at the occasion of the next transnational meeting. Two rapporteurs were appointed for each paper, an EU and Central American DAG member. Although there were exchanges of views from both sides, in the end no Central American trade unions contributed to the content of the documents [EUCS9]. Ultimately, the documents were not presented during the next meeting with the Board as two Central American business organisations opposed the content of the documents on Decent Work and CSR shortly before the meeting, even though they had been agreed upon in principle by the Central American rapporteurs and all EU DAG members [EUCS6].

Turning to the CSR seminars, we learned that the organisers (i.e., the European Commission, relevant EU delegations and respectively Costa Rica and Guatemala) had determined not to focus on labour rights violations as such. Instead, broader and more positive issues were put forward to address labour rights (e.g., social protection) [I3]. In Guatemala, during the workshop given by the ILO, participants were divided into small roundtable groups. Each table had governmental, business and trade union representatives who discussed several case studies [I3]. This resulted in dynamic dialogues between the participants and was evaluated as a positive experience [EU3,I3,EUCS5].

In sum, we find that local trade unions did not participate consistently or directly and were sometimes even excluded from meetings in all MSIs (Table A2 in Appendix B). We note that procedural participation of unions was intermediate in ETI-Fyffes, low in CSMs, and can even be considered very low in the Platform since unions dropped out. Regarding substantial participation, unions were somewhat able to provide information and raise concerns, whereas they were still constrained in the extent to which they could influence decision-making and their concerns were taken into account. In the case of ETI, intermediate substantial participation was observed as they gave more input compared to the low substantial participation in the CSMs. Again, this contrasts with the very low substantial participation found in the Platform where unions were not at all able to provide input and consequently were also not considered in the final decision-making of the action plan. In what follows, we explain what factors led to these low degrees of procedural and substantial participation, based on an assessment of the MSI design and implementation (structural factors) and trade union capacity (agency factors).

6.2. MSI Design and Implementation

6.2.1. Representativeness

To evaluate the representativeness in the three MSIs, their selection procedures were analysed with attention for the exclusion or categorisation of certain stakeholders groups.

First, in the ETI case, ETI members IUF and Bananalink, respectively a global trade union and an NGO, played the role of bridge builder and gatekeeper as only member organisations can raise concerns or file a complaint within this MSI. However, during the implementation of ETI's recommendations, the participation of the local trade unions was left to the local management of the plantation. The local union leader complained about the vague communication on the organisation of the meetings because they received the invitation to join the meeting with ETI only two days in advance [CRU2]. This resulted in exclusion and thus low representativeness. Second, in the context of the Platform, unclear selection criteria, active resistance against trade union participation by the business side and a preference for high-level participants resulted in very low representativeness of the unions. Third, the EU–Central America trade agreement specifies that members of the DAG should be independent representative organisations, and that economic, social and environmental stakeholders should be represented in a balanced way. However, the selection of the participants is left to the discretion of the governments, with no clarity on the criteria used. In Costa Rica, the invitation procedure has been faulty as some trade union representatives included in the members' list were not aware of their new role. Commercial interests had already been involved during the negotiation of the trade agreement and businesses had closer ties with the Ministry of External Trade. They were, therefore, better aware of the creation of the DAG. In addition, Costa Rica decided to subdivide its DAG in three separate groups, one for each stakeholder category (business, trade union and environment). This categorisation could potentially isolate less well coordinated actors, such as trade unions, and impede collaboration between the different interests. Trade unions were implicitly excluded from the first CSR seminar as the organisers had framed CSR as a business topic. During the preparation of the second seminar, trade unions were actively invited by the local EU delegations and a Guatemalan CSR association.

6.2.2. Procedural Fairness

This criterion is assessed through the examination of the way decision-making procedures allow for equal opportunities between participants to express their voice and be heard as well as funding and capacity building supporting the participation of weaker actors.

In the ETI case, rules of procedures regarding governance mechanisms and disciplinary measures are formalised for members and the implementation is strongly monitored by ETI members representing local trade unions. However, ETI does not cover the translation of relevant documents on the progress of the case in the language of the affected workers. In order to give the local trade unions the opportunity to be correctly informed, Bananalink dealt with this costly task [EUCS7]. Trade unions are exempted from paying ETI membership fees, but other financial support measures for local trade unions are limited. ETI did fund an ad hoc session to be given by consultants in Costa Rica to trade unions which was then obstructed by the local management. Since ETI does not actively promote local trade union participation along with a considerable margin of manoeuvre for local management to disregard ETI's efforts, the procedural fairness within ETI is low.

Even though the Platform was established to design a common action plan through the involvement of numerous stakeholders, no moderator or agreed decision-making procedure was foreseen. In the end, the content of the action plan was reached by consensus. However, by that time, trade unions were no longer involved in the Platform entailing the consensus was agreed upon by likeminded business actors. The absence of an entire stakeholder category was possible because the participation of the business side was considered more essential for the existence of the Platform [CRG4]. Funding of the Platform was used for the organisation of workshops, but the topics did not cover labour rights nor were transport costs reimbursed for union representatives coming from the pineapple-producing regions. It can therefore be concluded that no procedural fairness was pursued vis-a-vis trade unions and that the procedures were in favour of the pineapple producers.

Turning to procedural fairness in the CSMs, it should be noted that the Central American DAGs have not agreed upon rules of procedures. This entails that there are no clear rules on how decisions are supposed to be taken. Even though in practice decisions have been taken by consensus (see *infra*), business is in the majority to overrule the voice of other interests. During the transnational meetings all participants can express their concerns by raising their hand and they will be given the floor by the moderator. Since the outset, funding has been a critical point for the CSMs. Whereas the European Economic and Social Committee has taken up the role of secretariat in the EU and the European Commission makes travel funds available for at least one participant per stakeholder category, there is no funding whatsoever foreseen in Central America. This has been criticised heavily by EU and Central American civil society, because travel distances are rather important (within the Central American region or to Brussels) and not-for-profit actors have limited financial resources. To address these shortcomings, the EU has created a three-year project of three million euros to support civil society participation in the implementation of EU trade agreements [86]. At the time of writing the implementation of the project has not yet started. Regarding the CSR seminars, more EU funding was available for regional participation in the second event, which had a positive impact on local trade union participation [EU3,I3].

6.2.3. Consensual Orientation

To determine this final criterion, the pursuit of mutual agreement is considered as well as the communication attitude and trust among the different stakeholders.

Following the allegations against Fyffes, ETI facilitated a meeting between the unions and the local management. It was, however, not possible to reach a mutual agreement. In general, the communication attitude of Fyffes was perceived as rather hostile. Due to Fyffes unresponsiveness to the grievance in its Costa Rican pineapple plantation, Bananalink launched a public campaign against practices in Honduras. This was not appreciated by Fyffes, who claimed this was against the code of conduct of ETI members. Fyffes stated that they do not respond to public pressure and they "dug their heels in" concerning the recognition of trade unions [EUCS7]. Although building trust relationships is a central element of ETI's approach, trust has been broken both by Bananalink and Fyffes through their communication. In sum, even though consensual orientation is an important objective of ETI, it was impeded by the communication attitude and damaged trust on both sides.

In the Platform, the ILO mediated between trade unions and producers to find mutual agreement between them. This attempt was unsuccessful and trade unions left the Platform. In addition to irreconcilable positions, the negative and aggressive communication attitude, considered 'emotional' language, of trade unions was also part of the issue as they wanted to make denunciations and discuss labour rights violations. This stood in the way of dialogue and the evolution of the Platform as producers claimed this was not the right place for it. Moreover, there was an overall distrust in the neutrality of the Platform and a deep mutual distrust between the trade unions and producers. To conclude, even though there had been a mediation attempt by the ILO, consensual orientation could not be fulfilled due to miscommunication and a lack of trust.

Finally, there is a consensus-based approach in the CSMs. It is, however, uncertain if this approach of mutual agreement can be sustained as experience has shown that business interests do not shy away from vetoing the inclusion of labour proposals in statements from the transnational CSMs [EUCS10] as well as in joint working documents [EUCS6]. An internal reflection is being conducted, mainly by the EU side, to assess how collaboration should be continued [EUCS5]. Regarding the communication attitude, trade unions have made denunciations at several occasions concerning labour rights violations in specific companies such as Fyffes [EUCS11]. These efforts received little support, as other participants claimed that denunciations should not be done during the meetings as the DAGs are not supposed to deal with specific cases. Since the inception of the DAGs, members have been trying to build trust within and among the DAGs. The recent unexpected last minute veto by Central American business representatives against the submission of joint working documents to the Board was a serious blow to this trust. In addition, local trade unions—who have protested against the trade agreement during the negotiations—remain on their guard for co-optation as the CSMs and their participation could legitimise the agreement. In sum, the consensual orientation in the CSMs appeared to be rather vulnerable as mutual agreement is under pressure, there is a mismatch of communication attitudes, and trust has been damaged. Turning to the CSR seminars, both organisers and participants agreed that the format of the workshops invited the participants to collaborate constructively instead of the more traditional conflictive communication [EU3,EUCS5].

In sum, the three criteria explaining trade union participation through the MSI design and implantation score low to very low in each MSI (Table A3 in Appendix B). To have a more comprehensive picture on the enabling and constraining factors of this participation, we should also take more internal aspects of trade unions into account. In the following section the influence of their power resources on their participation will be examined.

6.3. Union Power Resources

6.3.1. Internal Solidarity

In general, plantation unions suffer from weak levels of member engagement, because not all members are willing to sacrifice time during weekends or after work for meetings [CRU4]. For example, in the case of ETI, the local union leader is most engaged in following up on complaints as other members do not play a prominent role due to their limited experience with and knowledge of legal procedures. Mobile phones are the main means of communication between members and local leaders, and not all members are literate. There is not a dense network of union representatives in the workplace and members are isolated in different teams spread across the plantation fields. At sectoral level, a major challenge is to foster a collective identity among plantation workers. Although workers' problems are of the same nature, the majority of plantation workers are Nicaraguan migrants which impedes their potential participation and membership to unions. They work to earn an income for their household, do not want to risk losing their job by forming or joining a union to fight their cause and may only be on the plantation on a temporary basis. Unions experience difficulties to mobilise new members to join the union and often lack a clear strategy on how to do so. The negative perception that unions destroy the economy and cause trouble discourages pineapple workers to join unions out of fear for reprisals [I2].

6.3.2. Network Embeddedness

The fragmentation of trade unions in the Costa Rican private sector can be traced back to two events affecting the country's political economy. First, the Communist Party and their labour confederation, who had succeeded in organising the banana workers, were outlawed shortly after the civil war ended in 1948 [55]. The loss of legal recognition of the Communist trade union left banana workers, who had had one of the strongest and most militant unions of Costa Rica, divided. This represented a first severe blow to trade unionism in the agricultural industry as the corporations did their utmost best to maintain the situation and prevented the emergence of another powerful union among its workers. Second, during the 1980s, an economic crisis and steep rise of foreign debt resulted in forced neoliberal policies promoting export sectors. This period had detrimental consequences for Costa Rican trade unions and the current anti-union culture stems from this context of deregulation and austerity measures in which private employers created evasive structures and adopted a strong anti-union attitude [87].

In the case of ETI, SINTRAPEM has strong ties with IUF and Bananalink who supported them in preparing the complaint and campaign against Fyffes. They are also connected to the Coordinating Body of Latin American Banana and Agro-industrial Unions (COLSIBA) to share experiences and strengthen their ability to fight violations internationally. In the context of the Platform, local unions did not leverage their ties with international unions. Moreover, the network of pineapple unions is spread over different plantations and decentralised without well-established ties to other unions, for example the stronger public sector unions. Unions act more independently, targeting specific companies with specific issues or demands in isolation. Costa Rican (and Central American) trade union participation during the CSMs is stimulated by EU trade unionists who have, on the one hand, together with EU NGOs, continuously been raising awareness about the CSMs in Central America in order to increase trade union participation [EUCS9]. On the other hand, they have repeatedly complained to the European Commission about the lack of Central American trade unions participating in the CSMs, hoping for EU pressure on the Central American governments to stimulate trade union participation. However, it should be noted that when Central American trade unions participate in the CSMs, they are most likely high-level representatives. In Costa Rica, they are representing national federations and consequently disconnected from the realities in the plantations.

The findings show that it has been difficult to build coalitions between local unions, however, trade unions were able to connect to international actors (in the case of ETI and CSMs) and to benefit from capacity-building activities.

6.3.3. Narrative Resources

Given the heritage of labour struggles in the country (see *supra*), unions follow a defensive narrative in the way they act and think. For example, they used the Platform as a forum to denounce anti-union practices by referring to anecdotes of discrimination and persecution, because there was no direct line of communication between workers and management in the plantations. Unions represent only a very small share of workers due to the anti-union campaign and management support for solidarist associations. They have to compete with the discourse of *solidarismo* which tries to win members through offering tangible benefits (e.g., credit opportunities or rain jackets) and are more convincing in the eyes of workers. Yet, solidarist associations do not recognise the right to collective bargaining since they are not allowed to negotiate collective agreements by law.

The ideological trade union background also informed their actions in MSIs. For example, in the CSMs, a union decided not to participate in the MSI because it would have interpreted its participation as approving the agreement and feared being co-opted [CRU5]. Some unions did not perceive MSIs as valuable channels to achieve their objectives. Unions also questioned the credibility of private voluntary standards and feared that it is 'big business', used as marketing strategy for companies and not to genuinely improve labour rights [CRU2]. This stock of negative experiences with certification audits translated into a general mistrust and disinterest towards mediation efforts and dialogue opportunities foreseen in MSIs.

6.3.4. Infrastructural Resources

Human resources for the daily functioning of unions are limited since offices are often run by one person and a secretary. The union leader needs to divide his time between representing workers in court, visiting the Ministry of Labour for mediation in the capital city, attending workers in the field and organising training sessions and meetings with the members [CRU2].

In general, being part of an MSI requires time and preparation, while in many cases unions are not able to send a representative because they have other priorities connected to their grassroots trade union activities. They may also not be familiar with the professional language (often English) used in those MSIs and lack the negotiation or communication skills needed to foster consensus. It is also more interesting for unions to directly negotiate with management than to participate in dialogue platforms with no immediate, concrete results.

Turning to the material resources, the costs of transport to the place where the MSIs are organised, often the capital city or abroad, are too high for unions. While some unions benefit from donor funding, other unions have limited operating resources coming from membership fees. Unions in the field have also limited organisational resources (such as computers, meeting rooms or cars) to communicate and interact with members and other actors.

The analysis of power resources of trade unions (Table A4 in Appendix B) in addition to MSI design and implementation allows for a more complete view of the determinants of trade union participation.

7. Discussion

Our findings endorse the concern that MSIs are not as inclusive as they aspire or pretend to be. Physical attendance does not necessarily imply participants will be heard. This confirms the relevance of distinguishing between procedural and substantial dimensions of participation when assessing how a (weaker) stakeholder is involved. In what follows, our findings are discussed and used to articulate practical recommendations, relevant for MSI organisers, participants and decision makers alike.

The three criteria assessed for the design and implementation of the MSIs, show how the participatory processes remain far from the deliberative ideal of collective communication and inclusiveness. The three initiatives experience several challenges constraining representativeness, procedural fairness and consensual orientation which explain in part the overall limited participation of trade unions. To achieve a better quality of participation and deliberation, power inequalities among its participants should be addressed by improving MSI design. Recommendations on the design and implementation of MSIs are deduced from our findings and clustered around each criteria.

First, the selection criteria for participation to the MSI should be clearly predefined and ensure the representativeness of the participants. Stakeholders should be identified together with a mapping of potential conflicts, expectations and their power resources [13]. These should then be taken into account by a neutral facilitator, for example an impartial secretariat, who can support the participation of a contested stakeholder category.

Second, regarding procedural fairness, clear goals and rules of decision-making should be set from the start and agreed by all stakeholders, stronger and weaker stakeholders alike [88]. This is a first exercise in redressing power inequalities and confirmed in other research on MSIs [7,13]. It should also be possible to reassess these rules at a later stage. Participants should feel that their input is considered and the use of vetoes that are not open for discussion, especially by powerful actors, should be refrained from. Practically, as also stated in Brown [14], resources should be made available for translation services and transport ensuring the participation of less resourceful stakeholders. Finally, as became clear in the ETI case as well as the CSMs, international actors play an important role as bridge builders pushing for local trade union participation and making their voice heard. This leverage effect has been confirmed in other studies [31].

Third, concerning the consensual orientation in MSIs, we see that building trust between actors with divergent positions is challenging. Therefore, the format of MSIs should recognise existing power differences and facilitate a rapprochement between business and unions, for example through small working groups and capacity-building events as suggested by Reed [15]. Yet, reaching a consensual orientation requires a constructive communication attitude and especially willingness from all parties to listen to different positions. An impartial moderator can help to preserve positive group dynamics, control dominant voices and ensure that less powerful actors can give input. If agenda items suggested by weaker participants are deliberately ignored, the credibility of the MSI is threatened and these participants can vote with their feet and withdraw [14]. Finally, the organisation of mediation and capacity-building events should be left to, or at least involve, a neutral actor to overcome entrenched positions between conflicting parties such as local management and unions.

In general, MSIs should be interpreted as a learning process and benefit from continuous internal evaluation and reflection on obstacles that impede the engagement of weaker actors. This need for iterative learning is also stressed in adaptive management approaches to long-term participatory processes as suggested by Stringer et al. [89]. In addition, our analysis showed how the local context often hampers deliberation and the rebalancing of interests. This was particularly the case in the Platform, where hardly any efforts were made to ensure that weaker actors could give their input and were listened to. Since every MSI is influenced by the (local) context in which it operates, it requires a customised and localised strategy that incorporates feedback from participations and is sensitive to signals showing the need for redesigning participatory procedures or capacity building adapted to weaker stakeholders. Finally, even though implementing changes is time and resource consuming, MSIs can benefit from a more bottom-up involvement of workers and unions, contrary to high-level representation, as has been demonstrated in recent developments in worker-driven social responsibility [88].

The analysis also indicates that the design of an MSI is not all-decisive as insights on trade union power resources also helped to explain their participation. We found that strong network embeddedness and improved infrastructural resources enhanced trade union participation, whereas the lack of internal solidarity and unfavourable narrative resources had a negative effect on their participation.

When looking for ways to boost union's power resources, the most feasible improvements can be found in network embeddedness and infrastructural resources. Strengthening ties with international organisations are an important enabling factor for trade union participation to MSIs. They can demand involvement in MSIs, facilitate meetings, and support local unions' infrastructural resources. Yet, dependency on international alliances can also become a pitfall if the need for better internal union solidarity is neglected and the union relies exclusively on external support.

Even though internal solidarity and narrative resources should not be ignored, changing a highly fragmented trade union landscape, the negative reputation of trade unions and local norms cannot happen overnight [27]. Therefore, it is essential that local unions join forces and build alliances or coalitions at sectoral level to deal with societal and managerial counter pressures and more actively engage in the dialogue spaces created by MSIs.

When linking the design and implementation of MSIs to the power resources of trade unions, two relevant interactions, implying practical takeaways, are observed. First, procedural fairness can be increased through network embeddedness and infrastructural resources. For instance, in the ETI case the international partners of the local trade unions strived for their involvement by assisting them in their communication and translating relevant documents. In the CSMs, EU trade unions have been very insistent upon encouraging the participation of their Central American counterpart. In addition, funding is being made available to ensure the participation of less affluent participants. Strong network embeddedness is missing in the Platform, which is also the initiative with the weakest trade union participation. Second, consensual orientation is very difficult to attain in a context of negative narrative resources where historical conflicts, conflictual communication and distrust between the stakeholders impede progress of the MSI. This was obvious in the Platform as well as the CSMs. In general, MSI design could not compensate for deficits concerning internal solidarity and narrative resources as they are deeply entrenched in the domestic context.

8. Conclusions

This article shed light on the participation of trade unions in MSIs by analysing three initiatives in the EU–Costa Rican pineapple supply chain. In line with previous studies on inclusiveness of

Sustainability **2018**, *10*, 4295

weaker actors in MSIs, the three initiatives confirm that trade unions can be procedurally allowed to participate but often fail to contribute substantially. While there was no substantial participation of unions in the case of the Platform, unions could express their position in the ETI-case. The Central American trade unions' substantial participation to the CSMs has been very limited, however, their procedural participation is on the rise in less formalised meetings.

Our main contribution lies in explaining trade union's participation by combining two dimensions: MSIs design and trade union power resources. First, the analysis of the MSIs design and implementation demonstrates that selection procedures can lead to the exclusion of local trade unions (representativeness), decision making rules to enhance equality and funding to enable participation of unions are rare (procedural fairness), and conflictual communication and distrust can also obstruct substantial participation (consensual orientation). Second, the analysis of union power resources highlights, on the one hand, how strong network embeddedness and better infrastructural resources are complementary to the design of MSIs for trade union participation. On the other hand, the lack of internal solidarity and adverse narrative resources of Costa Rican (pineapple) trade unions have a negative effect on their participation. MSI design could not compensate for these deficits as they are embedded in the local context and difficult to change.

This implies for practitioners involved in MSIs that improving the design of MSIs is necessary (see *infra* for recommendations) but not sufficient to enhance trade union participation. It stands or falls with the ability of unions to mobilize their resources and the willingness and commitment of all participants in the MSI to meaningfully engage in deliberation. Our paper calls for a continuous evaluation of MSI participatory processes (regarding representativeness, procedural fairness and consensual orientation) and strengthening of union power resources (internal solidarity, network embeddedness, narrative and infrastructural resources).

This paper has concentrated on the participatory processes in MSIs, however, additional research on the outcomes of such MSIs, especially concerning the promotion of labour rights, should be conducted. These outcomes should be scrutinised to know whether the MSI has ultimately strengthened weaker actors. Another interesting avenue for further research is the role of public actors in MSIs. Even though MSIs are often considered to be solely private mechanisms, governments are often involved as a creator or sponsor. Additional research on the (potential) influence of public actors, both in importing and exporting countries, would be useful in the assessment of power struggles at play in MSIs. In this light, a cross-country comparison with MSIs operating in labour repressive states embedded in different political economies can give a fuller account of how the institutional and political context influences opportunities for trade union participation in MSIs and how unions and MSIs deal with these context-specific challenges.

Author Contributions: D.M. and A.G. have contributed equally and therefore receive equal credit as first co-authors. Conceptualization, D.M., A.G. and J.O.; Formal analysis, D.M. and A.G.; Funding acquisition, J.O. and M.D.; Investigation, D.M., A.G., J.O. and M.D.; Methodology, D.M. and A.G.; Project administration, J.O. and M.D.; Supervision, J.O. and M.D.; Writing—original draft, D.M. and A.G.; Writing—review and editing, J.O. and M.D.

Funding: This research was financed by the Ghent University Special Research Fund for Interdisciplinary Research Projects.

Acknowledgments: This article greatly benefited from feedback of Diana Potjomkina and participants of the EADI General Conference 2017; in particular we wish to thank Gabriel-Siles Brügge and David Cichon for their constructive comments. We are grateful to all respondents who made time for answering our questions and to our local research assistants who helped collecting data. We would also like to thank the Centro de Estudios para el Desarrollo Rural (CDR) in San José, Costa Rica, for their logistical support. Finally, thank you to the three anonymous reviewers for their valuable comments.

Conflicts of Interest: The authors declare no conflict of interest.

Appendix A

Table A1. List of interviews, focus groups and observations.

Category	In-Text Reference	Date	Place	Category	In-Text Reference	Date	Place
Costa Rican unions (6)	CRU1	June 2015	San José	EU officials (3)	EU1	May 2015	San José
	CRU2	November 2016	San José		EU2	May 2015	San José
	CRU3	June 2015	San José		EU3	August 2018	Skype
	CRU4	June 2015	San José	EU civil society (12)	EUCS1	September 2016	Brussels
	CRU5	August 2018	Skype		EUCS2	November 2016	Brussels
	CRU6	June 2015	San José		EUCS3	March 2017	Brussels
Focus groups unions (3)	FG1	May 2015	Sarapiquí		EUCS4	October 2017	Brussels
	FG2	March 2016	Santa Rita		EUCS5	June 2018	Brussels
	FG3	June 2015	Limón		EUCS6	September 2018	Brussels
Costa Rican government (8)	CRG1	June 2015	San José		EUCS7	September 2018	Skype
	CRG2	May 2015	San José		EUCS8	September 2018	Skype
	CRG3	January 2016	San José		EUCS9	September 2018	Brussels
	CRG4	May 2016	San José		EUCS10	July 2015	Brussels
	CRG5	June 2015	San José		EUCS11	June 2017	Skype
	CRG6	June 2016	San José		EUCS12	February 2016	Brussels
	CRG7	June 2016	San José	Observations CSMs (8)	Transnational	June 2016	Tegucigalpa
	CRG8	June 2016	San Carlos		Transnational	June 2018	Brussels
Costa Rican business (5)	CRB1	February 2016	San Rafael		DAG to DAG	June 2016	Tegucigalpa
	CRB2	May 2015	San José		DAG to DAG	June 2017	Videoconference
	CRB3	May 2015	San José		EU DAG	March 2016	Brussels
	CRB4	January 2016	San Carlos		EU DAG	June 2017	Brussels
	CRB5	January 2016	San José		EU DAG	November 2017	Brussels
International Labour Organisation (ILO) officials (3)	I1	May 2015	San José		EU DAG	October 2018	Brussels
	I2	May 2016	San José				
	I3	June 2018	Geneva				

Appendix B

Table A2. Participation of trade unions in MSIs.

	ETI	Platform	CSMs
Procedural	Intermediate participation	Very low participation	Low participation
	- Representation through international ties with ETI member NGO and union - Participation of local trade union in capacity building session cancelled by management	- Unions represented only 1% of participants initially - Eventually withdrawal of trade unions	- 2 out of 7 trade union Domestic Advisory Group (DAG) members participate actively - All trade union federation secretaries listed, but not aware of membership - No trade union participation in first corporate social responsibility (CSR) seminar, more trade unions involved in second CSR seminar
Substantial	Intermediate substantial input	Very low substantial input	Low substantial input
	- Hosting visit to collect information and provide evidence - Express concerns to ETI - Failed meeting with management during capacity-building event	- Failed attempt to put freedom of association on the agenda - Labour rights removed from final action plan	- No consideration given to denunciations about labour rights violations - No input provided for joint working document on Decent Work and CSR - Discussion of decent work issues during roundtables at second CSR seminar

Table A3. Criteria for design and implementation of MSIs.

	ETI	Platform	CSMs
Representativeness	Low representativeness	Very low representativeness	Low representativeness
	- International union and NGO act as bridge builders - Vague communication and late meeting invitation by management	- Unclear selection criteria - Active resistance against trade union participation by the producers' side - Preference for high-level participants	- Legal text refers to inclusion of economic, social and environmental stakeholders in a balanced way - Selection left to government, no clear criteria - Faulty invitation procedure - Unclear invitation for unions in 1st CSR seminar, proactive call for union participation in 2nd CSR seminar
Procedural fairness	Low procedural fairness	Very low procedural fairness	Low procedural fairness
	- Only ETI members can file complaint - Dependence on international ties with ETI members for funding and monitoring - Translation not covered by ETI - ETI funding for capacity building session - Unions exempted from fees	- No moderator - No agreed decision making procedure - Voting about final action plan based on consensus with only business actors in the room - No funding for workshop on labour rights - Travel expenses difficult to overcome	- No clear rules of procedure - Consensus based decision making but business in majority - No funding in Central America - New funding project for civil society participation - Funding to cover travel expenses of unions to CSR seminar
Consensual orientation	Low consensual orientation	Very low consensual orientation	Low consensual orientation
	- Trust-building at the core of ETI - Hostile communication attitude by Fyffes - Broken trust by call for action and advocacy campaign	- Mediation by ILO failed - Producers veto the inclusion of labour proposals	- Consensus based approach at the outset - Veto business side to publish joint working document - Denunciations not appreciated - Unions cautious for co-optation - Promotion of constructive collaboration in CSR seminar

Table A4. Criteria for union power resources.

	ETI		Platform		CSMs
Network embeddedness	-	Strong international network (Coordinating Body of Latin American Banana and Agro-industrial Unions (COLSIBA), Bananalink, IUF)	-	Limited ties among unions in the pineapple sector and their federations No international network involved	-	EU trade unions support Central American trade unions Only high level representatives, no direct linkages with pineapple plantation unions
Internal solidarity	-	In general, difficulties mobilizing workers to join union, lack of a collective identity among workers				
	-	No dense network of trade union representatives, weak levels of member engagement, limited knowledge of rights				
Narrative resources	-	In general, historical heritage of struggle and frustration lie at the basis of the defensive narrative of trade unions				
	-	Competition with solidarist associations and employer repression feed into the conflictual stance of trade unions				
	-	Unions question the credibility of MSIs because of negative experiences and are cautious for co-optation				
Infrastructural resources	-	Human resources are limited, lack of communication and negotiation skills required in MSIs				
	-	Union leaders have different priorities and need to divide time between core union activities and preparations for MSIs				
	-	Unions depend on membership fees or donors for funding of transport, computers and organisational infrastructure				

References and Note

1. Cheyns, E.; Riisgaard, L. Introduction to the symposium: The exercise of power through multi-stakeholder initiatives for sustainable agriculture and its inclusion and exclusion outcomes. *Agric. Hum. Values* **2014**, *31*, 439–453. [CrossRef]

2. Take, I. Legitimacy in Global Governance: International, Transnational and Private Institutions Compared. *Swiss Polit. Sci. Rev.* **2012**, *18*, 220–248. [CrossRef]

3. O'Rourke, D. Multi-stakeholder Regulation: Privatizing or Socializing Global Labor Standards? *World Dev.* **2006**, *34*, 899–918. [CrossRef]

4. Fransen, L. Multi-stakeholder governance and voluntary programme interactions: Legitimation politics in the institutional design of Corporate Social Responsibility. *Socio-Econ. Rev.* **2011**, *10*, 163–192. [CrossRef]

5. Fransen, L.; Kolk, A. Global Rule-Setting for Business: A Critical Analysis of Multi-Stakeholder Standards. *Organization* **2007**, *14*, 667–684. [CrossRef]

6. Marin-Burgos, V.; Clancy, J.S.; Lovett, J.C. Contesting legitimacy of voluntary sustainability certifcation schemes: Valuation languages and power asymmetries in the Roundtable on Sustainable Palm Oil in Colombia. *Ecol. Econ.* **2015**, *117*, 303–313. [CrossRef]

7. Mena, S.; Palazzo, G. Input and Output Legitimacy of Multi-Stakeholder Initiatives. *Bus. Ethics Q.* **2012**, *22*, 527–556. [CrossRef]

8. Boström, M.; Tamm Hallström, K. Global multi-stakeholder standard setters: How fragile are they? *J. Glob. Ethics* **2013**, *9*, 91–110. [CrossRef]

9. Schouten, G.; Leroy, P.; Glasbergen, P. On the deliberative capacity of private multi-stakeholder governance: The Roundtables on Responsible Soy and Sustainable Palm Oil. *Ecol. Econ.* **2012**, *83*, 42–50. [CrossRef]

10. Brem-Wilson, J. Towards food sovereignty: Interrogating peasant voice in the United Nations Committee on World Food Security. *J. Peasant Stud.* **2015**, *42*, 73–95. [CrossRef]

11. Brouwer, H.; Hiemstra, W.; van Vugt, S.; Walters, H. Analysing stakeholder power dynamics in multi-stakeholder processes: Insights of practice from Africa and Asia. *Knowl. Manag. Dev. J.* **2013**, *9*, 11–31.

12. Utting, P. Regulating business via multi-stakeholder initiatives: A preliminary assessment. In *Voluntary Approaches to Corporate Responsibility: Readings and a Resource Guide*; UN Non-Governmental Liaison Service, UNRISD, Eds.; NGLS: Geneva, Switzerland, 2002; pp. 61–126.

13. Hiemstra, W. *Power Dynamics in Multistakeholder Processes: A Balancing Act*; Wageningen University and Research: Wageningen, The Netherlands, 2012.

14. Brown, P. Principles that Make for Effective Governance of Multistakeholder Initiatives: Updated, Final Version. Available online: https://www.business-humanrights.org/sites/default/files/media/bhr/files/Principles-for-effective-MSIs-6-7-Nov-2007.pdf (accessed on 20 November 2018).

15. Reed, M.S. Stakeholder participation for environmental management: A literature review. *Boil. Conserv.* **2008**, *141*, 2417–2431. [CrossRef]

16. Langille, B. *What is International Labour Law for*; International Institute for Labour Studies: Geneva, Switzerland, 2005.

17. Gereffi, G.; Mayer, F. Globalization and the demand for governance. In *New Offshoring Jobs and Global Development*; Gereffi, G., Ed.; International Institute for Labour Studies: Geneva, Switzerland, 2005.

18. Toffel, M.; Short, J.; Ouellet, M. Codes in context: How states, markets, and civil society shape adherence to global labor standards. *Regul. Gov.* **2015**, *9*, 205–223. [CrossRef]

19. Bloom, D.J. Civil Society in Hybrid Governance: Non-Governmental Organization (NGO) Legitimacy in Mediating Wal-Mart's Local Produce Supply Chains in Honduras. *Sustainability* **2014**, *6*, 7388–7411. [CrossRef]

20. Fuchs, D.; Kalfagianni, A.; Havinga, T. Actors in private food governance: The legitimacy of retail standards and multistakeholder initiatives with civil society participation. *Agric. Hum. Values* **2011**, *28*, 353–367. [CrossRef]

21. Larsen, R.K.; Osbeck, M.; Dawkins, E.; Tuhkanen, H.; Nguyen, H.; Nugroho, A.; Gardnera, T.A.; Zulfahm; Wolvekampe, P. Hybrid governance in agricultural commodity chains: Insights from implementation of 'No Deforestation, No Peat, No Exploitation' (NDPE) policies in the oil palm industry. *J. Clean. Prod.* **2018**, *183*, 544–554. [CrossRef]

22. Torfing, J.; Peters, G.B.; Pierre, J.; Sørensen, E. *Interactive Governance: Advancing the Paradigm*; Oxford University Press: New York, NY, USA, 2012.

23. Dentoni, D.; Bitzer, V.; Schouten, G. Harnessing Wicked Problems in Multi-stakeholder Partnerships. *J. Bus. Ethics* **2018**, *150*, 333–356. [CrossRef]

24. HLPE. *Multi-Stakeholder Partnerships to Finance and Improve Food Security and Nutrition in the Framework of the 2030 Agenda*; High Level Panel of Experts on Food Security and Nutrition of the Committee on World Food Security: Rome, Italy, 2018.

25. van Huijstee, M. *Multistakeholder Initiatives. A Strategic Guide for Civil Society Organizations*; SOMO: Amsterdam, The Netherlands, 2012.

26. ITUC. *2018 ITUC Global Rights Index: The World's Worst Countries for Workers*; International Trade Union Confederation: Brussels, Belgium, 2018.

27. Lévesque, C.; Murray, G. Understanding union power: Resources and capabilities for renewing union capacity. *Transfer* **2010**, *16*, 333–350. [CrossRef]

28. Alford, M.; Barrientos, S.; Visser, M. Multi-scalar Labour Agency in Global Production Networks: Contestation and Crisis in the South African Fruit Sector. *Dev. Chang.* **2017**, *48*, 721–745. [CrossRef]

29. Selwyn, B. Labour flexibility in export horticulture: A case study of northeast Brazilian grape production. *J. Peasant Stud.* **2009**, *36*, 761–782. [CrossRef]

30. Barrientos, S.; Kritzinger, A. Squaring the Circle—Global Production and the Infor-malisation of Work in South African Fruit Exports. *J. Int. Dev.* **2004**, *16*, 81–92. [CrossRef]

31. Bartley, T.; Egels-Zanden, N. Beyond decoupling: Unions and the leveraging of corporate social responsibility in Indonesia. *Socio-Econ. Rev.* **2016**, *14*, 231–255. [CrossRef]

32. Koch-Baumgarten, S.; Kryst, M. Trade unions and collective bargaining power in global governance. In *Global Governance of Labour Rights. Assessing the Effectiveness of Transnational Public and Private Policy Initiatives*; Marx, A., Wouters, J., Rayp, G., Beke, L., Eds.; Edward Elgar Publishing: Cheltenham, UK, 2015; pp. 150–169.

33. Anner, M. Two Logics of Labor Organizing in the Global Apparel Industry. *Int. Stud. Q.* **2009**, *53*, 545–570. [CrossRef]

34. Hahn, R.; Weidtmann, C. Transnational Governance, Deliberative Democracy, and the Legitimacy of ISO 26000: Analyzing the Case of a Global Multistakeholder Process. *Bus. Soc.* **2016**, *55*, 90–129. [CrossRef]

35. Zanella, M.A.; Goetz, A.; Rist, S.; Schmidt, O.; Weigelt, J. Deliberation in Multi-Stakeholder Participation: A Heuristic Framework Applied to the Committee on World Food Security. *Sustainability* **2018**, *10*, 428. [CrossRef]

36. Dryzek, J.S. *Foundations and Frontiers of Deliberative Governance*; Oxford University Press: Oxford, UK, 2010.

37. Hendriks, C.M. Deliberative governance in the context of power. *Policy Soc.* **2009**, *28*, 173–184. [CrossRef]

38. Habermas, J. Hannah Arendt's communications concept of power. *Soc. Res.* **1977**, *44*, 3–24.

39. Scharpf, F. *Governing in Europe*; Oxford University Press: Oxford, UK, 1999.

40. Dryzek, J.S. Democratization as deliberative capacity building. *Comp. Polit. Stud.* **2009**, *42*, 1379–1402. [CrossRef]

41. Luttrell, C. *Multi-Stakeholder Processes: Lessons for the Process of Timber Verification*; Overseas Development Institute: London, UK, 2008.

42. Dingwerth, K. *The New Transnationalism: Transnational Governance and Democratic Legitimacy*; Palgrave Macmillan: New York, NY, USA, 2007.

43. Delputte, S.; Williams, Y. Equal partnership between unequal regions? Assessing deliberative parliamentary debate in ACP-EU relations. *Third World Themat. TWQ J.* **2016**, *1*, 490–507. [CrossRef]

44. Schaller, S. *The Democratic Legitimacy of Private Governance: An Analysis of the Ethical Trading Initiative (INEF Report 91/2007)*; Institute for Development and Peace, University of Duisburg-Essen: Duisburg, Germany, 2007.

45. Boström, M. Regulatory Credibility and Authority through Inclusiveness: Standardization Organizations in Cases of Eco-labeling. *Organization* **2006**, *13*, 345–367. [CrossRef]

46. Cheyns, E. Making "minority voices" heard in transnational roundtables: The role of local NGOs in reintroducing justice and attachments. *Agric. Hum. Values* **2014**, *31*, 439–453. [CrossRef]

47. Risse, T. Transnational governance and legitimacy. In *Governance and Democracy: Comparing National, European and International Experiences*; Benz, A., Papadopoulos, Y., Eds.; Routledge: London, UK, 2006; pp. 179–199.

48. Friedrich, D. Democratic Aspiration Meets Political Reality: Participation of Organized Civil Society in Selected European Policy Processes. In *Civil Society Participation in European and Global Governance: A Cure for the Democratic Deficit*; Steffek, J., Kissling, C., Nanz, P., Eds.; Palgrave Macmillan: Basingstoke, UK, 2008.

49. Steffek, J.; Nanz, P. Emergent Patterns of Civil Society Participation in Global and European Governance. In *Civil Society Participation in European and Global Governance: A Cure for the Democratic Deficit*; Steffek, J., Kissling, C., Nanz, P., Eds.; Palgrave Macmillan: London, UK, 2008.

50. Habermas, J. *The New Conservatism*; MIT Press: Cambridge, UK, 1990.

51. Habermas, J. *Between Facts and Norms*; MIT Press: Cambridge, UK, 1996.

52. Bennet, E.A. Voluntary Sustainability Standards: A Squandered Opportunity to Improve Workers' Wages. *Sustain. Dev.* **2018**, *26*, 65–82. [CrossRef]

53. United Nations Conference on Trade and Development (UNCTAD). *Pineapple—An INFOCOMM Commodity Profile*; UNCTAD: Geneva, Switzerland, 2016.

54. Cámara Nacional de Productores y Exportadores de Piña (CANAPEP). *Nuestra Revista Piña de Costa Rica Edición 29*; CANAPEP: San José, Costa Rica, 2018.

55. Robert, J.A. *A History of Organized Labor in Panama and Central America*; Praeger Publishers: Westport, CT, USA, 2008.

56. Mosley, L. Worker's Rights in Open Economies: Global Production and Domestic Institutions in the Developing World. *Comp. Polit. Stud.* **2008**, *41*, 674–714. [CrossRef]

57. Riisgaard, L. International framework agreements: A new model for securing workers rights? *Ind. Relat.* **2005**, *44*, 707–736. [CrossRef]

58. International Trade Union Confederation (ITUC). *Internationally-Recognised Core Labour Standards in Costa Rica: Report for the WTO General Council Review of the Trade Policies of Costa Rica*; ITUC: Geneva, Switzerland, 2007.

59. International Labour Organisation (ILO). *CEARC, NORMLEX Right to Organise and Collective Bargaining Convention, 1949 (No. 98)—Costa Rica (Ratification: 1960) Individual Case (CAS)-Discussion: 2010*; Publication 99th ILC Session 2010; ILO: Geneva, Switzerland, 2010.

60. OECD. *OECD Reviews of Labour Market and Social Policies: Costa Rica*; OECD Publishing: Paris, France, 2017.

61. International Confederation of Free Trade Unions (ICFTU). *Costa Rica: Annual Survey of Violations of Trade Union Rights*; ICFTU: Brussels, Belgium, 2006.

62. Knudsen, J.S.; Moon, J. *Visible Hands: Government regulation and International Business Responsibility*; Cambridge University Press: Cambridge, UK, 2017.

63. ETI. ETI Disciplinary Procedure. Available online: https://www.ethicaltrade.org/resources/eti-disciplinary-procedure (accessed on 28 August 2018).

64. Make Fruit Fair Serious Abuses of Labour Rights in Costa Rica and Honduras. Available online: http://makefruitfair.org/serious-abuses-of-labour-rights-in-costa-rica-and-honduras/ (accessed on 8 August 2017).

65. Watts, J. Fyffes Melons at Centre of Labour Abuse Claims from Honduran Workers. Available online: https://www.theguardian.com/global-development/2016/nov/29/fyffes-melons-labour-abuse-claims-honduras-workers (accessed on 8 August 2017).

66. Fyffes Annual Report. 2015. Available online: http://ww7.global3digital.com/fyffesplc/uploads/finreports/FyffesAR2015.pdf (accessed on 8 August 2017).

67. Kollewe, J. Fyffes Banana Sale Unpeels Fortune for Irish Business Dynasty. Available online: https://www.theguardian.com/business/2016/dec/09/fyffes-banana-sale-unpeels-fortune-for-irish-business-dynasty (accessed on 9 August 2017).

68. Moyo, J. Update on Fyffes Suspension from ETI. Available online: http://www.ethicaltrade.org/blog/update-fyffes-suspension-eti (accessed on 5 September 2018).

69. INSP. Background: National Platform for Actions to Improve the Environmental and Social Performance of the Production in Costa Rica. Available online: http://www.pnp.cr/en/background-national-platform-actions-improve-environmental-and-social-performance-production-costa (accessed on 3 June 2018).

70. CABEI. Sistematización de Experiencias y Divulgación del Proceso de Diálogo Realizado en el Marco del Proyecto de la Plataforma Nacional de Producción y Comercio Responsable de Piña en Costa Rica: Documento de Sistematización. Available online: https://info.undp.org/docs/pdc/Documents/CRI/Sistematizaci%C3%B3n%20de%20experiencias%20(1).pdf (accessed on 3 June 2018).

71. Martens, D.; Van den Putte, L.; Oehri, M.; Orbie, J. Mapping Variation of Civil Society Involvement in EU Trade Agreements: A CSI Index. *Eur. Foreign Aff. Rev.* **2018**, *23*, 41–62.

72. Orbie, J.; Martens, D.; Van den Putte, L. *Civil Society Meetings in European Union Trade Agreements: Features, Purposes, and Evaluation*; Centre for the Law of EU External Relations: The Hague, The Netherlands, 2016.

73. COMEX; European Commission. *Agenda Cadenas de valor y el Desarrollo Sostenible: Oportunidades y Desafíos*; COMEX: San José, Costa Rica, 2017.

74. European Union; SICA. *Agenda Trabajo Decente, Responsabilidad Empresarial y el Acuerdo de Asociación UE-CA: Contribuyendo a un Crecimiento Económico Sostenible*; European Union: Guatemala City, Guatemala, 2018.

75. Young, J.C.; Rose, D.C.; Mumby, H.S.; Benitez-Capistros, F.; Derrick, C.J.; Finch, T.; Garcia, C.; Home, C.; Marwaha, E.; Morgans, C.; et al. A methodological guide to using and reporting on interviews in conservation science research. *Methods Ecol. Evol.* **2018**, *9*, 10–19. [CrossRef]

76. Schreier, M. *Qualitative Content Analysis in Practice*; Sage: London, UK, 2012.

77. Eisenhardt, K.M. Building Theories from Case Study Research. *Acad. Manag. Rev.* **1989**, *14*, 532–550. [CrossRef]

78. Liu, F.; Maitlis, S. Nonparticipant Observation. In *Encyclopedia of Case Study Research*; Mills, A.J., Durepos, G., Wiebe, E., Eds.; Sage: London, UK, 2010.

79. Trinczek, R. *How to Interview Managers? Methodical and Methodological Aspects of Expert Interviews as a Qualitative Method in Empirical Social Research*; Palgrave Macmillan: London, UK, 2009.

80. Lievens, P. Positive Developments in Response to ANEXCO Urgent Action Appeal. Available online: http://makefruitfair.org/positive-developments-in-response-to-anexco-urgent-action-appeal/ (accessed on 8 August 2017).

81. Euroban. Make Fruit Fair Letter to David McCann (Fyffes chairman): Fyffes Must Respect Labour Rights. Available online: http://makefruitfair.org/wp-content/uploads/2017/01/Letter-to-David-McCann-Fyffes-re-Labour-rights.pdf (accessed on 8 August 2017).

82. INSP National Monitoring Committee. Available online: http://www.pnp.cr/en/national-monitoring-committee (accessed on 3 June 2018).

83. PNUD. Plataforma Piña Costa Rica: Plenaria de Lanzamiento 25 Junio 2011. Available online: https://www.youtube.com/watch?v=K0wx3LdCyjA (accessed on 20 November 2018).

84. PNUD. Plataforma Piña Costa Rica: Taller de Revisión del Plan Acción con el Sector Productivo, Desarrollada en Febrero del 2014 en Muelle de San Carlos, Zona Norte de Costa Rica. Available online: https://www.youtube.com/watch?v=UTXfb_6mMn0 (accessed on 20 November 2018).

85. Título VIII Comercio y Desarrollo Sostenible Implementación del AdA UE-Centroamérica, Listado Grupos Asesores de Centroamérica. 2016.

86. European Commission. *Annex 13 of the Commission Implementing Decision on the 2017 Annual Action Programme for the Partnership Instrument: Action Fiche for Support to Civil Society Participation in the Implementation of EU Trade Agreements*; European Commission: Brussels, Belgium, 2017.

87. Frundt, H.J. Central American Unionism in the era of globalization. *Lat. Am. Res. Rev.* **2002**, *37*, 7–53.

88. O'Brien, C.M.; Dhanarajan, S. The corporate responsibility to respect human rights: A status review. *Account. Audit. Account. J.* **2016**, *29*, 542–567.

89. Stringer, L.C.; Dougill, A.J.; Fraser, E.; Hubacek, K.; Prell, C.; Reed, M.S. Unpacking "Participation" in the Adaptive Management of Social–Ecological Systems: A Critical Review. Available online: https://www.ecologyandsociety.org/vol11/iss2/art39/ (accessed on 20 November 2018).

Article

Investigating the Sustainability Performance of PPP-Type Infrastructure Projects: A Case of China

Shengqin Zheng, Ke Xu *, Qing He *, Shaoze Fang and Lin Zhang

School of Management Engineering, Shandong Jianzhu University, Jinan 250101, China;
zhshqin@sdjzu.edu.cn (S.Z.); fangshaoze@126.com (S.F.); zhanglin2007@sdjzu.edu.cn (L.Z.)
* Correspondence: xukeooop@163.com (K.X.); heqingzdsl@163.com (Q.H.); Tel.: +86-186-6895-8630 (K.X.)

Received: 9 October 2018; Accepted: 8 November 2018; Published: 12 November 2018

Abstract: In China, the demand for public infrastructure projects is high due to the acceleration of urbanization and the rapid growth of the economy in recent years. Infrastructures are mainly large scale, so local governments have difficulty in independently completing financing work. In this context, public sectors often seek cooperation from private sectors, in which public–private partnership (PPP) is increasingly common. Although numerous studies have concentrated on sustainable development, the unsustainability performances of infrastructures are often reported on various media. Furthermore, studies on the sustainability performances of PPP-type infrastructure (PTI) projects are few from the perspective of private sectors' behaviors. In this study, we adopted the modified theory of planned behavior and the structure equation model and conducted a questionnaire survey with 258 respondents for analyzing the sustainable behaviors of private sectors. Results indicated that behavioral attitude, perceived behavioral control, and subjective norm interact significantly. They have direct positive effects on behavioral intention and then indirectly influence actual behavior through this intention. Actual sustainable behaviors of private sectors have significantly positive effects on the sustainable development of cities. We offer theoretical and managerial implications for public and private sectors on the basis of the findings to ensure and promote the sustainability performances of PTI projects.

Keywords: infrastructure; PPP; sustainable development; sustainable behaviors

1. Introduction

Public–private partnership (PPP), as an innovative procurement mode, has been playing a vital role in developing public infrastructures in China [1,2], for instance, social (e.g., prisons, social housing, and hospitals) and economic (e.g., highways, bridges, and high-speed rails) infrastructures [3–5]. The demand for public infrastructure is continuously increasing due to the acceleration of urbanization and the rapid growth of the economy [3,6]. In 2014, the State Council of China published the "Guidance for Strengthening the Management of Local Government Debts", which restricted local governments' financing platforms and funding [7]. Faced with the shortage of funds [8], governments were compelled to seek cooperation from private sectors, who can provide a large amount of funds, to participate in public infrastructure construction [9,10]. Under this economic circumstance, PPP has experienced a rapid expansion and a boom period for the last five years in China [5,11]. As of 30 September 2017, the number of Chinese PPP projects recorded has reached 14,220. The gross investment in these projects has amounted to 17.8 trillion yuan [12].

However, a series of social issues appear when an increasing number of PPPs are applied in infrastructure development because private sectors are attracted to profits [6]. For instance, private sectors may lower the quality of infrastructures and public services for reducing construction costs, ignore environmental protection and corporate social responsibility (CSR), and pay further attention to projects with high financial returns [13]. As a result of disputes on the expense of pollution emission with the local government, Huijin, a wastewater treatment company, discharged more than one million tons of wastewater to the Songhua River, causing severe effects in social and environmental aspects [14]. Some private and even public sectors do not integrate the three aspects of economics, environment, and society into their implementation process [15,16]. Hence, the concept of sustainability must be considered to understand the serious implication of PPP projects [17].

Sustainable development is a serious challenge worldwide and for our future generations [18]. The importance of infrastructures, procured by governments or PPPs, can be witnessed by all sectors of the society and international policies on "green" and "social" public projects [19]. The principles of sustainable development are often divided into the triple bottom line, namely, environmental, economic, and social frameworks, for the activities of regions, corporations, and individuals [20–22]. Scholars, such as Ugwu and Kumaraswamy, have established a sustainability appraisal system in infrastructure projects and investigated the improvements, barriers, and determinations for sustainable development [23]. However, their concerns were focused largely on macrolevel policy planning but minimally on microlevel construction behaviors [24]. Numerous scholars have studied relationship governance [25], risk management [26,27], and performance appraisal [28] with regard to private sectors. However, the research on private sectors' sustainable behaviors is limited, which motivated us to investigate whether and how behaviors influence the sustainability performance of infrastructures provided via PPP modality [17,29] as one of the objectives of this study. Another objective is to propose corresponding strategies for improving the sustainability performance from the perspectives of governments and private sectors. To achieve the research goals, we use the modified theory of planned behavior (TPB), a questionnaire survey, and the structural equation modeling (SEM) method. We perform an empirical research on the influencing factors to investigate the sustainability influenced by private sectors' behaviors [30]. This paper can provide suggestions for local governments and relevant private sectors on how to improve the sustainability performance and facilitate the sustainable development of PPP-type infrastructure (PTI) projects [9]. Furthermore, this study can expand the research scope of the sustainability performance of PTI projects and provide the basis for future research on PPP and even sustainable development.

The paper is organized as follows. Section 2 lays out the literature review of sustainability and corresponding factors in PTI projects. Section 3 presents the theoretical model and research hypotheses. Section 4 elaborates the research methodology and questionnaire design. Data analysis, model test, and result discussion are given in Section 5. The final section concludes the research and provides some implications.

2. Literature Review

2.1. Understanding Sustainability in PTI Projects

As defined in the Brundtland Report "Our Common Future" in 1987 [31], the concept of "sustainable development" has been extensively supported and addressed by people from all walks of life and governments worldwide [32]. Evaluation not only on the macroscopic level (e.g., national strategy) but also on the microscopic level (e.g., project sustainability appraisal or feasibility study) [8,13,33] in the perspective of sustainable development is crucial. On one hand, infrastructure projects have non-negligible effects on the economy, environment, and society, as three bottom lines in sustainability [34,35], due to a massive investment and a large consumption of resources [18]. These projects can promote economic growth and dramatically provide conducive effects on social welfare [36]. On the other hand, Shen et al. highlighted that infrastructure projects can also balance social disparity and improve regional competitiveness in developed and developing countries [9]. Numerous scholars argued that the benefits of infrastructure projects for society are remarkable [37,38], but their long-range sustainability performance is sometimes neglected [39].

The shortage of government fiscal funds and the constraint of managerial experience have resulted in the rapid development of PPP mode for establishing and operating infrastructure projects [9,39]. PPPs emerged when public sectors cooperated with private sectors to construct large-scale projects on the basis of mutual trust, which is different from hierarchical relationships [40]. The increasing number of PPP projects has attracted the attention of scholars in related fields [41]. The infrastructure applications of PPP mode has been investigated in several approaches, including relation governance [25], concessionaire determinants [42], contract governance [43], risk allocation [26,27], critical factors [44,45], and sustainability performance [23,24,46]. In this context, numerous scholars are concerned with the unsustainability of PTI projects, so they explore appropriate research angles and methods to ensure and improve sustainability performances [9].

Through a questionnaire survey with stakeholders in a PPP, scholars from India discovered that the sustainability of PTI projects nearly depends on the contribution of private sectors to sustainable development, such as efficient project implementation, resource utilisation efficiency, and so on [47]. Similarly, Hueskes et al. summarized that if the procuring government prefers projects with further sustainability performance, then they should encourage private corporations involved in the contract to perform further sustainable behaviors. They also argued that PPPs are sometimes regarded as vehicles for achieving sustainability goals [19]. According to Xiong, innovation (either in terms of technology or business model), as the most important power in facilitating sustainable development, is easily implemented by private sectors [14]. In addition, some studies emphasized the importance of CSR to sustainable construction [48,49]. CSR stresses ethical behavior with regard to the economy, society, and environment, which is similar to the three pillars of sustainability [46]. If corporations place sustainability as a company objective, then they will propose CSR policies to conduct necessary procedures [13]. However, despite its capability to bring benefits across all sustainability aspects, CSR has been rarely considered [46]. Although private sectors are closely linked to project sustainability, investigations from this perspective are limited. As a result, this study aims to bridge the research gap.

2.2. Factors Related to Sustainable Behaviors in PTI Projects

Numerous studies analyze the sustainability performances of projects [50,51]. Zhang et al. introduced a new model for evaluating the sustainability of infrastructure projects and then compared it between urban and rural areas by focusing on efficiency and equity perspectives [52]. Belgian scholars compared the difference between strong sustainability and weak sustainability through an analysis of 27 PTI projects to find an effective method for improving sustainability performance. Moreover, their research showed that social dimensions of sustainability are often neglected due to the shortage of measurable social indicators [19]. Greek scholars investigated the social and environmental sustainability of infrastructure projects in rural areas on the basis of a local PPP scheme. They found that the sustainability performance of infrastructure projects procured under a PPP is often better than that procured in the traditional way. This result indicated that under a PPP contract, if the government implements moderate specifications and regulations on private sectors, then enhanced sustainability performance with improved cost-effectiveness, innovative technology, and "green" incentives will be demonstrated [53]. Shen et al. collected 87 large-scale project feasibility reports to measure sustainability performance. They constructed an evaluation system, including 18 economic indicators, 8 environmental indicators, and 9 social indicators, which can be used as guidance for assessing whether the constructing behaviors of private sectors are sustainable [13]. The vast majority of firms in China have paid minimal attention to the deep exploration of sustainability performance or sustainable behaviors. Australian scholars investigated three leading construction firms and identified 29 aspects of sustainable behaviors, including green innovation, corporate governance, and water conservation [54]. Similarly, when assessing the sustainability of a wastewater treatment system, Annelies et al. separately listed the economic, environmental, and social indicators. They found that operation costs, land area, and heavy metals are crucial for sustainability performance [55]. Meanwhile, the stimulation of sustainable behavior, as a social indicator, also plays a non-negligible role in promoting sustainability [55]. More than 500 sustainability indicators have been listed by the Compendium of Sustainable Development Indicator Initiatives, including global (67), national (103), provincial (72), and local (289) indicators. These indicators are used to evaluate whether the goals of various policies, infrastructure projects, and construction contracts are in accordance with the goals of sustainable development [56]. Nilesh et al. also established a sustainability criteria system of infrastructure development focused on the Indian PPP market, which is the second largest market in the world, so that private sectors could consider these criteria in implementing further sustainable management measures [47].

Scholars have also analyzed factors that lower the sustainability performance of infrastructure projects [39]. Ezeah indicated that unbalanced relationship among local, state, and private sectors, low funding efficiency, weak legal framework, and polices without clear strategies for realization are the main limitations of sustainability performance [57]. By studying the sustainability of infrastructure projects from a project management perspective, numerous scholars have identified various constraints, for instance, poorly trained administrators and workers, complicated managerial rules [58], lack of awareness in sustainable development [59], and weak executive operation [17]. Chang et al. stated that the awareness of construction companies in China on sustainable development remains insufficient, and whether companies are performing sustainably is often ignored [54]. Through a questionnaire survey completed by on-site personnel, Zhou et al. identified the gaps between awareness and actual behaviors in the adoption of sustainable construction, and sustainable practices need to be popularized to a great extent, which reflects the necessity of our research [60].

On the basis of the discussions of existing literature, this study aimed to analyze private sectors' behaviors, which closely connect with sustainability performance.

3. Theoretical Model and Research Hypotheses

3.1. Modified TPB

The TPB proposed by Icek Ajzen in the 1980s states that people's behaviors are the results after deep considerations [61]. By selecting the expectancy–value theory as the starting point, the TPB explains individual behavior preference and decision-making course after processing the acquired information [62]. The TPB indicates that behavioral attitude, subjective norm, and perceived behavioral control conjointly determine individual behavioral intention [63]. These three decisive factors are based on a latent belief structure, under which behavioral beliefs have beneficial or adverse effects on behaviors. Similarly, normative belief results in social pressure and subjective norm, and control belief may control actual behaviors at execution [61].

Specifically, two variables, namely, perceived usefulness and usability, which are introduced in the technology acceptance model (TAM), must be considered in technical practice due to their potential complementation and theoretical compatibility for increasing the TPB's explanatory power [64]. For private sectors, perceived usefulness mainly refers to enhancing the corporation's reputation and promoting industrial changes accompanied by private sectors' sustainable behaviors. Perceived usability is an important factor before considering sustainable behaviors. On the basis of TAM, when individuals apply a new process or product, they often compare it with the existing process or product. Hence, private sectors may compare the usefulness and usability perceptions of sustainable behaviors with traditional behavior, considering the advantages and disadvantages of the two approaches [65].

By retaining original variables, this study added perceived usefulness and usability as causal latent variables to maintain the good explanatory capability of the model. Lin et al. claimed that infrastructure sustainability considerably influences urban sustainable development [66]. Therefore, the sustainable development of a city is used as an ultimate latent variable in this study for measuring the influence of private sectors' sustainable behaviors on the city. Figure 1 shows the modified TPB conceptual model. The dashed line represents the original hypothesis of the theoretical model, and the solid line indicates the model hypothesis of this study.

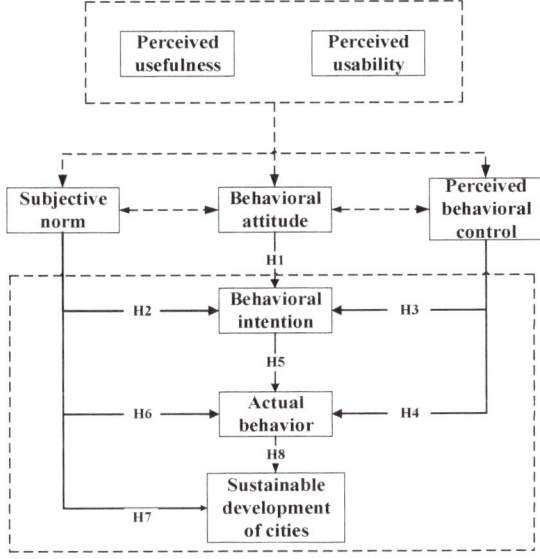

Figure 1. Conceptual model.

3.2. Research Hypotheses

3.2.1. Relationships among Behavioral Attitude, Subjective Norm, and Behavioral Intention

Behavioral attitude, as the important anterior variable of behavioral intention, can be defined as the overall evaluation on specific behavior [67]. This study regarded perceived usefulness and usability as extended elements in the TPB model which are used to assess the efficiency and convenience of sustainable behaviors, respectively. Behavioral intention is noted as the precondition and immediate determinant of actual behavior. Scholars have suggested that behavioral attitude positively affects behavioral intention. For instance, through a questionnaire survey completed by 3029 respondents on consumers' willingness to select electric vehicles, Hidrue et al. found that the more positive the behavioral attitude consumers have, the stronger the behavioral intention they will have [67].

Subjective norm refers to the perceived pressure from the society or groups who expect a subject to perform in a certain way [68]. In the context of this study, pressure includes the governments' strategies, evaluations from all sectors of society, and influences from other companies' behaviors. Kan et al. stated that a positive subjective norm will considerably promote behavioral intention [69]. In comparison with traditional ways, the subjective norm of sustainable behaviors is strong. For instance, if other companies decide to perform green behaviors, then following this decision is wise, considering corporate image and reputation, despite the high cost in the initial application stage.

Two hypotheses are proposed on the basis of previous considerations:

Hypothesis 1 (H1). *Behavioral attitude has significant positive effects on behavioral intention.*

Hypothesis 2 (H2). *Subjective norm has significant positive effects on behavioral intention.*

3.2.2. Relationships among Perceived Behavioral Control, Behavioral Intention, and Actual Behavior

Perceived behavioral control, which reflects individuals' previous experience and expected impediment, is defined as the degree of ease or difficulty perceived by individuals who want to perform specific behaviors [68]. In this context, perceived behavioral control includes perceptions of cost, time limit, quality, and safety.

When individuals think that they have additional resources or opportunities and less expected impediment, their perceived behavioral control will be fierce. Consistent with Axsen and Kurani's research conclusion, the more the ability individuals have to use resources and solve perceived problems, the more likely the intention and even the actual behaviors will be generated. As new behaviors may require new workers, relation governance is regarded as an observational variable of perceived behavioral control.

In the TPB model, behavioral intention is the immediate determinant of actual behavior. In accordance with the theory of organizational behavior, perceived behavioral control and behavioral intention conjointly determine the individual behavior of private sectors. Through a survey of Canadian office workers for reducing commuter car use, Abrahamse et al. found that perceived behavioral control moderated the relation and behavioral intention acted as the mediation between intention and actual behavior [70].

Three hypotheses are proposed on the basis of the previous considerations:

Hypothesis 3 (H3). *Perceived behavioral control has significant positive effects on behavioral intention.*

Hypothesis 4 (H4). *Perceived behavioral control has significant positive effects on actual behavior.*

Hypothesis 5 (H5). *Behavioral intention has significant positive effects on actual behavior.*

3.2.3. Relationships among the Subjective Norm, Actual Behavior, and Sustainable Development of a City

Intragenerational and intergenerational equities, the two key principles of sustainable development, emphasize that development should meet the needs of the present generation without compromising the capability of future generations to meet their own needs [47]. If the sense of sustainable development is deeply rooted in people from all walks of life, including construction of infrastructure projects, then sustainable development goals will be further implemented. Therefore, this study measured sustainability brought by the influence of sustainable behaviors, for instance, reducing air and water pollution, relieving noise pollution, reducing resource and energy consumption, and effecting other low-carbon behaviors.

Additional studies indicate that external pressure must be considered when promoting a new technology or behavior. In our work, subjective norm refers to the external environment and also the social influence to some extent. Greek scholars investigated 29 cases to examine how social innovation evolves and found that although actual behaviors drive social innovation, subjective norm brought by Greek government departments and the society is the main cause [71]. Subjective norm, often seen as a social pressure, will play a non-negligible role in promoting sustainable behavior and then will considerably affect the sustainable development of a city due to the minimal motivation to change and the profit-making mindset of private sectors [72].

Three hypotheses are proposed on the basis of the previous considerations:

Hypothesis 6 (H6). *Subjective norm has significant positive effects on actual behaviors.*

Hypothesis 7 (H7). *Subjective norm has significant positive effects on the sustainable development of a city.*

Hypothesis 8 (H8). *Actual behavior has significant positive effects on the sustainable development of a city.*

4. Research Methodology

4.1. Structure Equation Model

As SEM is widely used in numerous research areas, including social science, economics, marketing, management, and behavioral science, it has been proven to be efficient for analyzing and testing the causal relationship between observed and latent variables since the 1980s [73,74]. This method plays an excellent role in identifying key indicators and factors [39]. For example, Jiao et al. adopted SEM to identify the critical factors for sustainable urbanization in a case study of China [30]. Shen et al. applied SEM to analyze the most important factor that influences the passenger satisfaction with urban railway transit in Suzhou, China [75]. To compensate for the deficiency of traditional statistical approaches that cannot analyze latent variables, SEM has been one of the most important methods in the field of multivariate data analysis [76]. Therefore, we used SEM to understand the complex relationships between unobservable variables and the identified influencing factors. The AMOS 21.0 software was adopted for applying SEM during the research process.

4.2. Questionnaire

A questionnaire survey was conducted to collect respondents' first-hand information. Our survey consists of seven latent variables, namely, perceived usefulness, perceived usability, subjective norm, perceived behavioral control, behavioral intention, actual behavior, and sustainable development of a city. The five-point Likert scale was used to measure respondents' viewpoints, in which 1 represents negligible and 5 represents very important. This scale has been proven to be an efficient method for rating the importance among the factors by collecting respondents' opinions [77]. Considering that the survey items should be easy to understand, we requested 10 experts from the field of public management to test the readability of the questionnaire. We modified a few survey items and adjusted some descriptions on the basis of the advice provided by experts. Table 1 shows the final questionnaire of this study and Table 2 lists the characterization of the survey sample.

The number of distributed questionnaires was 280. The criteria for selecting the sample respondents were as follows: (1) they have hands-on experience in companies that participate in ongoing or recently completed PPP projects; (2) they come from multiple departments, such as design and site construction; and (3) they are willing to participate in the survey. By eliminating 22 questionnaires that were not completed or perfunctory, we obtained a total of 258 valid questionnaires. The rate of valid questionnaires was 92.1%, which meets the statistical requirements of SEM.

Table 1. Survey items of private sectors' behaviors and corresponding indices.

Variables and Survey Items	Factor Loading	Cronbach's Alpha	AVE	Literature
Perceived usefulness (PU1):				
1. It is suitable for me to take sustainable behaviors.	0.860			
2. Sustainable behaviors can increase construction efficiency.	0.852	0.791	0.655	[78,79]
3. Sustainable behaviors have positive effects on corporate image.	0.810			
Perceived usability (PU2):				
1. Companies can learn how to take sustainable behaviors quickly.	0.736			
2. Taking sustainable behaviors are easier than traditional ways.	0.766	0.810	0.591	[80]
3. The processes of sustainable behaviors are convenient to operate	0.671			
Subjective norm (SN):				
1. Other companies in the same field are taking sustainable behaviors.	0.830			
2. Sustainable behaviors get great social evaluation.	0.817	0.847	0.667	[63,81]
3. Sustainable behaviors are supported by governments strongly.	0.653			
Perceived behavioral control (PBC):				
1. I will consider cost increase accompanied by sustainable behaviors.	0.778			
2. I will consider possible construction delay accompanied by them.	0.833	0.905	0.672	[82,83]
3. I need govern new relations if I employ better trained workers and managers.	0.784			
4. I will take construction quality and safety into consideration.	0.723			
Behavioral intention (BI):				
1. I will take traditional behaviors unchangeably.	0.655			
2. I will take sustainable behaviors step by step.	0.681	0.750	0.504	[63,84]
3. I will take sustainable behaviors more frequently in later time.	0.665			
Actual behavior (AB):				
1. I just start taking sustainable behaviors in some aspects.	0.743			
2. I take sustainable behaviors in all aspects skillfully.	0.875	0.888	0.739	[84,85]
3. I advise other companies to take sustainable behaviors too.	0.835			
Sustainable development of cities (SD):				
1. Sustainable behaviors can reduce air, water, and noise pollution.	0.844			
2. Sustainable behaviors can reduce resource consumption in city.	0.880	0.891	0.632	[19,86]
3. Sustainable behaviors can reduce energy consumption in city.	0.797			
4. Private sector's behaviors can facilitate other low-carbon behaviors.	0.671			

Table 2. Characterization of survey sample.

Characterization	Type	Frequency	Percentage (%)
Gender	Male	182	70.54
	Female	76	29.46
Age	18–30 years old	54	20.93
	30–45 years old	141	54.65
	≥45 years old	63	24.42
Educational background	Senior high school or below	37	14.34
	Associate degree or bachelor's degree	169	65.50
	Master's degree or PhD	52	20.16
Monthly income	Less than 5000 yuan	34	13.18
	5000–10,000 yuan	146	56.59
	More than 10,000 yuan	78	30.23
Position	Administrative staff	64	24.81
	Basic staff	194	75.19
Related work years	≤5 years	32	12.40
	5–10 years	161	62.40
	≥10 years	65	25.20

5. Results and Discussions

5.1. Reliability and Validity Analysis

Reliability is regarded as the degree of consistency of the consequences of different test measurements. At present, scholars often use Cronbach's alpha coefficient (α) to test reliability. The closer the α is to 1, the more consistent the questionnaire items are with the corresponding variables, which indicates that questionnaire items are well designed. Generally, Cronbach's alpha coefficient is required to be more than 0.7. If α is more than 0.8, then the analysis is deemed to have a high degree of reliability [86]. SPSS20.0 was utilized to test the reliability of our study. The α of the questionnaire is 0.916 and the α of the seven latent variables ranges from 0.75 to 0.905. Therefore, the reliability of our questionnaire is great, regardless of holistic or part aspects.

Validity analysis contains convergent, discriminant, and content validities. Average variance extracted (AVE) values are used to test convergent and discriminant validity [87], and factor loadings after orthogonal rotation are utilized to test content validity. The AMOS20.0 software was adopted to calculate the AVE values. The AVE values of the seven latent variables are more than 0.5 (Table 1), so the convergent validity of our questionnaire is great. Table 3 shows that the square root of the AVE exceeds the correlation between the two different constructs for all construct pairs, which suggests that the discriminant validity is adequate. The factor loadings after the orthogonal rotation of indicators range from 0.653 to 0.880 (Table 1), so the content validity of our questionnaire is great.

Table 3. AVE and correlation matrix.

	AVE	1	2	3	4	5	6	7
1. PU1	0.655	0.81	–	–	–	–	–	–
2. PU2	0.591	0.39	0.77	–	–	–	–	–
3. SN	0.667	0.47	0.46	0.82	–	–	–	–
4. PBC	0.672	0.27	0.38	0.43	0.82	–	–	–
5. BI	0.504	0.18	0.29	0.37	0.46	0.71	–	–
6. AB	0.739	0.39	0.43	0.41	0.43	0.51	0.86	–
7. SD	0.632	0.56	0.41	0.18	0.27	0.44	0.57	0.79

5.2. Model Test

The AMOS20.0 was used to fit the model, and then we found that several main goodness-of-fit (GOF) measures did not meet the recommended levels which have been suggested in previous studies [88,89]. Thus, the initial SEM model needed to be refined and optimized. On the basis of various reports on SEM models, O'Rourke et al. stated that most models cannot meet all fit standards the first time due to deviations of collected data or deficiencies of the model itself [90]. We refined the model on the basis of the suggestions of GOF measures and the hypotheses proposed by TPB until the model presented a good fit and the GOF measures met the recommended levels. Table 4 shows the comparison of the GOF measures between initial and refined models. Figure 2 presents the action path of the private sectors' intention.

Table 4. Compatibility test before and after model modification.

GOF Measures	Recommended Levels	Before Refining	Evaluation	After Refining	Evaluation
χ^2/df	<3	2.258	Acceptable	1.964	Acceptable
RMR	<0.05	0.104	Unacceptable	0.048	Acceptable
RMSEA	<0.08	0.065	Acceptable	0.057	Acceptable
GFI	>0.9	0.879	Unacceptable	0.901	Acceptable
AGFI	>0.9	0.846	Unacceptable	0.912	Acceptable
RFI	>0.9	0.864	Unacceptable	0.927	Acceptable
TLI	>0.9	0.920	Acceptable	0.938	Acceptable
NFI	>0.9	0.884	Unacceptable	0.900	Acceptable
PGFI	>0.5	0.691	Acceptable	0.700	Acceptable
PNFI	>0.5	0.758	Acceptable	0.765	Acceptable

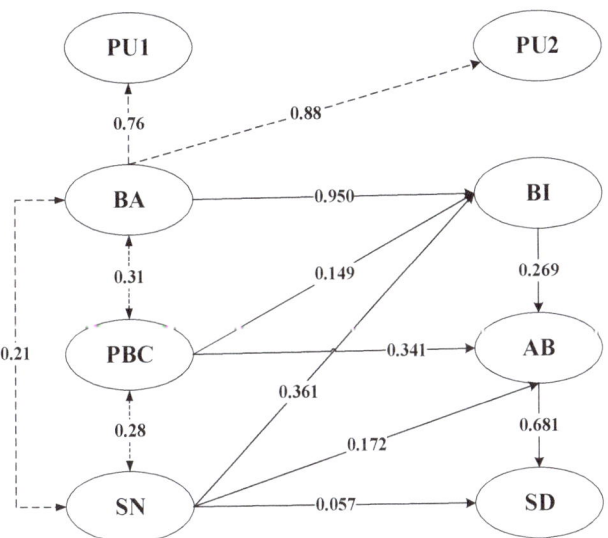

Figure 2. Action path.

At present, the academic circles often use composite reliability (CR) to test the degree of internal consistency of observable variables, in which CR meets the recommended level when its value is more than 0.7 [91]. The CR values can be obtained from the following equation:

$$\rho_c = \frac{(\sum \lambda)^2}{(\sum \lambda)^2 + \sum \theta}.$$

In this equation, ρ_c denotes the CR value; λ represents the standardized coefficient of observational variables, namely, factor loading; and θ indicates the error variance of variables. After calculation, the CR values range from 0.74 to 0.91, which exceed 0.7. Thus, the model has great internal quality.

5.3. Hypothesis Verification

Table 5 lists the path coefficients and consequences of hypothesis verification accompanied with refined SEM. We utilized a nonstandardized path coefficient for the analysis, which is meaningful in statistics. We need to verify the hypotheses on the basis of the empirical results.

Table 5. Path coefficients and test results.

Hypothesis Path	Path Coefficients	T	p	Test Results
BI←BA	0.950	5.129	***	Supported
BI←SN	0.361	3.561	***	Supported
BI←PBC	0.149	2.12	*	Supported
AB←PBC	0.341	5.58	***	Supported
AB←BI	0.269	3.476	***	Supported
AB←SN	0.172	2.926	**	Supported
SD←SN	0.057	0.800	0.424	Unsupported
SD←AB	0.681	6.423	***	Supported

Note: * denotes $p < 0.05$; ** indicates $p < 0.01$; *** represents $p < 0.001$.

On the basis of Table 5, behavioral attitude has significant positive effects on behavioral intention ($\beta = 0.95$, T value is 5.129, $p < 0.001$), so H1 is verified. Subjective norm has significant positive effects on behavioral intention ($\beta = 0.361$, T value is 3.561, $p < 0.001$), so H2 is verified. Perceived behavioral control has significant positive effects on behavioral intention ($\beta = 0.149$, T value is 2.12, $p = 0.034$), so H3 is verified. Perceived behavioral control has significant positive effects on actual behavior ($\beta = 0.341$, T value is 5.58, $p < 0.001$), so H4 is verified. Behavioral intention has significant positive effects on actual behavior ($\beta = 0.269$, T value is 3.476, $p < 0.001$), so H5 is verified. Subjective norm has significant positive effects on actual behaviors ($\beta = 0.172$, T value is 2.926, $p < 0.001$), so H6 is verified. Subjective norm does not have significant positive effects on the sustainable development of a city ($\beta = 0.057$, T value is 0.800, $p = 0.424$), so H7 is not verified. Actual behavior has significant positive effects on the sustainable development of a city ($\beta = 0.681$, T value is 6.423, $p < 0.001$), so H8 is verified. Except for H7, hypotheses are all verified.

5.4. Discussions

The SEM analysis indicates that perceived usefulness and usability conjunctively explain the variable–behavioral attitude, whose path coefficients are respectively 0.76 and 0.88, reflecting that they are the main influencing factors of actual behavior. Similar to the research conclusion of Fan et al., good perceptions of usefulness and usability are preconditions of strong behavioral attitude [65]. Behavioral attitude, perceived behavioral control, and subjective norm interact significantly. They have direct positive effects on behavioral intention and influence actual behaviors indirectly via behavioral intention.

Behavioral attitude→behavioral intention (0.95), with the most significant effect, reflects that behavioral attitude is the major factor influencing behavioral intention. Similar to the research conclusion of Gloukhovtsev, behavioral attitude considerably influences intention in ethical consumer behavior; moreover, perceived behavioral control, subjective norm, and moral intensity help bridge the attitude–intention and attitude–behavior gaps [92]. On the contrary, behavioral intention→actual behavior (0.269), with insignificant effect, indicates that despite a strong intention, actual behaviors are rarely found. Behavioral intention is restrained by subjective norm and perceived behavioral control under ideal conditions, so private sectors' behavioral intention is greater than the actual behavior at the present stage.

Moreover, perceived behavioral control and subjective norm have direct effects on actual behaviors, the values of which are 0.341 and 0.172, respectively. Perceived behavioral control influences actual behaviors in a more significant way than subjective norms. In our study, perceived behavioral control directly influences private sectors because they are attracted to profits. This situation remains until subjective norms are enforced by policies. When studying organic consumerism behaviors through TPB, Johe also emphasized the importance of perceived behavioral control on actual behaviors [93].

The path coefficient of the actual behavior→sustainable development of a city is 0.681, also with a considerable effect, suggesting the public knows the importance of promoting sustainable behaviors to facilitate the sustainable development of a city. However, the main contradiction is that intention is not transformed to actual behavior in a high degree. Therefore, an urgent problem to be solved is how to increase the transformation rate of intention→actual behavior steadily. Increasing the transformation rate by enforcing policies and regulations is simple but effective for governments. From a long-term perspective, the most appropriate approach is improving the CSR and awareness of sustainable development.

The path coefficient of the subjective norm→sustainable development of a city is only 0.057, but the subjective norm has significant effects on behavioral intention and actual behavior. This result indicates that the pressure of policies could facilitate the promotion of sustainable behaviors of private sectors, and to some extent, it will help generate other low-carbon behaviors in the city.

6. Conclusions and Implications

Research on the sustainable behaviors of private sectors is important for assisting the government in adopting strategies and policies to propel sustainable development, which also has a theoretical and practical significance in constructing PTI projects. An innovation in this research is to conduct an empirical analysis on the gaps between sustainable behavioral intention and actual behavior from the perspective of private sectors via modified TPB and questionnaire survey. To some extent, this work aims to compensate for the research deficiency in this field. This study shows the current situations and behavioral rules of private sectors' sustainable behaviors and presents strongly operational methods for governments and companies. These findings provide a useful reference for upper-level decision makers and governments to implement appropriate measures for improving infrastructure sustainability.

To facilitate the sustainable development of a city and enterprise transformation, we present management suggestions from the perspectives of the government and enterprises on the basis of the research findings and advice of the respondents:

(1) Perspective of the government: On one hand, introducing relevant laws and regulations is impending for governments to guide construction enterprises in performing as many as possible sustainable behaviors. Then, the transformation rate of intention→actual behavior is increased by the coerciveness of laws and regulations. On the other hand, under PPP mode, the government and private sectors establish a project company together. Although private sectors always operate the project company, public sectors can enforce necessary specifications and supervisions on private sectors to facilitate further sustainability performance. Governments can also provide reward incentives to corporations and present preferential policies to stimulate further sustainable behaviors; otherwise, corporations should be penalized. In addition, governments should emphasize the importance of sustainable behaviors to increase the subjective norm of private sectors.

(2) Perspective of the private sectors: Companies are required to undertake CSR, which refers to numerous aspects, such as pollution, safety, and environmental protection. Private sectors must bridge the gaps between intention and actual behavior on sustainable construction. For example, at the bidding stage, companies should implement relevant policies about the limits of investments for ensuring economic sustainability. At the construction stage, companies should adopt sustainable materials and concentrate further on saving energy and water and protecting the environment for ensuring environmental sustainability. At the operating stage, private sectors should maintain the infrastructure for improving social sustainability. These suggestions can increase the perceived behavioral control and behavioral intention of private sectors, and then further sustainable behaviors will be performed.

The primary limitation of this study is that the data are all collected in the Chinese context. Considering the differences in different social environments, whether the research conclusions are suitable for other countries or regions remains to be verified. Thus, some PPP cases in other countries or regions should be brought to follow-up studies.

Author Contributions: S.Z. and K.X. conceived the study, analyzed the data, and completed the paper. Q.H. and S.F. collected the data. L.Z. revised it critically for important content.

Funding: This research received no external funding.

Acknowledgments: The authors would like to thank the experts who reviewed the manuscript.

Conflicts of Interest: The authors declare no conflicts of interest.

References

1. Mukhopadhyay, C. A nested framework for transparency in Public Private Partnerships: Case studies in highway development projects in India. *Prog. Plan.* **2016**, *107*, 1–36. [CrossRef]
2. Patil, N.A.; Tharun, D.; Laishram, B. Infrastructure development through PPPs in India: Criteria for sustainability assessment. *J. Environ. Plan. Manag.* **2016**, *59*, 708–729. [CrossRef]
3. Ke, Y. Is public private partnership a panacea for infrastructure development? The case of Beijing National Stadium. *Int. J. Constr. Manag.* **2014**, *14*, 90–100. [CrossRef]
4. Grimsey, D.; Lewis, M.K. *Public Private Partnerships: The Worldwide Revolution in Infrastructure Provision and Projcet Finance*; E. Elgar: Cheltenham, UK, 2005.
5. Wang, H.M.; Xiong, W.; Wu, G.D.; Zhu, D.J. Public-private partnership in Public Administration discipline: A literature review. *Public Manag. Rev.* **2018**, *20*, 293–316. [CrossRef]
6. Koppenjan, J.F.M.; Enserink, B. Public-Private Partnerships in Urban Infrastructures: Reconciling Private Sector Participation and Sustainability. *Public Adm. Rev.* **2009**, *69*, 284–296. [CrossRef]
7. State Council of China. Guidance for Strengthening the Management of Local Government Debts. Available online: http://www.gov.cn/zhengce/content/2014-10/02/content_9111.htm (accessed on 2 October 2014). (In Chinese)
8. Anwar, B.; Xiao, Z.; Akter, S.; Rehman, R.U. Sustainable Urbanization and Development Goals Strategy through Public-Private Partnerships in a South-Asian Metropolis. *Sustainability* **2017**, *9*, 1940. [CrossRef]
9. Shen, L.; Tam, V.; Gan, L.; Ye, K.; Zhao, Z. Improving Sustainability Performance for Public-Private-Partnership (PPP) Projects. *Sustainability* **2016**, *8*, 289. [CrossRef]
10. Zhang, S.; Gao, Y.; Feng, Z.; Sun, W. PPP application in infrastructure development in China: Institutional analysis and implications. *Int. J. Proj. Manag.* **2015**, *33*, 497–509. [CrossRef]
11. Shi, J.G.; Si, H.Y.; Wu, G.D.; Su, Y.Y.; Lan, J. Critical Factors to Achieve Dockless Bike-Sharing Sustainability in China: A Stakeholder-Oriented Network Perspective. *Sustainability* **2018**, *10*, 2090. [CrossRef]
12. China Industrial Information. Transaction Amount of PPP Projects in China in 2017. Available online: http://www.chyxx.com/industry/201803/617299.html (accessed on 9 March 2018). (In Chinese)
13. Shen, L.Y.; Tam, V.W.Y.; Tam, L.; Ji, Y.B. Project feasibility study: The key to successful implementation of sustainable and socially responsible construction management practice. *J. Clean. Prod.* **2010**, *18*, 254–259. [CrossRef]
14. Xiong, W.; Zhu, D. The theory and practice of PPP mode oriented by sustainable development. *J. Tongji Univ.* **2017**, *28*, 78–84.
15. Marcelino-Sádaba, S.; González-Jaen, L.F.; Pérez-Ezcurdia, A. Using project management as a way to sustainability. From a comprehensive review to a framework definition. *J. Clean. Prod.* **2015**, *99*, 1–16. [CrossRef]
16. Schipper, R.P.J.; Silvius, A.J.G. Sustainability in project management: A literature review and impact analysis. *Syst. Bot.* **2014**, *4*, 63–96.
17. Shen, L.; Asce, M.; Wu, Y.; Zhang, X. Key Assessment Indicators for the Sustainability of Infrastructure Projects. *J. Constr. Eng. Manag.* **2011**, *137*, 441–451. [CrossRef]
18. Wu, G.; Duan, K.; Zuo, J.; Zhao, X.; Tang, D. Integrated sustainability assessment of public rental housing community based on a hybrid method of AHP-entropyweight and cloud model. *Sustainability* **2017**, *9*, 603.
19. Hueskes, M.; Verhoest, K.; Block, T. Governing public-private partnerships for sustainability: An analysis of procurement and governance practices of PPP infrastructure projects. *Int. J. Proj. Manag.* **2017**, *35*, 1184–1195. [CrossRef]

20. Edler, J.; Uyarra, E. *Public Procurement of Innovation*; Edward Elgar: Cheltenham, UK, 2012; pp. 224–237.
21. Elkington, J. Cannibals with forks: The triple bottom line of 21st century business. *Environ. Qual. Manag.* **2010**, *8*, 37–51. [CrossRef]
22. Institution, B.S. *Sustainability in Building Construction—General Principles*; British Standards Institution: London, UK, 2007.
23. Ugwu, O.O.; Kumaraswamy, M.M.; Wong, A.; Ng, S.T. Sustainability appraisal in infrastructure projects (SUSAIP): Part 2: A case study in bridge design. *Autom. Constr.* **2006**, *15*, 229–238. [CrossRef]
24. Ugwu, O.; Kumaraswamy, M.; Wong, A.; Ng, S. Sustainability appraisal in infrastructure projects (SUSAIP): Part 1. Development of indicators and computational methods. *Autom. Constr.* **2006**, *15*, 239–251. [CrossRef]
25. Zou, W.; Kumaraswamy, M.; Chung, J.; Wong, J. Identifying the critical success factors for relationship management in PPP projects. *Int. J. Proj. Manag.* **2014**, *32*, 265–274. [CrossRef]
26. Bing, L.; Akintoye, A.; Edwards, P.J.; Hardcastle, C. The allocation of risk in PPP/PFI construction projects in the UK. *Int. J. Proj. Manag.* **2005**, *23*, 25–35. [CrossRef]
27. Jin, X.H. Neurofuzzy Decision Support System for Efficient Risk Allocation in Public-Private Partnership Infrastructure Projects. *J. Comput. Civ. Eng.* **2014**, *24*, 525–538. [CrossRef]
28. Tieva, A.; Junnonen, J.M. Proactive contracting in finnish ppp projects. *Int. J. Strat. Prop. Manag.* **2009**, *13*, 219–228. [CrossRef]
29. Engel, E.; Fischer, R.; Galetovic, A. The economic or infrastructure finance: Public-Private Partnership versus public provision. *Eib Pap.* **2010**, *15*, 40–69.
30. Jiao, L.; Shen, L.; Shuai, C.; He, B. A Novel Approach for Assessing the Performance of Sustainable Urbanization Based on Structural Equation Modeling: A China Case Study. *Sustainability* **2016**, *8*, 910. [CrossRef]
31. Brundtland, G.H. Report of the World Commission on Environment and Development. *Environ. Policy Law* **1987**, *14*, 26–30.
32. Satolo, E.G.; Simon, A.T. Critical analysis of assessment methodologies for intraorganizational sustainability. *Manag. Environ. Qual.* **2015**, *26*, 214–232. [CrossRef]
33. Therese, B. Does Collaboration Lead to Sustainability? A Study of Public-Private Partnerships in the Swedish Mountains. *Sustainability* **2017**, *9*, 1685.
34. Jenkins, B.; Annandale, D.; Morrison-Saunders, A. The evolution of a sustainability assessment strategy for Western Australia. *J. Am. Dent. Assoc.* **2003**, *134*, 97–101.
35. Sheate, W.R.; Dagg, S.; Richardson, J.; Aschemann, R.; Palerm, J.; Steen, U. Integrating the environment into strategic decision-making: Conceptualizing policy SEA. *Environ. Policy Gov.* **2003**, *13*, 1–18. [CrossRef]
36. Fay, M.; Toman, M.; Benitez, D.; Csordas, S. Infrastructure and Sustainable Development. *Bone Marrow Transplant.* **2010**, *21*, 1071–1073.
37. Djukic, M.; Jovanoski, I.; Ivanovic, O.M.; Lazic, M.; Bodroza, D. Cost-benefit analysis of an infrastructure project and a cost-reflective tariff: A case study for investment in wastewater treatment plant in Serbia. *Renew. Sustain. Energy Rev.* **2016**, *59*, 1419–1425. [CrossRef]
38. Gil, N.A.; Biesek, G.; Freeman, J. Interorganizational Development of Flexible Capital Designs: The Case of Future-Proofing Infrastructure. *IEEE Trans. Eng. Manag.* **2016**, *62*, 335–350. [CrossRef]
39. She, Y.; Shen, L.; Jiao, L.; Zuo, J.; Tam, V.W.Y.; Yan, H. Constraints to achieve infrastructure sustainability for mountainous townships in China. *Habitat Int.* **2018**, *73*, 65–78. [CrossRef]
40. Naoum, S. An overview into the concept of partnering. *Int. J. Proj. Manag.* **2003**, *21*, 71–76. [CrossRef]
41. Mazher, K.M.; Chan, A.P.C.; Zahoor, H.; Khan, M.I.; Ameyaw, E.E. Fuzzy Integral-Based Risk-Assessment Approach for Public-Private Partnership Infrastructure Projects. *J. Constr. Eng. Manag.* **2018**, *144*, 15. [CrossRef]
42. Shen, L.Y.; Wu, Y.Z. Risk Concession Model for Build/Operate/Transfer Contract Projects. *J. Constr. Eng. Manag.* **2005**, *131*, 211–220. [CrossRef]
43. Klijn, E.H.; Koppenjan, J. The impact of contract characteristics on the performance of public-private partnerships (PPPs). *Public Money Manag.* **2016**, *36*, 455–462. [CrossRef]
44. Babatunde, S.O.; Opawole, A.; Akinsiku, O.E. Critical success factors in public-private partnership (PPP) on infrastructure delivery in Nigeria. *J. Facil. Manag.* **2012**, *10*, 212–225. [CrossRef]
45. Ismail, S. Critical success factors of public private partnership (PPP) implementation in Malaysia. *Asia-Pac. J. Bus. Adm.* **2013**, *5*, 6–19. [CrossRef]

46. Hutchins, M.J.; Sutherland, J.W. An exploration of measures of social sustainability and their application to supply chain decisions. *J. Clean. Prod.* **2008**, *16*, 1688–1698. [CrossRef]

47. Yu, Y.; Darko, A.; Chan, A.P.C.; Chen, C.; Bao, F.Y. Evaluation and Ranking of Risk Factors in Transnational Public-Private Partnerships Projects: Case Study Based on the Intuitionistic Fuzzy Analytic Hierarchy Process. *J. Infrastruct. Syst.* **2018**, *24*, 13. [CrossRef]

48. Hueting, R. Why environmental sustainability can most probably not be attained with growing production. *J. Clean. Prod.* **2010**, *18*, 525–530. [CrossRef]

49. Tam, V.W.Y.; Shen, L.Y.; Yau, R.M.Y.; Tam, C.M. On using a communication-mapping model for environmental management (CMEM) to improve environmental performance in project development processes. *Build. Environ.* **2007**, *42*, 3093–3107. [CrossRef]

50. Shen, L.Y.; Wu, M.; Wang, J.Y. A model for assessing the feasibility of construction project in contributing to the attainment of sustainable development. *J. Constr. Res.* **2012**, *30*, 989–994. [CrossRef]

51. Sun, X.; Liu, X.; Li, F.; Tao, Y.; Song, Y. Comprehensive evaluation of different scale cities' sustainable development for economy, society, and ecological infrastructure in China. *J. Clean. Prod.* **2015**. [CrossRef]

52. Zhang, X.; Wu, Y.; Skitmore, M.; Jiang, S. Sustainable infrastructure projects in balancing urban-rural development: Towards the goal of efficiency and equity. *J. Clean. Prod.* **2015**, *107*, 445–454. [CrossRef]

53. Manos, B.; Partalidou, M.; Fantozzi, F.; Arampatzis, S.; Papadopoulou, O. Agro-energy districts contributing to environmental and social sustainability in rural areas: Evaluation of a local public-private partnership scheme in Greece. *Renew. Sustain. Energy Rev.* **2014**, *29*, 85–95. [CrossRef]

54. Chang, R.D.; Zuo, J.; Soebarto, V.; Zhao, Z.Y.; Zillante, G.; Gan, X.L. Sustainability Transition of the Chinese Construction Industry: Practices and Behaviors of the Leading Construction Firms. *J. Manag. Eng.* **2016**, *32*, 05016009. [CrossRef]

55. Balkema, A.J.; Preisig, H.A.; Otterpohl, R.; Lambert, F.J.D. Indicators for the sustainability assessment of wastewater treatment systems. *Urban Water* **2002**, *4*, 153–161. [CrossRef]

56. Development, I.I.F.S. *Compendium of Sustainable Development Indicator Initiatives*; IISD: Geneva, Switzerland, 2006.

57. Ezeah, C.; Roberts, C.L. Analysis of barriers and success factors affecting the adoption of sustainable management of municipal solid waste in Nigeria. *J. Environ. Manag.* **2012**, *103*, 9–14. [CrossRef] [PubMed]

58. Chen, M.Q. Analysis on System Obstructions to Small Town Sustainable Development and Countermeasures in China. *China Popul. Resour. Environ.* **2004**, *1*, 60–63.

59. Qin, C.; Wang, J. On the Development of Mountain Economy of China's Western Regions: Based on Ecological Civilization. *Ecol. Econ.* **2012**, *10*, 62–71.

60. Zhou, J.; Tam, V.; Qin, Y. Gaps between Awareness and Activities on Green Construction in China: A Perspective of On-Site Personnel. *Sustainability* **2018**, *10*, 2266. [CrossRef]

61. Capwell, E.M. *Theory of Planned Behavior*; Springer: New York, NY, USA, 2013; pp. 179–211.

62. Ajzen, I. *From Intentions to Actions: A Theory of Planned Behavior*; Springer: Berlin/Heidelberg, Germany, 1985; pp. 11–39.

63. Ajzen, I. Perceived Behavioral Control, Self-Efficacy, Locus of Control, and the Theory of Planned Behavior. *J. Appl. Soc. Psychol.* **2002**, *32*, 665–683. [CrossRef]

64. Chen, C.F.; Chao, W.H. Habitual or reasoned? Using the theory of planned behavior, technology acceptance model, and habit to examine switching intentions toward public transit. *Transp. Res. Part F Traffic Psychol. Behav.* **2011**, *14*, 128–137. [CrossRef]

65. Fan, W.S.; Haung, Y.K.; Hsu, H.C.; Chen, C.C. An Analysis of the Blog-User Attitude Employing Structural Equation Modeling Combine TAM and TPB Model. In Proceedings of the International Conference on Information Technology and Management, Bucurestic, Romania, 20–23 January 2013; pp. 90–93.

66. Lin, G.; Shen, G.Q.; Sun, M.; Kelly, J. Identification of Key Performance Indicators for Measuring the Performance of Value Management Studies in Construction. *J. Constr. Eng. Manag.* **2011**, *137*, 698–706. [CrossRef]

67. Yunhi, K.; Han, H.S. Intention to pay conventional-hotel prices at a green hotel—A modification of the theory of planned behavior. *J. Sustain. Tour.* **2010**, *18*, 997–1014.

68. Ajzen, I. The theory of planned behavior, organizational behavior and human decision processes. *J. Leis. Res.* **1991**, *50*, 176–211.

69. Kan, M.P.H.; Fabrigar, L.R. *Theory of Planned Behavior*; Springer: Cham, Switzerland, 2017.

70. Abrahamse, W.; Steg, L.; Gifford, R.; Vlek, C. Factors influencing car use for commuting and the intention to reduce it: A question of self-interest or morality? *Transp. Res. Part F Traffic Psychol. Behav.* **2009**, *12*, 317–324. [CrossRef]

71. Angelidou, M.; Psaltoglou, A. An empirical investigation of social innovation initiatives for sustainable urban development. *Sustain. Cities Soc.* **2017**. [CrossRef]

72. El-Gohary, N.M.; Osman, H.; El-Diraby, T.E. Stakeholder management for public private partnerships. *Int. J. Proj. Manag.* **2006**, *24*, 595–604. [CrossRef]

73. Shah, R.; Goldstein, S.M. Use of structural equation modeling in operations management research: Looking back and forward. *J. Oper. Manag.* **2006**, *24*, 148–169. [CrossRef]

74. Shneif, M. *Principles and Practice of Structural Equation Modeling*; Guilford Press: New York, NY, USA, 2015.

75. Shen, W.; Xiao, W.; Wang, X. Passenger satisfaction evaluation model for Urban rail transit: A structural equation modeling based on partial least squares. *Transp. Policy* **2016**, *46*, 20–31. [CrossRef]

76. Xiong, B.; Skitmore, M.; Xia, B. A critical review of structural equation modeling applications in construction research. *Autom. Constr.* **2015**, *49*, 59–70. [CrossRef]

77. Chan, D.; Kumaraswamy, M.M. A comparative study of causes of time overrun in Hong Kong construction projects. *Int. J. Proj. Manag.* **1997**, *15*, 55–63. [CrossRef]

78. Jahangir, N.; Begum, N. The role of perceived usefulness, perceived ease of use, security and privacy, and customer attitude to engender customer adaptation in the context of electronic banking. *Afr. J. Bus. Manag.* **2008**, *2*, 32–40.

79. Jokar, N.K.; Noorhosseini, S.A.; Allahyari, M.S.; Damalas, C.A. Consumers' acceptance of medicinal herbs: An application of the technology acceptance model (TAM). *J. Ethnopharmacol.* **2017**, *207*, 203–210. [CrossRef] [PubMed]

80. Welsch, H.; Kühling, J. How Green Self Image is Related to Subjective Well-Being: Pro-Environmental Values as a Social Norm. *Ecol. Econ.* **2018**, *149*, 105–119. [CrossRef]

81. Liang, C.C.; Shiau, W.L. Moderating effect of privacy concerns and subjective norms between satisfaction and repurchase of airline e-ticket through airline-ticket vendors. *Asia Pac. J. Tour. Res.* **2018**, *23*, 1142–1159. [CrossRef]

82. Gellman, M.D.; Turner, J.R. *Perceived Behavioral Control*; Springer: New York, NY, USA, 2013; p. 1450.

83. de Bruijn, G.J.; Rhodes, R.E. Exploring exercise behavior, intention and habit strength relationships. *Scand. J. Med. Sci. Sports* **2011**, *21*, 482–491. [CrossRef] [PubMed]

84. Morwitz, V.G.; Fitzsimons, G.J. The Mere-Measurement Effect: Why Does Measuring Intentions Change Actual Behavior? *J. Consum. Psychol.* **2004**, *14*, 64–74.

85. Dublin. The Dublin Statement on Water and Sustainable Development. *Environ. Conserv.* **2017**, *19*, 6. [CrossRef]

86. Doloi, H.; Iyer, K.C.; Sawhney, A. Structural equation model for assessing impacts of contractor's performance on project success. *Int. J. Proj. Manag.* **2011**, *29*, 687–695. [CrossRef]

87. Fornell, C.; Larcker, D.F. Structural equation models with unobservable variables and measurement error: Algebra and statistics. *J. Mark. Res.* **1981**, *18*, 39–50. [CrossRef]

88. Bandalos, D.L. The effects of item parceling on goodness-of-fit and parameter estimate bias in structural equation modeling. *Struct. Equ. Model. A Multidiscip. J.* **2002**, *9*, 78–102. [CrossRef]

89. Meng, J.; Xue, B.; Liu, B.; Fang, N. Relationships between top managers' leadership and infrastructure sustainability. *Eng. Constr. Arch. Manag.* **2015**, *22*, 692–714. [CrossRef]

90. O'Rourke, N.; Hatcher, L. A Step-By-Step Approach to Using SAS System for Factor Analysis and Structural Equation Modeling. *Int. Stat. Rev.* **2013**, *83*, 325–326.

91. Bacon, D.R.; Sauer, P.L.; Young, M. Composite reliability in structural equations modeling. *Educ. Psychol. Meas.* **1995**, *55*, 394–406. [CrossRef]

92. Gloukhovtsev, A. Don't give me attitude: Can perceptions of social norms, behavioral control and moral intensity help bridge the attitude-behavior gap in ethical consumer behavior? *J. Microbiol. Methods* **2014**, *23*, 169–182.

93. Johe, M.H.; Bhullar, N. To buy or not to buy: The roles of self-identity, attitudes, perceived behavioral control and norms in organic consumerism. *Ecol. Econ.* **2016**, *128*, 99–105. [CrossRef]

Article

Drivers for Public–Private Partnerships in Sustainable Natural Resource Management—Lessons from the Swedish Mountain Region

Camilla Thellbro *, Therese Bjärstig[id] and Katarina Eckerberg

Department of Political Science, Umeå University, 901 87 Umeå, Sweden; therese.bjarstig@umu.se (T.B.); katarina.eckerberg@umu.se (K.E.)
* Correspondence: camilla.thellbro@umu.se; Tel.: +46-702-117-002

Received: 14 September 2018; Accepted: 24 October 2018; Published: 28 October 2018

Abstract: Sweden's mountain areas are sensitive ecosystems that are used by a wide range of stakeholders, and this raises multiple sustainability concerns. Collaborative governance solutions are becoming increasingly common in such situations to promote more sustainable practices. While the Swedish mountain area is indeed a hot spot for different forms of public–private partnerships (PPPs) related to natural resources management, as yet, little is known about the shaping of participation, leadership, and implementation of these processes. What are the drivers for implementing collaborative environmental partnerships, do the drivers differ, and if so, how? What role does the specific context play in the design of these PPPs? Are the PPPs useful, and if so, for what? To analyze those issues, we conducted 38 semi-structured interviews with project leaders from a sample randomly selected from a database of 245 public–private collaborative projects in the Swedish mountains. Our results indicate that consequential incentives in the form of funding and previous successful collaborations seem to be the major drivers for such partnerships. A critical discussion of the possibilities and limitations of public–private forms of governance in rural mountain areas adds to the ongoing debate on the performance of environmental PPPs in a regional context.

Keywords: collaboration; public–private partnership; drivers; process; implementation; sustainability; natural resource management; mountains; Sweden

1. Introduction

The Swedish mountain region is currently experiencing a high development pressure, which is threatening sensitive environments that are of interest for different land uses [1–3]. The prevalence of conflicts among the different stakeholders is identified as a major underlying problem. The realization of the Swedish National Environmental Quality Objectives (NEQO) of "a magnificent mountain environment", "flourishing lakes and streams", "sustainable forests", and "a rich diversity of plant and animal life" are at stake, and it is acknowledged that reaching the NEQOs will require considerable added efforts from a variety of social, political, and economic actors. Both in Sweden and internationally, various forms of collaborative governance are seen as promising ways to deal with "wicked problems" and policy failure, including the pooling of resources among multiple stakeholders and the use of deliberative management practices e.g., [4–7]. This trend is spurred on by the emphasis on participation in a range of relevant international environmental agreements, first and foremost in the Aarhus Convention and subsequently, in the Convention on Biological Diversity and the EU Biodiversity Strategy, the European Forest Action Plan, and the Water Framework Directive, to name a few. At a national level, the Swedish Government's Nature Protection Policy from 2001 reiterates the need to widen the scope and engage a broader range of actors, including local communities to achieve policy goals, in the form of public–private partnerships, and similar policies have been adopted in the forest, rural development, and water management sectors [8–11].

The specific focus of this paper is *environmental partnerships* which aim to improve the environmental quality or natural resource utilization, following the definition of Long and Arnold [12] (p. 6). They define environmental partnerships as *"voluntary, jointly-defined activities and decision-making processes among corporate, non-profit, and agency organizations that aim to improve environmental quality or natural resource utilization"*. The terms "public–private partnership", "public–private collaborative project", and "public–private project" are used interchangeably, all implying that actors from the public and private spheres are engaged and interacting. From now on, we use the abbreviation PPPs when referring to public–private partnerships and/or projects geared toward environmental and natural resource management.

In accordance with the argument of Van Huijstee et al. [13], the key analytical focus in the environmental partnership and governance literature is generally of a high spatial level, i.e., the global and international level (see also Reference [14]). Thus, applying the theoretical concepts to the regional and/or local level provides a contribution to this specific environmental partnership literature, as argued by Bjärstig and Sandström [8] and Widman [15]. There are also empirical arguments for bringing the analysis down to a more context-dependent level, for instance, the way ecosystems work [16] and the institutional and/or socioeconomic variations across spatial levels [17,18]. Furthermore, there is a research gap regarding the initiation of environmental partnerships and how the realization of partnerships takes place, which we will address in this study [15,19,20]. A previous paper by Bjärstig [21] covers sustainable output and the outcomes/effectiveness of PPPs on natural resource management in the Sweden mountain region, and studies by, for example, Bjärstig and Sandström and Zachrisson et al. [8,22] handle PPPs in natural resource management in rural areas in relation to the roles, relative power levels, and interactions between partners in a rural context. Within this literature, however, the rationale and drivers behind the PPPs are yet to be identified and analyzed.

The aim of this paper is to examine the shaping of participation, leadership, and the implementation of partnering processes on natural resource management, i.e., the realisation of these environmental PPPs in the Swedish mountain region. What are the drivers for implementing collaborative partnerships, do the drivers differ, and if so, how? What role does the specific context play in the design of these PPPs? Are the PPPs useful, and if so, for what?

The results presented are also relevant to other countries and/or regions with similar socio-economic contexts, i.e., sparsely populated areas rich in natural resources that wish to manage the sustainability of their natural resources through PPPs.

2. Drivers for Public–Private Partnerships

Partnerships are increasingly being used in sustainability governance worldwide [13,23–25]. There are various definitions of the PPP concept to be found. These depend on the disciplinary approach and policy area at hand (the concept originates in fields related to, e.g., infrastructure, economic development, and health/medicine), but they all share some common features [26,27]. In the context of our research, we define a PPP as a voluntary, agreed on collaboration between the state and a non-state actor(s). Moreover, in line with Bjärstig and Sandström [8], the partnership should be a formalized, long-term, or at least mutual, a commitment between partners with the purpose of complementing each other so that each partners' goals can be achieved more efficiently than would otherwise have been possible. Additionally, resources, risks, and rewards should be shared among the partners [28], and the aim of a PPP is often to provide some sort of public service or asset [20].

A considerable number of literature reviews have been made to find ways to sort and categorize PPPs (e.g., References [12,27,28]). Empirical studies have demonstrated that PPPs can appear in many different forms with different purposes. In some cases, PPPs are seen as a method by which to govern and/or manage specific objectives. In other cases, PPPs are described as an institutional arrangement for financial cooperation; a development strategy; an arrangement for crisis management and knowledge transfer; a tool for solving problems, conflicts, and providing community amenities; or a way to modernize the public sector [8].

In relation to categorizing environmental PPPs, it is interesting to address drivers to the partnering processes—the questions of when, where, and why these collaborative arrangements evolve. According to Emerson et al. [29] (p. 9), many frameworks for collaborative arrangements "conflate system context and conditions with the specific drivers of collaboration". Emerson et al. [29] presented a framework that distinguishes between contextual variables and essential drivers, which we will use as an analytical departure in this paper, with the purpose of mapping and analyzing drivers for partnerships in natural resource management in the Swedish mountains. Essential drivers are the force(s) without which the collaboration would not thrive. These drivers are *leadership, consequential incentives, interdependence,* and *uncertainty*. The more drivers present and acknowledged by the parties, the more likely it is that collaboration will commence.

Leadership refers to a present and identified leader who holds a position that allows him/her to initiate and aid in securing resources and support (e.g., by providing staffing, technologies, time, etc.) for a collaborative arrangement. It is crucial that the leader acts impartially with respect to the preferences of the collaborating participants [29]. Here, leadership is investigated in terms of the interviewed respondents' perceptions of the project organization; how and why the partnership was designed in the way it was; and how this has affected the partnering process/realization of the partnership.

Consequential incentives are positive or negative incentives that make leaders and participants engage collectively. Examples of such incentives are issues of great importance to the participants, including the fact that the timing to solve a problem is right and/or that negative effects might arise if the incentives are not attended to. Commonly perceived issues, resource needs, and/or crises or threats are examples of consequential incentives for the development of collaborative initiatives [29]. This is captured by the interviewed respondents' views on prevailing trust among partners, a previous policy failure (i.e., unsuccessful management and/or implementation), or a previous successful collaboration. It could also be an area/resource with a high level of conflict or an issue/area that otherwise would not be handled. Disagreement on the knowledge base and possibilities for receiving funding are also seen as consequential incentives.

Interdependence is the driver when individuals and organizations cannot achieve their objectives on their own [7]. Emerson et al. [29] (p. 9) expressed it as, in a sense, "*the ultimate consequential incentive*". This is particularly prevalent if many actors are affected and dependent on each other and therefore, is captured by responses regarding the number of actors affected and the shared responsibilities and engagement among the partners in the partnership.

Uncertainty can drive parties to collaborate in order to reduce, spread, and share risk(s). Uncertainty constitutes a particular challenge when managing "wicked" societal problems (such as environmental and sustainability issues) [29]. This is captured by the respondents' perceived presence and the level of shared risk among the partners in the partnership in handling issues related to the environment and to natural resource management in a more holistic and sustainable way.

3. Materials and Methods

Research Design, Study Area, and Background Context

This study builds upon 38 semi-structured interviews with representatives from environmental PPPs in the Swedish mountain region (see Reference [21] for an in-depth description). The mountain region is here geographically defined by the 15 so-called mountain municipalities (see Figure 1).

Figure 1. The mountain region (dark green area) of Sweden (light green area) extends over 15 municipalities in four counties: Norrbotten, Västerbotten, Jämtland, and Dalarna.

The 15 mountain municipalities cover an area of more than 155,000 km^2 (of which 13,000 km^2 is water), constituting nearly 30% of Sweden's total area. These municipalities currently contain less than 1.5% of the Swedish population of about 10 million people [30]. Bare mountains above the tree line cover about 20% of the region, and forests cover about 50% of the region. The rest of the area is mostly covered by wetlands. [31,32]. Large parts (about 11%) of the mountain region are formally protected as nature reserves or national parks [33]. Conventional forestry is practised on virtually all productive forest land owned by non-industrial private forest owners, forest companies, and by the state. Eight of the twelve large river systems are used for hydropower production. Land-based wind power production and the mining industry are currently expanding. Tourism and recreational activities (fishing, hunting, hiking, snowmobile driving, skiing, etc.) involve all types of land, and their use of this land is based on property rights and the right of public access in non-commercial as well as in commercial contexts. Reindeer husbandry is ongoing across the entire mountain area, and the Sami have both cultural rights and rights to self-determination in the mountain region, as the region constitutes a central part of the Sami traditional territories [34]. Consequently, it is obvious that nature and natural resources in the mountains are used for many purposes by numerous actors; this calls for coordination and collaboration [35,36]. However, the fact that the 15 rural municipalities that constitute the mountain region suffer from shrinking populations and diminishing financial resources makes it difficult to work strategically and take concrete actions with regard to natural resource management to achieve positive and sustainable societal development [35–37].

The semi-structured interviews were conducted from 2014 to 2016 (see supplementary material for interview manual). The random selection of the projects for further analysis originated from an extensive quantitative analysis of detailed information on 245 funded projects, all aimed at public–private collaboration in natural resource management in the four counties in the mountain region. For more information on the original compilation of the database of these 245 projects, see Eckerberg et al. [38]. The selection of the respondents, who represented the 38 environmental PPP projects, was based on official information from project leaders/contact persons. They represented a mix of public (14 respondents) and private actors (24 respondents) (see supplementary material for information on the respondents). All interviews were transcribed (following Reference [39]). To validate the study, the respondents were given the opportunity to read the transcribed interviews and to clarify and/or adjust their responses, but none of the respondents made any alterations (see Reference [40]).

The interviews were read in-depth and coded based on the questions/alternative responses and themes of the interview manual. They were then compiled according to contextual variables and the four essential drivers described above, i.e., *leadership, consequential incentives, interdependence,* and *uncertainty*, (see our operationalization of the drivers in the previous section and the interview manual in the supplementary material). To allow for discussions and conclusions regarding the general patterns and trends of the main drivers for PPPs on natural resource management, rather than providing in-depth descriptions of single PPPs and "hot spot analyses", the 38 projects were handled and analysed collectively, and this is presented in the results section. To illustrate and make the analysis transparent, representative quotes were identified and extracted, and these are displayed in the results section. No secondary data were used.

4. Results

The results section is organized in line with the four essential drivers for PPPs, followed by an analysis of the differences in drivers among the PPPs based on the themes for the collaborations. The section ends with a short note on the use of PPPs.

4.1. Leadership

In concurrence with Eckerberg et al. [38], this study found that voluntary organizations (76%) and municipalities (89%) were the most frequently represented partners in the 38 studied PPPs (Figure 2). According to the responses, different types of private companies take part in more than half (55%) of the partnerships. Nearly the same extent (53%) of, primarily, individuals, along with universities and foundations in the "Other" category, were stated as playing important roles in the collaborative efforts.

Figure 2. The partners in public–private partnerships (PPPs) related to environment and natural resource management in the Swedish mountain region (*n* = 38). PPP projects 1–7 were carried out in Norrbotten County, 8–18 in Västerbotten County, 19–31 in Jämtland County, and 32–38 in Dalarna County.

In most of the identified PPPs (39%), a voluntary organization was the initiator, followed by companies (26%), and municipalities (21%), which is in line with Eckerberg et al. [38]. The "Other" category (21%) had a mix of initiators such as municipal associations, universities, and other organizations or foundations (Figure 3). In 45% of the projects, the initiator was considered to be an enthusiast, while 47% of the projects were initiated as part of regular duties. For the rest of the projects, no information regarding this aspect was provided.

It was rather difficult to obtain a more general picture of project organization within PPPs from the conducted interviews. Most PPPs can be assumed to have some kind of formal steering committee or group, and this was commonly briefly mentioned by the respondents. The work of a project leader/coordinator and of active working groups and/or engaged individuals was more frequently described. Informality in project organization was widely applied. The main underlying reason for the applied, informal organization was stated to be "local conditions", including informal networks, geographical conditions, and aspects related to local traditions:

" ... it was not really in practice as it was formally stated in the application. [...] The steering group was initially engaged in many parts (of the work) and they were meticulous about results, but they let go relatively early on because it worked by itself". (Interview 29)

"No, there is no steering group. […] we don't have regular meetings, but deal with things simply if needed. […] There are so few people involved so there is no need for long debates". (Interview 13)

"It has been mostly informal […] she (the project leader) has been working with people that she knows are active. 'Okay, you're going there, but then maybe you can check this track?". (Interview 8)

"The team I have cooperated with is fantastic, and they had already anchored this in the area. Before they came to us (the municipality) they had already talked about which of the village teams were interested and which tracks were relevant (to restore) … so then we just sat down to write the application. […] Every village team has been designing its own track and drafting an action plan for it". (Interview 30)

The interviews suggest that enthusiasts—a few engaged individuals or one active part (often a voluntary organization)—are crucial for initiating and carrying out the planned activities within the project:

" … as I'm the driving force, I ended up … Well, I have done a large part of the job myself". (Interview 23)

"But it's just that the enthusiasts see it, but then to persuade people, that's something else … ". (Interview 32)

In 26% of the PPPs, the project organizations were said to depend on partners with various capabilities and opportunities to invest time and resources to the collaboration:

" … the tourism entrepreneurs (and the Sami entrepreneurs) who weren't in the area, there it was some problems with distance … ". (Interview 1)

"The authorities have participated and […] (organizations and larger companies in) the tourism industry … they have participated the whole time. Then there are small entrepreneurs, but they don't always have the resources to participate and be at every meeting". (Interview 22).

As mentioned, municipalities are partners in over 80% of the studied PPPs. Some quotes illustrated their roles:

" … what we (the municipality) experience concerning projects, in general, is that there are lots of ideas and initiatives, but that no-one wants to do the administrative accounting so we try to facilitate it, as much as it is possible". (Interview 28).

" … (the municipal project leader) is the administrator. It has been a way … The municipality has always been the one to help to apply for LONA-projects, to have (financial) liquidity and such … ". (Interview 30) and

"It is not certain that this project would have become if I (municipal official) had not been there as … not so much a carrier of ideas, that part was accounted for by the voluntary organization, but as an intermediary or the possibility to apply for grants". (Interview 24).

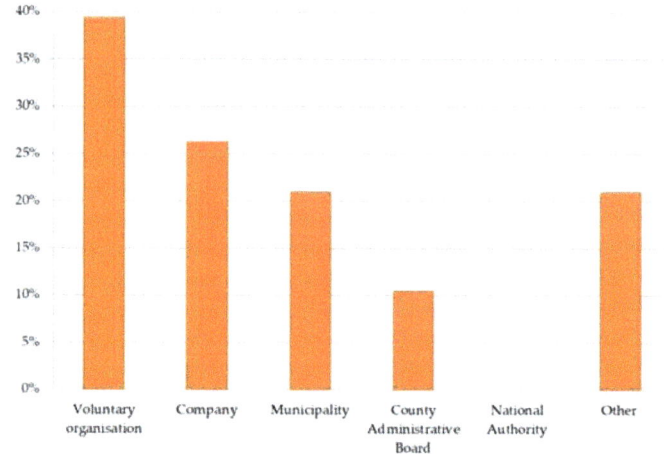

Figure 3. The initiators of PPPs on environmental and natural resource management in the Swedish mountain region. Note, some projects had more than one initiator.

Accordingly, in this context, the municipalities help to fulfil the requirements with regards to the public part in order to apply for funding and to act as administrators, i.e., they act as facilitators for the partnership (cf. Reference [8]). They also provide economical "safety nets" when it comes to liquidity since there can be a delay in the disbursement of funding. Thus, the driver of leadership—related to how the partnership was designed—appeared to be prevalent in most of the studied PPPs.

4.2. Consequential Incentives

Regional authorities, almost exclusively, the County Administrative Boards (CABs), play vital roles in regional funding (39%) and in the allocation of EU (37%) and national (24%) funding to environmental PPPs (Figure 4).

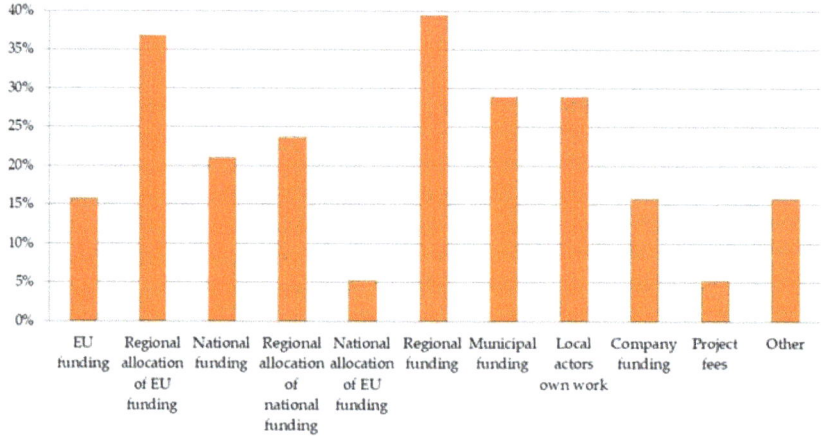

Figure 4. The funding sources for PPPs related to environmental and natural resource management (*n* = 38) in the Swedish mountain region. Most projects are funded by more than one source.

Figure 5 illustrates the combinations of funding in the 38 environmental PPPs. The PPPs with the regional allocation of national funding are all financed by SEPA (the Swedish Environmental

Protection Agency) through LONA (the Local Nature Protection Program, supporting local initiatives in nature conservation and recreation as they emerge from the local social context). LONA funding can be applied for by municipalities and local social partners, such as environmental and cultural organizations [41]. The EU Rural Development Program LEADER (Liaison entre actions de développement de l'économie rurale), is an approach that contributes to rural development by forming partnerships at a sub-regional level among the public, private, and civil sectors. A partnership is a prerequisite for retaining funding (cf. [38]). LEADER financed 11 of the 14 projects with a regional allocation of EU funding in this study.

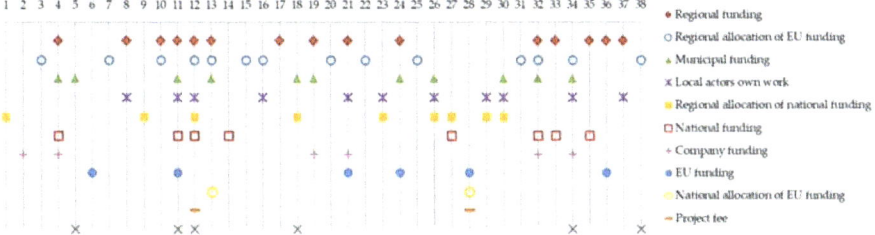

Figure 5. The combinations of funding in PPPs related to environmental and natural resource management in the Swedish mountain region (*n* = 38).

Figure 6 shows that the possibility to apply for external funding (50%) and the fact that the collaboration addresses an issue or area that would otherwise not be handled (42%) were the most commonly described reasons for initiating PPPs (i.e., the most common answer to the question "What was the triggering reason for choosing collaboration?"). Thus, consequential incentives appear to have been a very important driver for the studied PPPs:

"... when we saw that there was money, we applied for a project [...] our municipalities are so poor that we need (externally funded) projects if there is to be anything ... ". (Interview 9)

"... the need had been identified long since, [...] and when the money came, there was a possibility that this would fit, and then we started to work. Often, the issue is to find funding". (Interview 27)

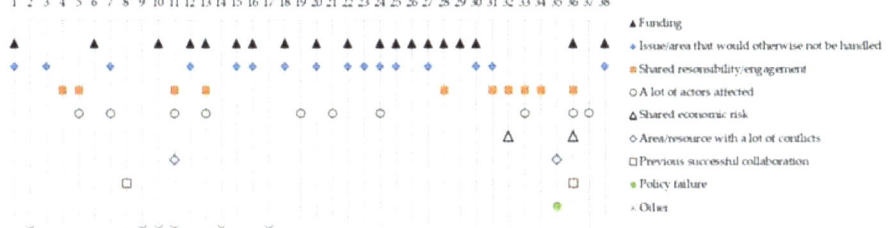

Figure 6. The catalyst reasons for initiating and implementing PPPs related to environmental and natural resource management in the mountain regions (*n* = 38).

Because the respondents often gave spontaneous presentations of previous and/or general circumstances, an attempt was made to present a contextual background (underlying reasons) for initiating and implementing the PPP projects (Figure 7). In 47% of the projects, the addressed PPP was clearly a result of previous successful collaboration(s):

"This is a long history, but the origin is a former restoration project ... ". (Interview 6)

"Our local project is an offshoot from the national project where our goal simply was to cooperate concerning the marketing of Swedish sports fishing tourism". (Interview 18)

"And then there were spin-offs from these projects, so this particular project [. . .] is just one of these projects". (Interview 35)

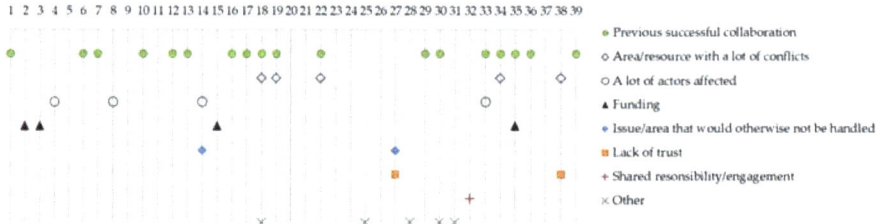

Figure 7. The contextual backgrounds (underlying reasons) for initiating and implementing PPPs related to environmental and natural resource management in the Swedish mountain region (*n* = 38).

The handling of an area/resource with a lot of conflicts and/or lack of trust was stated to be an underlying reason in merely six of the 38 PPPs, and this was almost exclusively in combination with a previous successful collaboration.

4.3. Interdependence and Uncertainty

Regarding interdependence, the most commonly cited reasons for initiating PPPs were shared responsibility (26%) and the fact that a lot of actors were affected by the purpose of the collaboration in one way or another (26%). Most often, these reasons were mentioned in combination with one or more other drivers (Figure 6).

Closely aligned to interdependence is the driver of uncertainty, but shared risk, in form of shared economic risk, in this case, was only put forward as the main reason for initiating the PPP in two of the studied PPPs. Our results thus suggest that reduction, spread, and/or sharing of risk, i.e., the driver of uncertainty is not central for PPPs aimed at environmental and natural resource management in the Swedish mountain region.

4.4. Differences in Drivers for PPPs

The PPPs related to environmental and natural resource management in the Swedish mountain region can be grouped in terms of the theme of the collaboration (i.e., the issue/area), for example, climate and energy, fishing, forest, hunting, landscape, local development, mining, nature and culture, nature protection, (collaborative) process, recreation, Sami and reindeer, tourism, tracks and access, water, and wind energy (see Reference [38]). In the database of the 245 projects, several themes could be attached to a project, but in this paper, we refined them and only associated one main theme with each of the 38 PPPs (see Figure 8). This was for analytical purposes, i.e., so that we could link drivers to specific themes.

The vast majority of the 38 projects concerned concrete actions or measures. The most common theme, which was present in about one-third (31%) of the projects, was collaboration on the development and improvement of tracks and access to nature/the landscape (Figure 8). Some PPPs were formed to develop or to restore values or facilities/constructions for tourism, nature and culture, water, and fishing. In many of these projects, recreation was an important additional theme (but not the main one, and thus, not a theme on its own in Figure 8). PPPs with process and the landscape as their main themes (18%) were focused on goals related to process development and dialogue. A few of the projects aimed to produce a product of some kind, e.g., a plan/program linked to climate and energy or nature protection, or a destination to generate local development.

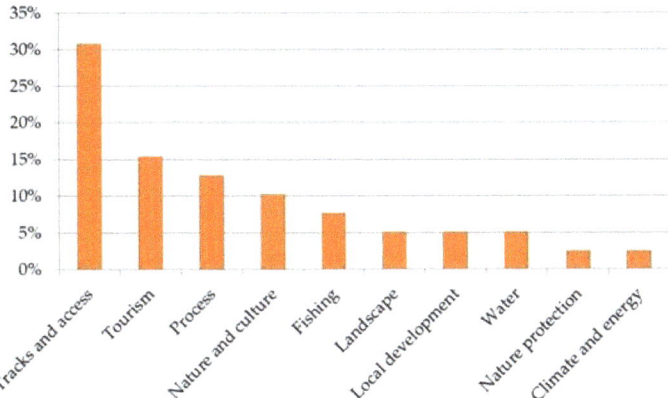

Figure 8. The main thematic focuses of the 38 PPPs related to environmental and natural resource management in the Swedish mountain region.

We did detect some differences in the drivers of the PPPs based on their different themes. Among the projects with nature and culture or nature protection as their main theme, the respondents all stated that the PPP deals with an issue/area that would otherwise not be handled and 60% of them highlighted the availability of funding as a central reason. Among the tourism-related PPPs, 67% were described as being driven by the fact that a lot of actors are or need to be involved. For projects concerning tracks and access, the most common theme was driven both by the available funding (67%) and by the fact that the issue/area would otherwise not be handled (50%). The results did not show any consistent reason(s) for collaborations on the process. There were few PPPs related to landscape or local development, with the single most important reason for collaboration stated as being shared responsibility and/or engagement. Regarding PPPs with landscape as their main theme, a lot of actors were also stated as being affected. Altogether, the results indicated that depending on the issue/area at hand, different drivers are at play when initiating and implementing environmental PPPs.

4.5. The Usefulness of Environmental PPPs

In concurrence with an earlier study by Bjärstig [21], based on the same interviews, our coding of the interview material showed that almost 58% of the respondents stated that their PPP had fulfilled its goals, and nearly 16% claimed that they had partially fulfilled them. In 18 (close to 16%) of the PPPs, the goals were not perceived to have been reached, while 10.5% of the respondents did not answer or left an inconclusive answer regarding goal fulfilment. Our results imply that out of the PPPs that had not reached their goals or who did not leave an answer/left an inconclusive answer, PPPs with more process-oriented goals; those with (collaborative) a process or landscape as their main theme were overrepresented (60%). Indeed, only one of the PPPs with a process as its main focus was perceived to have fulfilled its goals, suggesting that projects aimed at concrete measures are easier to evaluate than those with process goals. It is not unambiguous to draw conclusions with regard to the relationship between project drivers and goal fulfilment, but it should be mentioned that funding, as a consequential incentive, was not a primary driver for any of the PPPs that had failed to achieve their targeted goals. Furthermore, previous successful collaboration was only stated as an intermediate reason by one of these PPPs.

To summarize our results, it is clear that the initiation and implementation of PPP projects related to environmental issues and natural resource management in the Swedish mountain region most often engage a few enthusiastic actors. The PPPs often have an informal and pragmatic organization due to local circumstances and/or limited resources. The PPPs mainly aim for, and succeed in, conducting practical and concrete (outdoor) measures. Forming a PPP offers the possibility of accessing external funding, primarily EU funding, for activities and measures that voluntary organizations could not otherwise afford and that municipalities would not prioritize within their own budget.

5. Concluding Discussion

This study showed that consequential incentives constitute the most prevalent driver for initiating and implementing collaborative partnerships in environmental and natural resource management in the Swedish mountains, where funding, previous successful collaboration, and areas/issues that otherwise would not be handled stand out as the main reasons for the partnerships. Furthermore, leadership was shown to be an important driver, where the administrative capacity of municipalities and the presence of enthusiasts are of particular importance. Interdependence and uncertainty are less obvious drivers in environmental PPPs in a rural mountain context. This could be because many formal, mandatory, and institutionalized collaborations have already been instigated by law in high-level conflict issues/areas (such as hunting, land use planning, water management, etc.), putting less pressure on the formation of voluntary PPPs in such areas of high uncertainty and potential conflict (cf. Reference [38]). Thus, the studied PPPs were mainly "win-win" collaborations, where the involved actors all have the potential to gain and have little to lose. This concurs with the conclusions drawn by Zachrisson et al. [22], who stated that authorities initiate PPPs to solve conflicts and when there is distrust, while private actors build on previous successful collaborations to conduct straightforward and action-oriented PPPs.

The organization of projects in the form of PPPs is a prerequisite for access to some of the funding sources, especially EU funding, providing an important reason for so many municipalities to engage in PPPs. The involvement of municipalities also becomes essential for other reasons, namely, to provide leadership, administrative support, and accountability. Concerning leadership, however, we also saw many projects that were largely driven by a project leader and/or enthusiast alone, or that at least would not have materialized without this individual leadership. Indeed, the role of individual "fire-brands" in initiating bottom-up projects for sustainability actions is commonly cited [42]. The need to also mobilize additional resources from collaborating partners to provide the necessary public as well as private co-financing is evident, where the workforce and working hours of the private partners can also provide important assets. Often, the implementation of the PPPs is both informal and based on pragmatic concerns within the community context, partly because there are so few engaged actors and very long travel distances to other relevant stakeholders within the mountain region. Formal routines for a steering group to guide the project and to provide for systematic accountability along the project process (other than that required by the funding body), become difficult in this context. The scarce availability of resources, both in terms of personnel, time, and financing, therefore, makes the PPPs a somewhat ambiguous governance tool in this particular context (cf. Reference [8]).

In this study, we asked whether the drivers differ among environmental PPPs, and if so, how? Previous research of collaborative project governance in this region has found notable differences among the four counties in terms of the kinds of issues addressed as well as the partners included [40]. Interestingly, in this study, we did not see any significant differences among the counties in the mountain region with regard to the essential drivers. Still, and supported by previous research, we noticed that the PPPs in Dalarna were initiated due to both previous conflicts and the need to share economic risks to a higher degree than in the other counties, and had, as an intermediate reason, the lack of trust among partners, i.e., more of the independence and uncertainty drivers (cf. Reference [22]). However, we detected some differences among the drivers for PPPs related to the issue/area (theme) of the collaboration. All projects with nature and culture or nature protection as their main theme were stated to deal with an issue/area that would have otherwise not been handled, and the great majority of them highlighted the availability of funding as a central reason. This result shows the substantive influence of the funding emanating from the Local Nature Protection Program that has spurred on many small and rural municipalities, including in the mountain region, to protect and provide public access to local nature areas where they would otherwise not have had the needed resources to take action [41]. Thus, in terms of a consequential incentive, funding acts as a very important driver. However, focusing on funding opportunities as a primary base for a PPP constitutes a certain risk since economic incentives could turn the focus away from collaboration and the pursuit of shared goals. This did not seem to be the case in the studied projects; however, we advise caution, in line with Smith and Thomasson [43]. Regarding PPPs with tourism, landscape, or processes as their main theme, a vast number of actors were affected and engaged as partners in such partnerships, indicating that drivers such as interdependence and uncertainty also became highly relevant drivers for initiating and implementing those PPPs.

Another central question for this study was whether the PPPs were useful, and for what? Overall, the studied PPPs appeared to be complementary to other types of more formal and top-down initiated collaborations, and they mainly provide a way to "gets things done that otherwise would not be done", largely by enabling the partners to access external funding. It is also clear that the majority of the studied projects were action-oriented and practical projects (where the participants restore tracks, build a shelter, etc.). These projects were perceived to have fulfilled their objectives to a high degree (cf. Reference [21]). However, the few projects that were more of process/dialogue-oriented did not seem to achieve their goals to the same extent. This is a reasonable result because processes and dialogue can take more time; often there is no clear finish line, rather the continuance of the process is what is desired.

The analytical framework of essential drivers, as presented by Emerson et al. [29], was useful for analyzing the possibilities and limitations of PPPs for sustainable resource management in rural mountain areas. It provided new insights into both the partnering process/initiation and the implementation of the environmental PPPs in relation to the specific regional context. To summarize, our case study of the Swedish mountain region showed that the mountain municipalities have an important facilitating role with regard to the leadership driver. Furthermore, we identified consequential incentives as being a major driver for most of the PPPs, where funding, a previous successful collaboration, and the presence of an issue/area that otherwise would not be handled stood out as the main reasons. Shared engagement and responsibility were also put forward by the respondents to some extent, suggesting that interdependence and uncertainty are indeed important drivers, but often function as intermediate drivers and/or in combination with the two main drivers: leadership and consequential incentives. This finding is novel and adds important insight into the environmental partnership literature regarding the drivers for PPPs in relation to the specific contexts, socio-economic factors, and institutional realities that are prevalent in geographical areas similar to the Swedish mountain region. In particular, it helps to problematize the tendency in the literature on PPPs to emphasize the positive aspects of partnering and highlight the successful outcomes while downplaying how challenging it can be to establish a collaborative culture [44]. We, therefore, argue that further studies are needed that not only focus on projects with "positive" outcomes, but also on less successful ones, especially on those involving more long-term processes and continuous dialogue among public–private partners.

In addition, future research should be designed so that the drivers can be assessed in relation to one another, for example, indicating which of the four factors—uncertainty, interdependence, consequential incentives, and leadership—are necessary and sufficient to spur collaborative environmental and natural resource management efforts (cf. Reference [45]). An even larger sample of PPPs would allow the testing of hypotheses about the interdependence between and/or causal mechanisms with regard to those drivers. In particular, our understanding of the necessary prerequisites for the initiation of environmental PPPs in rural areas with a capital-weak private sector, such as that which is prevalent in mountain regions, needs to be strengthened. A previous study by Bjärstig and Sandström [8] showed that PPPs in a rural context differ in terms of their stated objectives. This difference implies that the partnerships will take different forms and will involve different sets of actors. Furthermore, their results indicate that public and private actors engage in partnerships on different terms. The public actors engage them as part of their regular work duties, while private actors, including civil society representatives, need to take time off from work and thus, may lose income due to their engagement in the partnership (cf. Reference [8]). More in-depth studies of these aspects in relation to environmental partnerships would add to the understanding of how to make these partnerships sustainable in the long-term. By broadening the scope to include more regions and additional environmental and sustainability problems, knowledge on what drivers for PPPs work under certain conditions could be substantially improved. A critical discussion of the benefits and constraints of environmental partnerships would add important insight into that discussion.

Supplementary Materials: The supplementary materials are available online at http://www.mdpi.com/2071-1050/10/11/3914/s1.

Author Contributions: Conceptualization, T.B. and C.T.; Methodology, C.T.; Validation, C.T., T.B. and K.E.; Formal Analysis, C.T. and T.B.; Investigation, T.B.; Data Curation, C.T.; Writing—Original Draft Preparation, C.T.; Writing—Review & Editing, C.T., T.B. and K.E.; Visualization, C.T.; Supervision, T.B.; Project Administration, T.B.; Funding Acquisition, K.E.

Funding: The research was funded by the Swedish Environmental Protection Agency as part of their research program *Storslagna fjäll* (Magnificent Mountains: www.storslagnafjall.se).

Acknowledgments: We are grateful to Anna Zachrisson whom we have worked closely with in the project *Expectations and Impacts of Collaborative Environmental Governance in the Swedish Mountain Region*, and who assisted in the development of the interview manual.

Conflicts of Interest: The authors declare no conflict of interest. The funding agency had no role in the design of the study; in the collection, analyses, or interpretation of data; in the writing of the manuscript, and in the decision to publish the results.

References

1. Bjärstig, T.; Zachrisson, A.; Svensson, J.; Thellbro, C. *Grön Översiktsplanering i Fjäll- och Fjällnära Landskap. Deltagande Planering för en Hållbar och Innovativ Översiktsplan för Vilhelmina Kommun*; Rapport 6811; Naturvårdsverket: Stockholm, Sweden, 2018; 120p., ISBN 978-91-620-6811-0. Available online: http://www.naturvardsverket.se/Documents/publikationer6400/978-91-620-6811-0.pdf?pid=21967 (accessed on 7 August 2018).

2. Wall-Reinius, S.; Fredman, P.; Dahlberg, A.; Svensson, D.; Sörlin, S.; Godtman Kling, K. *Vägar Till Mångfunktionella Landskap: En Pilotmodell i Jämtlandsfjällen*; Rapport 6820; Naturvårdsverket: Stockholm, Sweden, 2018; 66p., ISBN 978-91-620-6820-2. Available online: http://www.naturvardsverket.se/Documents/publikationer6400/978-91-620-6820-2.pdf?pid=22092 (accessed on 7 August 2018).

3. Swedish Environmental Protection Agency (SEPA). *Förslag Till en Strategi för Miljökvalitets Målet Storslagen Fjällmiljö. Redovisning av ett Regeringsuppdrag. [Strategy for the Magnificent Mountain Environment]*; NV-04173-13; Naturvårdsverket: Stockholm, Sweden, 2014; 220p., Available online: http://www.naturvardsverket.se/strategi-for-storslagen-fjallmiljo (accessed on 7 August 2018).

4. Bäckstrand, K.; Khan, J.; Kronsell, A.; Lovbrand, E. (Eds.) The promise of new modes of environmental governance. In *Environmental Politics and Deliberative Democracy*; Edward Elgar Publishing: Northampton, MA, USA, 2010; 239p., ISBN 978-1-84844-954-1.

5. Driessen, P.P.; Dieperink, C.; van Laerhoven, F.; Runhaar, H.A.; Vermeulen, W.J. Towards a conceptual framework for the study of shifts in modes of environmental governance–experiences from the Netherlands. *Environ. Policy Gov.* **2012**, *22*, 143–160. [CrossRef]

6. Rhodes, R.A. *Understanding Governance: Policy Networks, Governance, Reflexivity and Accountability*, 1st ed.; Open University Press: Buckingham, UK, 1997; 23p., ISBN 0-335-19727-2.

7. Ansell, C.; Gash, A. Collaborative governance in theory and practice. *J. Public Adm. Res. Theory* **2008**, *18*, 543–571. [CrossRef]

8. Bjärstig, T.; Sandström, C. Public-private partnerships in a Swedish rural context. *J. Rural Stud.* **2017**, *49*, 58–68. [CrossRef]

9. Widman, U.; Bjärstig, T. Protecting Forests' Social Values through Partnerships. *Scand. J. For. Res.* **2017**, *32*, 645–656. [CrossRef]

10. Mancheva, I. Which factors spur forest owners' collaboration over forest waters? *For. Policy Econ.* **2018**, *91*, 54–63. [CrossRef]

11. Benson, D.; Jordan, A.; Cook, H.; Smith, L. Collaborative environmental governance: are watershed partnerships swimming or sinking? *Land Use Policy* **2013**, *30*, 748–757. [CrossRef]

12. Long, F.J.; Arnold, M.B. *The Power of Environmental Partnerships*; Harcourt College Pub.: Fort Worth, TX, USA, 1995; 338p., ISBN 0-03011327-X.

13. Van Huijstee, M.M.; Francken, M.; Leroy, P. Partnerships for sustainable development: A review of current literature. *Environ. Sci.* **2007**, *4*, 75–89. [CrossRef]

14. Bovaird, T. Public-private partnerships: From contested concepts to prevalent practice. *Int. Rev. Adm. Sci.* **2004**, *70*, 199–215. [CrossRef]

15. Widman, U. Protecting Forests through Partnerships. Ph.D. Thesis, Department of Political Science, Umeå University, Umeå, Sweden, 2016.

16. Gunderson, L.H.; Holling, C.S. *Panarchy: Understanding Transformations in Systems of Humans and Nature*; Island Press: London, UK, 2002; 507p., ISBN 1-55963-856-7.

17. Galaz, V.; Olsson, P.; Hahn, T.; Folke, C.; Svedin, U. The problem of fit among biophysical systems, environmental and resource regimes, and broader governance systems: Insights and emerging challenges. In *Institutions and Environmental Change: Principal Findings, Applications, and Research Frontiers*, 1st ed.; Young, O.R., King, L.A., Schroeder, H., Eds.; The MIT Press: Cambridge, MA, USA, 2008; pp. 147–182, ISBN 978-0-262-74033-3.

18. Dressel, S.; Ericsson, G.; Sandström, C. Mapping social-ecological systems to understand the challenges underlying wildlife management. *Environ. Sci. Policy* **2018**, *84*, 105–112. [CrossRef]

19. Hodge, G.A.; Greve, C. Public-Private Partnerships: An International Performance Review. *Public Adm. Rev.* **2007**, *67*, 545–558. [CrossRef]

20. Khanom, N.A. Conceptual Issues in Defining Public Private Partnerships (PPPs). *Int. Rev. Bus. Res. Pap.* **2010**, *6*, 150–163.

21. Bjärstig, T. Does collaboration lead to increased sustainability? A study of public-private partnerships in the Swedish mountains. *Sustainability* **2017**, *9*, 1685. [CrossRef]

22. Zachrisson, A.; Bjärstig, T.; Eckerberg, K. When public officers take the lead in collaborative governance: To confirm, consult, facilitate, or negotiate? *Scand. J. Public Adm.* **2018**, accepted.

23. Hemmati, M. *Multi-Stakeholder Processes for Governance and Sustainability: Beyond Deadlock and Conflict*; Earthscan: London, UK, 2002; 312p., ISBN 1-85383-869-1.

24. Andonova, L. Public-private partnerships for the earth: Politics and patterns of hybrid authority in the multilateral system. *Glob. Environ. Politics* **2010**, *10*, 25–53. [CrossRef]

25. Glasbergen, P. Understanding partnerships for sustainable development analytically: The ladder of partnership activity as a methodological tool. *Environ. Policy Gov.* **2011**, *21*, 1–13. [CrossRef]

26. Peters, B.G. With a little help from our friends: Public-private partnerships as institutions and instruments. In *Partnership in Urban Governance. European and American Experiences*; Pierre, J., Ed.; Palgrave Macmillan: London, UK, 1998; pp. 11–33, ISBN 978-1-349-14410-5.

27. Glasbergen, P.; Biermann, F.; Mol, A.P. (Eds.) *Partnerships, Governance and Sustainable Development: Reflections on Theory and Practice*; Edward Elgar Publishing: Cheltenham, UK, 2007; 328p., ISBN 978-1-84720-405-9.

28. Kwak, Y.H.; Chih, Y.; Ibbs, C.W. Towards a comprehensive understanding of public private partnerships for infrastructure development. *Calif. Manag. Rev.* **2009**, *51*, 51–78. [CrossRef]

29. Emerson, K.; Nabatchi, T.; Balogh, S. An integrative Framework for Collaborative Governance. *J. Public Adm. Res. Theory* **2012**, *22*, 1–29. [CrossRef]

30. Djupdykning i Statistik om Sveriges Kommuner [Deep Diving in Statistics about Sweden's Municipalities]. Available online: http://www.scb.se/hitta-statistik/sverige-i-siffror/djupdykning-i-kommunstatistik/ (accessed on 11 September 2018).

31. Hedenås, H.; Christensen, P.; Svensson, J. Changes in vegetation cover and composition in the Swedish mountain region. *Environ. Monit. Assess.* **2016**, *188*, 452. [CrossRef] [PubMed]

32. GSD-Vägkartan, Vector. Available online: https://www.lantmateriet.se/sv/Kartor-och-geografisk-information/Kartor/Vagkartan/GSD-Vagkartan-vektor/ (accessed on 11 September 2018).

33. Skyddad Natur. Available online: http://www.scb.se/hitta-statistik/statistik-efter-amne/miljo/markanvandning/skyddad-natur/ (accessed on 11 September 2018).

34. Bjärstig, T.; Nygaard, V.; Riseth, J.Å.; Sandström, C. The institutionalisation of Sami interest in municipal comprehensive planning—A comparison between Norway and Sweden. *J. Environ. Policy Plan.* **2018**, submitted.

35. Bjärstig, T.; Thellbro, C.; Stjernström, O.; Svensson, J.; Sandström, C.; Sandström, P.; Zachrisson, A. Between protocol and reality—Swedish municipal comprehensive planning. *Eur. Plan. Stud.* **2018**, *26*, 35–54. [CrossRef]

36. Thellbro, C. Local Planning for Sustainable Rural Boreal Landscapes.–Prerequisites and Opportunities in the Encounter between Theory and Practice. Ph.D. Thesis, Swedish University of Agricultural Science, Umeå, Sweden, 2017.

37. Syssner, J.; Olausson, A. *Översiktsplanering i Kommuner som Krymper*; Statsvetenskaplig tidskrift 2016/2, årgång 118, 221–245; Statsvetenskapliga Förbundet: Lund, Sweden, 2016; pp. 221–245.

38. Eckerberg, K.; Bjärstig, T.; Zachrisson, A. Incentives for Collaborative Governance: Top-Down and Bottom-Up Initiatives in the Swedish Mountain Region. *Mt. Res. Dev.* **2015**, *35*, 289–298. [CrossRef]

39. Kvale, S. *Doing Interviews*; Sage: London, UK, 2008; 161p., ISBN 978-0-7619-4977-0.

40. Baxter, J.; Eyles, J. Evaluating qualitative research in social geography: Establishing 'rigour' in interview analysis. *Trans. Inst. Br. Geogr.* **1997**, *22*, 505–525. [CrossRef]

41. Eckerberg, K.; Bjärstig, T.; Miljand, M.; Mancheva, I. *Tio års Erfarenheter med Lokala Naturvårdssatsningen. En Utvärdering om Långsiktigt Intresse, Deltagande och Lärande i Kommunernas Arbete med Naturvård och Friluftsliv*; Rapport 6748; Naturvårdsverket: Stockholm, Sweden, 2017; 86p., ISBN 978-91-620-6748-9. Available online: http://www.naturvardsverket.se/Documents/publikationer6400/978-91-620-6748-9.pdf?pid=20245 (accessed on 7 August 2018).

42. Eckerberg, K. Sweden: Problems and Prospects at the leading edge of LA21 implementation. In *Sustainable Communities in Europe*; Lafferty, W.M., Ed.; Earthscan: London, UK, 2014; pp. 15–39, ISBN 1-85383-791-1.

43. Smith, E.M.; Thomasson, A. The Use of the Partnering Concept for Public–Private Collaboration: How Well Does it Really Work? *Public Organ. Rev.* **2018**, *18*, 191–206. [CrossRef]

44. Kadefors, A. Trust in project relationships—Inside the black box. *Int. J. Proj. Manag.* **2004**, *22*, 175–182. [CrossRef]

45. Hossu, C.A.; Ioja, I.C.; Susskind, L.E.; Badiu, D.L.; Hersperger, A.M. Factors driving collaboration in natural resource conflict management: Evidence from Romania. *Ambio* **2018**, 1–15. [CrossRef] [PubMed]

Article

Influence of Relational Norms on User Interests in PPP Projects: Mediating Effect of Project Performance

Xiaodan Zheng [1], Jingfeng Yuan [2,*] , Jiyue Guo [2], Mirosław J. Skibniewski [3,4,5] and Sujun Zhao [6]

[1] College of Management and Economics, Tianjin University, Tianjin 300072, China; zhengxiaodan@tju.edu.cn
[2] Department of Construction and Real Estate, School of Civil Engineering, Southeast University, Nanjing 210096, China; 220161160@seu.edu.cn
[3] Department of Civil and Environmental Engineering, University of Maryland, College Park, MD 20742, USA; mirek@umd.edu
[4] Institute for Theoretical and Applied Informatics, Polish Academy of Sciences, 44100 Gliwice, Poland
[5] Department of Civil Engineering, Chaoyang University of Technology, Taichung 41349, Taiwan
[6] Institute of Finance and Economics, Shanghai University of Finance and Economics, Shanghai 200433, China; Sujun332@163.com
* Correspondence: 101011337@seu.edu.cn; Tel./Fax: +86-25-8379-3251

Received: 17 May 2018; Accepted: 14 June 2018; Published: 15 June 2018

Abstract: Protecting user interests is one of the most important public sector responsibilities in PPP (public-private partnership) projects. However, user interests could be damaged by poor project performance. Therefore, this study focuses on the protection of user interests in PPP projects and analyzes the relationships among relational norms, project performance, and user interests in PPP projects. A questionnaire survey is conducted to collect the opinions of professionals from the public sector and private sector. Upon analyzing 109 valid questionnaires, the results demonstrate that the relational norms between the public sector and private sector have a positive effect on project performance, and project performance has a positive relationship on user interests. Moreover, project performance has a positive mediating effect on the relationships between relational norms and user interests. This finding can provide a theoretical foundation and suggest practical measures to help the public sector better protect user interests in PPP projects.

Keywords: user interests; relational norms; project performance; public-private partnership; PPP projects

1. Introduction

To meet the needs of citizens for public facilities and to relieve governments' financial pressure in developing public facilities to improve public services, governments introduce private sector companies into public projects by adopting a PPP (public-private partnership) [1].

However, many PPP projects have lower performance than traditional public procurement [2,3], which could result in higher charges or lower quality for users who use public facilities or public services provided by PPP projects [4]. This absolutely damages user interests, and users therefore lose confidence in PPP projects and the government. Moreover, user interests are critical elements of public interests in PPPs and should be properly addressed in PPP agreements [5]. If they are not, strong public resistance could occur due to serious concerns about the protection of public interests, as presented by the U.S. Government Accountability Office [6].

The needs of users should be first met when governments use PPPs to develop public facilities and provide public services [7]. Therefore, safeguards of user interests are an important responsibility of the government and one of the most important objectives in PPP projects [8–10]. It is essential for the government to understand how to protect user interests in PPP projects. However, prior studies have not focused on user interest protection. Prior studies have usually classified user interests as a part of the interests of the public sector. Thus, they have focused on how to protect the interests of the public sector without discussing user interest protection separately [11]. However, user interests are not identical with the interests of the public sector and, therefore, should not be replaced by them [12]. In PPP projects, the public sector, private sector, and users are three parties [12]. Thus, this study focuses on how to protect the interests of users in PPP projects.

User interests can be influenced directly by project performance because it influences the facility and service delivery and users directly use the facilities and services provided by PPP projects [10,13]. The public sector and private sector are contracting with concession contractors and executors to implement PPP projects together. According to the theory of relationship governance, project performance can be influenced significantly by relational norms between the public sector and private sector [14]. Therefore, to study how to protect user interests in PPP projects, this study discusses the effects of relational norms and project performance on user interests in PPP projects. The findings in this study can provide useful information to help governments effectively protect user interests in PPP projects.

The paper begins with a literature review in related fields followed by a series of hypotheses. Then, the research approaches used in the study are presented. By using a questionnaire survey, the proposed hypotheses are tested. Finally, the study finishes with a discussion and a conclusion.

2. Theory Background and Hypotheses

2.1. User Interests in Public-Private Partnerships (PPPs)

User interests in PPP projects include: (1) users can obtain information about PPP projects and can participate in project decisions and supervise project implementation; (2) users can access public facilities and services at reasonable prices; and (3) users can access high-quality public facilities and services [15]. The user interests in this study are different from the 'public interests' that are defined in public interest theory or in welfare economics [16]. In public interest theory or welfare economics, the public interests are societal interests. Public interests are described as the best possible allocation of scarce resources for individual and collective goods and services in society [17]. However, in this study, user interests are only the interests of end users who use the public facilities or public services provided by PPP projects; they do not include the interests of the public sector or private sector.

Meeting the needs of users is the ultimate motivation of governments in initiating PPP projects [7]. Therefore, protecting user interests is one of a government's most important responsibilities in PPP projects. The safeguards of user interests are also critical success factors in PPP projects [18,19].

In practice, there are many problems associated with low performance in PPP projects, including cost overruns, time delays, quality defects and safety hazards, all of which could lead to more money being paid by the users to use the public facilities or public services provided by PPP projects [4]. In other words, user interests can be damaged by poor performance in PPP projects. Prior studies have identified many key risks in PPP projects and have discussed how to allocate these risks between the public sector and private sector [20–22]. However, in PPP projects the ultimate objective of the private sector is to earn profits [23,24]. Once poor performance occurs and reduces the value to the private sector, the private sector can shift their losses to the users by increasing charges or lowering the quality of the public facilities and services [8]. Hence, in PPP projects, to protect user interests, poor performance must be avoided as far as possible.

2.2. Role of Project Performance on User Interests in PPPs

In a construction project, the most commonly used project performance indicators are the quality (i.e., construction quality), cost (i.e., construction cost), and time (i.e., completion time) [25,26]. For PPP projects, the project period usually includes the construction stage and operation stage [27]. Hence, it is necessary to expand the connotations of the three performance indicators (i.e., quality, cost, and time) from the construction stage to the operation stage in PPP projects. According to Yuan et al. [10], the quality of PPP projects refers to the quality of the public facilities and services provided; the cost of PPP projects refers to the life cycle cost, and the time of PPP projects refers to the construction completion time as well as the maintenance and repair time.

- If PPP projects can provide quality public facilities and services, users can continuously enjoy quality public facilities and services [10]. Ho and Tsui [9] demonstrate that PPP projects are usually public service/facility oriented and have significant influences on user interests. Moreover, users' health and safety and the social environment would be improved by high-quality public facilities and services [20,28]. Therefore, good quality can effectively safeguard user interests in PPP projects.

- If PPP projects can optimize the life-cycle cost, the private sector can reduce their costs and increase profits [20]. If the private sector can obtain reasonable profits from PPP projects, they would not need to decrease the quality or increase the price of public facilities and services to earn profits [23]. Sharma et al. [5] indicate that low private capital due to the uncertainties of traffic on toll roads could reduce the attractiveness of their PPPs. Thus, user interests can obtain protection through achieving a good quality and price for the public facilities and services provided by PPPs.

- If the construction of PPP projects is delayed, the time when users can access public facilities and services is also delayed [29]. The delay of PPP projects can also lead to private sector cost overruns and profit shrinkage [30]. In this case, the private sector may improve its profits through lowering the quality or increasing the price of public facilities and services so that users ultimately shoulder the delay risks and cost failures [8]. Thus, user interests are damaged. In addition, PPP projects have long concession periods. PPP projects need to be maintained and repaired during the concession periods. If PPP projects can be maintained and repaired on time, they can continue to provide quality public facilities and services to users during the long concession periods [31]. Thus, user interests are protected.

PPP project objectives can be achieved effectively if the projects have good performance in quality, cost, and time [32]; otherwise, the projects may fail [33]. If PPP projects fail, it can cause huge losses and severe harm to users [34]. Therefore, in PPP projects, good project performance can have a positive effect on user interests.

Although prior studies did not find direct relationships between project performance and user interests, their findings indicated indirect relationships. Liu et al. [35] evaluated performance improvements to realize the predetermined outcomes and benefits of PPPs, including user interests. Liu et al. [36] further indicated that stakeholder satisfaction is the most important indicator to measure the performance of PPP projects, within which more attention should be paid to user interests. Usually, the achievement of synergistic gains and positive spillover effects are expected when adopting PPPs, which greatly benefit users because the satisfactory performance of a PPP project would be costless [37].

2.3. Role of Relational Norms on Project Performance in PPPs

Relational norms refer to "behavioral expectations that are partially shared by a group of decision makers and directed toward collective or group goals" [38]. Relational norms include flexibility, information exchange, and solidarity [39–41]. Flexibility is the notion that two parties are willing to make adaptations because of circumstances changing. Information exchange is the idea that two parties are willing to share useful information with each other. Solidarity refers to the idea that two parties are willing to maintain a bilateral relationship [41].

The period of PPP projects is usually more than 10 years [27]. In the long term, various changes in circumstances may happen, such as price changes, inflation, interest rate fluctuations, and changes in market demand [42]. If these changes occur, the public sector and private sector need to adjust to them [43]. In fact, changes are inevitable. However, the initial VfM objectives for a PPP project should still be developed through project governance and control-related matters during the processes of ongoing management [44]. Hence, the fundamental principle is that a PPP project should have the necessary flexibility to adapt to future changes [45]. Moreover, the required flexibility can ensure appropriate service outcomes of PPP projects would be achieved over the full concession period [46]. Flexibility in relational norms enables the public sector and private sector to adjust to changing environmental conditions so that the project performance is not influenced negatively by these changes [40].

PPP projects require the public sector and private sector to have long-term cooperation [47]. If the public sector and private sector can proactively exchange information, it is beneficial to their understanding and communication with each other to reduce mutual suspicion [48]. Furthermore, it is beneficial to building and maintaining friendly and trustful relationships between the public sector and private sector [49]. Friendly and trustful cooperation can also promote the improvement of project performance [50]. PPP projects are complex [51]. During the project process, the public and private sectors may have divergences. Information sharing between the public and private sectors can help to diminish divergences and reduce conflicts [52]. Even though conflicts happen because of disagreement, information sharing and effective communication can promote conflict resolution in a quick way and reduce the negative effects of conflict on project performance [53]. Information exchange in the relational norms can also help the public and private sectors generate more innovative ideas to improve the performance of PPP projects [1,54].

Solidarity in the relational norms enables the public and private sectors to treasure the bilateral relationship and common interests rather than focusing on the maximization of self-interest [55]. Therefore, the private sector can regard its cooperation in PPPs as contributions to social stability and solidarity [56]. Solidarity reflects the synergistic effects of the public and private sectors [57]. In a PPP project, partners have extremely collaborative relationships as they share long-term and short-term goals and plans [58]. Rwelamila et al. [59] indicate that project failure in a traditional project can be related to a lack of solidarity between project stakeholders because of an inappropriate organizational structure, which could negatively affect project performance [60]. Thus, if PPP projects have problems, solidarity enables the public and private sectors to solve them from a perspective of common interest maximization in order to protect performance [40].

To sum up, relational norms include flexibility, information exchange, and solidarity. In PPP projects, flexibility, information exchange, and solidarity between the public and private sectors are all helpful in safeguarding and improving project performance. Thus, in PPP projects, the relational norms between the public and private sectors can have a positive effect on project performance.

2.4. Role of Relational Norms on User Interests in PPPs

According to the analysis of the preceding context, when the public and private sectors have good relational norms, PPP projects can be operated smoothly. This is because the public and private sectors can flexibly adjust to changing environmental conditions, can share information to reduce mutual suspicion and conflicts, and can make decisions based on project interests rather than self-interest [40,48,52,55]. If PPP projects are operated smoothly, it is easy to improve project performance [61,62]. Good project performance is beneficial to providing public facilities and services to users at a good quality and price. Thus, user interests can be protected.

In contrast, if the public and private sectors do not have good relational norms, it may be difficult to adjust to changing environmental conditions [40]. Moreover, the public and private sectors may be suspicious of each other and make decisions based on self-interest and, thus, have frequent conflicts [48,52,55]. As a consequence, imperfect relational norms between the public and private sectors would result in poor project performance [61,62]. If PPP projects have poor performance, they cannot provide public facilities and services to users at a good quality and reasonable price [34]. Thus, user interests are hurt.

Therefore, good relational norms can have an indirect positive effect on user interests through improving project performance.

2.5. Knowledge Gap

According to the literature review, in PPP projects, poor project performance, like cost overruns and time delays, is an important reason for user interests being impaired. Thus, it is possible for project performance to influence user interests in PPP projects directly. However, few studies have discussed the direct relationship between project performance and user interests in PPP projects. In addition, many studies have found that relational norms are beneficial to improving project performance. Thus, relational norms are likely to influence user interests in PPP projects indirectly through project performance. However, because few studies have explored the direct relationship between project performance and user interests in PPP projects, fewer studies have attempted to explore the indirect relationship between relational norms and user interests.

To fill this research gap, this study first verifies the effect of relational norms between the public and private sectors on project performance in PPP projects. It then probes the effect of project performance on user interests in PPP projects. Finally, it tries to connect relational norms with user interests to discuss the mediating effect of project performance in PPP projects.

2.6. Research Model and Hypotheses

According to the above analysis, Hypothesis 1, Hypothesis 2, and Hypothesis 3 can be proposed to verify the relationship among relational norms, user interests, and project performance in PPPs. Figure 1 shows the theoretical model in this study.

Hypothesis 1(H1). *In PPP projects, the relational norms between the public and private sectors have a positive relationship with project performance.*

Hypothesis 2(H2). *In PPP projects, project performance and user interests have a positive relationship.*

Hypothesis 3(H3). *In PPP projects, project performance has a positive mediating effect on the relationship between the relational norms and user interests.*

For H1, many prior studies in the field of business have found that good relational norms have positive effects on performance [40,61,62]. As a result, this study tests H1 to verify the effect of relational norms between the public and private sectors on project performance in PPP projects. For H2, prior studies only indirectly indicate that project performance can influence user interests [35,36], but do not directly investigate the relationships between project performance and user interests. Consequently, this study tests H2 to probe the effect of project performance on user interests in PPP projects. For H3, few studies have attempted to explore the relationship among relational norms, project performance, and user interests. Thus, this study tests H3 to innovatively explore the mediating effect of project performance on the relationship between relational norms and user interests in PPP projects.

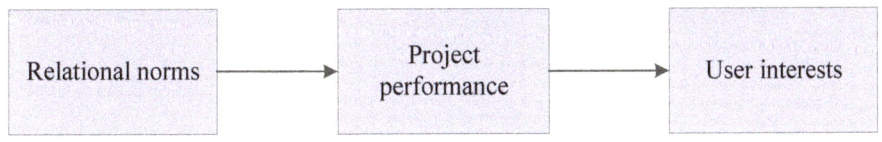

Figure 1. Proposed theoretical model.

3. Research Design

A questionnaire survey method was adopted to test the hypotheses proposed in this study. The questionnaire was designed based on the existing literature. The questionnaire included two parts. The first part was about respondents' experiences in PPP projects. The second part was the measurements of three variables including relational norms, project performance, and user interests. A questionnaire was shown in Appendix A.

Questionnaires were distributed using a stratified random sampling method. The target respondents were experts or professionals from the public and private sectors, because the questions in the questionnaire involved the relationships between the public and private sectors, so professionals from the two sectors were needed. User interests also need the input of the public and private sectors for them to be protected [5]. One author held a PPP conference in which many professionals from public sectors or private sectors participated. These professionals were invited to fill out the questionnaire. In addition, the author was invited to participate in some PPP workshops held by public sectors or private sectors. Many professionals from public sectors or private sectors also participated in these workshops, and these professionals were also invited to fill out the questionnaire.

Respondents were asked to fill out the questionnaire according to their general knowledge and work experience. In addition, the public and private sectors may have a bias in filling out the questionnaires because they prefer to believe that they provide good public facilities and services to users. To avoid this bias, all respondents were asked to complete the questionnaires from an open-minded perspective. The respondents were informed that their responses were only used for academic research rather than a project assessment. The information they provided was confidential.

The three variables (i.e., relational norms, project performance, and user interests) were latent variables and were measured by observed variables (i.e., measurement items). After data collection, an exploratory factor analysis was firstly used to select the most significant measurement items for each latent variable. The relationships between the latent variables and selected measurement items are referred to as the measurement model. The validity and reliability of the measurement model needed to be verified by survey data. A confirmatory factor analysis can verify whether the survey data supports the measurement model [63]. Additionally, a multiple regression analysis was used to test whether the three hypothetical relationships were supported based on the survey data. A regression analysis used a linear relation to provide explanations and predictions. A multiple regression analysis was used to consider more than one independent variable simultaneously in explaining and predicting a single dependent variable [63]. Finally, the results were discussed to provide theoretical contributions and practical implications.

4. Measurement Methods

Multiple variables in this study were identified from the existing literature to measure the relational norms, user interests, and project performance in PPPs as well as their relationships. Appropriate modifications were made to suit the research context. All the measurements were based on a five-point Likert scale, from 1 (strongly disagree) to 5 (strongly agree). Table 1 shows all the measurements of the relational norms, user interests, and project performance.

Table 1. The measurements of variables.

Variables		Measurements
Relational norms (RN)	RN1	Two sectors were willing to make adjustments in the ongoing relationship to cope with changing circumstances.
	RN2	Two sectors would cooperatively work out a new deal when some unexpected situation arose.
	RN3	Exchange of information in the relationship took place frequently and informally, and not only according to a pre-specified agreement.
	RN4	Two sectors kept each other informed about events or changes that might affect the other party in a timely fashion.
	RN5	Two sectors could provide any information if it could help the other party. Three measuring items were used to measure solidarity.
	RN6	Problems that arose in the course of this relationship were treated by two sectors as joint rather than individual responsibilities.
	RN7	Two sectors were committed to improvements that might benefit the relationship as a whole, and not only the individual.
	RN8	Two sectors in this relationship did not mind owing each other favors.

Table 1. *Cont.*

Variables		Measurements
Project performance (PP)	PP1	The project quality is within the quality scope specified in the contract.
	PP2	The life-cycle cost of PPP projects was within budget.
	PP3	PPP projects could complete construction on time or earlier, and could receive maintenance and repairs on time.
User interests (UI)	UI1	The information about PPP projects was available to the users and the users could participate in project decisions and supervise project implementation.
	UI2	PPP projects provided sufficient safeguards for users to ensure all users (including disadvantaged groups) can effectively access the public facilities and services at a reasonable price.
	UI3	PPP projects could ensure continuous supply of healthy, safe and convenient facilities and services to users.

4.1. Relation Norms

The independent variable for relational norms can be identified from the perspectives of flexibility, information exchange, and solidarity between the public and private sectors. The measurement of relational norms was based on Griffith and Myers [40] and Goo et al. [41], with appropriate wording modifications to fit the PPP environment. For flexibility, it can be measured by two items. The first item was that both public and private sectors would be willing to make adjustments in their ongoing relationship to cope with changing circumstances [40,41]. Another item was both public and private sectors would cooperatively work out a new deal when some unexpected situation arose [40]. Information exchange can be measured by three items. The first item is that the exchange of information in the relationship took place frequently and informally, which would obey a pre-specified agreement [40]. Then, both the public and private sectors kept each other informed about events or changes that might affect the other party in a timely way [40,41]. In addition, both the public and private sectors could provide any information that would help the other party [40]. Solidarity can be measured by three items. The first item was that the problems in the course of the relationship between the public and private sectors items could be treated by two sectors jointly rather than as individual responsibilities [40]. The second item was that the public and private sectors were committed to improvements that might benefit the relationship as a whole, and not only the individual [40,41]. The third item was that the public and private sectors in their relationships did not mind owing each other favors [40].

4.2. Project Performance

The mediating variable for project performance can be identified from the perspectives of time, cost and quality (TCQ). The iron triangle of TCQ is always employed to evaluate construction project performance [64,65]. However, Liu et al. [66] indicate that there is a widespread consensus among the interviewees that the conventional TCQ approach is simplistic and thus unable to capture the critical success factors and uncertainties of PPPs. Therefore, the items should not only focus on TCQ but also reflect the key features of PPP projects, including long-term operation and the delivery of public services. For example, Yuan et al. [67] identified 46 KPIs (Key Performance Indicators) of PPP projects, demonstrating that cost and time management during the construction and operation periods as well as high quality control are Top 10 important KPIs. Therefore, in this study, the performance of PPP projects can be measured by a three-item scale with appropriate modification of the scale of Yuan et al. [10]. The quality of PPP projects should be within the quality scope specified in the contract. The life-cycle cost (LCC) of PPP projects should be within budget. Moreover, PPP projects could complete their construction on time or earlier and could obtain maintenance and repairs on time [10].

4.3. User Interests

The dependent variables for user interests can be identified from the perspectives of information exposure, availability of public services, and the quality of public services. Based on the Partnerships Victoria Guidance Material [15], three measuring items were used to measure user interests in PPP projects, with appropriate wording modifications to fit the research context. First, the information about PPP projects should be available to users and users could participate in project decisions and supervise project implementation [15]. Ng et al. [12] and Anderson [68] found that information exposure is an important way for users to protect their own interests. PPP projects should also provide sufficient safeguards for consumers to ensure that all users (including disadvantaged groups) can effectively access the public facilities and services at a reasonable price [15]. Moreover, PPP projects should ensure a continuous supply of healthy, safe and convenient facilities and services to users [15]. The price and quality of public facilities and services have a direct impact on user interests in PPPs. The main reason why users perceive that their interests are damaged in PPPs is because they have to pay more money to use public facilities and services or they use a lower quality of public facilities and services provided by PPP projects than those public facilities and services provided by governments [4].

5. Research Survey and Results

The whole survey lasted 3 months. Approximately 500 questionnaires were distributed and 143 questionnaires were collected, with a response rate of 28.6%. After deleting records with missing data, 109 valid records were selected as the sample, with a valid response rate of 21.8%. This response rate is acceptable for social science research [69].

The respondents were Chinese project professionals from the public sector (58.41%) and private sector (41.59%). All respondents had experience in PPP projects. The PPP projects that respondents participated in included rail transportation projects, municipal road projects, underground pipeline projects, sewerage projects, hydraulic engineering projects, and refuse disposal projects; 75.25% of respondents had 1–5 years' work experience in PPP projects, 18.81% of respondents had 6–10 years' work experience in PPP projects, and 3.96% had above 10 years' work experience in PPP projects.

5.1. Exploratory Factor Analysis

The eight measurement items of relational norms (i.e., RN1–RN8) were analyzed using the exploratory factor analysis. The Kaiser–Meyer–Olkin (KMO) value was 0.889, above the 0.6 benchmark [70]. Thus, the eight measurement items were suitable for the exploratory factor analysis. In Table 2, the measure of sampling adequacy (MSA) value of each item was above the 0.5 benchmark. Thus, each item of relational norms should be used in the exploratory factor analysis [70]. Only one factor arose from the exploratory factor analysis, according to the method of the Eigen-value above 1. This factor included all the eight measurement items from RN1 to RN8. This factor can explain 58.165% variation. Therefore, this factor was relational norms.

Table 2. Results of the exploratory factor analysis for relational norms.

Items	Factor Loading	Measure of Sampling Adequacy (MSA)	Factor Title
RN4	0.803	0.859	
RN7	0.802	0.871	
RN1	0.790	0.905	
RN8	0.773	0.875	
RN3	0.772	0.918	Relational norms
RN6	0.732	0.921	
RN5	0.727	0.898	
RN2	0.695	0.871	
Explained variation (%)	58.165%		

The three measurement items of project performance (i.e., PP1-PP3) were analyzed using the exploratory factor analysis. The KMO value was 0.665, above the 0.6 benchmark [70]. Thus, the three measurement items were suitable for the exploratory factor analysis. In Table 3, the MSA value of each item was above the 0.5 benchmark. Thus, each item of project performance should be used in the exploratory factor analysis [70]. Only one factor arose from the exploratory factor analysis, according to the method of the Eigen-value above 1. This factor included all the three measurement items from PP1 to PP3. This factor can explain 58.110% variation. Therefore, this factor was project performance.

Table 3. Results of the exploratory factor analysis for project performance.

Items	Factor Loading	MSA	Factor Title
PP2	0.922	0.617	
PP3	0.675	0.696	Project performance
PP1	0.661	0.706	
Explained variation (%)	58.110%		

The three measurement items of user interests (i.e., UI1-UI3) were analyzed using the exploratory factor analysis. The KMO value was 0.710, above the 0.6 benchmark [70]. Thus, the three measurement items were suitable for the exploratory factor analysis. In Table 4, the MSA value of each item was above the 0.5 benchmark. Thus, each item of user interests should be used in the exploratory factor analysis [70]. Only one factor arose from the exploratory factor analysis, according to the method of the Eigen-value above 1. This factor included all the three measurement items from UI1 to UI3. This factor can explain 57.969% variation. Therefore, this factor was user interests.

Table 4. Results of the exploratory factor analysis for user interests.

Items	Factor Loading	MSA	Factor Title
UI2	0.786	0.695	
UI1	0.783	0.696	User interests
UI3	0.713	0.743	
Explained variation (%)	57.969%		

5.2. Validity and Reliability of the Measurement Model

To ensure the effectiveness of the measurement model, the validity and reliability of the measurement model were tested. A confirmatory factor analysis (CFA) with a structural equation model (using AMOS 20.0 software) was employed to explore the validity and reliability of the measurement model [63,71]. The structural equation model is shown in Figure 2. Table 5 shows the results of the CFA. In Table 5, the Cronbach's alpha value of the three variables was more than the 0.7 benchmark, which indicates that the measurements have good consistency and reliability [63]. This study used three indices, which were the standard factor loading (SFL), construct reliability (CR), and average variance extracted (AVE), to assess the convergent validity [63]. In Table 5, all the SFL values were above the 0.5 benchmark. The AVE value for every variable was above the 0.5 cutoff. The CR value for each variable was above the 0.7 benchmark. The values of the three indices indicate the good convergent validity of the measurements. To test the discriminant validity, the square root of AVE was compared with the off-diagonal correlation coefficients. As shown in Table 6, the square root value of the AVE of each variable was higher than the off-diagonal correlation coefficients, which indicates adequate discriminant validity of the measurements [63].

The structural equation model in Figure 2 is also needed to satisfy the recommended goodness-of-fit (GOF) [72,73]. The results of the GOF measures are shown in Table 7. The ratio of χ^2/degrees of freedom (Df) was 1.92, which is located in the range from 1 to 2. The root mean square error of approximation (RMSEA) value was 0.09, below the threshold level of 0.1. Furthermore, the Tucker–Lewis index (TLI) and comparative fit index (CFI) were above 0.9, and the normal fit index (NFI) was close to 0.9, which indicate a good fit [73–75]. Thus, the recommended GOF levels were satisfied and acceptable.

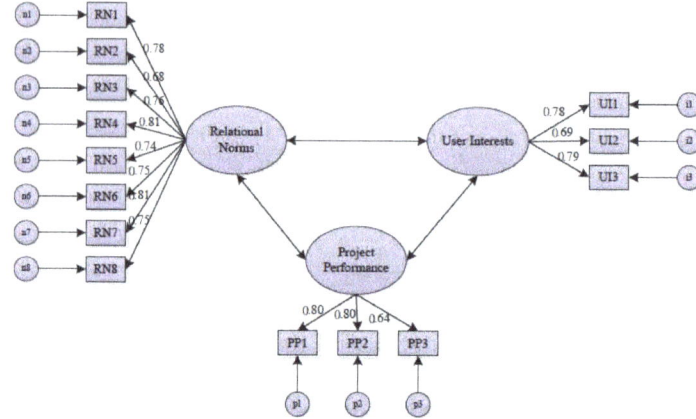

Figure 2. Structural equation model for confirmatory factor analysis (CFA).

Table 5. Results of validity and reliability of measurements.

Variables		Standard Factor Loading (SFL)
Relational norms (Cronbach's α = 0.92; CR = 0.92; average variance extracted (AVE) = 0.58)	RN1	0.78
	RN2	0.68
	RN3	0.76
	RN4	0.81
	RN5	0.74
	RN6	0.75
	RN7	0.81
	RN8	0.75
Project performance (Cronbach's α = 0.79; CR = 0.79; AVE = 0.56)	PP1	0.80
	PP2	0.80
	PP3	0.64
User interests (Cronbach's α = 0.80; CR = 0.80; AVE = 0.57)	UI1	0.78
	UI2	0.69
	UI3	0.79

Table 6. Pearson correlation matrix.

Variables	Relational Norms	Project Performance	User Interests
Relational norms	0.76	—	—
Project performance	0.72	0.75	—
User interests	0.72	0.72	0.75

Note: Bold numbers in diagonal row are square roots of AVE.

Table 7. Results of goodness-of-fit (GOF) measures.

Goodness-of-Fit Measure	Recommended Level of GOF Measure	SEM
χ^2/degree of freedom (Df)	Recommended level from 1 to 2	1.92
Root mean square error of approximation (RMSEA)	<0.05 indicates very good fit (Threshold level = 0.10)	0.09
Tucker-Lewis index (TLI)	0 (no fit) to 1 (perfect fit)	0.90
Comparative fit index (CFI)	0 (no fit) to 1 (perfect fit)	0.93
Normal fit index (NFI)	0 (no fit) to 1 (perfect fit)	0.86

5.3. Multiple Regression Analysis

Multiple regression analysis (using SPSS 18.0 software) was adopted to test the relationships among the relational norms, project performance, and user interests in PPP projects. Model 1 was tested to verify the effect of relational norms on project performance. Model 2 was tested to verify the effect of project performance on user interests. Model 3 was tested to verify the mediating effect of project performance on the relationship between relational norms and user interests. The results of the three models are shown in Table 8.

Table 8. Results of regression analysis.

Variables		Model 1	Model 2	Model 3
		Project Performance	User Interests	User Interests
Direct effects	Relational norms	0.72 ***	—	—
	Project performance	—	0.72 ***	—
Mediating effects	Relational norms	—	—	0.42 ***
	Project performance	—	—	0.42 ***
	F	114.02 ***	113.53 ***	79.30 ***
	R^2	0.52	0.52	0.60
	Adjusted R^2	0.51	0.51	0.59

Note: $N = 109$; *** $p < 0.001$.

Model 1 showed that relational norms had a significant positive impact on project performance ($\beta = 0.72$, $p < 0.001$). Consequently, Hypotheses 1 was supported, which indicates that the relational norms between the public and private sectors had a positive relationship with project performance in PPPs. This finding supported the previous studies that found that good relational norms could facilitate performance [58,76,77]. Model 2 showed that project performance had a significant positive relationship with user interests ($\beta = 0.72$, $p < 0.001$). This result supported Hypothesis 2 well, illustrating that project performance and user interests have a positive relationship in PPPs. This finding shows that project performance was an important factor influencing user interests in PPP projects. Model 3 showed that project performance had a mediating effect on the relationship between relational norms and user interests ($\beta = 0.42$, $p < 0.001$). Therefore, Hypothesis 3 was supported, indicating that project performance is a mediating bridge to link relational norms and user interests in PPPs. This finding reveals the mechanism of relational norms affecting user interests in PPP projects. In other words, relational norms between the public and private sectors can indirectly influence user interests. It also illustrates that achieving user interest protection in PPPs needs both the public and private sectors, rather than only the public sector, which provides a new perspective to study user interest protection in PPPs.

In addition, although the R^2 of multiple regression analysis in this study was not high, the R^2 (around 0.5) was acceptable [78].

6. Discussion

6.1. Directly Protecting User Interests through Improving Project Performance

The research result demonstrates that project performance has a direct effect on user interests in PPP projects. The improvement of project performance (i.e., better quality, lower costs, and shorter time) can effectively facilitate user interests in PPP projects. This finding illustrates that the precondition of user interest protection is achieving success in PPP projects. If PPP projects have poor performance in quality, cost, and time, user interest protection cannot be achieved. This finding also supports Soomro and Zhang's [34] point that the failure of PPP projects can cause huge losses.

The findings of this study can provide guidance for governments to protect user interests in PPP projects. Governments can protect user interests by controlling project performance in PPP projects.

Specifically, it is difficult to quantify user interests using specific indicators in the concession contracts of PPP projects [79]. Actually, user interest protection may be a vague region in the concession contracts of PPP projects. Therefore, it is difficult for the public sector to use contracts to control the private sector to protect user interests during project execution because user interests should be an extensive concept [79]. However, the project performance of PPP projects can usually be quantified using specific indicators in detail [26,67]. The public sector can stipulate project performance in the concession contracts and use the contracts to control the private sector in implementing the project performance during project execution [13,80]. In this way, the public sector can improve project performance to achieve user interest protection in PPP projects.

6.2. Good Relational Norms Improve Project Performance

The positive effect on project performance in PPP projects by good relational norms between the public and private sectors has been verified. This finding is consistent with previous studies [40,61,62], which indicate that project performance can also be influenced by relational norms between the public and private sectors, although project performance is stipulated in the concession contracts and is controlled through the implementation of the concession contracts in PPP projects. Contracts are a formal governance mechanism, and relational norms are an informal governance mechanism [81–83]. The informal governance mechanism can effectively supplement and enhance the functions of the formal governance mechanism to safeguard and improve project performance [14,55,80]. This finding indicates that the public and private sectors should build good relational norms to improve project performance in PPPs.

6.3. Indirectly Protecting User Interests by Good Relational Norms

Our study also finds that project performance has a mediating effect on the relationship between relational norms and user interests in PPP projects. This finding also indicates that relational governance should be of concern besides project performance for user interest protection in PPP projects. Good relational norms between the public and private sectors can indirectly help protect user interests by improving project performance. This finding connects relational governance with user interest protection in PPP projects to provide a new perspective for studies about user interest protection in PPP projects. It also illustrates that achieving user interest protection in PPPs needs coordination between the public and private sectors, rather than only depending on the public sector.

The findings drawn from the study can also help facilitate the promotion of user interests in PPP projects. The public sector can protect user interests in PPP projects not only through using the concession contracts to control project performance but also through building friendly relationships with the private sector. Specifically, in the process of getting along with the private sector, the public sector can use good relational norms (i.e., flexibility, information exchange, and solidarity) to assist in the implementation of the concession contracts [65,84], ensuring the good performance of PPP projects and indirectly achieving the goal of user interest protection.

7. Case Study

This section introduces a case of the Hong Kong Western Harbor Tunnel PPP project to show the effect of relational norms on project performance and user interests in PPP projects.

In the late 1980s, the Hong Kong government forecasted that the number of cross-harbor trips would grow greatly. Specifically, the Hong Kong government forecasted that the number of daily cross-harbor person trips would increase by 86% from 1.4 to 2.6 million, and goods vehicle trips by 129% from 34,000 to 78,000 over the same period [85]. However, by the early 1980s, the two existing harbor tunnels were carrying far more vehicles per day than their design capacity. To relieve growing traffic congestion on the two existing harbor tunnels and to develop the transport infrastructure, the Hong Kong government decided to build the Hong Kong Western Harbor Tunnel (HKWHT).

The Hong Kong government also decided to use the PPP mode to introduce the private sector in order to build, operate, and maintain the HKWHT [86].

In the HKWHT PPP project, the public sector and the private sector had too many debates, from the signing stage, to the construction and operation stages. These debates resulted in the public sector and the private sector being unable to openly exchange views and solidly make decisions. As a result, the project planning was unsuccessful. The HKWHT was poorly integrated with the road infrastructure in HK to create inconvenience for the users. Moreover, the project costs experienced an overrun mainly because of the associated buildings and roads [86]. Because of the cost overrun, the private sector of the HKWHT PPP project priced the toll charge high in order to ensure their internal rate of return (IRR) was not below 15% [87]. Because the toll charge of the HKWHT was high and the HKWHT was inconvenient for connecting the road network in HK, the general public still preferred to use the other two tunnels despite severe congestion, rather than to use the HKWHT [88]. Thus, the actual traffic volumes in the HKWHT were significantly below estimates. Because the traffic volumes were low, the private sector of the HKWHT PPP project decided to increase the toll charge in order to ensure their profits. However, this decision only resulted in further reductions in the traffic volumes [87]. In fact, the HKWHT PPP project could not provide convenient and low-price traffic services for the users, and did not successfully reduce traffic congestion. User interests were seriously hurt in the HKWHT PPP project. Therefore, many citizens in Hong Kong were asking for early termination of the PPP contract and the early return of the tunnel [89].

The case of the HKWHT PPP project illustrated that in a PPP project, if the public sector and the private sector have too many debates without good relational norms, these two sectors cannot openly exchange views and solidly make decisions. It would easily result in poor performance and damage user interests in the PPP project.

8. Potential Applications for Public Administration

This study can provide some specific suggestions for public administration to help protect user interests in PPP projects.

- The public sector can set the project performance of PPP projects in the concession contracts in detail. For example, the public sector can determine the quality standards of the public facilities and services that are provided by the private sector and that can be measured by user satisfaction as an important standard. In this case, the public sector can closely connect user interests with project performance.

- Moreover, the public sector can determine not only the concession periods but also the construction periods in the concession contracts to ensure that the private sector can finish the construction and maintenance on time and provide public facilities and services as early as possible.

- Additionally, the public sector can increase informal contact with the private sector to promote good relational norms between them during the process of PPP projects. For example, the public sector can work on the same location as the private sector to increase opportunities for communication and mutual understanding while working. The public and private sectors can also work on the same working system to enhance information exchange and sharing. The same working location and working system can help the public and private sectors build flexible, solid, and shared relational norms.

- Furthermore, the public sector can increase opportunities for public participation and extend the interaction among users, the public sector and the private sector in PPP projects. For example, the public sector can hold public hearings at different stages of PPP projects so that users can directly contact the public and private sectors. The public and private sectors can also understand users' needs and satisfaction with the PPP projects. Additionally, the public and private sectors can establish websites for PPP projects and open up information on PPP projects online. In this way, users can understand the PPP projects better and can supervise them. In this case, building information model (BIM) technologies can be further adopted to help the public sector, private sector and users work together, share information and improve the performance of PPP projects [90].

9. Conclusions

The primary objective of this paper was to discuss user interest protection in PPP projects. Using a sample of 109 questionnaires from Chinese project professionals who had experience with PPP projects, this research examined the relationships among the relational norms between the public and private sectors, project performance, and user interests in PPP projects. The results showed that relational norms between the public and private sectors had a positive relationship with project performance, and project performance could facilitate the protection of user interests. This research also indicated that project performance had a positive mediating effect on the relationship between relational norms and user interests. This study provided a theoretical foundation to understand user interest protection from a relational norms perspective and to clarify project performance as a mediating path of relational norms affecting user interests. Moreover, this study provided two important measures to enhance the government's ability to protect user interests in PPP projects, including using the concession contracts to control project performance and building friendly relational norms with the private sector.

There are some limitations and future research topics in this study. All respondents in this study were from China. However, there are cultural differences among countries [91]. The functions of relational norms may be affected by cultural differences, so that the effects of relational norms on project performance and user interests may be different in different cultures [92]. Thus, future studies can collect data from several countries and compare the relationships among relational norms, project performance, and user interests among different countries to help achieve user interest protection in global PPP projects. Additionally, this study focused on the effects of relational norms on project performance and user interests in PPP projects. However, this study also noted that project performance was determined in the concession contracts and was controlled by using these contracts during the implementation stage. In addition, the relationships between the public and private sectors are formed based on the concession contracts. Thus, the concession contracts may influence project performance and user interests in PPP projects. However, this study does not discuss the effects of the contracts. Future studies may try to discuss user interest protection in PPP projects from a contractual governance perspective in order to offer useful suggestions to governments. Finally, this study discusses the mediating effect of project performance on the relationship between relational norms and user interests in PPP projects. However, there may be other mediating paths in the relationship between relational norms and user interests. Future studies can continue to explore and find more mediating variables to clarify the mechanism of relational norms affecting user interests, in order to facilitate the protection of user interests better in PPP projects.

Author Contributions: J.Y. conceived and designed the study; S.Z. collected the data; X.Z. and J.G. analyzed the data; M.J.S. did the English editing; X.Z. wrote the paper, J.Y. reviewed the paper.

Funding: The National Natural Science Foundation of China (NSFC-71472037, and 71671042); the Social Foundation of China (14AJY013); the Program for Outstanding Young Teachers of Southeast University (2242015R30009); the Fundamental Research Funds for the Central Universities.

Acknowledgments: The authors' special thanks go to all reviewers of the paper and to the National Natural Science Foundation of China (NSFC-71472037, and 71671042); the Social Foundation of China (14AJY013); the Program for Outstanding Young Teachers of Southeast University (2242015R30009); and the Fundamental Research Funds for the Central Universities for financially supporting this research.

Conflicts of Interest: The authors declare no conflict of interest.

Appendix A

Part 1 Personal experiences in PPP projects	
1	Your role in PPP projects: (1) the public sector, (2) the private sector
2	You participated in PPP projects, including: (1) rail transportation projects; (2) municipal road projects; (3) underground pipeline projects; (4) sewerage projects; (5) hydraulic engineering projects; (6) refuse disposal projects
3	Working experiences in PPP projects: (1) 1–5 years; (2) 6–10 years; (3) above 10 years

Part 2 Measurements
1 (strongly disagree), 2 (disagree), 3 (neutrality), 4 (agree), 5 (strongly agree)

Relational norms

1	Both sectors were willing to make adjustments in the ongoing relationship to cope with changing circumstances.	1	2	3	4	5
2	Both sectors would cooperatively work out a new deal when some unexpected situation arose.	1	2	3	4	5
3	Exchange of information in the relationship took place frequently and informally, and not only according to a pre-specified agreement.	1	2	3	4	5
4	Both sectors kept each other informed about events or changes that might affect the other party in a timely way.	1	2	3	4	5
5	Both sectors could provide any information if it could help the other party. Three measuring items were used to measure solidarity.	1	2	3	4	5
6	Problems that arose in the course of this relationship were treated by two sectors as joint rather than individual responsibilities.	1	2	3	4	5
7	Both sectors were committed to improvements that might benefit the relationship as a whole, and not only the individual.	1	2	3	4	5
8	Both sectors in this relationship did not mind owing each other favors.	1	2	3	4	5

Project performance

1	The project quality is within the quality scope specified in the contract.	1	2	3	4	5
2	The life-cycle cost of PPP projects was within budget.	1	2	3	4	5
3	The PPP project could complete construction on-time or earlier, and could receive maintenance and repairs on time.	1	2	3	4	5

User interests

1	The information about the PPP project was available to the users and the users could participate in project decision and supervise project implementation.	1	2	3	4	5
2	The PPP project provided sufficient safeguards for users to ensure all users (including disadvantaged groups) can effectively access the public facilities and services at a reasonable price.	1	2	3	4	5
3	The PPP project could ensure continuous supply of healthy, safe and convenient facilities and services to users.	1	2	3	4	5

References

1. Chan, A.P.; Lam, P.T.; Chan, D.W.; Cheung, E.; Ke, Y. Drivers for adopting public private partnerships—Empirical comparison between China and Hong Kong special administrative region. *J. Constr. Eng. Manag.* **2009**, *135*, 1115–1124. [CrossRef]
2. Shaoul, J. The Private Finance Initiative or the Public Funding of Private Profit? In *The Challenge of Public-Private Partnerships: Learning from International Experience*; Hodge, G., Greve, C., Eds.; Edward Elgar: Cheltenham, UK, 2005.
3. Blanc-Brude, F.; Goldsmith, H.; Valila, T. *Ex Ante Construction Costs in the European Road Sector: A Comparison of Public-Private Partnerships and Traditional Public Procurement*; Economic and Financial Report; European Investment Bank: Luxembourg, 2006.
4. Greve, C. When Public–Private Partnerships Fail: The Extreme Case of the NPM-inspired Local Government of Farum in Denmark. In Proceedings of the EGPA Conference, Oeiras, Portugal, 3–6 September 2003.
5. Sharma, D.; Cui, Q.; Chen, L.; Lindly, J. Balancing private and public interests in public-private partnership contracts through optimization of equity capital structure. *Transp. Res. Rec. J. Transp. Res. Board* **2010**, *2151*, 60–66. [CrossRef]
6. Gao, S.Y. *Highway Public-Private Partnerships: Securing Potential Benefits and Protecting the Public Interest Could Result from More Rigorous Up-Front Analysis*; U.S. Government Accountability Office: Washington, DC, USA, 2008.
7. Tang, L.; Shen, Q. Factors affecting effectiveness and efficiency of analyzing stakeholders' needs at the briefing stage of public private partnership projects. *Int. J. Proj. Manag.* **2013**, *31*, 513–521. [CrossRef]
8. Kumaraswamy, M.M.; Zhang, X.Q. Governmental role in BOT-led infrastructure development. *Int. J. Proj. Manag.* **2001**, *19*, 195–205. [CrossRef]
9. Ho, S.P.; Tsui, C.W. The transaction costs of Public-Private Partnerships: Implications on PPP governance design. In Proceedings of the Lead 2009 Specialty Conference: Global Governance in Project Organizations, South Lake Tahoe, CA, USA, January 2009; Available online: http://academiceventplanner.com/LEAD2009/papers/Ho_Tsui.pdf (accessed on 15 June 2018).
10. Yuan, J.; Zeng, A.Y.; Skibniewski, M.J.; Li, Q. Selection of performance objectives and key performance indicators in public–private partnership projects to achieve value for money. *Constr. Manag. Econ.* **2009**, *27*, 253–270. [CrossRef]
11. Kwak, Y.H.; Chih, Y.; Ibbs, C.W. Towards a comprehensive understanding of public private partnerships for infrastructure development. *Calif. Manag. Rev.* **2009**, *51*, 51–78. [CrossRef]
12. Ng, S.T.; Wong, J.M.; Wong, K.K. A public private people partnerships (p4) process framework for infrastructure development in Hong Kong. *Cities* **2013**, *31*, 370–381. [CrossRef]
13. Robinson, H.S.; Scott, J. Service delivery and performance monitoring in PFI/PPP projects. *Constr. Manag. Econ.* **2009**, *27*, 181–197. [CrossRef]
14. Lu, P.; Guo, S.; Qian, L.; He, P.; Xu, X. The effectiveness of contractual and relational governances in construction projects in China. *Int. J. Proj. Manag.* **2015**, *33*, 212–222. [CrossRef]
15. *Partnerships Victoria Guidance Material: Practitioners' Guide*; The Victorian Department of Treasury and Finance: Victoria, Australia, 2001.
16. WIKIPEDIA. Public Interest Theory. Available online: https://en.wikipedia.org/wiki/Public_interest_theory (accessed on 17 May 2018).
17. Pigou, A.C. *The Economics of Welfare*; McMillan&Co.: London, UK, 1920.
18. Osei-Kyei, R.; Chan, A.P. Review of studies on the Critical Success Factors for Public–Private Partnership (PPP) projects from 1990 to 2013. *Int. J. Proj. Manag.* **2015**, *33*, 1335–1346. [CrossRef]
19. Węgrzyn, J. The Perception of Critical Success Factors for PPP Projects in Different Stakeholder Groups. *Entrep. Bus. Econ. Rev.* **2016**, *4*, 81–92. [CrossRef]
20. Shen, L.Y.; Platten, A.; Deng, X.P. Role of public private partnerships to manage risks in public sector projects in Hong Kong. *Int. J. Proj. Manag.* **2006**, *24*, 587–594. [CrossRef]
21. Ke, Y.; Wang, S.; Chan, A.P.; Lam, P.T. Preferred risk allocation in China's public–private partnership (PPP) projects. *Int. J. Proj. Manag.* **2010**, *28*, 482–492. [CrossRef]
22. Xu, Y.; Yang, Y.; Chan, A.P.; Yeung, J.F.; Cheng, H. Identification and allocation of risks associated with PPP water projects in China. *Int. J. Strateg. Prop. Manag.* **2011**, *15*, 275–294. [CrossRef]

23. Li, B.; Akintoye, A.; Edwards, P.J.; Hardcastle, C. Critical success factors for PPP/PFI projects in the UK construction industry. *Constr. Manag. Econ.* **2005**, *23*, 459–471. [CrossRef]

24. Brinkerhoff, D.W.; Brinkerhoff, J.M. Public–private partnerships: Perspectives on purposes, publicness, and good governance. *Public Adm. Dev.* **2011**, *31*, 2–14. [CrossRef]

25. Chan, A.P.; Chan, A.P. Key performance indicators for measuring construction success. *Benchmarking Int. J.* **2004**, *11*, 203–221. [CrossRef]

26. Liu, J.; Love, P.E.; Davis, P.R.; Smith, J.; Regan, M. Performance measurement framework in PPP projects. In Proceedings of the International Conference on PPP Body of Knowledge in Preston, University of Central Lancashire, Lancashire, UK, 18–20 March 2013.

27. Ng, S.T.; Xie, J.; Cheung, Y.K.; Jefferies, M. A simulation model for optimizing the concession period of public–private partnerships schemes. *Int. J. Proj. Manag.* **2007**, *25*, 791–798. [CrossRef]

28. Song, J.; Song, D.; Zhang, X.; Sun, Y. Risk identification for PPP waste-to-energy incineration projects in China. *Energy Policy* **2013**, *61*, 953–962. [CrossRef]

29. Doloi, H. Understanding impacts of time and cost related construction risks on operational performance of PPP projects. *Int. J. Strateg. Prop. Manag.* **2012**, *16*, 316–337. [CrossRef]

30. Soomro, M.A.; Zhang, X. Roles of private-sector partners in transportation public-private partnership failures. *J. Manag. Eng.* **2015**, *31*, 04014056. [CrossRef]

31. Javed, A.A.; Lam, P.T.; Zou, P.X. Output-based specifications for PPP projects: Lessons for facilities management from Australia. *J. Facil. Manag.* **2013**, *11*, 5–30. [CrossRef]

32. Zhang, X. Critical success factors for public–private partnerships in infrastructure development. *J. Constr. Eng. Manag.* **2005**, *131*, 3–14. [CrossRef]

33. Zhang, X.; Soomro, M.A. Failure path analysis with respect to private sector partners in transportation public-private partnerships. *J. Manag. Eng.* **2015**, *32*, 04015031. [CrossRef]

34. Soomro, M.A.; Zhang, X. Evaluation of the functions of public sector partners in transportation public-private partnerships failures. *J. Manag. Eng.* **2015**, *32*, 04015027. [CrossRef]

35. Liu, J.; ED Love, P.; Smith, J.; Regan, M.; Sutrisna, M. Public-Private Partnerships: A review of theory and practice of performance measurement. *Int. J Product. Perform. Manag.* **2014**, *63*, 499–512. [CrossRef]

36. Liu, J.; Love, P.E.; Davis, P.R.; Smith, J.; Regan, M. Conceptual framework for the performance measurement of public-private partnerships. *J. Infrastruct. Syst.* **2014**, *21*, 04014023. [CrossRef]

37. Jacobson, C.; Choi, S.O. Success factors: Public works and public-private partnerships. *Int. J. Public Sect. Manag.* **2008**, *21*, 637–657. [CrossRef]

38. Liu, Y.; Luo, Y.; Liu, T. Governing buyer–supplier relationships through transactional and relational mechanisms: Evidence from China. *J. Oper. Manag.* **2009**, *27*, 294–309. [CrossRef]

39. Heide, J.B.; John, G. Do norms matter in marketing relationships? *J. Mark.* **1992**, *56*, 32–44. [CrossRef]

40. Griffith, D.A.; Myers, M.B. The performance implications of strategic fit of relational norm governance strategies in global supply chain relationships. *J. Int. Bus. Stud.* **2005**, *36*, 254–269. [CrossRef]

41. Goo, J.; Kishore, R.; Rao, H.R.; Nam, K. The role of service level agreements in relational management of information technology outsourcing: An empirical study. *MIS Q.* **2009**, *33*, 119–145. [CrossRef]

42. Cheung, E.; Chan, A.P. Risk factors of public-private partnership projects in China: Comparison between the water, power, and transportation sectors. *J. Urban Plan. Dev.* **2011**, *137*, 409–415. [CrossRef]

43. Zhang, C.; Cavusgil, S.T.; Roath, A.S. Manufacturer governance of foreign distributor relationships: Do relational norms enhance competitiveness in the export market? *J. Int. Bus. Stud.* **2003**, *34*, 550–566. [CrossRef]

44. Cruz, C.O.; Marques, R.C. Flexible contracts to cope with uncertainty in public–private partnerships. *Int. J. Proj. Manag.* **2013**, *31*, 473–483. [CrossRef]

45. Martins, J.; Marques, R.C.; Cruz, C.O. Maximizing the value for money of PPP arrangements through flexibility: An application to airports. *J. Air Transp. Manag.* **2014**, *39*, 72–80. [CrossRef]

46. Ferrari, C.; Parola, F.; Tei, A. Governance models and port concessions in Europe: Commonalities, critical issues and policy perspectives. *Transp. Policy* **2015**, *41*, 60–67. [CrossRef]

47. Ke, Y.; Wang, S.; Chan, A.P.; Cheung, E. Research trend of public-private partnership in construction journals. *J. Constr. Eng. Manag.* **2009**, *135*, 1076–1086. [CrossRef]

48. Givens, A.D.; Busch, N.E. Realizing the promise of public-private partnerships in US critical infrastructure protection. *Int. J. Crit. Infrastruct. Prot.* **2013**, *6*, 39–50. [CrossRef]

49. Laan, A.; Noorderhaven, N.; Voordijk, H.; Dewulf, G. Building trust in construction partnering projects: An exploratory case-study. *J. Purch. Supply Manag.* **2011**, *17*, 98–108. [CrossRef]

50. Cheung, S.O.; Yiu, T.W.; Man, C.L. Interweaving trust and communication with project performance. *J. Constr. Eng. Manag.* **2013**, 941–950. [CrossRef]

51. Van Marrewijk, A.; Clegg, S.R.; Pitsis, T.S.; Veenswijk, M. Managing public–private megaprojects: Paradoxes, complexity, and project design. *Int. J. Proj. Manag.* **2008**, *26*, 591–600. [CrossRef]

52. Moye, N.A.; Langfred, C.W. Information sharing and group conflict: Going beyond decision making to understand the effects of information sharing on group performance. *Int. J. Confl. Manag.* **2004**, *15*, 381–410. [CrossRef]

53. Koza, K.L.; Dant, R.P. Effects of relationship climate, control mechanism, and communications on conflict resolution behavior and performance outcomes. *J. Retail.* **2007**, *83*, 279–296. [CrossRef]

54. Maurer, I. How to build trust in inter-organizational projects: The impact of project staffing and project rewards on the formation of trust, knowledge acquisition and product innovation. *Int. J. Proj. Manag.* **2010**, *28*, 629–637. [CrossRef]

55. Poppo, L.; Zenger, T. Do formal contracts and relational governance function as substitutes or complements? *Strateg. Manag. J.* **2002**, *23*, 707–725. [CrossRef]

56. Wettenhall, R. The rhetoric and reality of Public–Private Partnerships. *Public Organ. Rev. Glob. J.* **2003**, *3*, 77–107. [CrossRef]

57. Fandel, G.; Giese, A.; Mohn, B. Measuring synergy effects of a Public Social Private Partnership (PSPP) project. *Int. J. Prod. Econ.* **2012**, *140*, 815–824. [CrossRef]

58. Arranz, N.; Arroyabe, J.C. Effect of formal contracts, relational norms and trust on performance of joint research and development projects. *Br. J. Manag.* **2012**, *23*, 575–588. [CrossRef]

59. Rwelamila, P.D.; Talukhaba, A.A.; Ngowi, A.B. Tracing the African project failure syndrome: The significance of "Ubuntu". *Eng. Constr. Arch. Manag.* **1999**, *6*, 335–346.

60. Ika, L.A. Project management for development in Africa: Why projects are failing and what can be done about it. *Proj. Manag. J.* **2012**, *43*, 27–41. [CrossRef]

61. Pinto, J.K.; Slevin, D.P.; English, B. Trust in projects: An empirical assessment of owner/contractor relationships. *Int. J. Proj. Manag.* **2009**, *27*, 638–648. [CrossRef]

62. Addae-Boateng, S.; Wen, X.; Brew, Y. Contractual Governance, Relational Governance, and Firm Performance: The Case of Chinese and Ghanaian and Family Firms. *Am. J. Ind. Bus. Manag.* **2015**, *5*, 288. [CrossRef]

63. Qiu, H.Z. *Quantitative Research and Statistical Analysis: Examples of SPSS (PASW) Data Analysis*; Chongqing University Press: Chongqing, China, 2013. (In Chinese)

64. Hodge, G.A.; Greve, C. Public–private partnerships: An international performance review. *Public Adm. Rev.* **2007**, *67*, 545–558. [CrossRef]

65. Zheng, J.; Roehrich, J.K.; Lewis, M.A. The dynamics of contractual and relational governance: Evidence from long-term public–private procurement arrangements. *J. Purch. Supply Manag.* **2008**, *14*, 43–54. [CrossRef]

66. Liu, J.; LovE, P.E.; Smith, J.; Matthews, J.; Sing, C.P. Praxis of performance measurement in public-private partnerships: Moving beyond the iron triangle. *J. Manag. Eng.* **2016**, *32*, 04016004. [CrossRef]

67. Yuan, J.; Wang, C.; Skibniewski, M.J.; Li, Q. Developing Key Performance Indicators for Public-Private Partnership Projects: Questionnaire Survey and Analysis. *J. Manag. Eng.* **2012**, *28*, 252–264. [CrossRef]

68. Anderson, J.E. *Public Policy Making*; Cengage Learning: Boston, MA, USA, 2014.

69. De Vaus, D.A. *Research Design in Social Research*; Sage: London, UK, 2001.

70. Kaiser, H.F.; Rice, J. Little Jiffy, Mark Iv. *J. Educ. Psychol. Meas.* **1974**, *34*, 111–117. [CrossRef]

71. Blunch, N. *Introduction to Structural Equation Modeling Using IBM SPSS Statistics and AMOS*, 2nd ed.; Sage: London, UK, 2012.

72. Molenaar, K.; Washington, S.; Diekmann, J. Structural equation model of construction contract dispute potential. *J. Constr. Eng. Manag.* **2000**, *126*, 268–277. [CrossRef]

73. Doloi, H.; Iyer, K.C.; Sawhney, A. Structural equation model for assessing impacts of contractor's performance on project success. *Int. J. Proj. Manag.* **2011**, *29*, 687–695. [CrossRef]

74. Jin, X.H.; Doloi, H.; Gao, S.Y. Relationship-based determinants of building project performance in China. *Constr. Manag. Econ.* **2007**, *25*, 297–304. [CrossRef]

75. Ng, S.T.; Wong, Y.M.; Wong, J.M. A structural equation model of feasibility evaluation and project success for public–private partnerships in Hong Kong. *IEEE Trans. Eng. Manag.* **2010**, *57*, 310–322. [CrossRef]

76. Lee, Y.; Cavusgil, S.T. Enhancing alliance performance: The effects of contractual-based versus relational-based governance. *J. Bus. Res.* **2006**, *59*, 896–905. [CrossRef]

77. Narasimhan, R.; Mahapatra, S.; Arlbj, J.S. Impact of relational norms, supplier development and trust on supplier performance. *Oper. Manag. Res.* **2008**, *1*, 24–30. [CrossRef]

78. Malhotra, D.; Lumineau, F. Trust and collaboration in the aftermath of conflict: The effects of contract structure. *Acad. Manag. J.* **2011**, *54*, 981–998. [CrossRef]

79. Bozeman, B. *Public Values and Public Interest: Counterbalancing Economic Individualism*; Georgetown University Press: Washington, DC, USA, 2007.

80. Ning, Y. Combining formal controls and trust to improve dwelling fit-out project performance: A configurational analysis. *Int. J. Proj. Manag.* **2017**, *35*, 1238–1252. [CrossRef]

81. Cannon, J.P.; Achrol, R.S.; Gundlach, G.T. Contracts, norms, and plural form governance. *J. Acad. Mark. Sci.* **2000**, *28*, 180–194. [CrossRef]

82. Cani, M.C.; Gelderman, C.J.; Vermeulen, N.P. The interplay of governance mechanisms in complex procurement projects. *J. Purch. Supply Manag.* **2012**, *18*, 113–121.

83. Lumineau, F.; Henderson, J.E. The influence of relational experience and contractual governance on the negotiation strategy in buyer–supplier disputes. *J. Oper. Manag.* **2012**, *30*, 382–395. [CrossRef]

84. Faems, D.; Janssens, M.; Madhok, A.; Looy, B.V. Toward an integrative perspective on alliance governance: Connecting contract design, trust dynamics, and contract application. *Acad. Manag. J.* **2008**, *51*, 1053–1078. [CrossRef]

85. Kong, T.D.O.H. *Hong Kong Second Comprehensive Transport Study*; Government Printer: Hong Kong, China, 1989.

86. OMEGA Centre. Project File: Hong Kong West Harbour Crossing. 2012. Available online: http://www.omegacentre.bartlett.ucl.ac.uk/wp-content/uploads/2014/12/HK_WEST_HARBOUR_PROFILE.pdf (accessed on 17 May 2018).

87. Yuan, J.; Chan, A.P.; Xia, B.; Skibniewski, M.J.; Xiong, W.; Ji, C. Cumulative Effects on the Change of Residual Value in PPP Projects: A Comparative Case Study. *J. Infrastr. Syst.* **2016**, *22*, 05015006. [CrossRef]

88. LCPTHK. Proposed Measures to Improve the Traffic Distribution among the Road Harbour Crossings. 2013. Available online: http://www.legco.gov.hk/yr12-13/english/panels/tp/papers/tp0222cb1-544-3-e.pdf (accessed on 17 May 2018).

89. Wilbur Smith Associates. Consultancy Services for Providing Expert Advice on Rationalising the Utilization of Road Harbour Crossings. 2010. Available online: http://www.thb.gov.hk/tc/policy/transport/policy/consultation/RHC_Final_Report_Sep2010.pdf (accessed on 17 May 2018).

90. Love, P.E.; Liu, J.; Matthews, J.; Sing, C.P.; Smith, J. Future proofing PPPs: Life-cycle performance measurement and building information modelling. *Autom. Constr.* **2015**, *56*, 26–35. [CrossRef]

91. Hofstede, G.; Hofstede, G.J.; Minkov, M. *Cultures and Organizations: Software of the Mind, Revised and Expanded*; McGraw-Hill: New York, NY, USA, 2010.

92. Estrin, S.; Prevezer, M. The role of informal institutions in corporate governance: Brazil, Russia, India, and China compared. *Asia Pac. J. Manag.* **2011**, *28*, 41–67. [CrossRef]

Article

Public and Private Governance in Interaction: Changing Interpretations of Sovereignty in the Field of Sustainable Palm Oil

Greetje Schouten [1,*] and Otto Hospes [2]

[1] Partnerships Resource Centre, Rotterdam School of Management, Erasmus University,
    P.O. Box 1738, 3000 DR Rotterdam, The Netherlands
[2] Public Administration and Policy Group, Wageningen University and Research,
    P.O. Box 100, 6708 PB Wageningen, The Netherlands; Otto.Hospes@wur.nl
*   Correspondence: schouten@rsm.nl

Received: 15 October 2018; Accepted: 20 November 2018; Published: 17 December 2018

Abstract: Since the 1990s, non-governmental organizations (NGOs) and businesses have gained prominence as architects of new forms of transnational governance creating Voluntary Sustainability Standards (VSS). The legitimacy and effectiveness of VSS are dependent on interactions with public authorities and regulation. While studies suggest that the (perceived) gain or loss of sovereignty by a state shapes public–private interactions, we have little understanding on how states use or interpret sovereignty in their interactions with VSS. In this paper, we explore what interpretations of sovereignty are used by states at different ends of global value chains in interactions with VSS. Based on a comparative and longitudinal study of interactions of Indonesian and Dutch state actors with the Roundtable on Sustainable Palm Oil, we conclude that states strategically use different and changing notions of sovereignty to control the policy and debate regarding sustainable palm oil. When interactions between public and private governance are coordinative in nature, notions of interdependent sovereignty are used. However, when interactions are competitive, domestic and Westphalian notions of sovereignty are used. Our results show conflicting interpretations and usages of sovereignty by different states, which might negatively impact the regulatory capacity within an issue field to address sustainability issues.

Keywords: VSS; public–private interactions; sovereignty; sustainability; palm oil

1. Introduction

Since the 1990s, non-governmental organizations (NGOs) and businesses have gained prominence as architects of new forms of governance to address sustainability issues [1–5]. Challenging or bypassing the territory-based sovereignty of the state, they have claimed central positions as new rule-making authorities and standard-setting bodies at the global level [6]. As a result, many Voluntary Sustainability Standards (VSS) have emerged to address a wide variety of issues, including sustainable forestry [7,8], biofuels [9], aquaculture [10], sustainable agricultural commodities [11], and responsible mining [12,13].

With the implementation of the VSS at national and local level, both stakeholders and scholars have more and more realized that these standards do not operate in isolation, but rather interact with state-based regimes and regulations [14]. Their legitimacy and effectiveness are dependent on these regimes and regulations [15,16]. Thus, the understanding of the operation of transnational private regulation requires the inclusion of the state into the analysis of VSS [2,14,17–20].

There is an increasing body of literature that investigates interactions of VSS with public authorities and regulation. These studies show that interactions between private and public governance can result in complementarity, substitution, or antagonism [21]. Complementarity occurs when governance systems are mutually reinforcing one another; substitution occurs when a governance system replaces VSS regulation; while antagonistic governance systems undermine each other [21]. Studies that pay attention to state responses to the emergence of private governance show that interactions with states at the consuming end of the value chain (e.g. [22,23]) may differ tremendously from interactions with states at the production end (e.g. [24–28]). On the one hand, we see dynamics of mutual reinforcement (that is, complementarity) between public and private actors, when the state uses VSS for implementing regulations or attaining public policy objectives [22,29]. On the other hand, we see that antagonistic dynamics of state actors with VSS can occur in the context of their limited respect for national regulatory sovereignty and weak alignment with national economic priorities, which might lead to the establishment of rival (public) sustainability standards [28]. Thus, the type of public–private interactions that occur seem to relate to the (perceived) gain or loss of sovereignty by a state in relation to the VSS.

While studies suggest that the (perceived) gain or loss of sovereignty by a state shapes public–private interactions [28], we have little understanding on how states use or interpret sovereignty over time in their interactions with VSS. However, most studies focus on either states at the consumer end or producer end of global value chains. Therefore, this paper analyzes how states that are connected to different positions of a global value chain interpret sovereignty over a longer period of time in their interactions with transnational private governance. More specifically, this paper studies the interactions of Indonesian and Dutch state actors with the Roundtable on Sustainable Palm Oil (RSPO), which is a global private governance initiative that developed a VSS for the palm oil industry. The next section details our analytical framework on sovereignty and governance interactions. Section 3 subsequently explains our research approach, data collection, and analysis methods. Sections 4 and 5 present the empirical findings of our longitudinal study. The paper concludes with a reflection on the relationship between state sovereignty and public–private interactions in the context of VSS.

2. Analytical Framework

VSS are often presented as a reaction to decreasing capacities of states to solve the various problems posed by globalization processes [11,30]. The proliferation of non-state actors as new governance agents are thereby challenging the state as the supreme authority within a territory [31–33]. Due to increasing cross-border trade flows, states have increasingly shared their sovereignty over territory and transactions with market actors [34], and therefore cannot simply ignore private governance arrangements [35]. At the same time, private governance arrangements are often dependent on local public governance when it comes to the implementation of the VSS at the local level [10,36,37]. However, public–private relations related to the emergence of VSS are very different in nature [29]. Wijaya and Glasbergen [26] distinguished four different types of relations between VSS and state actors. The first relationship is a distant one, as it regards sustainability issues in commodity chains as a responsibility of the market itself and not of the state (see also [38]). The second recognizes the interdependencies between VSS and public strategies (see also [39]), while the third is about seeking congruence between private and public regulation. The fourth one is of quite a different nature, as in this conceptualization, the state is reclaiming its authority by developing rival strategies [27,28]. These four different observed relationships assert a different meaning to state sovereignty in relation to VSS.

Krasner [40] distinguished four meanings of state sovereignty: domestic sovereignty, interdependence sovereignty, international sovereignty, and Westphalian sovereignty. *Domestic sovereignty* refers to "the organization of public authority within a state and to the level of effective control exercised by those holding authority" [40] (p. 9). *Interdependence sovereignty* refers to the ability to control cross-border flows of goods, persons, ideas, etc. *International legal sovereignty* is concerned with the mutual recognition of states or other entities. *Westphalian sovereignty* refers to the principle of territoriality and the exclusion of external actors from domestic authority configurations. Whilst enjoying sovereignty on one dimension can be a precondition for establishing another, the relationships between these four dimensions are not self-evident.

For instance, a state can enjoy a high degree of international legal sovereignty, but have difficulties in demonstrating domestic sovereignty. The four types of sovereignty indicate that every state faces the challenge of working on all different dimensions of sovereignty in different arenas.

The emergence of VSS has complicated the challenges of states to demonstrate or negotiate sovereignty in terms of all four dimensions. States have to decide whether or not to share rule-making authority with VSS that exercise control over cross-border flows. Krasner's four dimensions of sovereignty and the related diversity of matters (territory, transactions, markets, people, culture, beliefs) over which a holder of authority can be sovereign [32] form a repertoire for states to interpret sovereignty in particular ways. These interpretations of sovereignty are both a tool and an outcome of interactions between state and non-state actors [41].

As explained before, public–private interactions can take a variety of forms. Eberlein et al. [42] classified four types of governance interactions: competition, coordination, cooptation, and chaos. We use this categorization to analyze and compare interactions of state actors with VSS. Competition can refer to rivalry between standards, but also to the issue of what institutional actor has the legitimate authority to regulate a certain issue field. Coordination can vary from active collaboration to mutual agreement on division of labor. Cooptation can range from convergence on norms and activities to meta-regulation and hegemony or subordination, through which certain governance arrangements achieve a quasi-monopolistic position [42,43]. Chaos is characterized by undirected and unpredictable interactions that display no clear pattern. Interactions are dynamic and may change over time: chaos may develop into competition and into coordination; vice versa, coordination might develop into competition or chaos [42]. The type of interaction of a particular state with a VSS is indicative of their interpretation of sovereignty: coordination and cooptation are indicative of shared sovereignty of state and non-state actors, whereas competition and chaos show that a state actor is trying to (re)claim its sovereignty or deny the sovereignty of a non-state actor. These interpretations of sovereignty are not given but may change over time, which may reflect changes in interactions. This paper aims to shed light onto how these different types of interactions relate to different interpretations of sovereignty.

3. Materials and Methods

Palm oil is a globally consumed vegetable oil that is used for food, feed, biofuel, and industrial purposes. The production of palm oil is regarded by many as a threat to the land and social rights of local communities, biodiversity, and the environment in general [44]. The RSPO, which was initiated in 2002, is generally regarded as a prominent VSS. To study the interactions of different states with the RSPO over time, two specific countries were selected: Indonesia and the Netherlands. Indonesia is the biggest palm oil producer in the world. The Netherlands is the biggest importer of palm oil in Europe, and Netherlands-based actors have played a key role in developing the RSPO [45].

Our research consisted of several phases. The first phase was exploratory and served to gain an initial understanding of the public–private interactions taking place between the Indonesian or Dutch state actors and the RSPO. For this purpose, we scanned public reports of the RSPO annual conference to explore whether state actors were invited as chairs or (key note) speakers. In addition, we scanned press releases of the RSPO as well as newspaper articles of Indonesian government officials. Based on this initial scan, we identified two rather distinctive episodes in which the type of interactions shifted significantly. The first episode took place during the rule formation process of the RSPO (2003–2009). The second episode started with the announcement and development of a national Indonesian standard: the Indonesian Sustainable Palm Oil (ISPO) standard (2010–2017). The Indonesian Ministry of Agriculture launched the ISPO as an obligatory standard in 2010 to support its international commitments to greenhouse gas reduction and enhance the competitiveness of Indonesian palm oil in the world market [46].

The second phase consisted of data collection to gain a deeper understanding of the kind of interactions during the two periods. For the first episode, we made use of the database "RSPO and the role of the state", including data on the participation of public authorities in different groups and RSPO teams compiled by Rebecca Howard and Otto Hospes in 2010. For both episodes, we conducted a desk study of the minutes of RSPO Executive Board meetings and RSPO general assemblies, which are publicly available through the RSPO website. The analysis of these archival data were complemented with participatory observations at several conferences on sustainable palm oil organized by the RSPO, the Dutch government, or the Indonesian government. Then, semi-structured interviews with a total of 31 key actors in the palm oil industry were conducted. These included officials of the RSPO, ISPO, and Dutch government, as well as multinational companies and NGOs playing a key role in the RSPO.

4. Episode 1: The Rise of a Single Standard Regime (2003–2009)

In the early 2000s, WWF Switzerland began to explore the possibility of a partnership with the private sector to address the sustainability challenges associated with the palm oil industry. To this end, the WWF assembled a group of 25 European stakeholders—retailers, food manufacturers, palm oil processors, traders, and financial institutions—in London [47]. During this meeting, these stakeholders agreed to start promoting sustainable palm oil, which led to the establishment of the Roundtable on Sustainable Palm Oil (RSPO).

Given that palm oil production is mostly concentrated in Indonesia and Malaysia, most of the stakeholders felt that an initiative consisting of only European actors would not be very effective [48]. Therefore, WWF Switzerland invited the Malaysian Palm Oil Association (MPOA) to join the RSPO. This private national industry association called its Indonesian counterpart, GAPKI, to affiliate with the RSPO as well [47]. Both associations have strong relations with their respective national governments. One of the main reasons for GAPKI to join the RSPO was to avoid reputational damages, counter negative claims about palm oil, and discuss possible price premiums, market access, and preferential purchasing policies [15].

In 2004, the RSPO was officially registered as a foundation. The RSPO organized a multi-stakeholder process and agreed on global principles and criteria for sustainable palm oil production, a verification and certification process, and mechanisms for supply chain traceability. After field testing, the RSPO principles and criteria were adopted at the General Assembly of 2007. The RSPO currently counts over 4,000 members. Within the RSPO, only businesses and NGOs have decision-making power. However, many public–private interactions took place during the rule formation phase. We first outline the interactions between Indonesian state actors and the RSPO, and thereafter the interactions of Dutch state actors and the RSPO.

4.1. Interactions between the RSPO and Indonesian State Actors

4.1.1. Annual Conferences of the RSPO

Various interactions took place during annual RSPO conferences to which Indonesian state actors participated either as observers or speaker at the annual conferences of the RSPO. During the second annual RSPO meeting (RT2) in 2004, the Indonesian Minister of Agriculture gave a keynote address in which he expressed his specific and positive expectations about the RSPO: *"[I] conclude my short remarks by proposing a special request to the organizer that this roundtable should also discuss steps toward [the] development of a protocol of good agricultural practice in the palm oil industry. I understand this is not an easy task. But I am optimistic the participants of this roundtable are highly competent for such an important task"* [49] (in 2011, the then former Minister of Agriculture was appointed as special advisor of the RSPO). State actors were also involved in organizing RT2; the chair of the organizing committee was the chair of the Indonesian Palm Oil Commission (IPOC), a special commission falling under the auspices of the Ministry of Agriculture [50]. From that roundtable meeting onwards, the Indonesian Ministry of Agriculture and particularly its officials from the Directorate General for Estates and IPOC would be regular contributors, by providing keynotes and presentations, as well as by chairing sessions.

Not only Indonesian state actors were active in the roundtable meetings; other producing countries were invited to participate as well. At the fifth roundtable meeting in 2007, the Minister of Plantation

Industries and Commodities of Malaysia held the closing address in which he praised the efforts of the RSPO: "*The progress achieved by RSPO is indeed laudable, and I believe this is largely due to the multi-stakeholder approach (. . .) I would like to urge all growers to implement the RSPO principles and criteria for sustainable palm oil production diligently*" [51]. However, the Minister was very critical about the positions of smallholders vis-à-vis the RSPO: "*[Small-holders] will find it impossible to meet the standards required by the RSPO criteria*".

4.1.2. Thematic Working Groups

Interactions also took place at working groups organized by the RSPO to get consensus on contentious issues and organize collaborative action. Indonesian government officials participated in several of working groups, including the Biodiversity Technical Committee [52], the Greenhouse Gases Working Group, and the Smallholder Task Force. Representatives from the Indonesian Ministry of Agriculture wanted to discuss "the best approach in coordinating and expediting the Smallholders Task Force (STF)-related activities specifically for Indonesia" [53]. As a result of their work in the Smallholders Task Force, the Ministry of Agriculture signed a memorandum of understanding with the RSPO in 2009 to collaborate on training trainers of smallholders. In two periods, a total of 40 local facilitators (*Facilitator Daerah*) were instructed on how to train smallholders on the RSPO principles and criteria (interview with RSPO officer in Indonesia). More than 400 smallholders were trained by these agricultural extension officers on the RSPO principles and criteria.

4.1.3. National Interpretation Working Group of Indonesia

A specific working group in which Indonesian state actors were particularly active is the national interpretation working group Indonesia. The general purpose of this group was to adapt the global RSPO principles to the national context of Indonesia [54] and ensure that its implementation was congruent or compatible with the norms, laws, and values of Indonesia as a sovereign state [55].

The national interpretation team of Indonesia consisted of 65 members, of which 21 government officials of six Ministries—the Ministry of Agriculture, the Ministry of Environment, the Ministry of Industry, the Ministry of Labor and Transmigration, the Ministry of Economy, Finance, and Industry, and the Ministry of Trade—and of the Indonesian Palm Oil Commission (IPOC) and the National Land Agency (BPN) [56]. The IPOC was the group leader of the thematic commission on Environment and Natural Resources within the national interpretation team.

4.1.4. Interactions and Interpretations of Sovereignty

During Episode 1, the interactions of the Indonesian government with the RSPO could be characterized by processes of coordination and even cooptation. Coordination in this period became visible in the collaborative attitude of the Indonesian government (taking part in annual conferences, thematic working groups, and national interpretation groups) toward the RSPO. However, the RSPO is in the lead of the interactions and determines the rules of the game for developing a global standard for sustainable palm oil. Therefore, the interactions are also characterized by cooptation, wherein the RSPO is the dominant governance arrangement regarding sustainable palm oil.

The collaboration of the Indonesian government with the RSPO suggests that during this time, they were willing to share the control of cross-border flows of palm oil with a private regulatory arrangement. The Indonesian government implicitly practiced a notion of interdependence sovereignty, in which state and non-state actors share control over cross-border flows of goods.

During Episode 1, the RSPO uses the word sovereignty to explain the rationale behind national interpretation groups. This suggests that the RSPO to some degree respects the domestic sovereignty of the Indonesian government. Moreover, the RSPO seems to acknowledge international legal sovereignty by referring to state laws and regulations in their standard, and by inviting state actors to participate in public meetings and working groups. However, they do not allow state actors to engage in their formal decision-making procedures. Indonesian civil servants did not participate in decision-making processes regarding verification and certification processes and mechanisms for supply chain traceability. This suggests that the RSPO regards itself as sovereign over the palm oil supply chain.

4.2. Interactions between the RSPO and Dutch State Actors

4.2.1. Political Support

Dutch state actors have not been involved in hosting annual conferences of the RSPO or providing keynote addresses at such conferences. Yet, the Dutch government has been an outspoken supporter of the RSPO from the beginning onwards, expressing support for the RSPO as a form of self-regulation. In 2008, the Dutch Minister of Agriculture, Nature, and Food Quality communicated that *"the RSPO is an example of a promising international voluntary initiative of producers, consumers, and NGOs (. . .)"* making it redundant to formulate regulatory and legislative frameworks by the Dutch government to address the import of unsustainable palm oil [57].

4.2.2. Thematic Working Groups

The Dutch Product Board for Margarine Fats and Oils (MVO) has been a member of the RSPO since November 2005. Until the end of 2014 Dutch products boards were semi-public organizations in the agricultural sector: they were authorized to develop policies and instruments on behalf of the government, and at the same time articulate the interests of the sector (as per 1 January 2015, the 11 Dutch product boards were abolished by law; the product board MVO was transformed into a private agency). Membership in the MVO was mandatory for all Dutch companies in the margarine, fats, and oil sectors and had—and still has—a large emphasis on driving sustainability in the sector. The MVO was active in several working groups, and chaired the working group on trade and traceability, and was in that capacity part of the RSPO Executive Board meetings [55].

4.2.3. Financing of the Rule-Formation Process

This positive attitude of the Netherlands and other European Union (EU) countries toward the RSPO has resulted in another important role of governments in the development of the RSPO: financing of the rule-formation process. For example, the Task Force for the Smallholder Certification Support Network was funded by the Sustainable Trade Initiative (IDH), which is an organization established by the Dutch government. The IDH receives funding from the Dutch, Swiss, and Danish governments. Another example is the funding of the 'framework for drafting criteria for sustainable palm oil' by the GTZ, which is the German development cooperation organization under the German federal government [47].

In 2005, the governments of the Netherlands, Indonesia, and Malaysia agreed to start "an agricultural trilateral cooperation in order to stimulate market access and sustainable development (amongst others) in the palm oil sector" [58] (p. 149). With money from this partnership, an RSPO satellite office was opened in Jakarta, and a number of projects were funded aimed at implementing RSPO certification [59].

4.2.4. Interactions and Interpretations of Sovereignty

During Episode 1, the interactions of the Dutch government with the RSPO could be characterized by processes of coordination, although they are more indirect than the interactions of the Indonesian government with the RSPO. The Dutch government itself is not participating in meetings or working groups; at best, it participates in an indirect way through the Dutch product board for margarines, fats, and oil. The collaborative attitude manifests itself most prominently in the financial support by the Dutch government of RSPO projects.

These interactions show that the Dutch government uses and interprets sovereignty in the same ways as the Indonesian government, that is, to emphasize interdependent sovereignty. Theoretically put, they believe that sovereignty regarding cross-border flows of goods needs to be shared with private regulatory arrangements, such as the RSPO. This means that the RSPO is seen as sovereign over the global palm oil value chain.

5. Episode 2: The Rise of a Plural Standard Regime (2010–2017)

While the Indonesian government adopted a positive and collaborative attitude toward the RSPO during its rule-formation process, this drastically changed around 2010. Governments and palm oil producer associations of Indonesia and Malaysia began to overtly challenge the effectiveness and legitimacy of the RSPO to contribute to sustainable palm oil production in their country [28,54].

Whilst the change of attitude of the Indonesian government was drastic, this change has to be seen as the cumulative effect of a series of encounters of Indonesian government officials and palm oil producers with the RSPO. Shortly after the launch of the ISPO, various Indonesian government officials and stakeholders of the Indonesian palm oil industry aired their grievances about the RSPO principles and procedural rules: they felt that the economic benefits of palm oil production at the producer and country level were not articulated well enough; having a minority vote, the producers felt that their suggestions at (preparations of) annual meetings were often overruled [54]. Offermans and Glasbergen [60] indeed found that knowledge supply within the RSPO is strongly dominated by NGOs. The interactions between the Indonesian government and palm oil producers with the non-state members of the RSPO gradually led to more conflicted interactions. The Indonesian government did not only gradually distance itself from the RSPO, it also prepared the launch of a national standard. This example was soon followed by the government of Malaysia. The emergence of national standards marked the rise of a plural standard regime.

That the principles of the ISPO are lookalikes of those of the RSPO shows that the Indonesian government, similar to the RSPO, adheres to the idea of setting sustainability standards for palm oil. However, this cannot be seen as an acceptance of the sovereignty of the RSPO, which is also because the criteria of the ISPO offer more room for producers to expand into high conservation areas and peatland than those of the RSPO [27,28].

5.1. Interactions between the RSPO and Indonesian State Actors

5.1.1. Announcing a Competing Standard at an RSPO Conference

In the opening address on behalf of the new Indonesian Minister of Agriculture at the 2010 RSPO conference in Jakarta, the Indonesian Sustainable Palm Oil (ISPO) standard was announced: "*ISPO [provides] guidance on sustainable oil palm development based on existing legislation in Indonesia. (. . .) [T]he provisions of ISPO are mandatory for plantation actors in Indonesia. The goals of ISPO are: (1) increasing awareness of the importance of producing sustainable palm oil, (2) increasing competitiveness of sustainable oil palm production, and (3) supporting the commitment of Indonesia in conserving natural resources and the environment. We can add that ISPO is proof of company compliance toward legislation as well as proof of the concern of Indonesian oil palm plantation players to carry out sustainable oil palm development*" [61].

The president of the RSPO reported that 19 RSPO memberships were terminated immediately after the launch of the ISPO [62]. One of the organizations that resigned was GAPKI. The leadership of this Indonesian Palm Oil Association explicitly mentioned in the Jakarta Post (5 October 2011) that it wanted to support the ISPO as the public standard for sustainable palm oil. GAPKI felt that the organizational structure of the RSPO was biased in favor of manufacturers and retailers, while putting producers at a disadvantage (interview with special advisor of the RSPO; and interview with executive director of GAPKI). Producers have to pay the main part of the certification costs, while the uptake of certified palm oil has so far been very low (interview with industry representative; interview with executive director of GAPKI). The official argument for the establishment of ISPO is that the RSPO has a poor outreach, and cannot be effective in making palm oil production sustainable in Indonesia: only a fraction of the palm oil growers are members of the RSPO, and compliance to RSPO rules is voluntary [63].

The ISPO standard was the result of interdepartmental consultation between the Ministries of Agriculture, Environment, and Forestry, facilitated by the Indonesian Palm Oil Committee (IPOC) [27]. The standard is based on Indonesian laws and regulation, and therefore, neither business nor civil society was involved in drafting the criteria. However, businesses and NGOs are involved in the certification process itself.

The ISPO commission presented Indonesia as the sovereign power that has the exclusive right to regulate issues within its territorial boundaries: *"We do not listen to pressure from the European market. This is our palm oil and this is what we do. We are sovereign"* (interview with executive chairperson ISPO). The ISPO underlines that Indonesia is not giving in to foreign pressures for environmental protection at the cost of their own producers (interview with executive chairperson ISPO). *"This [the ISPO] is Indonesia's definition of sustainability. When a company complies with ISPO, they are sustainable according to the law"* (interview with industry representative). *"The government believes that it is our right as a country to address sustainability"* (interview with Indonesian NGO representative). The Indonesian government wants to make a clear statement that the promotion of sustainable palm oil production in Indonesia belongs to the national scale and is not a matter of governance at the global level [54].

5.1.2. Seeking International Recognition for the ISPO Next to the RSPO

At the 2010 RSPO conference, the Indonesian government also announced that it wanted to get the ISPO standard recognized by the Word Trade Organization as well as international standard organizations, such as the International Organization for Standardization (ISO) [63]. However, seeking international recognition presents a challenge to the ISPO, because as large group of buyers of palm oil consider the RSPO standard to be the only credible one. Moreover, buyers feel that the RSPO standard is stricter than that of ISPO. *"[The] RSPO is at least the best thing there is. It is accepted; ISPO is not. Of our clients, no one is actually interested in ISPO"* (interview with international consultant). In a report of the 2010 roundtable meeting, a representative of the Association of Southeast Asian Nations (ASEAN) Oleochemicals Manufacturers Group writes: *"It [ISPO] is seen as a watered down version of the RSPO P&C [principles and criteria]. (. . .) It is not known what measures the government would undertake to make the ISPO and its certification process internationally accepted as credible"* [64].

The aim of the Ministry of Agriculture is to have all companies ISPO-certified by the end of 2014. However, an article in the Jakarta Post (3 March 2014, p.13) stated that only 40 out of roughly 2500 plantations have secured a government-issued certificate on sustainability, and another 153 applied for certification. The executive director of the ISPO commission declared in the article that the commission would not revise the deadline or launch specific initiatives to push the remaining plantations to apply for the certification. Yet, at the national level, the Ministry of Agriculture is confronted with a lack of resources, while at the local level, enforcement of the rules is difficult because of the high level of corruption in Indonesia. *"The Indonesian state cannot even ensure the enforcement of their own laws, then why should ISPO be able?"* (interview with international consultant). *"Law implementation and enforcement is a very big problem in this country [Indonesia]. It is very unusual for the government to rely on third-party certification to enforce their law"* (interview with United Nations Development Programme employee). Hidayat et al. [65] concluded that ISPO faces a lack of authority, while at the same time, there is a lack of incentives for local governments to enforce ISPO regulation.

To attain international recognition, the ISPO commission has approached importing countries directly by asking for bilateral support and approval. A team of representatives from ISPO visited governments, NGOs, and businesses in Europe, the US, China, and India (interview with executive chairperson of ISPO). While China and India are thus far not particularly interested in buying certified sustainable palm oil, many countries in Europe exclusively focus on the RSPO to make their imports more sustainable (see Section 5.2 below).

5.1.3. Developing a Joint ISPO–RSPO Study

Despite the tense relationship of the Indonesian government with the RSPO after the launch of the ISPO standard, several efforts were made to develop working relationships between the RSPO and ISPO. Under the auspices of the UNDP, the RSPO and the ISPO commission of the Indonesian Ministry of Agriculture signed an agreement in October 2013 to explore the differences and similarities between the two standards through a joint study. The study was supposed to be finished by December 2013, but was only published in February 2016, reportedly because the ISPO commission and the RSPO could not agree on the findings.

The report of the study is entitled "Similarities and Differences of the ISPO and the RSPO Certification Systems" [66]. One of the key recommendations of the study is to use the common elements required by both certification systems as a basis to conduct a joint audit process to reduce the duplicity of efforts [66]. However, the former executive director of the ISPO commission claimed that this is impossible, as the ISPO standard is an implementation of state law, and can therefore never be combined with market-driven certification (interview with executive chairperson of ISPO). Other stakeholders, including the executive director of GAPKI, do firmly believe in this strategy.

During the launch of the study, the new chairperson of the ISPO Secretariat took the opportunity to promote ISPO by saying: "This study marks a turning point in the international community's effort to support and work with Indonesia's laws and regulations relating to the palm oil sector. We are looking forward to strengthening the Indonesia Sustainable Palm Oil certification standard and improving market access for the industry" [66]. This statement does not reflect an intention of ISPO to increase collaboration with the RSPO.

5.1.4. Interactions and Interpretations of Sovereignty

During Episode 2, the interactions of the Indonesian government with the RSPO could be characterized by processes of competition. The Indonesian government explicitly distanced itself from the RSPO and established a competing sustainability standard.

The changing nature of the interactions indicates that the notions of interdependence sovereignty have faded, and have been replaced by notions of domestic and Westphalian sovereignty. The ISPO standard appeals primarily to domestic audiences and refers to national values [28]. However, the Indonesian government also tries to attain international sovereignty by seeking recognition for their governance strategy regarding sustainable palm oil from international organizations (e.g., the World Trade Organization and ISO) and from other states. The Indonesian government no longer wants to share sovereignty over the sustainability of palm oil that is produced on its territory.

The joint study does not mark the end of Episode 2, as the reactions to it show that the Indonesian government is not willing to share sovereignty over sustainable palm oil with foreign, non-state actors.

5.2. Interactions between the RSPO and Dutch State Actors

While the Indonesian government changed its sustainable palm oil strategy and its interactions with the RSPO drastically from 2009 onwards, the Dutch government maintained its collaborative and supportive attitude toward the RSPO.

5.2.1. High-Level Business Meeting Supporting RSPO

In 2010, the Dutch and United Kingdom (UK) governments convened a high-level business meeting of leaders from the palm oil sector in London. During these meetings, a declaration on sustainable palm oil was formulated, in which the objective was stipulated: "*We are committed to underpinning the continued rapid growth in the production and use of RSPO-certified palm oil and derivative products, and contributing to the overall mainstreaming of certified products*" [67].

5.2.2. The Amsterdam Declaration in Support of a Fully Sustainable Palm Oil Supply Chain

In trying to attain international recognition for their standard, representatives of ISPO visited the Netherlands several times (interview with executive chairperson of ISPO; interview with executive director of GAPKI; participant observations in The Hague, 2015). However, the Dutch government explicitly keeps supporting the RSPO and not the ISPO. In December 2015, five ministers (of the Netherlands, Denmark, France, Germany, and the UK) signed the Amsterdam Declaration in Support of a Fully Sustainable Palm Oil Supply Chain, which stated: *"As European countries and as member states of the European Union, we take note and declare ourselves supportive of the private sector-driven "Commitment to Support 100% Sustainable Palm Oil in Europe", as signed by [the] European national sector organizations engaged with the palm oil supply chain at the Amsterdam Conference on the "EU and Global Value Chains"* [68]. The commitment that is supported in this declaration explicitly mentioned the RSPO as the preferred way to achieve sustainability in the sector: *"We declare to work together and support each other in transforming toward a 100% sustainable palm oil supply chain in Europe by 2020. We aim to achieve this through actions such as the following: defining sustainable palm oil as a stepping stone approach, working toward RSPO-certified (or equivalent) at minimum (. . .)"* [69].

The rationale behind the Amsterdam declaration is explained as follows: "As the world's largest economy, Europe has an opportunity and responsibility to move the global economy to a more sustainable path. Europe is the second largest global import market for palm oil, and home to some of the world's biggest brands and companies. Europe can be an important 'game changer' when it comes to a sustainable palm oil supply chain for the world. This can only be achieved if all of the public and private stakeholders work together in a coherent way according to each role and responsibility. This includes [the] industry parties, civil society, and governments of producing and consuming countries" [68].

5.2.3. Reactions to the Joint ISPO–RSPO Study

At the presentation of the joint study, the IDH and government representatives from Denmark, Norway, the UK, the United States, and Switzerland were present, *"some of who used the study's launch as an opportunity to express concerns to the Indonesian government on behalf of the world's palm oil buyers"* [66], as is illustrated by this quote of the Senior Forestry Advisor at the UK's Department for International Development (DFID): *"Currently, we recognize [the] RSPO, but not ISPO. Why? Because there is a communication issue; we don't know where the palm oil comes from. There's also a credibility issue; [there are] problems with governance and transparency. We will recognize ISPO when it is a true multi-stakeholder standard, when it is audited independently . . . ideally we would love to recognize ISPO"*.

5.2.4. Interactions and Interpretations of Sovereignty

In contrast to the Indonesian government, the interactions of the Dutch government with the RSPO continue to be characterized by processes of coordination during Episode 2. The Dutch government maintained its strategy to show their public support for the RSPO through for example the Amsterdam Declaration.

The Dutch government keeps granting interdependence sovereignty to the RSPO. By seeking other EU countries to acclaim the sovereignty of the RSPO, they also grant international sovereignty to the initiative. By holding on to this interpretation of sovereignty and preferring the RSPO over ISPO, the Dutch government disregards the Westphalian interpretation of sovereignty on the part of Indonesia. The Netherlands, as a large importer of palm oil, feels entitled and responsible to exert influence abroad in this field. The reactions to the publication of the joint study show that this event does not mark the end of Episode 2, but that the two opposing interpretations of sovereignty continue to exist.

6. Discussion

Different types of interactions of state actors with the RSPO indicate different interpretations and uses of sovereignty over sustainable palm oil. Coordinative interactions of Indonesian and Dutch state actors with the RSPO reflect notions of interdependent sovereignty. Competitive interactions of Indonesian state actors with the RSPO reflect different uses of sovereignty: domestic and Westphalian sovereignty. Table 1 below summarizes the results of our analysis.

Table 1. Interpretations of sovereignty.

	Episode 1	Episode 2
Indonesia	• Interdependent sovereignty: seeking control over cross-border flows. Sharing this type of sovereignty with the RSPO • Domestic sovereignty: taking part in national interpretation processes	• Domestic sovereignty/Westphalian sovereignty: by disregarding the RSPO and focusing on national audiences. • International sovereignty: getting the ISPO standard recognized
The Netherlands	• Interdependence sovereignty: seeking control over cross-border flows via the RSPO	• 'Denial' of Westphalian sovereignty on the part of Indonesia by disregarding ISPO • Interdependence sovereignty: seeking control over cross-border flows via the RSPO
RSPO	• International legal sovereignty: inviting states to cooperate • Interdependence sovereignty: seeking shared control of cross-border flows • Recognition of minimal type of domestic sovereignty: national interpretation teams	• International legal sovereignty: inviting states to cooperate • Interdependence sovereignty: seeking shared control of cross-border flows

Not only states have a specific interpretation of their sovereignty vis-à-vis a private governance arrangement; also, the private governance arrangement has a specific interpretation of state sovereignty. However, this interpretation seems to be quite stable over time.

Our analysis both confirms and extends the argument of Vandergeest and Unno [24], who argued that private regulatory arrangements overlook more territorially embedded forms of legitimacy and public authorities whose mandates and claims overlap with certification standards. The RSPO acknowledges the existing legal system, but still claims rule-making and rule-enforcement authority in a specific territory. Hereby, private regulatory governance replicates key aspects of colonial-era extraterritoriality by contributing to "the creation of a variegated sovereignty in which the state does not have exclusive or absolute sovereignty", because private certification is justified through a narrative of deficient states [24] (p. 9). Based on our research, we are able to extend this argument by looking at the ways in which two different states interact with one private regulatory arrangement, each using different and changing notions of sovereignty to exert control in the issue area of sustainable palm oil. Dutch state actors seem to use the extraterritoriality of the RSPO to indirectly claim some form of sovereignty in Indonesia as the major palm oil producing country of the world. The government of Indonesia shifted its interpretation and use of sovereignty to reclaim its shared sovereignty from the RSPO. Thus, interpretations and uses of sovereignty are not carved in stone. When the Indonesian government realized that the RSPO might actually hamper the economic interests of Indonesian producers, they began to interact differently with the RSPO and started to develop a national standard. To rationalize this, they changed their interpretation and use of sovereignty: sovereignty was not any longer interpreted by the Indonesian government as shared and interdependent, but rather as exclusive and Westphalian.

7. Conclusions

Our analysis shows that sovereignty is not a static concept; instead, it is used strategically by different state actors, and its use changes over time. Conducting a longitudinal study allowed us to see changing pattern of interactions, showing a dynamic picture of sovereignty. Interpretations and uses of sovereignty can be derived by looking at the actions of a governance arrangement—be it public or private—and its interactions with other governance arrangements.

Interestingly, the changing interpretation and use of sovereignty by the Indonesian and Dutch state supports Krasner's original argument on the political use of sovereignty by rulers: rulers are motivated by a desire to stay in power, not by some abstract adherence to international principles. In our case, the Indonesian state showed a desire to stay in power regarding the palm oil produced on its territory, rather than adhering to and accepting transnational private regulation. The implementation of transnational private regulation that was felt to inadequately address the views and interests of Indonesian producers prompted the Indonesian government to shift its use of sovereignty from shared to exclusive, and from interdependent to Westphalian.

Different interpretations of and strategies toward sovereignty do not necessarily lead to direct conflicts between states. During Episode 2, Indonesia contested the RSPO, reclaiming domestic sovereignty, while the Netherlands promoted it—claiming interdependent sovereignty. This however indicates an antithesis between commodity producing and consuming countries. This duality might decrease the regulatory capacity and outreach of private and state-initiated regulatory complexes. The development of rival standards by producing countries may create a further differentiation and fragmentation of the governance of sustainable agricultural commodities (cf. [38]), especially when consuming states focus solely on promoting private VSS. Aligning the public strategies of different countries and private strategies with one another might increase regulatory coherence to increase sustainable practices in global value chains. Future research could focus on the consequences of different and possibly conflicting frames on sovereignty on the regulatory capacity within an issue field.

Author Contributions: Conceptualization, G.S. and O.H.; Methodology, G.S. and O.H.; Software, G.S.; Validation, G.S and O.H.; Formal Analysis, G.S.; Investigation, G.S. and O.H.; Resources, G.S. and O.H.; Data Curation, G.S. and O.H.; Writing-Original Draft Preparation, G.S. and O.H.; Writing-Review & Editing, G.S. and O.H.; Visualization, G.S.; Supervision, G.S. and O.H.; Project Administration, G.S.; Funding Acquisition, O.H.

Funding: This research was funded by the Interdisciplinary Research and Education Fund (INREF) of Wageningen University (SUSPENSE).

Acknowledgments: The authors would like to thank research assistant Rebecca Howard for compiling the archive "RSPO and the role of the state" (see Materials and Methods) and Johanna Deike for conducting field research on the re positioning of the Indonesian and Malaysian state in Sustainable Palm Oil Governance. The authors would also like to thank the Interdisciplinary Research and Education Fund (INREF) of Wageningen University for financially supporting the research for this paper.

Conflicts of Interest: The authors declare no conflicts of interest.

References

1. Van Kersbergen, K.; Van Waarden, F. 'Governance' as a bridge between disciplines: Cross-disciplinary inspiration regarding shifts in governance and problems of governability, accountability and legitimacy. *Eur. J. Political Res.* **2004**, *43*, 143–171. [CrossRef]
2. Falkner, R. Private environmental governance and international relations: exploring the links. *Glob. Environ. Politics* **2003**, *3*, 72–87. [CrossRef]

3.   Bartley, T. Institutional Emergence in an Era of Globalization: The Rise of Transnational Private Regulation of Labor and Environmental Conditions. *Am. J. Sociol.* **2007**, *113*, 297–351. [CrossRef]

4.   Biermann, F.; Pattberg, P. Global environmental governance: Taking stock, moving forward. *Annu. Rev. Environ. Resour.* **2008**, *33*, 277–294. [CrossRef]

5.   Abbott, K.W.; Snidal, D. The governance triangle: Regulatory standards institutions and the shadow of the state. In *The Politics of Global Regulation*; Princeton University Press: Princeton, NJ, USA, 2009; pp. 44–88.

6.   Fuchs, D.; Kalfagianni, A.; Havinga, T. Actors in private food governance: The legitimacy of retail standards and multistakeholder initiatives with civil society participation. *Agric. Hum. Values* **2011**, *28*, 353–367. [CrossRef]

7.   Cashore, B.; Auld, G.; Newsom, D. Legitimizing political consumerism: The case of forest certification in North America and Europe. In *Politics, Products, and Markets: Exploring Political Consumerism Past and Present*; Transaction Press: New Brunswick, NJ, USA, 2004; pp. 181–199.

8.   Marx, A.; Cuypers, D. Forest certification as a global environmental governance tool: What is the macro-effectiveness of the Forest Stewardship Council? *Regul. Gov.* **2010**, *4*, 408–434. [CrossRef]

9.   Schleifer, P. Orchestrating sustainability: The case of European Union biofuel governance. *Regul. Gov.* **2013**, *7*, 533–546. [CrossRef]

10.   Schouten, G.; Vellema, S.; van Wijk, J. Diffusion of global sustainability standards: The institutional fit of the ASC-shrimp standard in Indonesia. *RAE Revista de Administracao de Empresas* **2016**, *56*, 411–423. [CrossRef]

11.   Bitzer, V. Partnering for change in chains: The capacity of partnerships to promote sustainable change in global agrifood chains. *Int. Food Agribus. Manag. Rev.* **2012**, *15*, 13–38.

12.   Grant, J.A.; Taylor, I. Global governance and conflict diamonds: The Kimberley Process and the quest for clean gems. *Round Table* **2004**, *93*, 385–401. [CrossRef]

13.   Meidinger, E. Beyond Westphalia: Competitive legalization in emerging transnational regulatory systems. In *Law and Legalization in Transnational Relations*; Routledge: New York, NY, USA, 2007; pp. 121–143.

14.   Bartley, T. *Rules without Rights: Land, Labor, and Private Authority in the Global Economy*; Oxford University Press: Oxford, UK, 2018.

15.   Schouten, G.; Glasbergen, P. Private multi-stakeholder governance in the agricultural market place: An analysis of legitimization processes of the roundtables on sustainable palm oil and responsible soy. *Int. Food Agribus. Manag. Rev.* **2012**, *15*, 53–78.

16.   D'Hollander, D.; Marx, A. Strengthening private certification systems through public regulation: The case of sustainable public procurement. *Sustain. Account. Manag. Policy J.* **2014**, *5*, 2–21. [CrossRef]

17.   Mol, A.P. Bringing the environmental state back in: Partnerships in perspective. In *Partnerships, Governance and Sustainable Development: Reflections on Theory and Practice*; Edward Elgar: Cheltenham, UK, 2007; p. 214.

18.   Knorringa, P.; Meijerink, G.; Schouten, G. *Voluntary governance initiatives and the challenges of inclusion and upscaling. Value Chains, Social Inclusion and Economic Development: Contrasting Theories and Realities*; Routledge: London, UK, 2011; pp. 42–60.

19.   Marques, J.C. Private regulatory fragmentation as public policy: Governing Canada's mining industry. *J. Bus. Ethics* **2016**, *135*, 617–630. [CrossRef]

20.   Pacheco, P.; Schoneveld, G.; Dermawan, A.; Komarudin, H.; Djama, M. Governing sustainable palm oil supply: Disconnects, complementarities, and antagonisms between state regulations and private standards. *Regul. Gov.* **2018**. [CrossRef]

21.   Lambin, E.F.; Meyfroidt, P.; Rueda, X.; Blackman, A.; Börner, J.; Cerutti, P.O.; Walker, N.F. Effectiveness and synergies of policy instruments for land use governance in tropical regions. *Glob. Environ. Chang.* **2014**, *28*, 129–140. [CrossRef]

22.   Gulbrandsen, L.H. Dynamic governance interactions: Evolutionary effects of state responses to non-state certification programs. *Regul. Gov.* **2012**, *8*, 74–92. [CrossRef]

23.   Bendell, J.; Miller, A.; Wortmann, K. Public policies for scaling corporate responsibility standards: Expanding collaborative governance for sustainable development. *Sustain. Account. Manag. Policy J.* **2011**, *2*, 263–293. [CrossRef]

24.   Vandergeest, P.; Unno, A. A new extraterritoriality? Aquaculture certification, sovereignty, and empire. *Polit. Geogr.* **2012**, *31*, 358–367. [CrossRef]

25.   Bartley, T. Transnational governance and the re-centered state: Sustainability or legality? *Regul. Gov.* **2014**, *8*, 93–109. [CrossRef]

26. Wijaya, A.; Glasbergen, P. Toward a new scenario in agricultural sustainability certification? The response of the Indonesian national government to private certification. *J. Environ. Dev.* **2016**, *25*, 219–246. [CrossRef]

27. Hospes, O. Marking the success or end of global multi-stakeholder governance? The rise of national sustainability standards in Indonesia and Brazil for palm oil and soy. *Agric. Hum. Values* **2014**, *31*, 425–437. [CrossRef]

28. Schouten, G.; Bitzer, V. The emergence of Southern standards in agricultural value chains: A new trend in sustainability governance? *Ecol. Econ.* **2015**, *120*, 175–184. [CrossRef]

29. ISEAL. *R079 Governmental Use of Voluntary Standards: Innovation in Sustainability Governance*; ISEAL Alliance: London, UK, 2008.

30. Dentoni, D.; Bitzer, V.; Schouten, G. Harnessing wicked problems in multi-stakeholder partnerships. *J. Bus. Ethics* **2018**, *150*, 333–356. [CrossRef]

31. Hajer, M. Policy without polity? Policy analysis and the institutional void. *Policy Sci.* **2003**, *36*, 175–195. [CrossRef]

32. Comaroff, J.L.; Comaroff, J. Reflections on the anthropology of law, governance and sovereignty. In *Rules of Law and Laws of Ruling*; Routledge: London, UK, 2009; pp. 31–59.

33. Sassen, S. *Losing Control?: Sovereignty in the Age of Globalization*; Columbia University Press: New York, NY, USA, 1996.

34. Mikler, J. Sharing sovereignty for global regulation: The cases of fuel economy and online gambling. *Regul. Gov.* **2008**, *2*, 383–404. [CrossRef]

35. Pramudya, E.P.; Hospes, O.; Termeer, C.J.A.M. Friend or foe? The various responses of the Indonesian state to sustainable non-state palm oil initiatives. *Asian J. Sustain. Soc. Responsibil.* **2018**, *3*, 1. [CrossRef]

36. Auld, G.; Renckens, S.; Cashore, B. Transnational private governance between the logics of empowerment and control. *Regul. Gov.* **2015**, *9*, 108–124. [CrossRef]

37. Bush, S.R.; Belton, B.; Hall, D.; Vandergeest, P.; Murray, F.J.; Ponte, S.; Kruijssen, F. Certify sustainable aquaculture? *Science* **2013**, *341*, 1067–1068. [CrossRef]

38. Glasbergen, P.; Schouten, G. Transformative capacities of global private sustainability standards: A reflection on scenarios in the field of agricultural commodities. *J. Corp. Citizsh.* **2015**, *58*, 85–102. [CrossRef]

39. He, W.; Yang, W.; Choi, S.J. The interplay between private and public regulations: Evidence from ISO 14001 adoption among Chinese firms. *J. Bus. Ethics* **2018**, *152*, 477–497. [CrossRef]

40. Krasner, S.D. *Sovereignty: Organized Hypocrisy*; Princeton University Press: Princeton, NJ, USA, 1999.

41. Mikler, J. Sharing sovereignty for policy outcomes. *Policy Soc.* **2011**, *30*, 151–160. [CrossRef]

42. Eberlein, B.; Abbott, K.W.; Black, J.; Meidinger, E.; Wood, S. Transnational business governance interactions: Conceptualization and framework for analysis. *Regul. Gov.* **2014**, *8*, 1–21. [CrossRef]

43. Büthe, T. Engineering Uncontestedness? The Origins and Institutional Development of the Inter-national Electrotechnical Commission (IEC). *Bus. Politics* **2010**, *12*, 1–62.

44. Hospes, O.; Kroeze, C.; Oosterveer, P.; Schouten, G.; Slingerland, M. New generation of knowledge: Towards an inter-and transdisciplinary framework for sustainable pathways of palm oil production. *NJAS-Wagen. J. Life Sci.* **2017**, *80*, 75–84. [CrossRef]

45. Nikoloyuk, J.; Burns, T.R.; de Man, R. The promise and limitations of partnered governance: The case of sustainable palm oil. *Corp. Gov. Int. J. Bus. Soc.* **2010**, *10*, 59–72. [CrossRef]

46. Indonesian Palm Oil Commission (IPOC). *The Introduction of the ISPO: Towards Sustainable Palm Oil 2011*; Ministry of Agriculture of the Republic of Indonesia: Jakarta, Indonesia, 2011.

47. Schouten, G.; Glasbergen, P. Creating legitimacy in global private governance: The case of the Roundtable on Sustainable Palm Oil. *Ecol. Econ.* **2011**, *70*, 1891–1899. [CrossRef]

48. RSPO. Minutes of the Preparatory Meeting Hayes (London), 20 September 2002. Available online: https://www.rspo.org/sites/default/files/Minutes_London_2002_09_20.pdf (accessed on 10 December 2016).

49. Saraghi, B. *Keynote Speech of the Minister of Agriculture of the Republic of Indonesia in the Roundtable on Sustainable Palm Oil, 5 October 2004, Grand Hyatt hotel Jakarta*; Ministry of Agriculture of the Republic of Indonesia: Jakarta, Indonesia, 2004.

50. IPOC. Letter of the Indonesian Palm Oil Commission. Available online: http://www.rspo.org/files/pdf/RT2/Invitation%20to%20RT2%20(IPOC).pdf (accessed on 24 March 2014).

51. Kui, Y.D.P.C.F. *Keynote Address by Y.B Datuk Peter Chin Fah Kui Minister of Plantation Industries and Commodities at the Closing Session of the 5th Roundtable Meeting on Sustainable Palm Oil in Kuala Lumpur*; Minister of Plantation Industries and Commodities: Putrajaya, Malaysia, 2007.
52. RSPO. Composition and Description of Team Members. Available online: http://www.rspo.org/?q=page/537 (accessed on 17 November 2014).
53. RSPO. Available online: http://www.rspo.org/en/indonesia_smallholder_ni_working_group (accessed on 24 March 2014).
54. Hospes, O.; Kentin, A. Tensions between Global Scale and National Scale Governance: The Strategic Use of Scale Frames to Promote Sustainable Palm Oil Production in Indonesia. In *Scale-Sensitive Governance of the Environment*; Wiley-Blackwell: Hoboken, NJ, USA, 2014; pp. 203–219.
55. Hospes, O. Private law making at the round table on sustainable palm oil. In *Private Food Law Governing Food Chains through Contract Law, Self-Regulation, Private Standards, Audits and Certification Schemes*; van der Meulen, B., Ed.; Wageningen Academic Publishers: Wageningen, The Netherlands, 2011.
56. RSPO. Available online: http://www.rspo.org/sites/default/files/NI_INANIWG_Final_English_May2008_ver01.pdf (accessed on 22 November 2018).
57. Tweede Kamer. Antwoord op vragen van het lid Ouwehand (PvdD) aan de ministers van Landbouw. In Proceedings of the Natuur en Voedselkwaliteit en voor Ontwikkelingssamenwerking Overde Schadelijke Gevolgen van de Productie van Palmolie in Indonesië voor de Orang-Oetan en Biodiversiteit, Den Haag, The Netherlands, 8 July 2008.
58. van Dijk, M.P. Using a partnership to achieve sustainable development of the palm oil value chain in Malaysia. In *Global Value Chains: Linking Local Producers from Developing Countries to International Markets*; Amsterdam University Press: Amsterdam, The Netherlands, 2012; pp. 137–162.
59. Hospes, O.; Stattman, S.L.; de Pooter, S. Groen en geel zien: Private partnerschappen voor duurzame productie van soja en palmolie. In *Governance in de Groen-Blauwe Ruimte. Handelingsperspectieven voor Landbouw, Landschap en Water*; Van Gorcum: Assen, The Netherlands, 2009; pp. 244–258.
60. Offermans, A.; Glasbergen, P. Boundary work in sustainability partnerships: An exploration of the Round Table on Sustainable Palm Oil. *Environ. Sci. Policy* **2015**, *50*, 34–45. [CrossRef]
61. Suswono, H. *Opening Speech of the Minister of Agriculture of the Republic of Indonesia at the 8th Roundtable Meeting on Sustainable Palm Oil, 9 November 2010, Hotel Mulia Senayan Jakarta*; Ministry of Agriculture of the Republic of Indonesia: Jakarta, Indonesia, 2010.
62. Vis, J.K. *Summary of RT8 Results by Jan Kees Vis President of the RSPO and Sustainable Sourcing Development Director*; Unilever: London, UK, 2010.
63. Suharto, R. Why Indonesia Needs ISPO. The Jakarta Post, Supplement. 2 December 2010. Available online: http://www.thejakartapost.com/news/2010/12/02/why-indonesia-needs-ispo.html (accessed on 10 October 2013).
64. Seng, Q.K. November 2010 update on Roundtable on Sustainable Palm Oil. Available online: http://www.aomg.org.my/images/content/november2010_update_on_rspo.pdf (accessed on 11 November 2017).
65. Hidayat, N.K.; Offermans, A.; Glasbergen, P. Sustainable palm oil as a public responsibility? On the governance capacity of Indonesian standard for sustainable palm oil (ISPO). *Agric. Hum. Values* **2018**, *35*, 223–242. [CrossRef]
66. InPOP. ISPO-RSPO Comparative Study, 23 February 2016. Available online: http://www.inpop.id/en/news/read/02-23-2016-ispo-rspo-comparative-study (accessed on 22 November 2018).
67. Proforest. Palm Oil Leadership Group Meeting. In Proceedings of the 2010 Global business of Biodiversity Conference, Excel Conference Centre, London, UK, 13 July 2010.
68. Amsterdam Declaration. The Amsterdam Declaration in Support of a Fully Sustainable Palm Oil Supply Chain by 2020, 7 December 2015, Amsterdam, The Netherlands. Available online: http://www.euandgvc.nl/documents/publications/2015/december/7/declarations-palm-oil (accessed on 22 November 2017).
69. IDH & MVO. *Commitment to Support: 100% Sustainable Palm Oil in Europe by 2020, 7 December 2015*; IDH: Utrecht, The Netherlands, 2015.

Article

Signalling Responsibility? Applying Signalling Theory to the ISO 26000 Standard for Social Responsibility

Lars Moratis [1,2]

[1] The Netherlands & Sustainable Transformation Lab, NHTV Breda University of Applied Sciences, 4817 JT Breda, The Netherlands
[2] Corporate Social Responsibility, Antwerp Management School, 2000 Antwerpen, Belgium; lars.moratis@ams.ac.be

Received: 17 September 2018; Accepted: 8 November 2018; Published: 13 November 2018

Abstract: Many global challenges cannot be addressed by one single actor alone. Achieving sustainability requires governance by state and non-state market actors to jointly realise public values and corporate goals. As a form of public–private governance, voluntary standards involving governments, non-governmental organisations and companies have gained much traction in recent years and have been in the limelight of public authorities and policymakers. From a firm perspective, sustainability standards can be a way to demonstrate that they engage in corporate social responsibility (CSR) in a credible way. To capitalise on their CSR activities, firms need to ensure their stakeholders are able to recognise and assess their CSR quality. However, because the relative observability of CSR is low and since CSR is a contested concept, information asymmetries in firm–stakeholder relationships arise. Adopting CSR standards and using these as signalling devices is a strategy for firms to reduce these information asymmetries, by revealing their true CSR quality. Against this background, this article investigates the voluntary ISO 26000 standard for social responsibility as a form of public-private governance and contends that, despite its objectives, this standard suffers from severe signalling problems. Applying signalling theory to the ISO 26000 standard, this article takes a critical stance towards this standard and argues that firms adhering to this standard may actually emit signals that compromise rather than enhance stakeholders' ability to identify and interpret firms' underlying CSR quality. Consequently, the article discusses the findings in the context of public-private governance, suggests a specification of signalling theory and identifies avenues for future research.

Keywords: corporate social responsibility; signalling theory; information asymmetry; ISO 26000; sustainability standards; private governance; public-private governance

---

1. Introduction

Whether it is on a local, national or global level, achieving sustainability requires governance by state and non-state market actors. In fact, scholars, policymakers and business leaders have recognised that, as forms of "governance beyond government", private governance and public-private governance are key for effectively dealing with some of the most pressing social and ecological challenges, such as combatting climate, eradicating poverty and deforestation [1]. In this context, corporate social responsibility (CSR) initiatives taken by firms, including codes of conduct, sustainability reporting, and the adoption of voluntary standards in the social and ecological domain, can be seen as a manifestation of private governance. In efforts to jointly realise public values and corporate goals, voluntary CSR and sustainability standards involving governments, non-governmental organisations and companies have emerged as a promising form of public-private governance. The uptake of these forms of public-private governance has gained much traction in recent years and has increasingly received recognition from public authorities and policymakers. As a result, public-private governance has become an integral part of the repertoire of policy arrangements [2–4].

In addition to contributing to societal goals, firms seek to realise financial and economic value from their CSR activities. To capitalise on their efforts, firms need to ensure their stakeholders are able to recognise and assess their "CSR quality", understood as a firm's CSR commitments, actions and performance. Firms encounter at least two problems here. First, the relative observability of an organisation's CSR quality is generally low due its dominant orientation on internal processes [5–8]. Second, the essentially-contested nature of the CSR concept implies that firms need to develop idiosyncratic interpretations of CSR, based on their respective characteristics and contexts [9–11]. The co-existence of many firm-specific meanings attributed to CSR may compromise stakeholders' ability to gauge these interpretations.

These problems cause information asymmetries in firm-stakeholder relationships. To reduce information asymmetries, firms pursue sensegiving and sensemaking communication strategies using a variety of media and messages to reveal their true CSR quality [12,13]. However, research indicates that a majority of stakeholders appears to believe firms do not communicate about CSR honestly [14] and demonstrations of symbolic CSR implementation and corporate misconduct have raised concerns about firms' credibility [15,16].

1.1. Sustainability Standards

Efficacious signalling of CSR quality thus is a key challenge for firms. As a manifestation of private governance in the context of public goals, voluntary sustainability standards [2,17] represent a way for firms to demonstrate that they engage in CSR in a credible way. Defined by Rasche ([18], p. 263) as *"predefined rules and procedures for organizational behavior with regard to (…) issues that are usually not required by law"*, CSR standards in this context not only have a function in disciplining firm behaviour, but also function as a signalling device.

Being a prominent example of a voluntary corporate sustainability standard, the ISO 26000 standard for social responsibility covers subjects across the entire CSR domain, providing guidance instead of being a certifiable management systems standard that contains requirements and propagates a dominantly moral rather than strategic perspective on CSR [3,19]. As such, it represents an innovation in standards development [20,21]. ISO 26000 is the result of a global stakeholder-inclusive development process that took place under the auspice of the International Organisation for Standardisation (ISO), providing the standard with a high level of legitimacy [19,22,23]. Various reports [24–27] show that ISO 26000 has become a commonly used standard by companies worldwide and that the interest for adhering to the standard is steadily growing. In addition, ISO standards are an integral part of public policy in both environmental and social domains and are, for instance, used in public procurement processes and applied to stimulate effective sustainability governance in international trade [28].

However, despite these positive signs several characteristics of ISO 26000 may cause it to suffer from severe signalling problems. Firms adhering to the standard could consequently well emit signals that compromise rather than enhance stakeholders' ability to identify and interpret firms' underlying CSR quality and thus may engage in adverse CSR communication that maintains information asymmetries. This article investigates this proposition by examining literature on CSR standards, ISO 26000 and developments in the practical realm of the standard through the lens of signalling theory (ST). Focusing on firm behaviour, CSR communication, firm-stakeholder interaction and information asymmetries, the framework of ST allows for a relevant and critical examination of ISO 26000 that relates to (potential) problems associated with this standard. Taking a critical stance, this article develops arguments based on the type of standard ISO 26000 represents, its contents and developments in the CSR standards environment that have followed since its publication.

1.2. Academic and Practical Contribution

This article aims to make an academic contribution in several ways. Its main contribution is that it provides one of the few empirical applications of ST in the context of CSR, answering the call of Connelly et al. [29] to tap ST's potential in the field of sustainability and to explore further specifications of ST. Against the background that ISO standards are a "coagulated" manifestation of public-private governance, the analysis may also offer novel insights for the field of public-private governance. Notably, ISO 26000 makes a particularly interesting case for analysis since it differs significantly from other instruments in the public-private governance realm, including reporting standards, certification schemes, labelling and roundtables. In addition, focussing on ST provides an additional lens to examine CSR (communications) beyond the commonly used lenses of legitimacy theory, institutional theory, stakeholder theory and accountability [30]. Finally, while others have examined ISO 26000 from the perspective of developing it as a guidance or certifiable standard [31] and have hinted on signalling aspects of the standard [20], this article is the first to assess ISO 26000 from the perspective of ST. In addition, in addition, applying ST to ISO 26000 gives rise to a further specification of theoretical concepts within the ST framework for analysing patterns of CSR communication.

Practical relevance of this article lies in the implications of analysing ISO 26000 as a problematic signal for firms that want to demonstrate their CSR quality to secure legitimacy through the standard or which are requiring ISO 26000 adherence from suppliers and subcontractors. The analysis points at the necessity of using additional signalling strategies for ISO 26000-adhering firms, contains advice to standardisation and certification organisations that aim to design efficacious CSR standards, and provides suggestions for policy makers that want to encourage corporate transparency on CSR.

The article starts by discussing ST's theoretical basis, distinguishing between two central types of information asymmetry. Next, it provides an account of ISO 26000, including its main characteristics and consequences in the CSR standards environment. It then turns to analysing ISO 26000 with ST concepts. Finally, the article reflects on the analysis and suggests both a specification of ST and avenues for future research.

2. Signalling Theory: Focus and Key Concepts

Sprouted from the work of Akerlof [32], Spence [33], and Stiglitz [34], ST relates to a substantial body of academic work in economical contract theory focusing on information asymmetries between multiple entities, such as individuals or organisations. In particular, ST is concerned with how one entity—the agent or insider—may undertake actions to signal its underlying quality to reduce information asymmetries. This underlying quality is often hard to observe or unobservable to another entity—the principal or outsider [29]. ST therefore revolves around *"problems of social selection under conditions of imperfect information"* ([29], p. 63).

Signals can be defined as snapshots pointing to unobservable signaller qualities at a given point in time [35]. They constitute messages or images communicated from one entity to another. Quality refers to attributes or abilities of the signaller to fulfil the needs or demands of an outsider observing the signal [29].

A central assumption behind ST is that the entity that does not have certain information at its disposal is usually willing to pay a(n) (in)tangible premium to the entity that reveals its attributes through signals. ST essentially formulates propositions about strategies for (in)action in the context of costs and benefits under different levels of opacity or transparency, on the side of both the signaller and the signal receiver. ST suggests that firms provide information that could be used by individuals or constituent groups that are seeking to form impressions about the firm, its values and its overall future direction [36]. It primarily addresses *"the deliberate communication of positive information in an effort to convey positive organizational attributes"* ([29], p. 44) that represent imperceptible underlying qualities and can be a powerful explanation for the conduct of firms and their constituents and their patterns of interaction.

2.1. ST concepts

In their review of ST, Connelly et al. [29] distilled several key theoretical concepts. These include: (1) signals of quality and intent; (2) the efficacy of signalling by high-quality and low-quality firms; (3) signal honesty and signal fi; and (4) signal frequency and consistency.

Signals of quality and intent. In ST, a basic distinction is made between information signalling the quality and intent of an organisation. Signals of quality relate to the communication of a certain organisational characteristic in order to obtain legitimacy with signal receivers (e.g., CSR quality). Signals of intent *"indicate future action, possibly conditional on the receiver's response"* ([29], p. 60). Through these signals, firms inform stakeholders about their aspirations or resolutions.

Efficacy of signalling by high-quality and low-quality firms. Though important, the fact that a signal is observable is not a sufficient condition for it to be efficacious. Connelly et al. [29] wrote that signals need to have the characteristic of being costly as well. Signals that incur costs from signallers show that some signallers may be better able to absorb the associated costs than others. Some firms may pursue social initiatives even if they imply economic losses [37,38]. The signal may hence send the message that the signaller be perceived as more credible or honest in its claim to possess a certain quality.

Signal honesty and signal fit. Signal honesty relates to the coupling of formal plans and subsequent actions and is defined as *"the extent to which the signaller actually has the underlying quality associated with the signal"* ([29], p. 45), bearing some similarity to the previously addressed distinction between signal intent and signal quality. Signal fit can be defined as the degree to which a signal correlates with the unobservable quality of the signaller. This notion implies that situations may occur in which a signaller sends out signals that do not correlate well with the signaller's unobservable quality [39,40]. In the context of CSR, such misalignment is usually perceived as greenwashing [41,42]. The discrepancy between the signal and the quality of the signaller—either actual or perceived—is hence due to poor signalling, which may either be caused by the quality of the signal or the integrity of the signaller. Signal fit and signal honesty together comprise signal reliability, which closely relates to the notion of credibility [29].

Signal frequency and consistency. Firms can enhance the effectiveness of their signalling by means of sending a larger spectrum of observable signals or by increasing the number of signals emitted, which is called signal frequency. Connelly et al. [29] pointed at the possibility for signallers to signal repetitively to keep reducing information asymmetries and increase the effectiveness of the signalling process. This especially applies when a firm uses multiple types of signals to convey the same message [43]. A related concept to signal frequency is that of signal consistency, which Connelly et al. defined as the agreement between multiple signals from one particular source. Signal consistency may help mitigate the problem of communication becoming less effective as uncorresponding or conflicting signals confuse the receiver [44,45].

While other concepts can be distinguished in literature on ST, Connelly et al. [29] considered the above to cover key categories within ST. This article takes these categories as its point of reference for analysing ISO 26000 from a signalling perspective (Although these categories may partly overlap, for purposes of analysis, they are treated as conceptually separate in this article).

2.2. Observing CSR Signals: Within-Firm and between-Firm Information Asymmetries

Voluntary in nature, CSR represents an integral part of corporate strategy and is concerned with the responsibility a firm takes for the social and environmental impacts of its (in)actions and its responsiveness to the legitimate concerns and expectations of its stakeholders and broader society about these impacts [46,47]. CSR discourse is dominated by instrumental and strategic approaches rather than moral orientations towards CSR, emphasising the economic benefits that firms can gain by addressing their social and environmental responsibilities [48,49]. In this context, CSR is an important underlying quality to signal to stakeholders as firms seek to capitalise on their investments in managing sustainability impacts, product and business model innovation and corporate philanthropy. As Johnston ([5], p. 7) put it: *"[u]nless firms can find a credible signal of CSR, the positive potential of the market may go unrealized"*. Literature has pointed at the value of signalling CSR as a beneficial firm characteristic that sends investors the message that they can anticipate future firm profits, that helps building a good corporate image and reputation among customers, (future) employees and regulators, cultivates trust among corporate constituents and that can enhance the credibility of CSR claims [5,50–54]. Scholars have also suggested that organisations may signal their CSR quality in response to stakeholder demands or to differentiate themselves from competitors, providing them with greater legitimacy in the marketplace [13,30,55–59].

In its simplest form, ST's primary focus is on information asymmetries between two entities, the signaller and the signal receiver. However, in the realm of CSR, firms experience strong incentives to signal their CSR quality. Receiver attention for signals of CSR quality has surged. A recent survey by Globescan [14] demonstrates that a large majority of corporate stakeholders are interested to learn about firms' CSR engagement. Connelly et al. ([29], p. 60) rightfully argued that the field of CSR presents an interesting research area from the perspective from ST: *"as many stakeholders such as host communities, employees, and customers become increasingly concerned about sustainability, how can firms signal their commitment to a sustainable enterprise?"* This has led to a proliferation of signals, including the use product labels, advertising responsible products, sponsoring worthy causes, issuing press releases about CSR initiatives, engaging in strategic stakeholder dialogue and publishing comprehensive sustainability reports, making competitive signalling important. In the face of information asymmetry, firms with good performance will try to find ways of signalling the relative superiority of their performance to increase observability [60].

Consequently, this spree of CSR communication causes relationships between firms and their stakeholders to be characterised by two types of information asymmetries in particular: within-firm and between-firm information asymmetries. Within-firm information asymmetries concern the inherent opacity of underlying CSR quality and its relative unobservability to stakeholders. In many cases, a firm's CSR quality is hard to observe or even unobservable for transacting partners due to the prevalent orientation of CSR activities on internal business processes rather than its integration in the development of new products, the exploration of new markets and the innovation of business models [5–8]. To the extent firms communicate their CSR engagement to reduce information asymmetry, only a part of signal receivers appear to think that companies communicate honestly about CSR [14]. As Lydenberg ([61], p. 61] observed: *"Although an increasing number of corporations publish environmental and health and safety reports, many are simply token efforts—greenwashing—and few address the full range of social issues necessary to asses adequately a corporation's behaviour."* In other words, the inconvenient truth for firms here is that assumptions of greenwashing seem to be a starting point in assessing communication on their social and environmental responsibilities. These conjectures thus point at a subtler concept of unobservability: while a firm tries to signal its CSR quality to reduce problems of information asymmetry, many stakeholders tend to think that the information revealed to them does not reflect the organisation's true underlying quality or may be communicated to consciously obscure rather than reveal observability. Signalling CSR then results in maintaining information asymmetries as stakeholder perception may trump truth.

A second type of information asymmetries relates to between-firm observability and concerns the idiosyncrasy of the CSR concept. The contested, multifaceted, and vague nature of CSR [10,11,62,63] requires company-specific interpretations of the concept to acquire meaning [9,64]. While such interpretations may benefit stakeholders' understanding of the CSR quality of a particular firm, this also implies that substantial differences between management approaches to, incomparable renditions of, and widely varying communications strategies for CSR, even of similar firms that are in direct competition with each other, are scattered around the marketplace [13,65,66]. As a result, CSR (minimum) norms and performance benchmarks are unclear to signal receivers, making it hard for stakeholders to gauge, differentiate between and make inferences about companies' signals about their comparative CSR quality. This leads to preservation of information asymmetries in business-stakeholder relationships.

3. A Standard for Signalling CSR: Understanding ISO 26000

In this context, CSR standards can serve as efficacious signalling devices for firms to reduce information asymmetries. By increasing the observability of firms' underlying CSR quality and through providing common frameworks for interpreting and implementing CSR, they enable firms and their stakeholders to cope with problems associated with within-firm and between-firm observability of CSR. CSR standards offer a shared point of orientation and an agreed-upon language in a fragmented domain and thus carry a legitimising function for guiding CSR behaviour [67–70]. Terlaak [71] argued that standards may create order without law in settings characterised by incomplete consensus and information and capture in a written and codified form "how things should be done". Several standards allow firms to obtain certification for their demonstrated compliance through second- or third-party auditing. Certification functions as an enforcement mechanism that cultivates accountability and disciplines corporate conduct, ensuring—at least to a certain extent—signal honesty and fit. Certification allows firms to explain and justify their behaviour, enabling stakeholders to pass better informed judgments and facing sanctions when they do not comply with the designated norms [72].

Over the past two decades, the CSR domain has witnessed a proliferation of complementary and competing standards. Representing exclusive or exhaustive categories, types of standards that have emerged include principle-based standards, reporting-based standards, certification standards, process standards and integrating guidance-based standards [17,73,74]. Amidst the proliferation of CSR standards, ISO took the initiative to develop ISO 26000, a comprehensive CSR standard that offers guidance for understanding and interpreting CSR, formulating and implementing CSR policy and communicating CSR. Published in late 2010, the standard marks a deviation from the closely related category of management systems standards in the CSR realm (e.g., ISO 14001, ISO 9001, OHSAS 18001, SA 8000) which contain process and performance requirements and are certifiable. Whereas widely used standards such as the United Nations Global Compact (UNGC) and the Global Reporting Initiative guidelines through their own enforcement mechanisms (communication on progress requirement and application levels respectively) mandate firm behaviour, ISO 26000 contains no enforcement mechanisms at all. Hahn [20] labels ISO 26000 as an innovation in standards development, *"intended to enhance (or induce) a [management system] with regard to content and structure by systematically promoting (or introducing) continuous discourse processes"* ([20], p. 720). This type of standards focuses on providing guidance on contents, process and dialogue, facilitating stakeholder interaction and organisational learning.

ISO 26000 was developed in the largest-ever stakeholder consultation process, involving institutional stakeholders from more than 90 countries and hundreds of international delegates and experts in the field of CSR that deliberated and negotiated on aspects of the standards for more than five years. This inclusive nature and procedural fairness of the development process, its consensual orientation, and its transparency led the standard to possess a high level of legitimacy [19,22,23,75].

Its broad-based contents were inspired by many other authoritative standards, conventions, guidelines, codes of conduct, etc. ISO 26000 specifies expectations and related actions for guiding firm behaviour in the realm of CSR in order to *"provides guidance on the underlying principles of social responsibility, recognizing social responsibility and engaging stakeholders, the core subjects and issues pertaining to social responsibility and on ways to integrate socially responsible behaviour into the organization"* ([26], p. vi). The standard has a strong stakeholder orientation [76,77] and, although recognising the business imperative for addressing social and environmental responsibilities, takes a dominantly moral instead of an instrumental or strategic approach to CSR. The standard builds on the idiosyncratic character of the CSR concept encouraging firms to develop their own interpretation of CSR within the general confinements of the principles and CSR subjects it specifies [3,78]. As such, it can be considered as a multi-stakeholder initiative to create a form of public-private governance in the context of the roles or organisations in achieving sustainability.

In a comparison of ISO 26000 vis-à-vis other standards, Hahn [20] argued that ISO 26000 provides opportunities for signalling CSR beyond certification on a direct level of interaction with stakeholders: *"While possible de-coupling tendencies in third-party certificates might induce a loss of confidence in the respective conventional standards, such alternative modes of signalling potentially enable a more credible implementation [of CSR]"* (p. 724). He also concluded that ISO 26000 holds particular value for firms that are in the beginning stages of CSR implementation. Webb [79] argued that ISO 26000 is an innovative rule instrument that contains bridging functions in addressing public and private transnational business governance interactions, including the standard's compatibility with other global CSR standards and the function of the standard as an emerging global CSR custom to address firm behaviour.

The standard seems to be well-received by firms. A recent report of the European Commission [25] based on research among 200 European companies shows that 40 per cent refer to at least one internationally recognised CSR standard, while 33 per cent of the companies in the research refer to at least the UNGC, the OECD Guidelines for Multinational Enterprises (MNEs) or ISO 26000. ISO post-publication surveys indicate that adoption of the standard is gaining traction worldwide [24,26,27].

The characteristics of the standard have led to various responses by organisations in the CSR standards environment, including national standardisation bodies and certification organisations. As many firms seek to certify their CSR engagement, various national standardisation bodies (e.g., in Denmark, Portugal, and Brazil) have developed certifiable CSR management systems based on ISO 26000 standards, such as the Danish DS 49001. A consortium of internationally active certification organisations have developed and launched a certifiable management systems standard as response to the publication of ISO 26000, called the CSR Performance Ladder. Other standardisation bodies (e.g., in the Netherlands, Sweden, and France) have initiated the development of a self-declaration strategies to evidence the CSR claims of firms adhering to ISO 26000 in a systematic way. The Dutch national standardisation body has developed a self-declaration protocol which was laid down in a guideline that now serves as the basis for a proposal to formally acknowledge this strategy within the international ISO network. A self-declaration contains structured information about an organisation's claim that it works in accordance with ISO 26000 and can be subjected to an external audit. Accompanying this initiative is the availability of an online publication platform for organisations to issue an ISO 26000 self-declaration.

4. Analysing ISO 26000 with ST

The nature, contents and consequences of the ISO 26000 standard on the one hand and its promise and take-up by firms on the other hand occasion investigating the signalling value of ISO 26000. In the next sections, ISO 26000 is examined with ST along the lines of the earlier mentioned concepts. The analysis subsequently focuses on the extent to which ISO 26000 can be viewed as a signal of quality and intent, to what extent the standard is an efficacious signal, signal honesty and fit, and signal frequency and consistency. The analysis incorporates aspects related to the nature and the contents of the standard as well as their consequences in the CSR standards environment.

4.1. Signal of Quality and Intent

Adherence to ISO 26000 may dominantly signal a company's intent to engage in CSR. Rather than containing requirements for taking appropriate action or specifying performance levels, it merely offers guidance to firms in interpreting CSR and formulating their CSR policy and CSR implementation. Although the standard emphasises *"the importance of results and improvements in performance"* ([80], p. vi), it neither specifies performance levels for companies in terms of reducing negative social and environmental impacts nor provides accepted or general benchmarks. Hahn [20], in this respect, pointed at the possibility that the adoption of standards as institutionalised rules does not necessarily improve operational efficiency [81–83]. Similar fears were expressed by Schwartz and Tilling [84] who argued that ISO 26000 focuses *"on management techniques and related rituals, rather than on actual outcomes in terms of more responsible actions*" ([84], p. 292). This means that a firm's intention to engage in CSR is decoupled from its actual engagement in CSR and its performance, or CSR quality.

In the absence of appropriate governance or enforcement mechanisms (e.g., certification, required communication on progress), there are few thresholds for claiming ISO 26000 adherence and the standard may even tempt firms that do not possess the CSR quality to signal. This is especially the case when relationships between firms and their stakeholders are characterised by within-firm and between-firm observability of CSR. The low exigencies of ISO 26000 imply the presence of a risk of incongruence between a firm's CSR claim and its actual CSR actions, compromising the credibility of the firm that communicates that it adheres to the standard, the CSR concept in general and the standard itself [85,86]. Information that signals a firm's actual CSR quality (e.g., relative or absolute reduction of carbon emissions, measures the company has taken to find alternatives for the use of deplete-prone natural resources, and information on the working conditions in overseas factories) rather than its intent ultimately determine its credibility in the marketplace.

In the realm of standards, performance can also be conceived of in another way. Various authors have placed ISO 26000 within quality management-oriented approaches towards CSR [20,67,87]. Such approaches are known for their focus on continuous improvement from a systematic plan-do-check-act perspective [87–89] and may be considered to constitute a commitment to improving performance and optimising the efficiency of internal business operations rather than the achievement of ambitious performance levels and innovation. The option of ISO 26000 self-declaration does not solve these problems as this self-declaration is essentially only an exercise in illustrating adherence to the standard, not in performance (see also Section 4.3).

In his analysis of ISO 26000, Hahn [20] concluded that the standard is particularly suited for firms that are in the beginning stages of CSR implementation. He argued that ISO 26000 "*can serve as an introduction into the main concepts of [CSR] and it can help by introducing relevant instruments, initiatives and core elements of an management system for those organizations which are still in the initial stage of implementing [CSR] into orderly management processes. (. . .) For companies beginning to realize their [social responsibilities], ISO 26000 with its content-focus can be a starting point for implementing it into organizational management processes*" ([20], pp. 722–724). While firms in early stages of CSR development may possess a certain CSR quality, it can be assumed that this quality is still underdeveloped and can be considered to be primarily reflecting an intention to further develop their CSR quality. ISO 26000 thus seems to signal intent over performance.

4.2. Efficacy of the Signal

ISO 26000's lack of proper verification and enforcement mechanisms hampers the ability of signal receivers to distinguish between firms with different CSR quality. Such mechanisms can function as useful discriminators between companies of high and low quality [29,70,90]. Related to the cost aspect of efficacious signalling, certification or other second- or third-party conformity assessments provides an illustration of this: high-performing firms generally incur lower certification costs because their practices are already up to par and because better firm capabilities contribute to the reduction of costs related to making the necessary adjustments to qualify for certification [8,29,90,91]. In the case of ISO 26000, however, producing the signal would incur little cost and claiming adherence to the standard would merely require symbolic or selective implementation of change from the organisation. From the perspective of ST, poor-performing firms may experience superior benefits from signalling over non-signalling too and conclude that these benefits outweigh the minor costs involved. High-quality firms are consequently not motivated by arguments of costly signalling to claim that they are working according to ISO 26000 as it does not offer them a comparative advantage vis-à-vis the proverbial cheap talk of low-quality firms. ISO 26000 is thus likely to lead to an uninformative "pooling equilibrium" instead of a "separating equilibrium" in which firms can be clearly distinguished [56,92].

The costs incurred by firms as a result of going through an ISO 26000 self-declaration protocol, such as the ones that are available in the Netherlands, Sweden and France, will probably not be a burden for low-quality firms to signal their adherence to the standard. Although there is a fee involved in publishing a firm's self-declaration on the Dutch ISO 26000 publication platform, and even though the exercise to comply with the applicable guideline requires effort from firms, these burdens may prove to be too low for firms to become reluctant to adhering to the standard in the face of the benefits of doing so.

A final observation on the cost characteristic of signal efficacy relates to the standard's interpretation of CSR. Since this interpretation is dominantly normatively-oriented rather than reflecting a strategic or business case orientation towards CSR, one could argue that, by adhering to ISO 26000, firms choose to respond to stakeholders' and society's expectations primarily from a moral point of view rather than through aligning these interests with their own from a profit-seeking motive [77,78]. As such, adhering to ISO 26000 could indicate that firms opt for a mode of CSR that signals they are prepared to sacrifice profits in the public interest [37,53], leading the standard to account for a costly signal.

The absence of required verification mechanisms such as certification and communications on progress requirement also relate to the observability aspect of efficacious signalling as firms are unable to make their CSR quality visible through these mechanisms. The observability of the CSR quality of ISO 26000-adhering firms is further hampered as neither a public register of companies that adhere to the standard nor a clearinghouse system for ISO 26000 exists. While ISO post-publication surveys have observed a substantial increase in the number of firms that seem to be interested in and adopting ISO 26000 [26,27], it is impossible to determine how many firms and which firms have adopted the standard or even obtain a sensible proxy of this. While not being available for ISO 26000, such provisions are available for many certifiable standards, enabling stakeholders to obtain detailed information on for instance a firm's certification and related data, including the scope of its certification, prior certifications, the period through which the certification is valid, non-conformances, possibly related certifications and firms' management declarations on the topic. Initiatives have however been taken in the context of ISO 26000 that aim to do exactly the opposite: blacklisting companies that wrongfully claim that they have been ISO 26000 certified or are saying that they intend to obtain certification with the standard and showcasing bad practice [93].

As a final point, one of the ways firms can increase the observability of their CSR quality is through disclosing their CSR quality in greater clarity, whereas firms with poor performance will obfuscate their poor quality by using complex and difficult wording, a phenomenon known as the obfuscation hypothesis [94,95]. In a way, ISO 26000 permits vague wording as the standard allows for idiosyncratic approaches to and interpretations of CSR. Any interpretation of CSR is in fact acceptable for the standard as long as it remains within the general confinements of the standards' CSR definition, CSR principles and CSR core subjects. Similarly, Hemphill [21], in this regard, said that ISO 26000 is too broad in its scope, implying that it cannot serve a useful purpose in the context of specific industries and sectors in terms of being a meaningful CSR signal.

4.3. Signal Honesty and Fit

Lacking verification and enforcement mechanisms and the fact that there are hardly any costs involved in signalling adherence to ISO 26000 for firms, make the standard susceptible for false signalling, thereby compromising signal honesty. The low exigencies of ISO 26000 make it easy for companies to polish or even fake underlying qualities and may tempt or encourage firms spitefully wanting to claim an engagement in CSR to only partly implement changes for cosmetic purposes [41,69]. As high-quality firms may be discouraged to signal when low-quality firms can easily send the same signal, the standard could even become a symbol of false signalling, inferior norms and outright deceit. This could lead to dire adverse effects in the face of the standard's objectives, including consciously misinforming stakeholders and obscured purposeful corporate misconduct.

In addition, and as illustrated above, ISO 26000 is particularly concerned with signalling a firm's intention to engage in CSR rather than its CSR performance, rendering it difficult for stakeholders to distinguish between the different signals they receive from different companies and assess these by gauging the extent to which these signals fit firms' underlying CSR quality. Stakeholder assessment of the honesty of a firm's CSR signals is further impeded by the tendency of the standard to decouple action from performance [78,84], making the standard subject to moral hazard as a result of opportunistic firm behaviour. At its best, ISO 26000 would enable stakeholders to differentiate organisations based on their intent to engage in CSR initiatives rather than their actual engagement in these initiatives or the social and environmental effects their engagement engenders. However, it is clear that judging firms based on their intentions may be a precarious exercise in the first place; the litmus test for distinguishing between credible companies ultimately lies in demonstrating CSR performance and hence in evidenced information that signals a firm's quality. Signal honesty thus seems hard to determine in the context of firms that adhere to ISO 26000, especially when compared to, for example, the certifiable environmental management systems standard ISO 14001 and the certifiable variants for ISO 26000 that have been developed to date. ISO 26000 hence upholds between-firm asymmetries.

The aforementioned is inextricably linked to problems in determining the degree to which the signal emitted by firms about their adherence to ISO 26000 correlates with their underlying CSR quality (i.e., signal fit). This may be considered an inherent flaw resulting from the type of standard and the approach to CSR that ISO 26000 represents and points to a phenomenon that can be called the paradox of idiosyncrasy. As the standard leaves a lot of interpretation and application of the CSR concept up to individual firms, the messages that are communicated by firms about their supposed CSR quality may actually reflect their CSR quality well, indicating a high level of signal fit. However, exactly because of the fact that ISO 26000 revolves around company-specific CSR interpretations and implementation, signal fit is very hard to determine for stakeholders and may lead to confusion when they compare even similar firms to each other [9,64]. ISO 26000 may represent a range of CSR interpretations that are used by firms, leading the same signal (i.e., a firm's adherence to ISO 26000) to reflect very different approaches to interpreting and implementing CSR and thus hamper the reduction of between-firm information asymmetries.

The notion of signal fit becomes even more problematic when one takes into account the results of empirical research by Perera [96] on the relevance of the contents of ISO 26000 for SMEs. These results indicate that only a small number of the CSR principles, core subjects and issues that are specified by ISO 26000 are seen as being of sufficient material importance for SMEs. This is attributed to the lack of involvement of SME representatives in the ISO 26000 development process [76,97].

4.4. Signal Frequency and Consistency

Under the condition that signals correspond with each other, signalling effectiveness can be enhanced by sending a larger number of observable signals or increasing the number of signals emitted to reduce information asymmetry [29]. In terms of signal frequency and consistency, ISO 26000 in itself does not necessarily give rise to any particular signalling problems: a firm can signal its adherence to the standard at will and in myriad ways (e.g., through press releases, sustainability reports, corporate presentations or social media) under the homogenous label of ISO 26000. However, ISO 26000 does not have the advantage of offering the possibility to communicate about the results of mandatory periodic conformity assessments such as external audits, re-certification, voluntary assurance statements or regular progress reports that other CSR standards offer. ISO 26000-adhering firms may thus be missing out on opportunities to signal about formal milestones on fixed intervals related to their standards adherence. The fact that alternative standards that have been developed for ISO 26000 are certifiable may therefore reinforce the competitive signalling dynamics in favour of these alternatives, further reducing the relative degree of observability of ISO 26000 (between-firm information asymmetries).

Another aspect of signal frequency lies in the signalling environment of ISO 26000. The Dutch context proves a case-in-point: communications by the national standards body NEN on organisations that have adopted ISO 26000, for instance, seem to be much less frequent than that of the certification institutions that have developed the CSR Performance Ladder, a prominent substitute CSR management systems standard in the Netherlands that was inspired by ISO 26000 and which is certifiable. Certification institutions arguably have stronger marketing and business incentives to communicate about their product and related supporting and certification services as they will financially benefit from both the process leading to certification and the certification itself. This incentive has become even stronger as the CSR Performance Ladder is not endorsed by NEN or the national CSR knowledge centre in the Netherlands. Without this institutional backing, certification organisations are required to put more effort in marketing communications. As consultancies may also benefit from market demand for obtaining certification according to the CSR Performance Ladder through offering advisory, implementation and audit services, they have an incentive to communicate about this standard as well [98].

Despite the standard itself not representing problems in signal consistency for firms, ISO 26000 may well give rise to such problems to occur. For ISO 26000-adhering firms to make their CSR quality better observable and reduce information asymmetries between them and their stakeholders, engaging in additional signalling strategies is required [4]. As illustrated above, the standard only allows for limited signalling, both in terms of the number and diversity of signals. Firms that work with ISO 26000 have multiple options to strengthen their signals, including the adoption of issue-based CSR standards (e.g., SA 8000 and ISO 14001) or adhering to other comprehensive CSR standards that are either mandatorily or voluntary subject to enforcement mechanisms (e.g., Global Compact, DS 49001, CSR Performance Ladder, and Global Reporting Initiative).

Such approaches to strengthen corporate CSR signals may have drawbacks, however. One drawback is that a firm's CSR signals proliferate too much and comprise a diversity of signals that may consequently confuse stakeholders' perception of what a firm actually stands for or focuses on in the context of CSR. A second drawback of this approach relates to signal consistency. As a firm needs to manage an intricate constellation of partly overlapping CSR commitments and performance requirements to manage, it not only risks confusing stakeholders, but also increases the risks of emitting inconsistent signals. This may increase suspicion among stakeholders about the firm's CSR claims. A firm may for instance emit inconsistent signals as both the scope of the contents and the perceived status of the standards it adheres to differ to a certain extent. For instance, ISO 14001 focuses exclusively on environmental management and the DS 49001 that was directly modelled onto ISO 26000 includes the subject of animal welfare. In addition, while ISO 26000 is a worldwide standard based on global consensus, the CSR Performance Ladder was particularly aimed at Dutch firms and the certification institutions involved have only just begun to enter an international playing field with the standard. The signalling firm may even confuse signal receivers in terms of the value it attaches to certification for CSR purposes, since this is something that is not uncontested in practice and an ongoing debate among academics [20,31].

5. Discussion, Theoretical Reflection and Research Suggestions

The analysis through an ST lens in this article shows that, particularly due to its guidance orientation, its focus on intention, its tendency to decouple action from performance and the absence of enforcement mechanisms ISO 26000 may neither be an efficacious signal nor have a high signal fit. However, several points of discussion and reflection arise.

A first point of discussion relates to the mixed results of research on the value of certifications. While some scholars have found labels and certifications in the context of CSR to cause separating equilibriums [56,99], others have however empirically found or argued that certification may not always possess high levels of signal fit either. King et al. [100] found that poor rather stellar performers opt for certification, while Terlaak [71] observed "satisficing signalling" by firms indicating mere compliance with requirements by well-performing subunits rather than aspirations to realise better performance for all subunits. Using certification as a signal may thus have drawbacks as well. Persuaded by the drawbacks of certification, including inconclusiveness in findings whether adopters actually do outperform non-adopters, an undesirable focus on compliance rather than on performance in many organisations and using certification to raise trade barriers and execute power in global networks, Castka and Balzarova [31] earlier concluded that ISO 26000 should indeed have been designed as a guidance standard. However, these authors did not include a signalling perspective in their analysis. From a related angle, Duflo et al. [12] provided experimental empirical evidence that auditors routinely make unethical decisions favouring client interests. Auditors' financial dependence of client firms leads to conflicts of interest and poor incentives to tell the truth and make objective observations on firms' compliance. When this type of information is available in the marketplace, certifications may not turn out to be efficacious mechanisms to create a separating equilibrium and equip firms with a signal of limited value [101]. Evidence of greenwashing by companies that have subscribed to the UNGC or other CSR-related initiatives that involve enforcement mechanisms such as communications on progress may have similar effects as firms obscure their true quality by a smokescreen of signals. This may, in turn, be beneficial for ISO 26000 as it may increase its value relative to CSR management standards that have enforcement mechanisms. The adoption of ISO 26000 in practice could however prove to be the ultimate referee: when it is clear that firms that do possess underlying CSR quality adopt ISO 26000, the standard will gain empirical legitimacy [75]. ISO 26000 may be particularly adopted by firms that already have (certified) social, environmental and quality management systems in place and thus are already well under way with realising the CSR agenda. In addition, while the reputed ISO label may serve as an attractive label or cover for firms that aim to mislead stakeholders and still gain legitimacy in the context of addressing their social and environmental responsibilities, assumptions about the organisational implications of ISO 26000 (e.g., the implementation of a perceived management systems standard and substantive change) may also scare and fence off those uninformed.

A second point of discussion relates to the constitutive function that adhering to ISO 26000 may have for firms despite it being a dysfunctional signal. While intention may not necessarily lead to action or performance, organisational CSR aspirations may yield behavioural dynamics that help guide and build performance by "communicating the organisation into being" [86,102]. In this sense, a firm claiming to adhere to ISO 26000 while not yet possessing adequate underlying CSR quality may perhaps be better able to live up to its own claim and do so more committedly precisely because of its adherence to the standard. Both from the viewpoint of firm-supplier relationships and the perspective of public policy for stimulating transparent and responsible business behaviour, managers and policymakers may thus encourage the use of ISO 26000, although they should be well aware that, to an extent, they intentionally allow and embolden a certain level of loose coupling between intention and action or, as it has been called, corporate hypocrisy [86]. In any case, and illustrated by this latter argument, using ISO 26000 as an instrument in public-private governance requires accountability mechanisms to discipline firm behaviour and prevent excessive opportunism and patterns of free-riding behaviour. In line with the standard's orientation on stakeholder engagement, a firm adhering to ISO 26000 could be disciplined in aligning their intentions, actions and performance and their signalling activity by engaging in sensemaking processes with critical stakeholders, such as NGOs, employees, client panels and public authorities. As such, an approach may minimise risks of greenwashing it may also enable firms in coping with the paradox of idiosyncrasy observed in this article.

5.1. Further Specification of ST Concepts

Analysing ISO 26000 along the lines of key concepts from ST seems to give rise to a further specification of the applied concepts.

ST distinguishes between signalling the quality and signalling the intent of an organisation. One could even say that a firm's intention to engage in CSR using the contents of ISO 26000 as a point of reference perhaps constitutes the main quality of the firm that is signalled, blurring the analytical distinction between signals of quality and intent. Although both types of signals can be observed apart from each other, one could argue that in a CSR context these types of signals may be mutually conditioning. For instance, communicating CSR commitments (intent) without communicating action, demonstrating CSR performance or accountability for social or environmental impacts (quality) leads companies to run the risk of being accused of greenwashing. This distinction resembles the concept of credibility which Becker-Olsen et al. [85] defined as the difference between a company's CSR claim and its CSR action. In addition, the distinction between intent and quality may prove theoretically tangled and consequently difficult to discern in the context of CSR as the mere intent of a firm to behave socially responsible may be perceived as one of its qualities [103]. In addition, the nature of a firm's orientation towards CSR (e.g., public-serving, profit-serving or a combination thereof; see [85]) reveals information about its intent, which may be relevant in stakeholders' assessments. Such a position could even be dependent on stakeholders' orientations towards CSR: some stakeholders may find a firm more credible when it pursues a business case approach to CSR, while others would prefer the firm to be engaged in CSR purely for the betterment of society. Instead of distinguishing between signals of intent and signals of quality, perhaps a more useful distinction in this context could be between a signal of intent on the one hand and signals of action, performance and impact on the other [86]. Signals of quality could then also be perceived as a construct that encompasses these different signals and constitute a proxy for the level of within-firm information asymmetries in the context of CSR and even the alignment of signals of intent and signals of quality. In this latter case, one may speak of signal of fit, not be confused with signal fit.

A second suggestion relates to a specification of the concepts of signal frequency and consistency. Signal diversity may be a more appropriate label than signal frequency as the latter is concerned with repeatedly sending out one and the same signal (which may be called "signal iteration"), while the former is concerned with emitting a greater variety of signals (which may be called "signal proliferation"). Signal iteration relates more to the timing of signals, for instance, making sure that signals have good reach among relevant stakeholders without overloading receivers with information. Signal proliferation then is the phenomenon that gives rise to investigating signal consistency, as this may increase the risk of emitting conflicting signals resulting in a diffuse or polymorph aggregate signal for receivers. In fact, from a theoretical point of view, it is proposed that "signal congruence" may be a better term for the phenomenon described by Connelly et al. [29] than signal consistency. To illustrate this in a CSR context: signal consistency seems to apply more to a situation in which a company publishes a sustainability report with irregular intervals (e.g., not consistently on an annual or bi-annual basis) or in which a company publishes sustainability reports that are not always accompanied by assurance statements or include accounts resulting from stakeholder consultations (i.e., inconsistencies in data quality). The degree of signal congruence hence focuses on the extent to which different signals present corresponding messages or contents.

5.2. Research Suggestions

This article has argued that, because of the existence of within-firm and between-firm information asymmetries, it may prove hard for stakeholders to interpret and assess signals relating to unobservable qualities such as CSR, even when companies signal their adherence to standards. A first suggestion would therefore be to focus research on identifying strategies for different types to stakeholders to evaluate corporate CSR claims that are based on non-certifiable standards. This is also a relevant research question for companies themselves, as companies that take their CSR commitments seriously would probably be interested in learning how to inform their stakeholders effectively. Obviously, stakeholder engagement strategies and stakeholder dialogue may prove useful as signals are created, attributed meaning to and institutionalised in the process of continuously interacting parties [13,104,105]. However, what if a firm provides only limited options for such engagement and dialogue? Would the fact that it does so, and thereby breaches a principle behind many CSR standards, be a signal that becomes stakeholders' main source for dismissing its CSR claim?

A second research project could be guided by the question whether signal fit is higher with non-certifiable CSR standards than with certifiable management systems. Non-certifiable may have lower exigencies, but may fence off firms with low CSR signal fit as they prefer to send a signal that is more costly. Since scholarly work appears to show mixed results on this issue, research could be guided by the question "are companies that adhere to non-certifiable CSR standards more likely to possess the unobservable qualities than those that adhere to certifiable CSR standards?"

Thirdly, as signal strength appears to be dependent on various aspects (not only certification), research could focus on empirically assessments of the signal strength of various CSR standards, both certifiable and non-certifiable and with different enforcement mechanisms (e.g., ISO 26000, UNGC, SA 8000, and AA 1000 series), using the ST concepts used and refinements suggested in this article. In addition, research could be directed at the emerging competitive landscape of CSR standards, investigate what standards will surface for what reasons and the degree to which signal strength possesses explanatory value for this phenomenon. In particular, future research may not only be directed towards different types of CSR management standards, but also aim at exploring related frameworks that are widely used by firms to communicate about their social and environmental performance. From a signalling perspective, sustainability and integrated reporting frameworks may serve as prominent signalling devices for firms, in terms of both adopting such frameworks and the type of information firms communicate in their reports. While several scholars have recently investigated the relationship between firms' sustainability reporting and other types of disclosure (e.g., greenhouse gas emissions) on the one hand and information asymmetries on the other hand in general terms [59,106,107], none of them have endeavoured into applying ST in detail to this type of corporate communication.

The main research question that imposes itself based on this article, however, is what effective signal-enhancing strategies can be formulated in the context of ISO 26000 and other non-certifiable CSR standards. Given the weak signal that ISO 26000 has been argued to be, what strategies can firms pursue to strengthen the signal they emit by adhering to this standard? Speculating on these strategies, and next to an (externally assured) ISO 26000 self-declaration, firms could opt for a certifiable variant of ISO 26000, although these have mainly been developed in several national contexts by standardisation bodies until now. A second strategy for firms could be to obtain certification according to substitute certifiable comprehensive CSR standards developed by other organisations, or use these in combination with ISO 26000. A third option concerns adhering to multiple certifiable standards in CSR-related domains, such as quality, environment, accountability, and occupational health and safety. A fourth strategy for firms could be to have their claim to adhere to ISO 26000 or their self-declaration externally assured [4]. Empirical research could focus on determining whether and under what conditions firms would consider different signal-enhancing strategies, the efficacy of (combinations of) these strategies and the perceptions of stakeholders of them. These strategies are, again, not limited to the adoption of standards, but also include the application of reporting frameworks and engaging in other types of sustainability-related disclosures. In these research efforts, scholars may particularly pay attention to issues related to signal frequency and consistency, including the refinements suggested in this article. As Connelly et al. noted in this respect: "*Sending different signals from the same signaller, or the same signal from different signallers, could change the way receivers interpret those signals*" ([29], p. 59).

6. Conclusions

In the context of public-private governance for sustainability, CSR and sustainability standards have a particular and potentially promising role to play as form of "governance beyond government". Firms have clear incentives to signal their underlying CSR quality and many have opted for adhering to CSR standards as way of reducing information asymmetries in their relationships with stakeholders. The ISO 26000 standard is a prominent case in point and may, in the context of realising both public values and business goals, serve as a signalling device for firms aiming to communicate their CSR quality. However, despite the high level of legitimacy ISO 26000 possesses based on its inclusive, multi-stakeholder-oriented development process and the practical value its CSR framework offers adopters, firms adhering to the standard risk emitting a rather weak signal. Analysing the standard with ST shows that the standard satisfies neither characteristic of an efficacious signal (observability and costliness) and signal honesty and signal fit may be rather low. In addition, the standard appears to lead to problems of signal frequency and signal consistency. The low exigencies of ISO 26000, including it lacking an enforcement mechanism, are a root cause of these problems. Firms may consequently be tempted to signal underlying CSR qualities that they actually do not possess. This can lead ISO 26000 to become a signal of companies with poor CSR performance and even a standard for greenwashing. In addition, the idiosyncratic approach to CSR that the standard propagates requires a lot of effort from stakeholders to observe and assess the CSR quality of ISO 26000-adhering firms. The standard thus adds proof to the obfuscation hypothesis and by creating uninformative pooling equilibriums does not seem to be suited for differentiation purposes. Against this background, when adopting or encouraging the use of ISO 26000, firms and governments may well compromise the promise of public-private governance of sustainability.

The fact that ISO 26000 was not developed as a certifiable management systems standard has led to the emergence of other CSR standards that make CSR better observable, thus enhancing between-firm information asymmetries to its disadvantage. The analysis in this article points at the necessity of using of additional signalling strategies for firms that adhere to ISO 26000, including self-declaration and the adoption of certifiable (issue-based) CSR standards. However, as the standard necessitates firms to turn to alternative signalling strategies, stakeholders may be more likely to misinterpret and get confused by a firms CSR signals.

From the perspective of public-private governance, the question should hence be raised whether ISO 26000 is an appropriate standard to further engage firms (and other organisations that want to use this guidance) in the sustainability agenda, for instance by policymakers in the social and environmental realm. Interestingly, governments have been a contributor to the multi-stakeholder process that has led to the creation of ISO 26000, too, and the interest of public authorities in private governance has been on the increase. In addition, certification is not a solution for the signalling problems voluntary standards engender per se [1]. In the final analysis, it may be said that the differentiating characteristics of ISO 26000, including the fact that it is not certifiable and allows for idiosyncratic interpretations of CSR, can easily compromise its value. Images of realising public values may actually be not much more than a cover for achieving the same business goals as ever. In the context of public-private governance, such greenwashing may well tarnish not only the credibility of business, but also that of other partners involved, including governments and non-governmental organisations. Against the background of the results of the numerous studies mentioned in this article that point at the drawbacks of private and public-private governance in general and CSR and sustainability-related standards in particular, the question then is: Where does this leave the potential value of ISO 26000 for public-private governance? Perhaps a starting point for getting to the most viable answer to this question can be found in the conclusion reached by Mayer and Gereffi ([108], p. 19) on private governance: *"unless private governance is supplemented and reinforced by public institutions of governance, it cannot provide adequate governance capacity for the global economy"* However, to avoid solely resorting to the route of legislation and in order to honour the central idea of public-private governance, ISO 26000 may function as a platform for public and private institutions to discuss, negotiate and mutually enforce the responsibilities, initiatives and outcomes of both firms, governments and non-governmental organisations in achieving sustainability. This may take the form of continuous and transparent stakeholder dialogue as a way of aligning interests and securing accountability mechanisms that may make the signals emitted credible and less susceptible to misinterpretation. The agenda offered by the United Nations Sustainable Development Goals (SDGs) and the consequent initiatives taken by governments, non-governmental organisations (including citizen-led initiatives) and firms worldwide to promote and achieve this agenda may be an emerging (although embryonic) example in this regard. Such an approach may result in the adoption of a variety of idiosyncratic public-private governance arrangements, each characterised by their own signalling strategies [4], including the involved parties auditing each other and communicating the results of this process in a fully transparent way. Inclusive, global partnerships, either directly targeted at activities to tackle the SDGs or aimed at creating new public-private governance arrangements (including standards) may be an example of this.

Paradoxically, as the analysis in this article has shown, ISO 26000 may discourage precisely those investments that are necessary to develop and send credible signals of current and future CSR performance that reduce information asymmetries in firm-stakeholder relationships that firms need in order to capitalise on their CSR efforts. Not being able to capitalise on their efforts may hinder taking up their role in the public-private governance of sustainability beyond complying with legislation. However, this does not say that ISO 26000 will not be taken up by firms worldwide—surveys among businesses actually indicate that the adoption of the standard has gained traction—or that the standard will be discouraged through public policy or supported by non-governmental organisations. Firms, their stakeholders, governments and organisations involved in the standardisation of business conduct should be aware of the signals firms emit by ISO 26000 in order to not let the standard become part of the problems it set out to solve and exacerbate rather than reduce problems in public-private governance.

Funding: This research received no external funding.

Conflicts of Interest: The authors declare no conflicts of interest.

References

1. Marx, A.; Cuypers, D. Forest certification as a global environmental governance tool: What is the macro-effectiveness of the Forest Stewardship Council? *Regul. Gov.* **2010**, *4*, 408–434. [CrossRef]
2. Marx, A. Global governance and the certification revolution: Types, trends and challenges. In *Handbook on the Politics of Regulation*; Levi-Faur, D., Ed.; Edward Elgar: Cheltenham, UK, 2011; pp. 590–603.
3. Moratis, L. Signalling strategies for ISO 26000: A firm-level approach. *Int. J. Oper. Prod. Manag.* **2016**, *36*, 512–531. [CrossRef]
4. Moratis, L. Consequences of collaborative governance in CSR: An empirical illustration of strategic responses to institutional pluralism and some theoretical implications. *Bus. Soc. Rev.* **2016**, *121*, 415–446. [CrossRef]
5. Johnston, J. *Signaling Social Responsibility: On the Law and Economics of Market Incentives for Corporate Environmental Performance*; Regulatory Policy Program Working Paper RPP-2006-01; University of Pennsylvania Law School: Philadelphia, PA, USA, 2005.
6. Malik, M. Value-enhancing capabilities of CSR: A brief review of contemporary literature. *J. Bus. Ethics* **2015**, *127*, 419–438. [CrossRef]
7. Perez-Batres, L.; Doh, J.; Miller, V.; Pisani, M. Stakeholder pressures as determinants of CSR strategic choice: Why do firms choose symbolic versus substantive self-regulatory codes of conduct? *J. Bus. Ethics* **2012**, *110*, 157–172. [CrossRef]
8. Terlaak, A. Satisficing Signalling: Corporate Social Strategy and Certified Management Standards. In *Academy of Management Best Paper Proceedings*; Academy of Management: Briarcliff Manor, NY, USA, 2007.
9. Cramer, J.; Van der Heijden, A.; Jonker, J. Corporate social responsibility: Making sense through thinking and acting. *Bus. Ethics A Eur. Rev.* **2006**, *15*, 380–389. [CrossRef]
10. Matten, D.; Moon, J. 'Implicit' and 'explicit' CSR: A conceptual framework for a comparative understanding of corporate social responsibility. *Acad. Manag. Rev.* **2008**, *33*, 404–424. [CrossRef]
11. Okoye, A. Theorizing corporate social responsibility as an essentially contested concept: Is a definition necessary? *J. Bus. Ethics* **2009**, *89*, 613–627. [CrossRef]
12. Duflo, E.; Greenstone, M.; Pande, R.; Ryan, N. *Truth-Telling by Third-Party Auditors and the Response of Polluting Firms: Experimental Evidence from India*; MIT Department of Economics Working Paper No. 13–17; MIT: Cambridge, MA, USA, 2013.
13. Morsing, M.; Schultz, M. Corporate social responsibility communication: Stakeholder information, response and involvement strategies. *Bus. Ethics A Eur. Rev.* **2006**, *15*, 323–338. [CrossRef]

14. Globescan. Credibility Gap Persists around Companies' CSR Communications. Available online: http://www.globescan.com/commentary-and-analysis/featured-findings/entry/credibility-gap-persists-around-companies-csr-communications.html (accessed on 15 September 2018).

15. Basu, K.; Palazzo, G. Corporate social responsibility: A process model of sensemaking. *Acad. Manag. Rev.* **2008**, *33*, 122–136. [CrossRef]

16. Jahdi, K.; Acikdilli, G. Marketing communications and corporate social responsibility: Marriage of convenience or shotgun wedding? *J. Bus. Ethics* **2009**, *88*, 103–113. [CrossRef]

17. Rasche, A. Collaborative governance 2.0. *Corp. Gov.* **2010**, *10*, 500–511. [CrossRef]

18. Rasche, A. Corporate responsibility standards. In *Continental Philosophy and Business Ethics*; Painter-Morland, M., Ten Bos, R., Eds.; Cambridge University Press: Cambridge, UK, 2011; pp. 263–284.

19. Idowu, S.; Sitnikov, C.; Moratis, L. (Eds.) *ISO 26000: A Standardized View on Corporate Social Responsibility*; Springer: Heidelberg, Germany, 2018.

20. Hahn, R. Standardizing social responsibility? New perspectives on guidance documents and management system standards for sustainable development. *IEEE Trans. Eng. Manag.* **2012**, *59*, 717–727. [CrossRef]

21. Hemphill, T. The ISO 26000 guidance on social responsibility international standard: What are the business governance implications? *Corp. Gov.* **2013**, *13*, 305–317. [CrossRef]

22. Mena, S.; Palazzo, G. Input and output legitimacy of multi-stakeholder initiatives. *Bus. Ethics Q.* **2012**, *22*, 527–556. [CrossRef]

23. Mueckenberger, U.; Jastram, S. Transnational norm-building networks and the legitimacy of corporate social responsibility. *J. Bus. Ethics* **2010**, *97*, 223–239. [CrossRef]

24. AFNOR. *Engaging in Dialogue—Focus on Our Social Responsibility*; AFNOR: Paris, France, 2018.

25. European Commission. *An Analysis of Policy References Made by Large EU Companies to Internationally Recognised CSR Guidelines and Principles*; European Commission: Brussels, Belgium, 2013.

26. ISO. *ISO 26000 Post-Publication Survey 2011*; ISO: Geneva, Switzerland, 2011.

27. ISO. *ISO 26000 Post-Publication Survey 2012*; ISO: Geneva, Switzerland, 2012.

28. ISO. *ISO 26000 and OECD Guidelines—Practical Overview of the Linkages*; ISO: Geneva, Switzerland, 2017.

29. Connelly, B.; Certo, T.; Ireland, D.; Reutzel, C. Signaling theory: A review and assessment. *J. Manag.* **2011**, *37*, 39–67. [CrossRef]

30. Frynas, J.; Yamahaki, C. Corporate social responsibility: Review and roadmap of theoretical perspectives. *Bus. Ethics A Eur. Rev.* **2016**, *25*, 258–285. [CrossRef]

31. Castka, P.; Balzarova, M. Social responsibility standardization: Guidance or reinforcement through certification? *Hum. Syst. Manag.* **2008**, *27*, 231–242.

32. Akerlof, G. The market for "lemons": Quality uncertainty and the market mechanism. *Q. J. Econ.* **1970**, *84*, 488–500. [CrossRef]

33. Spence, M. Job market signalling. *Q. J. Econ.* **1973**, *87*, 355–374. [CrossRef]

34. Stiglitz, J. Information and economic analysis: A perspective. *Econ. J.* **1985**, *95*, 21–41. [CrossRef]

35. Davila, A.; Foster, G.; Gupta, M. Venture capital financing and the growth of startup firms. *J. Bus. Vent.* **2003**, *18*, 689–708. [CrossRef]

36. Jones, R.; Murrell, A. Signaling positive corporate social performance: An event study of family-friendly firms. *Bus. Soc.* **2001**, *40*, 59–78. [CrossRef]

37. Reinhardt, F.; Stavins, R.; Vietor, H. Corporate social responsibility through an economic lens. *Rev. Environ. Econ. Policy* **2008**, *2*, 219–239. [CrossRef]

38. Windsor, D. The future of corporate social responsibility. *Int. J. Org. Anal.* **2001**, *9*, 225–256. [CrossRef]

39. Busenitz, L.; Fiet, J.; Moesel, D. Signaling in venture capitalist–new venture team funding decisions: Does it indicate long-term venture outcomes? *Entrep. Theory Pract.* **2005**, *29*, 1–12. [CrossRef]

40. Zhang, Y.; Wiersema, M. Stock market reaction to CEO certification: The signaling role of CEO background. *Strateg. Manag. J.* **2009**, *30*, 693–710. [CrossRef]

41. Laufer, W. Social accountability and corporate greenwashing. *J. Bus. Ethics* **2003**, *43*, 253–261. [CrossRef]

42. Marquis, C.; Toffel, M. *When do Firms Greenwash? Corporate Visibility, Civil Society Scrutiny, and Environmental Disclosure*; Harvard Business School Working Paper 11–115; Harvard Business School: Boston, MA, USA, 2012.

43. Balboa, M.; Marti, J. Factors that determine the reputation of private equity managers in developing markets. *J. Bus. Vent.* **2007**, *22*, 453–480. [CrossRef]

44. Chung, W.; Kalnins, A. Agglomeration effects and performance: A test of the Texas lodging industry. *Strateg. Manag. J.* **2001**, *22*, 969–988. [CrossRef]

45. Fischer, E.; Reuber, R. The good, the bad, and the unfamiliar: The challenges of reputation formation facing new firms. *Entrep. Theory Pract.* **2007**, *31*, 53–75. [CrossRef]

46. Carroll, A. Corporate social responsibility: Evolution of a definitional construct. *Bus. Soc.* **1999**, *38*, 268–295. [CrossRef]

47. Dahlsrud, A. How corporate social responsibility is defined: An analysis of 37 definitions. *Corp. Soc. Responsib. Environ. Manag.* **2008**, *15*, 1–13. [CrossRef]

48. Carroll, A.; Shabana, K. The business case for corporate social responsibility: A review of concepts, research and practice. *Int. J. Manag. Rev.* **2010**, *12*, 85–105. [CrossRef]

49. Lee, M. Review of the theories of corporate social responsibility: Its evolutionary path and the road ahead. *Int. J. Manag. Rev.* **2008**, *10*, 53–73. [CrossRef]

50. Cui, J.; Jo, H.; Na, H. Does corporate social responsibility affect information asymmetry? *J. Bus. Ethics* **2018**, *148*, 549–572. [CrossRef]

51. Daugherty, E. Public relations and social responsibility. In *Handbook of Public Relations*; Heath, R., Ed.; Sage: Newcastle upon Tyne, UK, 2001; pp. 389–402.

52. Fan, Y. Ethical branding and corporate reputation. *Corp. Commun. Int. J.* **2005**, *10*, 341–350. [CrossRef]

53. Lys, T.; Naughton, J.; Wang, C. Signaling through corporate accountability reporting. *J. Acc. Econ.* **2015**, *60*, 56–72. [CrossRef]

54. Pfau, M.; Haigh, M.; Sims, J.; Wigley, S. The influence of corporate social responsibility campaigns on public opinion. *Corp. Reputat. Rev.* **2008**, *11*, 145–154. [CrossRef]

55. Clarke, J.; Gibson-Sweet, M. The use of corporate social disclosures in the management of reputation and legitimacy: A cross sectoral analysis of UK Top 100 Companies. *Bus. Ethics A Eur. Rev.* **1999**, *8*, 5–13. [CrossRef]

56. Etilé, F.; Teyssier, S. Signaling corporate social responsibility: Testing third-party certification vs. brands. *Scand. J. Econ.* **2016**, *118*, 397–432. [CrossRef]

57. Gugerty, M. Signaling virtue: Voluntary accountability programs among nonprofit organizations. *Policy Sci.* **2009**, *42*, 243–273. [CrossRef]

58. Scherer, A.; Palazzo, G. The new political role of business in a globalized world: A review of a new perspective on CSR and its implications for the firm, governance, and democracy. *J. Manag. Stud.* **2011**, *48*, 899–931. [CrossRef]

59. Wang, Z.; Tien-Shih, H.; Sarkis, J. CSR performance and the readability of CSR reports: Too good to be true? *Corp. Soc. Responsib. Environ. Manag.* **2018**, *25*, 66–79. [CrossRef]

60. Rutherford, B. Obfuscation, textual complexity and the role of regulated narrative accounting disclosure in corporate governance. *J. Manag. Gov.* **2003**, *7*, 187–210. [CrossRef]

61. Lydenberg, S. Envisioning socially responsible investing: A model for 2006. *J. Corp. Citizensh.* **2002**, *7*, 57–77. [CrossRef]

62. Frankental, P. Corporate social responsibility—A PR invention? *Corp. Commun. Int. J.* **2001**, *6*, 18–23. [CrossRef]

63. Moon, J.; Crane, A.; Matten, D. Can corporations be citizens? Corporate citizenship as a metaphor for business participation in society. *Bus. Ethics Q.* **2005**, *15*, 427–451. [CrossRef]

64. Murillo, D.; Lozano, J. SMEs and CSR: An approach to CSR in their own words. *J. Bus. Ethics* **2006**, *67*, 227–240. [CrossRef]

65. Barth, R.; Wolff, F. *Corporate Social Responsibility in Europe: Rhetoric and Realities*; Edward Elgar: Cheltenham, UK, 2009.

66. Perera, L.; Chaminda, J. Corporate social responsibility and product evaluation: The moderating role of brand familiarity. *Corp. Soc. Responsib. Environ. Manag.* **2012**, *20*, 245–256. [CrossRef]

67. Castka, P.; Balzarova, M. The impact of ISO 9000 and ISO 14000 on standardisation of social responsibility—An inside perspective. *Int. J. Prod. Econ.* **2008**, *113*, 74–87. [CrossRef]

68. Mijatovic, I.; Stokic, D. The influence of internal and external codes on CSR practice: The case of companies operating in Serbia. *J. Bus. Ethics* **2010**, *94*, 533–552. [CrossRef]

69. Mueller, M.; Dos Santos, V.; Seuring, S. The contribution of environmental and social standards towards ensuring legitimacy in supply chain governance. *J. Bus. Ethics* **2009**, *89*, 509–523. [CrossRef]

70. Pflugrath, G.; Roebuck, P.; Simnett, R. Impact of assurance and assurer's professional affiliation on financial analysts' assessment of credibility of corporate social responsibility information. *Audit. A J. Pract. Theory* **2011**, *30*, 239–254. [CrossRef]

71. Terlaak, A. Order without law: The role of certified management standards in shaping socially desired firm behaviors. *Acad. Manag. Rev.* **2007**, *32*, 968–985. [CrossRef]

72. Bovens, M. Analyzing and assessing accountability: A conceptual framework. *Eur. Law J.* **2007**, *13*, 447–468. [CrossRef]

73. Gilbert, D.; Rasche, A.; Waddock, S. Accountability in a global economy: The emergence of international accountability standards. *Bus. Ethics Q.* **2011**, *21*, 23–44. [CrossRef]

74. Waddock, S. Building a new institutional infrastructure for corporate responsibility. *Acad. Manag. Perspect.* **2008**, *22*, 87–108. [CrossRef]

75. Hahn, R.; Weidtmann, C. Transnational governance, deliberative democracy, and the legitimacy of ISO 26000: Analyzing the case of a global multi-stakeholder process. *Bus. Soc.* **2016**, *55*, 90–129. [CrossRef]

76. Balzarova, M.; Castka, P. Stakeholders' influence and contribution to social standards development: The case of multiple stakeholder approach to ISO 26000 development. *J. Bus. Ethics* **2012**, *111*, 265–279. [CrossRef]

77. Johnston, A. *Constructing Sustainability through CSR: A Critical Appraisal of ISO 26000*; University of Oslo Faculty of Law Research Paper No. 2011–33; University of Sheffield: Sheffield, UK, 2011.

78. Moratis, L. Out of the ordinary? An appraisal of the ISO 26000 definition of (corporate) social responsibility. *Int. J. Law Manag.* **2013**, *58*, 26–47. [CrossRef]

79. Webb, K. *ISO 26000: Bridging the Public/private Divide in Transnational Business Governance Interactions*; Osgoode Hall Law School Research Paper Series No. 21/2012; Osgoode Hall Law School: Toronto, ON, Canada, 2012.

80. ISO. *ISO 26000—Guidance on Social Responsibility*; ISO: Geneva, Switzerland, 2010.

81. DiMaggio, P.; Powell, W. The iron cage revisited: Institutional isomorphism and collective rationality in organizational fields. *Am. Soc. Rev.* **1983**, *48*, 147–160. [CrossRef]

82. Meyer, J.; Rowan, B. Institutionalized organizations: Formal structure as myth and ceremony. *Am. J. Soc.* **1977**, *83*, 340–363. [CrossRef]

83. Westphal, J.; Zajac, E. Decoupling policy from practice: The case of stock repurchase programs. *Adm. Sci. Q.* **2001**, *46*, 202–228. [CrossRef]

84. Schwartz, B.; Tilling, K. 'ISO-lating' corporate social responsibility in the organizational context: A dissenting interpretation of ISO 26000. *Corp. Soc. Responsib. Environ. Manag.* **2009**, *16*, 289–299. [CrossRef]

85. Becker-Olsen, K.; Cudmore, A.; Hill, R. The impact of perceived corporate social responsibility on consumer behaviour. *J. Bus. Res.* **2006**, *59*, 46–53. [CrossRef]

86. Christensen, L.; Morsing, M.; Thyssen, O. CSR as aspirational talk. *Organization* **2013**, *20*, 372–393. [CrossRef]

87. Castka, P.; Balzarova, M. A critical look on quality through CSR lenses: Key challenges stemming from the development of ISO 26000. *Int. J. Qual. Reliab. Manag.* **2007**, *24*, 738–752. [CrossRef]

88. McAdam, R.; Leonard, D. Corporate social responsibility in a total quality management context: Opportunities for sustainable growth. *Corp. Gov.* **2003**, *3*, 36–45. [CrossRef]

89. Van der Wiele, T.; Kok, P.; McKenna, R.; Brown, A. A corporate social responsibility audit within a quality management framework. *J. Bus. Ethics* **2001**, *31*, 285–297. [CrossRef]

90. Terlaak, A.; King, A. The effect of certification with the ISO 9000 quality management standard: A signaling approach. *J. Econ. Behav. Organ.* **2006**, *60*, 579–602. [CrossRef]

91. Riley, J. Silver signals: Twenty-five years of screening and signalling. *J. Econ. Lit.* **2001**, *39*, 432–478. [CrossRef]

92. Kirmani, A.; Rao, A. No pain, no gain: A critical review of the literature on signaling unobservable product quality. *J. Mark.* **2000**, *64*, 66–79. [CrossRef]

93. Henriques, A. *Standards for Change: ISO 26000 and Sustainable Development*; International Institute for Environment and Development: London, UK, 2012.

94. Bakar, A.; Ameer, R. Readability of corporate social responsibility communication in Malaysia. *Corp. Soc. Responsib. Environ. Manag.* **2011**, *18*, 50–60. [CrossRef]

95. Barkemeyer, R.; Comyns, B.; Figge, F.; Napolitano, G. CEO statements in corporate sustainability reports—Substantive information or background noise? *Acad. Manag.* **2012**, *38*, 241–257. [CrossRef]

96. Perera, O. *How Material is ISO 26000 Social Responsibility to Small and Medium-Sized Enterprises?* IISD: Winnipeg, MB, Canada, 2008.

97. Egyedi, T.; Toffaletti, S. Standardising social responsibility: Analysing ISO representation issues from an SME perspective. In *Proceedings 13th EURAS Workshop on Standardisation*; Jakobs, K., Soederstroem, E., Eds.; Wissenschafts Verlag Mainz: Aachen, Germany, 2008; pp. 121–136.

98. Delmas, M.; Montes-Sancho, M. An institutional perspective on the diffusion of international management system standards: The case of the environmental management standard ISO 14001. *Bus. Ethics Q.* **2011**, *21*, 103–132. [CrossRef]

99. Miles, M.; Munilla, L. The potential impact of social accountability certification on marketing: A short note. *J. Bus. Ethics* **2004**, *50*, 1–11. [CrossRef]

100. King, A.; Lenox, L.; Terlaak, A. The strategic use of decentralized institutions: Exploring certification with the ISO 14001 management standard. *Acad. Manag. J.* **2005**, *48*, 1091–1106. [CrossRef]

101. Delmas, M. Barriers and incentives to the adoption of ISO 14001 in the United States. *Duke Environ. Law Policy Forum* **2000**, *11*, 1–38.

102. Schoeneborn, D.; Trittin, H. Transcending transmission: Towards a constitutive perspective on CSR communication. *Corp. Commun. Int. J.* **2011**, *18*, 193–211. [CrossRef]

103. Idowu, S.; Papasolomou, I. Are the corporate social responsibility matters based on good intentions or false pretences? An empirical study of the motivations behind the issuing of CSR reports by UK companies. *Corp. Gov.* **2007**, *7*, 136–147. [CrossRef]

104. Basdeo, D.; Smith, K.; Grimm, C.; Rindova, V.; Derfus, P. The impact of market actions on firm reputation. *Strateg. Manag. J.* **2006**, *27*, 1205–1219. [CrossRef]

105. Nijhof, A.; Jeurissen, R. A sensemaking perspective on corporate social responsibility: Introduction to the special issue. *Bus. Ethics A Eur. Rev.* **2006**, *15*, 316–322. [CrossRef]

106. Borghei, Z.; Leung, P.; Guthrie, J. Does voluntary greenhouse gas emissions disclosure reduce information asymmetry? Australian evidence. *Afro-Asian J. Finnanc. Acc.* **2018**, *8*, 123–147. [CrossRef]

107. Michaels, A.; Grüning, M. Relationship of corporate social responsibility disclosure on information asymmetry and the cost of capital. *J. Manag. Control* **2017**, *28*, 251–274. [CrossRef]

108. Mayer, F.; Gereffi, G. Regulation and economic globalization: Prospects and limits of private governance. *Bus. Polit.* **2010**, *12*, 1–25. [CrossRef]

Article

The Impacts of Cocoa Sustainability Initiatives in West Africa

Verina Ingram [1,2,]*[⬤], Fedes van Rijn [2], Yuca Waarts [2] and Henk Gilhuis [3]

[1] Forest & Nature Conservation Policy Group, Wageningen University and Research, P.O. Box 100, 6708 PB Wageningen, The Netherlands

[2] Wageningen Economic Research, Wageningen University and Research, P.O. Box 100, 6708 PB Wageningen, The Netherlands; fedes.vanrijn@wur.nl (F.v.R.); Yuca.Waarts@wur.nl (Y.W.)

[3] Rainforest Alliance, De Ruyterkade 6, 1013 AA, Amsterdam, The Netherlands; HGilhuis@ra.org

* Correspondence: verina.ingram@wur.nl; Tel.: +31-6-1461-5485

Received: 20 October 2018; Accepted: 4 November 2018; Published: 17 November 2018

Abstract: To tackle the multiple challenges facing the cocoa sector, voluntary sustainability standards and corporate initiatives, largely focusing on farm and farmer group scale, are often implemented by public–private–civil society partnerships of stakeholders further in the value chain. This paper looks at the social, economic, and environmental effects of such initiatives, based on empirical evidence from large-scale, mixed-method studies using a suite of socioeconomic, agronomic, and environmental indicators to compare the situation of UTZ certified with non-certified farmers in 2012 and 2015 in Ghana, and 2013 and 2017 in Ivory Coast. The results show that, on average, outcomes are mixed and generally modest. However, significant cocoa productivity and income increases were experienced by certified farmers receiving a full package of services. However, the type and intensity of services has changed over time, decreasing for half of the farmers, and productivity and income increases are levelling off. These findings suggest that whilst partnerships have created new governance arrangements with an increased focus on sustainable value chains, initiatives which result in a living income and optimise productivity, whilst limiting environmental impacts, require sectoral transformation, continued partnerships, plus a range of other policy instruments to address the persistent, wicked problems in cocoa production.

Keywords: cocoa; value chain; voluntary sustainability standards (VSS); governance; public–private partnerships

---

1. Introduction

1.1. Wicked Problems Converge on Cocoa Farms

The context of cocoa farming has changed little in the last sixty years during which cocoa has been traded as an international commodity [1]. Whilst the term cocoa means "the food of the gods", at farm level, the cocoa sector faces a number of deeply embedded, interrelated challenges. These include old trees, pests and diseases, which lower tree productivity [2–4]; low farmer and worker profits and incomes [5–8]; persistent poor labour conditions; the use of child and forced labour [9,10]; negative environmental impacts, such as deforestation, soil degradation, and soil and water pollution [11]; coupled with political instability in many of the origin countries [12–15]. These wicked problems have proved difficult to solve because of incomplete, contradictory, and changing views on how sustainability has been defined in the cocoa sector [16]. Small-scale farmers continue to dominate cocoa production, particularly in West Africa, where they produced an estimated 73% of total production in 2015 [17]. These farmers generally rely on cocoa for a major proportion of their household income [18], and form part of a highly segmented value chain: selling dried and fermented cocoa beans to individual traders or cooperatives, who sell to traders and exporters. Traders then sell to processors and confectionary companies which process cocoa into intermediate products (cocoa powder, butter, and liquor) and, then, into food and cosmetic products [19].

1.2. The Growth of Voluntary Sustainability Standards and Services to Farmers

In contrast to the cocoa farm household scale, at a value chain level, virtually every dimension of international cocoa value chains has changed in the last two decades [20]. In major producing countries, such as Ivory Coast, Ghana, Indonesia, and Cameroon, since the 1990s, exports, market power, and price setting have been largely determined by the private sector. Sufficient quality supply has increasingly become an issue due to growing demand [7,21] and supply variability, due to large annual fluctuations in cocoa production caused by multiple factors, particularly the weather. The tight relationship between supply and long-term cyclical recession and expansion booms has affected global market and farm gate prices [12–15]. Bean quality has generally been increasing, due to training, increasing use of drying equipment, and market and regulatory standards. The governance of production and quality aspects, input credit and supply, extension services and market infrastructure, has been state-controlled in the main West African producing countries. However, producing country governments have gradually lost their ability to manage the international cocoa market and shape their own domestic markets. Since the late 1990s, a market-based corporate governance and price negotiation system has developed in many production countries, with the breakdown of national institutions, low yielding cocoa harvests, and pressure from international financial institutions for economic structural adjustment. Foreign companies have increased their investments, integration, and position in the chain. Exporters and major traders, such as Cargill, Barry Callebaut, Olam, and Armajaro, then began to buy and sell using London Cocoa Futures market prices. This liberalised system left farmers exposed to global price fluctuations and resulted in reforms in Ghana and Ivory Coast in 1999 and 2012, respectively, including privatising buying and setting minimum export prices [22,23]. Increases in cocoa prices have been more fully and rapidly transmitted to consumers than decreases, indicating the market power of traders and chocolate manufacturers [24–26] and the increasing concentration due to mergers, and vertical and horizontal integration. Processors Barry Callebaut and Cargill account for 70% to 80% of cocoa processing worldwide, with traders and grinders Barry Callebaut, Cargill, Olam, Ecom, Sucden, Touton, CEMOI, Cocoanect, and Blommer accounting for 60% to 80% of global cocoa processing. The six largest chocolate manufacturers (Mondelēz International, Nestlé, Mars, Hershey's, Ferrero, Lindt und Sprüngli) transform 40% of chocolate products worldwide [14,26,27]. Despite large fluctuations in demand and supply [15], demand for cocoa grew by 3.3% annually from 2002 to 2011 [8,27,28].

These institutional, economic, and market changes and restructuring in the cocoa and chocolate value chain have created space for innovation, particularly new partnerships and sustainability initiatives [29], defined broadly in the terms embraced by the United Nations sustainable development goals as including ending poverty and hunger; improving health and education, water, and sanitation; reducing inequalities; decent work and economic growth; combating climate change; responsible consumption and production; protecting and restoring marine and terrestrial ecosystems; and reversing degradation and biodiversity loss.

As Figure 1 shows, the majority of sustainability initiatives started in the mid-2000s, and have grown significantly, mainly by replication of similar projects and initiatives by different companies, NGOs, and service providers. They have focused on the two main producing countries, Ivory Coast and Ghana, with outscaling to other larger producer countries. Precise numbers of farmers and cooperatives participating, and volumes produced, are not available, as farmers can join more than one trader's initiative and have multiple certifications.

Four types of sustainability initiatives are found in the cocoa value chain to address these multiple, long-running "wicked" problems [29,30]:

(1) Voluntary sustainability standards (VSS) have a programmatic nature, and consist of different interlocking mechanisms of which the most important are standards (codes of conduct), internal management system requirements to allow for group certification, traceability requirements, and systems, independent verification, and consumer facing labels. VSS are usually owned and governed by different stakeholders, including producers, retailers, and NGOs [30]. Retailers, chocolate product manufacturers, traders, and processors have all adopted VSS, which is the main force driving the adoption by producers.

(2) Individual corporate initiatives are a form of corporate social responsibility and self-regulation, whereby a business monitors and ensures active compliance with the spirit of the law, ethical standards, and national or international norms. A firm may engage in actions that appear to further a social or environmental good, beyond the interests of the firm and that required by law [31]. Corporate programmes have increasingly been used by traders-exporters, processors, and manufacturers since the mid-2000s, who have offered packages of interventions or services (such as organising farmers into groups, training, credit, and farm inputs (fertilisers, agrochemicals, cocoa seedlings, equipment) to farmers and their organisations, as a way to secure supplies of cocoa beans of specific quality, produced in specific, often traceable, environmental and social conditions.

(3) Platforms, networks, and associations refer to partnerships of private, public, research, and/or civil society (CSO) or non-governmental (NGO) organisations collaborating on a common goal of sustainability with a declared policy or programme and plan of action.

(4) NGO and CSO campaigns have aimed to raise awareness and lobbied for changes on a sector and chain scale.

Many of these sustainability initiatives overlap: platforms, networks and associations have been used to launch VSS and support the introduction of corporate initiatives. VSS have often been accompanied by packages of services, provided by CSOs, NGOs, and/or government agencies. There exist both producer country agencies, such as via the Ghana Cocoa Board (COCOBOD) in Ghana, and the Fonds Interprofessionnel pour la Recherche et le Conseil Agricole (FIRCA) and Conseil du Café Cacao in Ivory Coast; and consumer country government agencies, such as the Dutch Sustainable Trade Initiative (IDH), and embassy programs, such as German Development Cooperation (GIZ) and Swiss Economic and Development Cooperation (SECO). There have also been projects and programmes funded by international organisations, such as United Nations Food & Agriculture Organisation (FAO) and the United Nations Development Program (UNDP), and World Bank. Traders have also collaborated in a variety of national and international associations and platforms with certifiers, and partnered with research organisations, as well as with government organisations [29].

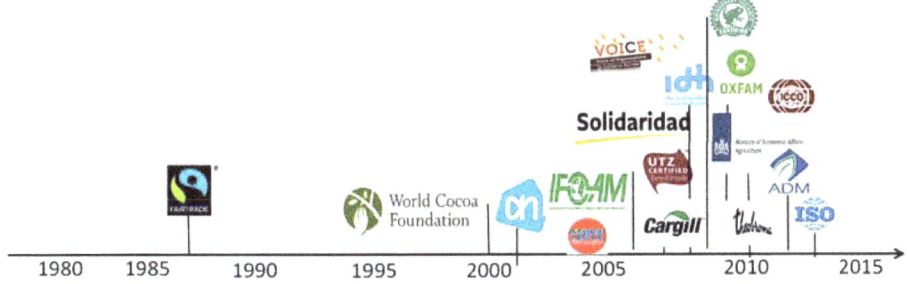

Figure 1. Timeline of cocoa sustainability initiatives in West Africa.

Voluntary sustainability standards have been some of the most notable sustainability initiatives in terms of their increase in scope, scale, and growing coverage of value chain stakeholders. UTZ is a certification program and a label for sustainable farming. UTZ merged with Rainforest Alliance in 2017. UTZ, followed by Fairtrade and Organic, have been the most popular VSS adopted by cocoa traders, chocolate manufacturing, and retail companies from 1987 onwards, shown in Figure 2. In West Africa, UTZ certified cocoa grew sevenfold from 2010 to 2017, by which time 329,978 farmers in Ivory Coast and 144,007 in Ghana were certified, producing 671,854 tons and 176,200 tons i.e., 34% and 19% respectively of the 2016/2017 national production [32–35]. The UTZ standard focuses on mainstreaming sustainability in farming practices, promoting improving farmer's agricultural and management practices, with a chain of custody approaches, traceability, and transparency reflecting concerns by consumers and NGOs about chain governance. Seven of the main trader-exporters and processors in West Africa have adopted UTZ and, often, a second certification scheme.

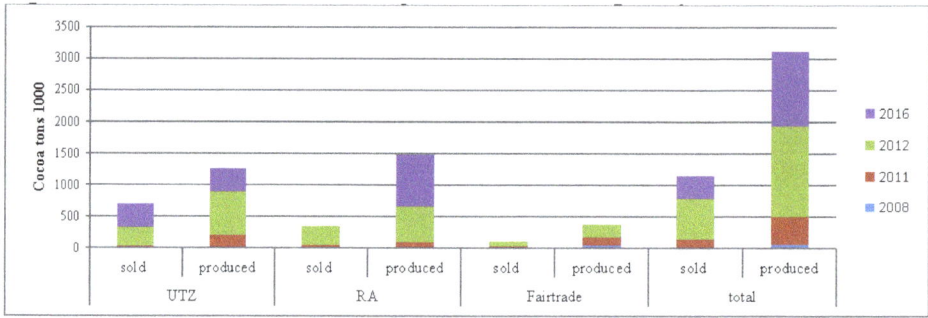

Figure 2. Growth of voluntary sustainability standards (VSS) certified cocoa production and sales globally, from 2008 to 2016. Source: [14,35].

Despite the growing body of literature assessing the impacts of sustainability initiatives [32,36–38], questions remain about whether voluntary sustainability standards and associated interventions are effective, and with what environmental and social-economic outcomes. Many evaluations attempting to answer these questions have been small scale, limited to specific locations, certification standards, and countries; cover a limited time period; and have been published as grey literature, where the methodology and robustness is often unclear. To fill this gap, this study uses a large sample of stakeholders in the two largest cocoa production countries, rigorous qualitative and quantitative methods to investigate the impacts of voluntary certification and related packages of services, asking what has been the impact of sustainability-focused interventions on cocoa farmers in West Africa?

2. Materials and Methods

2.1. Data Collection

To analyse the contribution of sustainability initiatives to farmer livelihoods, panel data were collected from over 778 cocoa farming households in Ghana and Ivory Coast between 2012 and 2017, 18 focus group interviews with farmers, and 22 interviews with other stakeholders in the value chain. Two rounds of farmer household surveys were implemented in each country among UTZ and non-certified farmers (see Table 1). In Ghana, a total of 385 farmers belonging to six cooperatives were interviewed in 2012, and 352 farmers were interviewed, again, in 2015. Two-thirds of the farmers were UTZ certified in both years. In Ivory Coast, 725 farmers belonging to 97 cooperatives were interviewed in 2013 and, in 2017, 426 farmers in 42 cooperatives. The sample size used is considered representative with the majority of farmers (80%) being UTZ certified in both rounds. High attrition rates and the share of farmers no longer certified prevented a random selection of the 2017 Ivory Coast sample. Tests were conducted to explore differences between this sample in 2014 and in 2017. Using regression analysis, the 2017 sample had more farmers in the "good agro-ecological zone", owning a larger portion of their land and with a slightly higher share of cocoa income in their total gross income. These differences, however, did not bias the overall representativeness of findings.

To obtain a representative sample, UTZ farmers and comparable non-certified farmers were selected. Certified farmers were selected randomly from lists provided by UTZ and traders. Non-certified farmers (i.e., neither UTZ or certified by other certification schemes) were selected from lists of households in the community held by village chiefs and, in some cases, by snowball sampling. This group of comparison farmers were selected as being outside the direct influence of UTZ activities and living in communities far enough (at least 15 km) from certified farmers, such that they would not be affected by possible spillover effects. In both countries, UTZ farmers and non-certified farmers were sampled from three different agro-ecological climatic zones for cocoa production (excellent, good, and poor) [39], to allow representative findings at country level.

Table 1. Number of farmers interviewed.

		Sample 2012/2013			Sample 2015/2017	
		Number of Cooperatives	Number of Farmers	Status in 2017	Number of Cooperatives	Number of Farmers
Ivory Coast	UTZ in 2013 & 2017	91	788	606	37	339
	Non-UTZ 2013 & 2017	6	156	156	8	79
	UTZ 2013, Non-UTZ 2017			166		5
	Unobtainable			16		237
	Total	97	944	944	45	426
Ghana	UTZ in 2012 & 2015	6	258	235	6	235
	Non-UTZ 2012 & 2015	3	127	117	3	117
	UTZ 2012, Non-UTZ 2015			0		
	Unobtainable			33		
	Total	9	385	352	9	352
Total		106	1329	1296	54	778

Table 2 provides an overview of the characteristics of certified and non-certified households in the baseline situation. These characteristics were used to compare certified and non certified farmers because they constitute the main observable characteristics of cocoa farmers which are not expected to be directly influenced by certification. In Ghana, certified farmers had a lower share of hired labour and slightly more farms. Certified respondents were also more often female. However, generally, households were fairly similar in the baseline with no statistical differences for 11 of the 14 characteristics. In Ivory Coast, significant differences between certified and non-certified farmers were found, but were limited in size, with non-certified farmers having significantly smaller household sizes and smaller farm sizes (through relatively more under ownership), being older, more often living in agro-ecological zone 2 or 3, and being less dependent on cocoa as a source of income in 2013. These results confirm that the sampled certified and uncertified farmers were fairly comparable.

In addition to the farmer household survey, to increase validity [40], a mixed-method approach was taken, with qualitative data collected in focus group discussions and stakeholder interviews using structured questionnaires. In total, 18 focus group meetings were conducted in the communities where farmers and their cooperatives are located (10 in Ivory Coast in 2013 and 14 in 2017, 8 in Ghana in 2015). In-depth interviews were also conducted with cooperative managers in both periods (6 in Ivory Coast), traders (7 in Ivory Coast and 5 in Ghana), support organisations (2 in Ivory Coast and 2 in Ghana), and school teachers (6 in Ivory Coast).

2.2. Indicators

Indicators for data collection were established based on theory of change impact logics for both countries, developed together with UTZ, IDH, Solidaridad (for Ghana and Ivory Coast) and, also, Cargill (Ivory Coast). The impact logic draws on UTZ's "Better farming, better future" theory of change. These indicators were transposed into the survey, focus group, and stakeholder interview questionnaires. In both countries, environmental, economic, and social indicators, shown in Table 3, were used to measure the outcomes of sustainability activities implemented.

Table 2. Certified and non-certified farmers in the baseline.

Ivory Coast			Ghana		
Variable	Non-Certified	UTZ Certified	Variable	Non-Certified	UTZ Certified
Female respondent	4%	3%	Female respondent *	13%	20%
Household size ***	7	8	Household size	6	6
Farm size ** (ha)	4	5	Farm size (ha)	3.78	4.58
Ownership *	85%	77%	Share of land owned	59%	51%
Oldest plot (years)	23	22	Year establishment farm	1996	1994
Farmer age	52	50	Farmer age	50	49
Agro-ecological Excellent (Zone 1)	51%	50%	Time to farm in minutes	36	35
Agro-ecological Good (Zone 2) **	49%	36%	Number of farms **	59%	71%
Agro-ecological Marginal (Zone 3) ***	0%	15%	Respondent household head	94%	93%
Share of cocoa income ***	82%	93%	Hiring labour	80%	81%
Share cocoa as total land area ***	48%	66%	Household member is purchasing clerk	8%	10%
			Share of female adults	30%	30%
			Education in years household head	7.3	6.7
			Share hired labour ***	9%	4%

Statistical significance: *** ($\alpha = 0.01$), ** ($\alpha = 0.05$), and * ($\alpha = 0.10$).

Table 3. Outcome areas and indicators.

UTZ Outcome Area	Indicators at Farm Scale
Better incomes, better crops (Economic Indicators)	Production practices score [1] Productivity per hectare Production costs per hectare Profit per hectare Total cocoa income
Better lives (Social Indicators)	Social practices score [2] Children working on hazardous farm activities Use of Personal Protective Equipment
Better environment (Environmental Indicators)	Environmental practices score [3] Use of compost Use of shade trees Use agrochemical and waste chemical management

[1] Good agricultural practices defined in UTZ Code of Conduct for Cocoa [41–43] and associated training in relation to plant nurseries, weeding, cocoa tree spacing, input use, frequency of input use, record keeping on input use, management of diseased pods, harvesting practices, use of shade trees, and distance between shade trees. [2] Practices defined in UTZ Code of Conduct for Cocoa [41–43] and associated training in relation to use of protective clothing, with two indicators on chemical waste management (related to safety and health) and on the use of child labour (nominal value 0 to 1). [3] Good agricultural practices defined in UTZ Code of Conduct for Cocoa [41–43] and associated training in relation to shade trees, distance between shade trees, with three indicators concerning treatment of chemical waste and soil quality.

2.3. Farmer Household Data Analyses

The farmer household survey data was quantitatively analysed. To empirically test for the contribution of UTZ certification using the farm household data, a difference-in-difference analysis was conducted. The difference-in-difference analysis compares the change in the performance of the outcome indicators between two moments in time (the first difference) for UTZ certified farmers, compared to changes in the same time period among uncertified farmers (the second difference). The change in outcome indicators (Y), shown in Tables 3–5, is a function of being UTZ certified in both years (UTZ), with (X) differing between Ghana and Ivory Coast, and subscripts i and t denoting household and time period (baseline and endline measurement), respectively. Differences over time might be the consequence of factors other than UTZ certification or the implementation of associated projects, such as specific farmer characteristics. To control for this influence, in our estimation of impact we include a set of farmer characteristics (aside from those controlled for in the sampling design and using panel data), as presented in Table 2. Equation (1) is estimated using ordinary least squares (OLS).

$$\Delta Y_{i,t} = Y_{i,t=0} - Y_{i,t=1} == fn(UTZ_i, X_{i,t=0}) \tag{1}$$

Equation (1) assumes UTZ certification is a one-size-fits-all "treatment", which is not the case (see Introduction). Different farmers received different packages of services alongside certification, such as training, agricultural inputs, and/or credit. As all farmers in the process of certification in 2013 were fully certified by 2017, the associations between the types of services farmers received and different outcomes were evaluated. Four levels of service intensity were identified based on the farmer questionnaires. The services included were finance (advance payments on cocoa or credit), agricultural ("good agricultural practices" (GAPs) as defined in the UTZ Code of Conduct for cocoa) training, cooperative training, management training, social training, access to farm inputs via cooperative or service providers, and free farm inputs. In Ghana, this analysis was not conducted, due to the different context in which certification and associated services occurred. However, the influence of specific certification-related variables was evaluated: whether farmers participated in the certification-related training, the total number of training activities they participated in, and whether or not farmers are lead farmers in certification-related activities.

To empirically test the contribution of different service intensities on the performance of selected indicators, the change in outcome indicators (Y), in Table 3, as a function of service intensity Z, and a selection of farm household characteristics (X), was estimated using Equation (2), where subscripts i and t denote household and time period (baseline and endline measurement) respectively:

$$\Delta Y_{i,t} = Y_{i,t=0} - Y_{i,t=1} == fn(z_i, X_{i,t=0}) \text{ (Ivory Coast, UTZ farmers only)} \tag{2}$$

Equation (2) uses ordinary least squares (OLS) for UTZ certified farmers only, excluding non-UTZ farmers, as the number of farmers receiving higher intensity services levels was too small for advanced statistical analysis. As in Equation (1), a set of farmer characteristics was controlled for. Estimates from Equation (2) should not be interpreted as causal relations as some farmers may have decided to participate in some service packages and some types of farmers may be more likely to become certified than others.

2.4. Building the Counterfactual: Robustness Analysis and Validation

To build a strong counterfactual i.e. "What would have happened without UTZ certification and associated interventions?", the results from Equations (1) and (2) were tested for robustness and combined with the results of qualitative data analysis to triangulate, validate, and explain differences or lack thereof. In Tables 3–5, we indicate results are robust if the quantitative models, discussed below, show similar results in terms of sign and significance.

In Ghana, the models were tested for robustness in two ways. First, an alternative OLS estimation (Equation (1)) using propensity score matching (PSM) was used. The propensity score, defined as the probability of receiving a treatment given observable covariates, was determined using a two-step process. First, the extent to which certified and non-certified farmers are comparable on a range of observable characteristics ("common support") was tested, with common support high (see Table 2), indicating that certified and uncertified farmers are highly comparable. The second robustness test used clustered error terms at village level, to ensure the model was not biased by the similarity of farmers in the same community tending to be more similar than farmers in different communities. In Ivory Coast, as certification programs had started before baseline data was collected, the first test was a simple OLS model to explore baseline and endline differences in isolation. Secondly, Equation (1) was tested for robustness by including the number of years certified in the model. Thirdly, an effect model at the household level was used to control for omitted variable bias. The results are considered as robust when the results of all these models indicate the same direction in terms of sign (positive or negative) and statistical significance. Common support was tested (see Table 2) and found to be high.

Qualitative data were transcribed from interviews and coded based on the indicators, then analysed using content analysis and simple statistical analysis. These results were used to triangulate, validate, and explain results from the quantitative analysis. Preliminary results of all datasets were presented and verified at meetings in Ivory Coast and Ghana attended by cooperative managers, traders, government, and UTZ representatives after each data collection round. During these meetings, an assessment of external and unexpected influences which could affect farmers' performance on the indicators—such as the Ivorian government's reform of the sector and weather effects on cocoa production—was also conducted. Participants also triangulated and interpreted the findings, particularly when different data sources provided different results. Qualitative data was also used to interpret potential spillover effects.

3. Results

The results are presented for the three outcomes areas on the indicators. For each indicator, for the results of the farmer household survey the difference-in-difference coefficient, and whether it is statistically significant is reported and, also, whether the effect is robust to different model specifications and whether there are relationships between the difference-in-difference analyses. Results from the stakeholder interviews are also presented.

3.1. Better Incomes, Better Crops—Economic Indicators

Table 4 presents the status of certified and non-certified farmers on the five economic indicators: production practices, productivity per hectare, production cost per hectare, profit per hectare, and total cocoa income.

Farmers improved the implementation of good agricultural practices related to production over time. While uncertified farmers started at a slightly lower level, their implementation of good agricultural practices increased at the same pace. UTZ farmers perform slightly better, but far from optimal (a score of one). The change over time is slightly higher for non-certified farmers, but differences are not statistically significant. In Ivory Coast, the improvement over time is significantly bigger for farmers receiving the most complete packages of services in the past year.

Cocoa production per hectare increased over time for Ghana and Ivory Coast, although the increase is more prevalent in Ivory Coast. However, overall productivity levels continue to be generally low for all farmers, with an average of 321 kg/ha in Ghana and 480 kg/ha in Ivory Coast. In Ghana, the current level of production, as well as changes over time, were similar for UTZ and non-certified farmers. Whether farmers participated in the programme-related training, the total number of training activities they participated in, and whether or not farmers are lead farmers in the programme, were not related to changes over time. In Ivory Coast, UTZ farmers had significantly higher productivity, in 2013 and in 2017, than non-certified farmers. The average production of UTZ farmers stayed the same between 2013 and 2017, whilst non-UTZ farmers' productivity increased considerably, to 146 kg/ha on average. Since non-UTZ farmers' productivity increased, the difference in productivity between UTZ and non-certified farmers has become smaller. Results are robust for different models. The more services UTZ farmers received, the higher their yield in 2017. For farmers receiving the highest service package intensity, the difference between 2013 and 2017 is statistically significant compared to the changes in cocoa production of farmers receiving no services. Stakeholder interviews and the focus group discussions all highlighted that external factors affect productivity both positively and negatively, particularly weather conditions, with no clear trends for agro-ecological zones, and affecting both UTZ and non-UTZ farmers.

Table 4. Results Economic Indicators.

	Economic Indicators Equation (1)	UTZ		Non-Certified		Effect Equation (1)	Robust	Modalities
		Baseline t = 0	Endline t = 1	Baseline t = 0	Endline t = 1			
Ghana	Production practices score	0.45	0.56	0.39	0.49	0.009		No effects found
	Productivity per/hectare	282.5	311.2	262.5	321.2	−47	Yes	No effects found
	Production costs per/hectare	127.3	385.7	163.8	542.8	−104	Yes	↑ With trainings
	Profit per/hectare	956.5	1274	822.3	1441	−355 **	Yes	No effects found
	Total cocoa net income	3826	5094	3289	5765	−1419 **	No	No effects found
Ivory Coast	Production practices score	0.446	0.497	0.346	0.403	−0.01	Yes	Higher for group 4
	Productivity per/hectare	520	500	256	411	−179 ***	Yes	Higher for group 4
	Production costs per/hectare	22,720	31,125	29,467	33,966	3056.85	Yes	No effects found
	Profit per/hectare	377,238	527,857	160,907	425,113	−116,515**	Yes	No effects found
	Total cocoa gross income	1,692,480	2,575,645	747,808	1,767,034	−128,710	Yes	No effects found

Statistical significance: *** (α = 0.01) and ** (α = 0.05). The model includes the set of covariates as defined in Table 2. Results are robust when all 4 models, defined in Sections 2.3 and 2.4, show similar results in terms of sign and significance.

Overall total net cocoa income increased over time. Farmers experienced a significant increase in total production costs per hectare, attributed to the significant increase in labour costs. The cost of farmer's and their household members own labour is not included in production cost calculations. In Ghana, production costs were higher for farmers participating in training more often. Cocoa price increases offset rising costs of production (especially for hired labour) and increased cocoa profitability, per hectare, for all farmers. The increase in production costs per hectare, profit per hectare, and total income from cocoa (net in Ghana, and gross in Ivory Coast) was not significantly different for certified and uncertified farmers. Profit per hectare and total cocoa income was higher for UTZ farmers than uncertified farmers. The few differences in cocoa income between UTZ and non-certified farmers were attributed to non-certified farmers also having access to farm inputs, services, and training, with increased income attributed to productivity increases as well as, in Ivory Coast, to the sector reform.

In 2017, Ivorian cocoa farmers had, on average, one other source of income, ranging from one to four sources, with 72% of farmers having a second source of income. In contrast, fewer Ghanaian farmers reported other sources of income in 2014 than in 2011 and, those who did, had fewer sources than in 2011. More farmers depended entirely on cocoa in 2014, with no differences in the change in average income earned from other sources for certified and uncertified farmers over time.

3.2. Better Lives—Social Indicators

Table 5 presents the status of UTZ and non-certified farmers regarding three social indicators: implementation of social practices; whether children conduct hazardous activities; and farmers' use of personal protective equipment. For each indicator, the difference-in-difference coefficient and whether it is statistically significant are reported, whether the effect is robust to different model specifications, and whether relations between the difference-in-difference analyses support modalities.

Table 5. Results Social Indicators.

	Social Indicators Equation (1)	UTZ		Non-Certified		Effect	Robust	Modalities
		Baseline t = 0	Endline t = 1	Baseline t = 0	Endline t = 1			
Ghana	Social practices score	0.33	0.44	0.25	0.39	−0.023	Yes	Higher for certified farmers
	Days children <18 on hazardous activities	0	0.12	0.66	1.36	−0.25	Yes	No effect
	Days children <14 on hazardous activities	n.a.	0.17	n.a.	0.66	n.a.	Yes	No effect
	Use of protective equipment	0.34	0.57	0.44	0.63	−0.05	Yes	Higher for certified farmers
Ivory Coast	Social practices score	0.49	0.6	0.41	0.51	−0.01	Yes	No effect
	Days children <18 on hazardous activities	0.25	0.16	0.18	0.14	−0.04	Yes	No effect
	Use of protective equipment	0.21	0.46	0.17	0.35	0.06	Yes	No effect

No statistical significance was found at ($\alpha = 0.01$), ($\alpha = 0.05$) or ($\alpha = 0.10$). The model includes the set of covariates as defined in Table 2. Results are robust when all 4 models, defined in Sections 2.3 and 2.4, show similar results in terms of sign and significance.

The implementation scores for good social practices increased over time in both countries. Certified farmers performed slightly better, but no significant differences were found in improvements over time. A similar pattern emerges for indicators on child labour, use of protective equipment, and waste management. In both countries, there was a reduction in the number of farmers that report using child labour. In Ghana, children under the age of 14 worked significantly fewer days doing hazardous work than children on uncertified farms in 2014 and, for both groups, the number of days is extremely limited: 0.15 days versus 0.6 days per year, respectively, on average. There were no differences in the use of child labour between certified and uncertified farmers in 2011 and 2014, nor was there a noticeable change over time. In Ivory Coast, the proportion of all farmers reporting using child labour decreased over time, however, 14% of uncertified farmers and 16% of UTZ farmers reported children conduct activities prohibited by the UTZ Code of Conduct, which only permits children under 18 to conduct light work on family farms for a limited number of hours, as long as the work does not jeopardise their physical and mental well-being, or interfere with their schooling. In Ivory Coast, 35% of UTZ farmers knew the minimum age for children to work on the farm, compared to 18% of non-certified farmers. On average, 32% of farmers knew the correct minimum age. Knowing the minimum age is weakly positively correlated with being an UTZ certified farmer. The small decrease in the use of child labour was attributed in stakeholder interviews and focus group discussions to improved knowledge about child labour rights and schooling children due to projects and programmes, however, they also highlighted the continuing, general low awareness of farmers in respect of (inter)national labour standards.

In Ghana, few differences over time were found between certified and non-certified farmers in the use of personal protective equipment (PPE). In focus group discussions, most certified farmers attributed positive changes in their health to better health and safety practices, and training on chemical use, waste management, and PPE use. In Ivory Coast, UTZ certified farmers reported better implementation of GAPs on protective clothing than non-UTZ farmers, with no differences between UTZ farmers related to service intensity. UTZ farmers scored 0.46 points (on 0 to 1 scale), which indicates there is room for improvement as farmers do not use all protective items. The difference over time was higher for UTZ farmers, but not statistically significant once other farm and household characteristics were controlled for. Ivorian cooperative managers reported improved working conditions attributed to certification, such as the use of spraying gangs to apply farm chemicals, GAP training, and the presence of first aid kits, combined with community projects which included health centres.

3.3. Better Environment—Environmental Indicators

Table 6 presents the status of farmers from certified versus non-certified farmers regarding 3 different types of social indicators: (1) implementation of environmental practices, (2) whether farmers use compost on cocoa farms, (3) whether farmers have shade trees on cocoa farms, and (4) how they manage chemical waste.

The implementation of good environmental practices increased over time in both countries, although only very marginally in Ghana. Certified farmers performed slightly better than non-certified farmers, and have been catching up to the levels of certified farmers. Cooperative managers and focus groups indicated that soil and water quality had improved, mainly due to less or better input use and implementation of GAPs, and to better water pumps, partly provided by cooperatives and trader partners. In non-certified cooperatives, no such outcomes on environmental indicators were noted.

Table 6. Results Environmental Indicators.

Environmental Indicators Equation (1)		UTZ		Non-Certified		Effect	Robust	Modalities
		Baseline $t = 0$	Endline $t = 1$	Baseline $t = 0$	Endline $t = 1$			
Ghana	Environmental practices score	0.17	0.24	0.13	0.22	−0.039	Yes	No effects found
	Shade trees	0.18	0.33	0.15	0.30	−0.01	Yes	No effects found
	Waste management	0.21	0.33	0.15	0.30	−0.06	Yes	Lower increase for farmers receiving more training
Ivory Coast	Environmental practices score	0.49	0.53	0.46	0.48	0.02	Yes	No effect
	Compost	0.14	0.21	0.04	0.18	−0.08	Yes	No effect
	Shade trees	0.28	0.27	0.19	0.14	0.05	Yes	No effect
	Waste management	0.70	0.75	0.55	0.70	−0.11 ***	Yes	No effect

Statistical significance: *** ($\alpha = 0.01$). The model includes the set of covariates as defined in Table 2. Results are robust when all 4 models, defined in Sections 2.3 and 2.4, show similar results in terms of sign and significance.

In Ivory Coast, more farmers used compost than in 2013 with, on average, 21% of UTZ and 18% of non-UTZ farmers using compost in 2017, compared to 14% and 4%, respectively, in 2013. There is no statistically significant difference between UTZ and non-certified farmers. Regarding shade trees, UTZ certified farmers perform much better but, also on this indicator, non-certified farmers are catching up. In 2013, 19% of UTZ farmers reported planting shade trees in the previous two years, compared to 0.5% of non-UTZ. In 2017, 27% UTZ and 2% non-certified farmers reported planting shade trees in the previous two years. In 2017, 18% of all farmers (of which 85% were UTZ farmers) did not plant shade trees because they already had enough shade trees on the farm. The results in Ghana are contrary to

Ivory Coast (where there was no increase in GAP related to shade trees), but was an improvement in both groups, albeit not statistically significantly different. Scores on five questions regarding how farmers apply and manage agrochemicals and chemical waste were combined into a score between zero and one, with one indicating 100% compliance with GAP. UTZ farmers score higher in both years, although this difference decreased over time as non-certified farmers caught up. UTZ farmers scored 7.2 out of 10 on handling agrochemicals and waste, and non-certified farmers scored 7 out of 10. In the focus group discussions, the majority of farmers noted improved waste management practices and attributed this to training from the Agence Nationale d'Appui au Développement Rural (ANADER)—as part of certification and for non-certified cooperatives. Most cooperative managers also indicated that farmers had improved waste management practices.

3.4. Changes in Service Packages and Intensity

Certification in West Africa was increasingly accompanied by packages of services in the time period studied. In Ghana in 2011, 61% of UTZ farmers indicated that their producer organisation provided at least one additional service other than buying cocoa; in 2015, this increased to 67%. Trader data indicate that service delivery, in terms of the number and intensity of services and number of farmers using them, increased over time, but that not all farmers use the services every year. Certified and uncertified farmer's satisfaction with the services provided over time increased, although not significantly. Numerous projects were implemented in the study area—providing training, seedlings, farm inputs, and community support, similar to that received by certified farmers, for example, the World Cocoa Foundation's Cocoa Livelihoods Program and farmer business schools. In Ivory Coast, since 2012, traders, the Conseil Café-Cacao, and partners, have been supporting farmer organisation, with an estimated 33% [44] to 50% [45] farmers in groups. A growth in the number of projects by government agencies, international donor agencies, traders, grinder-processors, and cocoa manufacturers, as well as by intermediary buyers known as pisteurs, and cooperatives, was perceived. In focus group discussions, in both countries, it was noted that it takes time for some interventions, such as access to farm inputs, and especially seedlings, to have an effect on cocoa productivity and incomes.

4. Discussion

Given these results, the impacts of voluntary certification and related packages of services on cocoa farmers in West Africa are discussed first, followed by the extent to which these outcomes meet sustainability challenges.

4.1. Positive, Mixed, and Modest Impacts of Certification and Service Packages for Farmers

UTZ certified farmers have productivity rates of on average 321 kg/ha in Ghana and 480 kg/ha in Ivory Coast, with farmers achieving up to 1491 kg/ha in Ghana and 1400 kg/ha in Ivory Coast. As production nationally averages between 500 to 600 kg/ha, with potential for 1900 kg/ha in West Africa [1], this finding suggest there continues to be room for major productivity improvements. However, the costs of making these improvements, both financially and in terms of changing farming systems, the effects and trade-offs for other crops and food produced for subsistence use [18], and environmental impacts—such as biodiversity [46,47], need to be taken into account. Certified farmers receiving more intensive service packages have higher productivity levels. Input provision, combined with targeted training, appear to be the most effective interventions. The reliance on one predominant species and dominance of low-yielding cocoa varieties may contribute to low yields, and increases the risk of vulnerability to pests and diseases [48–50]. UTZ farmers in Ivory Coast and Ghana continue to have significantly higher net cocoa income and profit, and higher production and labour efficiency than non-certified farmers, but this decreased slightly in the endline measurements in both countries. Farmers attribute income changes in part due to productivity, but also to external factors such as price reforms, and the weather—highlighting how important short-term, but also longer-term, resilience in responding to climate changes is. Notably, in both countries, farmers faced increased costs—particularly for labour—which decreased profits for all groups, pointing to the importance of looking at cocoa farming as just one part of the resilience of household income generating strategies, a factor highlighted in recent studies [18,25]. Again, over time, non-certified farmer's incomes caught up with UTZ farmers. These findings, related to increased productivity and incomes for certified farmers, match those of other certified commodities [32,36–38].

UTZ certified farmers, however, seem to have reached a plateau in terms of production and income, aided by packages of training and high intensity services. These results suggest that it is difficult to go beyond this ceiling to achieve significant income improvements that result in a living income for the majority of cocoa farmers with the current approach. Also, that scaling up that results in moving a larger group of farmers towards a higher income and profitability has not been possible, although non-certified farmers are catching up to this celling. Productivity increases by non-certified farmers are explained by the fact they have also received similar services and organisational support, although not with the same intensity as the UTZ certified cooperatives. Services are now also being offered to non-certified farmers by pisteurs and traitants (types of intermediary trader-wholesalers) as an incentive to ensure farmer loyalty. Cooperatives have been created and certified as a means to access markets, rather than in the cooperative spirit common in the early years of the UTZ and company programmes. These aspects help explain why farmers are less satisfied with their cooperatives. However, farmers are still happy to have received "new" services and, particularly, the premiums that cooperatives receive are valued and used for a variety of local cocoa, but also, social community development initiatives.

Reasons why non-certified farmers have caught up with certified farmers are that uncertified farmers have also received training, which allowed them to develop in a similar way as certified farmers. such mainstreaming also appears over time for other certified commodities [38]. The impact of input services provided by traders also probably has not taken effect yet, as not all farmers use these services yet, and it takes time for fertiliser applications, pruning, and planting seedlings to affect productivity. Unfavourable climatic conditions were indicated to have negatively influenced productivity in 2014, affecting both uncertified and certified farmers and, thus, was not the impact of certification.

4.2. Sustainability Initiatives: Separating Certification from "Certification Plus"

Both prior to, and during, UTZ certification, there have and continue to be over 40 sustainability interventions [51–54]. Many interventions occur both nationally and on a very local scale, implemented by multiple partners. There is significant similarity between these interventions, and those implemented as part of UTZ, Rainforest Alliance, and Fairtrade certification, which makes it difficult to attribute changes specifically to UTZ certification. Specific activities implemented by traders participating in the UTZ certification programmes included cooperative capacity building, farmer training, farm and farmer professionalisation, provision of inputs and equipment, financial support and enabling access to credit, cooperative, and community development. Strong differences were found between traders' approaches to implementing certification as a stand-alone activity, or as part of a package of activities.

Service packages appear to lead to positive socioeconomic impacts, with specific packages (the "agricultural training + one input" package, and the "agricultural training + pesticides and fertiliser" package) being significantly associated with increased productivity and net cocoa income improvement for UTZ farmers. UTZ farmers with a complete agricultural service package earn a significantly higher net cocoa income and a higher net cocoa income per hectare in 2017. Cocoa income is also higher for UTZ farmers who received a fuller agricultural service package (agricultural training + one input, agricultural training + pesticides and fertiliser). UTZ certified farmers receive more intensive service packages: the majority received more than two services. However, 47% of UTZ farmers experienced a decreased intensity of services in 2017 compared to 2013, which has implications for their productivity and income in the short-term future, which could be expected to remain static.

4.3. Spillover from Certification

Certification provided a means to rapidly upscale sustainable cocoa production and allow farmers to access to certified markets where they aim to benefit from premium prices, as an additional price reward for sustainable cocoa production practices. Certification has promoted more professional producer associations, which farmers perceive as providing a wider range of benefits. Although farmers are generally satisfied, they indicated that services can be improved.

By revitalising the sector, certification appears to have contributed to making cocoa farming more attractive. Other outcomes of certification were that it provided a means for traders, grinders-processors, and manufacturers to rapidly upscale the volumes of certified cocoa production, and allowed farmers to access certified markets where they can benefit from premium prices. However, depending on the standard, between 40% and 80% of cocoa produced as certified gets sold as certified [14]. Certification promoted professional producer associations, which farmers perceive as providing a range of benefits, although some of which farmers and cooperatives indicated these could be improved.

Certification in general, and specifically UTZ in the cases measured, has created ripples at company and service provider level, creating a "cooperative + service package" model that is now common in both the corporate cocoa sector, as well as in government extension service provision. Certification can be seen as a vehicle to which services have been attached, enabling an increased intensity and broader package of services to be provided.

The growth of cocoa certification in Ghana and Ivory Coast since the baseline measurements has meant that there is more chance that non-certified farmers, who are cooperative members and, plausibly, also farmers who are not members of cooperatives, come into contact with certified farmers. This was evidenced by the UTZ data on cooperative growth and locations, the qualitative data, and verification meeting. This means that the chance of spillover of knowledge and practices from certified to non-certified farmers has increased. Farmer data also indicate that certified farmers share lessons from training they have received with other farmers. When farmers share knowledge, they notice that others changed their practices. Therefore, although not anticipated in the UTZ theory of change, spillover effects contribute to the impact of certification.

4.4. Positive Outcomes, but Still Insufficient?

The need for sectoral transformation to achieve "sustainable" cocoa has been heatedly debated, for example, in the annual World Cocoa Conferences, which have brought together many stakeholders in the chain since 2012. Transformation models, so far, have used a supply chain or a sector approach, but despite considerable progress, have not yet led to the desired results [55,56]. Whilst innovations in the sector (particularly certification and public–private partnerships) and upscaling of investment occurring in the cocoa sector on sustainability are recognised, the risk of continuing these current, mainly voluntary, often non-inclusive and unaligned approaches, in the "broken" cocoa supply chain [57], is that only incremental change in the sector will occur. This risk has been emphasised not only by academics [56], but also by cocoa farmer groups [58] and civil society organisations [14,26]. The private sector continues to emphasise the use of public private partnerships to accelerate change [59]. However, these current approaches, whilst sustaining the industry, do so under deteriorating conditions, leading to decreased farmer socioeconomic and environmental system resilience, without enabling smallholders to claim rights, have a voice and greater representation (i.e., transition), or tackle the fundamental causes of smallholder vulnerability. Current approaches also fall short of increasing the resilience of producers to climate change (i.e., transformation) [56], and addressing structural problems in the supply of good quality sustainable cocoa. Sectoral reforms in West Africa have, in contrast, shifted away from the market liberalisation in the 1980s towards more state involvement and regulation of the value chain—including market and pricing mechanisms, licensing buyers and exports, controlling cocoa genetic materials, capacity building of farmers, and aligning private and civil society interventions in the sector.

Sustainable sector transformation, therefore, needs to be holistic, relying not just on public–private partnerships, but on a much wider societal partnership, with public–private–civil society–producer–research engagement. Such a societal partnership needs to recognise conflicts of interests and trade-offs, to address drivers and conditions for change (strengthening demand; sector alignment and accountability; organisation of service providers and the production base; and public and private sector governance) [55], guided by recognition that transformation can occur only if market and regulatory incentives encourage continuous improvement, and if there is sufficient value at farmer level to (re)invest in the sector with limited external assistance.

5. Conclusions

This study shows that the impact of sustainability-focused interventions in the form of voluntary certification and related packages of services on farmers in West Africa has been mixed and modest. On average, the outcomes in terms of farmers' incomes, optimising cocoa productivity, farmer's and farm workers' living and working conditions, agricultural practices and environmental effects have been modest, when assessed over time and in terms of the outcomes experienced by certified farmers compared to non-certified farmers, in similar agro-ecological regions. However, for a smaller group of certified farmers receiving an intensive package of services and farm inputs, certification has had positive, significant impacts on incomes, crops, lives, and the environment. A notable spillover effect is that certification has paved the way for programs that offer more comprehensive service packages, which have resulted in a change in the sector.

These findings suggest that public–private partnerships have created new possibilities by developing voluntary governance arrangements that focus on improving sustainability in value chains. The use of voluntary sustainability standards and supporting corporate initiatives have been extensively scaled up by traders in Ivory Coast and Ghana, with support from chocolate manufacturers, retailers, and tacitly supported by consumer country government organisations in the Netherlands, Germany and Switzerland. These voluntary sustainability standards were then later combined with different initiatives financed and implemented by government agencies, trader's corporate initiatives, CSOs and NGOs, and network, platforms, and associations.

The extent that these voluntary sustainability certification initiatives and associated corporate initiatives have had modest outcomes for the majority, indicates their limits. These findings also point to a need for broad sectoral transformation (in cocoa and agriculture), continued partnerships, plus a range of other policy instruments to address the persistent, wicked problems in cocoa production.

Although pathways to impact foreseen in the theories of change in both countries are largely confirmed, there remains a gap between what certification alone has been expected to deliver and actually has been delivered. Impacts have not been felt by all certified farmers, and the level of impacts have generally been marginal for certified farmers, in general, in terms of crop productivity, incomes, and the environment. Lessons learnt from this study are that, firstly, certification alone has not led to impacts such as improving farmers' livelihoods beyond poverty levels and assuring social risk-free cocoa. A reason is that productivity and income increases are levelling off, which suggests that productivity increases for UTZ certified farmers have plateaued, while non-certified farmers are catching up with UTZ certified farmers. This is also as result of positive spillover effects, which itself can also been seen as an indirect positive impact, not foreseen in the impact logics.

Secondly, pathways to impacts at different scales (farmer level and farmer group) were largely as foreseen: well-functioning cooperatives and trader-led groups formed a vehicle to certification, providing packages of services to members. Training and adherence to the UTZ Code of Conduct was generally associated with better crops, incomes, and environmental outcomes and knowledge applied, in practice.

Thirdly, there were also unanticipated outcomes at producer and company level: a professionalisation of farmers and cooperatives; increased intensity and broader range of services provided mainly by private sector (sometimes hiring in public sector agencies such as ANADER in Ivory Coast) alongside certification and increased farmer satisfaction with cooperatives. There appear to be positive spillover effects as certification activities have been scaled up and certification-related practices (particularly attention on the good agricultural and social practices embodied in the UTZ Codes of Conduct for cocoa) have also been replicated by government, resulting in non-UTZ farmers coming into contact with certified farmers and certification-inspired practices, learning and adopting similar techniques to generate higher productivity and cocoa-related income. Certification can, therefore, be seen as a vehicle to which more services have been attached, enabling an increased intensity and broader package of services to be provided.

These conclusions lead to the following recommendations for societal partnerships implementing sustainability initiatives in the cocoa sector:

(1). Focus on topics that matter most: target interventions more closely to match farmers' varying demographic, economic, and farm characteristics, with tailored mixes of service packages that focus on farmers' specific needs and the most problematic practices relating to child labour, input use, shade trees, and waste management.

(2). Address the specific barriers (such as farmer uncertainty about investing in cocoa related to tenure and fluctuating prices, farm renewal costs) and enablers (such as targeted access to farm inputs and training, taking a farm household approach rather than focusing only on cocoa) to improve sustainable cocoa production and livelihoods of cocoa farmers.

(3). Current incentives of certification and associated services are insufficient to motivate all value chain actors: higher cocoa productivity often entails higher costs for farmers, while not all certified farmers receive a premium, since not all certified produce is sold as certified, due to low market uptake. A stronger uptake of certified cocoa by the industry is needed to reward and compensate certified groups and farmers for their sustainability investments. These factors suggest that investments are needed to close sustainability gaps and reinvent tools to sufficiently and adequately implement and diagnose and address sustainability gaps and underlying causes. This includes tensions of (over)supply and low prices, which harm farmer incomes, risk mitigation and accessing more profitable value chains, and enabling access to credit.

(4). Combine high intensity packages of good agricultural practice training with farm inputs to have higher economic impact. The most successful service delivery models have provided training via cooperatives free of charge for farmers, with fertilisers and agrochemicals generally provided on credit, paid for with cocoa beans. The main risks of this model for farmers and cooperatives are being locked into a supply chain or purchasing contracts that, depending on prices and premiums, may not be attractive. For traders and service providers, there are also risks of providing services and farm inputs to farmers and cooperatives who eventually may default.

(5). Certification organisations, and grinders/processors, traders, and manufacturers providing services, could engage with the government and CSOs to ensure a holistic, complementary, and aligned sector, value chain, and landscape scale interventions. An example is the Cocoa & Forests Initiative, which started in 2017 in Ghana and Ivory Coast, where the majority of public and private stakeholders are involved, and local, national, and international scales of action are connected to address cocoa related deforestation and degradation holistically.

(6). Focus on combining bottom-up farmer and top-down industry and government visions for a sustainable cocoa sector. The current imbalances in power in the value chain between stakeholders in the value chain mean that hearing farmers' and their organisations' voices and visions in partnerships is imperative. Initiatives that strengthen farmers' engagement in societal partnerships, such as emergence of stronger national and international cocoa farmer's organisations, such as the merger between World Cocoa Farmers Organization (WCFO) and the International CoCoa Farmers Organization (ICCFO) are, therefore, critical.

(7). Take a transformational approach to provoke systemic change in the West African cocoa sector. A systemic transformation should address at least the issues of environmental degradation, farmer households, and living incomes, worst forms of labour, and the interlinks between national, regional, and international cocoa market economics and politics, that are currently largely unaffected by certification and corporate sustainability programs.

Author Contributions: Conceptualisation: V.I., Y.W., F.v.R.; Methodology, F.v.R., V.I., Y.W.; Formal Analysis: F.v.R., V.I.; Writing—Original Draft Preparation: V.I., F.v.R., Y.W.; Writing—Review & Editing: V.I., F.v.R., Review: H.G.; Project Administration: V.I., Y.W.; Funding Acquisition: V.I., Y.W.

Acknowledgments: Funding for fieldwork, analysis and separate reports on the panel data for Ivory Coast and Ghana was provided by UTZ, Solidaridad and the Initiative for Sustainable Trade (IDH).

Conflicts of Interest: UTZ, Solidaridad and IDH were funders of separate baseline and endline studies [52,53,60,61] on the impact of UTZ certification and IDH cocoa programs in Ghana and Ivory Coast, the datasets of which have been combined and analysed for this paper. The funders did not have a role in the design of the analyses or data interpretation in this paper and did not cover publication costs of this article.

References

1. Wessel, M.; Quist-Wessel, P.M.F. Review: Cocoa production in West Africa, a review and analysis of recent developments. *NJAS Wagen. J. Life Sci.* **2015**. [CrossRef]
2. Ruf, F. *The Cocoa Sector. Expansion, or Green and Double Green Revolutions*; ODI: London, UK, 2007; p. 3.
3. KPMG. *Cocoa Certification A Study on the Costs, Advantages and Disadvantages of Cocoa Certification*; The International Cocoa Organization (ICCO): Den Haag, The Netherlands, 2012; p. 99.
4. Mejia, R. Increasing Productivity of Cocoa in Côte d'Ivoire, Ghana, Indonesia and Colombia. Master's Thesis, Purdue University, West Lafayette, IN, USA, 2011.
5. Quarmine, W.; Haagsma, R.; Huis, A.V.; Sakyi-Dawson, O.; Obeng-Ofori, D.; Asante, F. Did the price-related reforms in Ghana's cocoa sector favour farmers? *Int. J. Agric. Sustain.* **2014**, *12*, 248–262. [CrossRef]
6. Kessler, J.J.; Brons, J.; Braam, L.; Kuijk, M.V.; Pelders, P. *Social & Economic Effects of Value Chains of Tropical Agro-Commodities & Sustainability Initiatives. Final Report*; Aidenvironment-Planbureau voor de Leefomgeving (PBL): Amsterdam, The Netherlands, 2012; p. 192.
7. FAO. Governance, Coordination and Distribution along Commodity Value Chains. In Proceedings of the FAO Commodties and Trade, Rome, Italy, 4–5 April 2006; Trade and Markets Division, Food and Agriculture Organization of the United Nations: Rome, Italy, 2007; p. 297.
8. Squicciarini, M.P.; Swinnen, J. *The Economics of Chocolate*; Oxford University Press: Oxford, UK, 2016.
9. Owusu-Amankwah, R. *Certifications, Child Labour and Livelihood Strategies: An Analysis of Cocoa Production in Ghana*; Wageningen University: Wageningen, The Netherlands, 2015.
10. Wilson, S.; Vigneri, M.; Serra, R.; Cardenas, A.L. *Researching the Impact of Increased Cocoa Yields on the Labour Market and Child Labour Risk in Ghana and Côte d'Ivoire*; International Cocoa Initiative: Châtelaine, Switzerland, 2016.
11. Ruf, F.; Schroth, G. *Chocolate Forests and Monocultures: A Historical Review of Cocoa Growing and Its Conflicting Role in Tropical Deforestation and Forest Conservation*; Schroth, G., Gustavo, A., Fonseca, B., Harvey, C.A., Gascon, C., Vasconcelos, H.L., Izac, A.-N., Eds.; Island Press: Washington, DC, USA, 2004; pp. 107–134.
12. Matissek, R.; Reinecke, J.; Von Hagen, O.; Manning, S. Sustainability in the Cocoa Sector-Review, Challenges and Approaches. Available online: https://www.researchgate.net/profile/Stephan_Manning/publication/255726498_Sustainability_in_the_Cocoa_Sector_-_Review_Challenges_and_Approaches/links/004635355e173d3e55000000/Sustainability-in-the-Cocoa-Sector-Review-Challenges-and-Approaches.pdf (accessed on 4 November 2018).
13. Nkamleu, G.B.; Nyemeck, J.; Gockowski, J. *Technology Gap and Efficiency in Cocoa Production in West and Central Africa: Implications for Cocoa Sector Development*; African Development Bank: Abidjan, Côte d'Ivoire, 2010.
14. Fountain, A.C.; HUTZ-Adams, F. Cococa Barometer. VOICE Network, FNV Mondiaal, Südwind, HIVOS, Solidaridad, The Netherlands. 2015; p. 48. Available online: http://www.cocoabarometer.org/Cocoa_Barometer/Download_files/Cocoa%20Barometer%202015%20.pdf (accessed on 4 November 2018).
15. Ruf, F.; Siswoputranto, P. *Cocoa Cycles: The Economics of Cocoa Supply*; Woodhead Publishing: Cambridge, UK, 1995.

16. Umaharan, P. *Achieving Sustainable Cultivation of Cocoa*; Burleigh Dodds Science Publishing: Cambridge, UK, 2018.

17. ICCO. World cocoa bean production, grindings and stocks. *ICCO Q. Bull. Cocoa Stat.* **2016**, *XLII*. Available online: https://www.icco.org/about-us/icco-news/317-may-2016-quarterly-bulletin-of-cocoa-statistics.html (accessed on 4 November 2018).

18. Bymolt, R.; Laven, A.; Tyzler, M. *Demystifying the Cocoa Sector in Ghana and Côte d'Ivoire*; The Royal Tropical Institute (KIT): Amsterdam, The Netherlands, 2018.

19. Abbott, P.; Wilcox, M.; Muir, W.A. *Corporate Social Responsibility in International Cocoa Trade*; Purdue University: West Lafayette, IN, USA, 2005.

20. Wilcox, M.D.; Abbott, P.C. Market Power and Structural Adjustment: The Case of West African Cocoa Market Liberalization. In Proceedings of the American Agricultural Economics Association Annual Meeting, Denver, CO, USA, 1–4 August 2004.

21. Eberhard Krain, E.M.; Konan, E.; Servat, E. *Trade and Pro-Poor Growth: Introducing Rainforest Alliance Certification to Cocoa Production in Côte d'Ivoire*; Deutsche Gesellschaft für Internationale Zusammenarbeit (GIZ) GmbH: Eschborn, Germany, 2011.

22. Vellema, S.; Laven, A. Chain governance, sector policies and economic sustainability in cocoa: How to bring the state back in? In Proceedings of the First Conference on Economics and Politics of Chocolate, Leuven, Belgium, 16–19 September 2012.

23. Vellema, S.; Admiraal, L.; Valk, O.V.D. *Quality Control in Cross-Border Agro-Based Supply Chains; Modes of Regulation in Coffee, Cocoa, Bananas, Palm Oil, Timber and Aquaculture*; Agricultural Economics Research Institute (LEI): The Hague, The Netherlands, 2006; p. 37.

24. Jean-François, B.; Bonjean, C.A. Chocolate Price Fluctuations May Cause Depression: An Analysis of Price Pass-through in the Cocoa Chain. Available online: https://halshs.archives-ouvertes.fr/halshs-01074157 (accessed on 4 November 2018).

25. Oomes, N.; Tieben, B.; Laven, A.; Ammerlaan, T.; Appelman, R.; Biesenbeek, C.; Buunk, E. *Market Concentration and Price Formation in the Global Cocoa Value Chain*; SEO Amsterdam Economics: Amsterdam, The Netherlands, 2016.

26. Fountain, A.; Huetz-Adams, F. *Cocoa Barometer 2018*; Voice Network, HIVOS: Amsterdam, The Netherlands, 2018.

27. ICCO. *The World Cocoa Economy: Past and Present*; ICCO: London, UK, 2012; p. 43.

28. Naprta, M. Discussing chocolate market trends. *Agro Food Ind. Hi-Tech* **2015**, *26*, 24–27.

29. Ingram, V.; Waarts, Y.; van Rijn, F. Cocoa sustainability initiatives: The impacts of cocoa sustainability initiatives in West Africa. In *Achieving Sustainable Cultivation of Cocoa*; Umaharan, P., Ed.; Burleigh Dodds: Cambridge, UK, 2018; Volume 5.

30. Salmon, G. *Round Table on Sustainable Development. Voluntary Sustainability Standards and Labels (VSSLs): The Case for Fostering Them*; Organisation for Economic Co-operation and Development: Paris, France, 2002; p. 14.

31. McWilliams, A.; Siegel, D. Corporate social responsibility: A theory of the firm perspective. *Acad. Manag. Rev.* **2001**, *26*, 117–127. [CrossRef]

32. International Trade Centre (ITC). *The State of Sustainable Markets: Statistics and Emerging Trends 2015*; ITC: Geneva, Switzerland, 2015; p. xviii. 148p.

33. UTZ. *10 Years in Coffee, Cocoa and Tea. From Good to Better. Utz Certified Annual Report 2012*; UTZ: Amsterdam, The Netherlands, 2013.

34. ICCO. Production of cocoa beans. *ICCO Q. Bull. Cocoa Stat.* **2017**, *XLIII*. Available online: https://www.icco.org/about-us/icco-news/380-quarterly-bulletin-of-cocoa-statistics-november-2017.html (accessed on 4 November 2018).

35. UTZ. UTZ Cocoa Statistics Report Cocoa 2017. Available online: https://UTZ.org/?attachment_id=13234 (accessed on 30 April 2018).

36. Blackman, A.; Rivera, J. The Evidence Base for Environmental and Socioeconomic Impacts of 'Sustainable'Certification. SSRN 1579083. Available online: https://www.researchgate.net/publication/46456069_The_Evidence_Base_for_Environmental_and_Socioeconomic_Impacts_of_Sustainable_Certification (accessed on 4 November 2018).

37. Potts, J.; Lynch, M.; Wilkings, A.; Huppe, G.; Cunningham, M.; Voora, V. The State of Sustainability Initiatives Review 2014: Standards and the Green Economy. Available online: https://www.iisd.org/pdf/2014/ssi_2014.pdf (accessed on 4 November 2018).

38. Oya, C.; Schaefer, F.; Skalidou, D.; McCosker, C.; Langer, L. Effects of Certification Schemes for Agricultural Production on Socio-Economic Outcomes in Low- and Middle-Income Countries A Systematic Review. Available online: http://www.3ieimpact.org/media/filer_public/2017/03/15/sr34-certification-schemes-agricultural-production_yNjL1OW.pdf (accessed on 4 November 2018).

39. Läderach, P.; Martinez-Valle, A.; Schroth, G.; Castro, N. Predicting the future climatic suitability for cocoa farming of the world's leading producer countries, Ghana and Côte d'Ivoire. *Clim. Chang.* **2013**, *119*, 841–854. [CrossRef]

40. Ton, G. The mixing of methods: A three-step process for improving rigour in impact evaluations. *Evaluation* **2012**, *18*, 5–25. [CrossRef]

41. UTZ Certified. *UTZ CERTIFIED Good Inside Code of Conduct for Cocoa Version 1.0—April 2009*; UTZ Certified Foundation: Amsterdam, The Netherlands, 2009; p. 33.

42. UTZ Certified. *UTZ Certified Good Inside Code of Conduct for Cocoa. Annex: Guidance Document. Version 1.0—July 2009*; UTZ Certified Foundation: Amsterdam, The Netherlands, 2009; p. 18.

43. UTZ. *UTZ Code of Conduct Cocoa Module 1.1-2015*; UTZ: Amsterdam, The Netherlands, 2017.

44. EMC. *Ce Qu'il Faudrait Anticiper*; EMC: Abidjan, Cote d'Ivoire, 2016.

45. GEFAK. *Study on the State of Farmer Cooperatives in the Cocoa Sector of Côte d'Ivoire*; GEFAK: Marburg, Germany, 2015; p. 90.

46. Sonwa, D.J.; Weise, S.F.; Schroth, G.; Janssens, M.J.; Shapiro, H.-Y. Plant diversity management in cocoa agroforestry systems in West and Central Africa—Effects of markets and household needs. *Agrofor. Syst.* **2014**, *88*, 1021–1034. [CrossRef]

47. Gockowski, J.; Sonwa, D. Cocoa Intensification Scenarios and Their Predicted Impact on CO_2 Emissions, Biodiversity Conservation, and Rural Livelihoods in the Guinea Rain Forest of West Africa. *Environ. Manag.* **2011**, *48*, 307–321. [CrossRef] [PubMed]

48. Läderach, P. *Predicting the Impact of Climate Change on the Cocoa-Growing Regions in Ghana and Cote d'Ivoire Final Report*; Climate Change Agriculture and Food Security, International Centre for Tropical Agriculture CIAT: Managua, Nicaragua, 2011; p. 35.

49. Medina, V.; Laliberte, D. *A Review of Research on the Effects of Drought and Temperature Stress and Increased CO_2 on Theobroma cacao L., and the Role of Genetic Diversity to Address Climate Change*; Bioversity International: Rome, Italy, 2017.

50. Medina, V.; Meter, A.; Demers, N.; Laliberte, B. *Review of the CFC/ICCO/Bioversity Project on Cacao Germplasm Evaluation (1998–2010)*; Bioversity International: Rome, Italy, 2017.

51. Ingram, V.; van Rijn, F.; Waarts, Y.; Selten, M. Cocoa farmer models and practices in Ghana and Ivory Coast. In Proceedings of the World Cocoa Conference 2016, Bavaro, Dominican Republic, 22–25 May 2016.

52. Ingram, V.; Waarts, Y.; Ge, L.; van Vugt, S.; Wegner, L.; Puister-Jansen, L.; Ruf, F.; Tanoh, R. *Impact of UTZ Certification of Cocoa in Ivory Coast Assessment Framework and Baseline*; LEI Wageningen UR: Den Haag, The Netherlands, 2014; p. 174.

53. Ingram, V.; Waarts, Y.; Ge, L.; van Vugt, S.; Wegner, L.; Puister-Jansen, L.; Ruf, F.; Tanoh, R. *Towards Sustainable Cocoa. Assessment of Cargill and Solidaridad Farmer Support Activities in Ivory Coast 2008–2012*; LEI Wageningen UR: Den Haag, The Netherlands, 2014; p. 24.

54. Hatløy, A.; Kebede, T.A.; Adeba, P.J.; Elvis, C. *Towards Côte d'Ivoire Sustainable Cocoa Initiative (CISCI) Baseline Study Report*; FAFO: Oslo, Norway, 2012.

55. Molenaar, J.W.; Gorter, J.; Heilbron, L.; Simons, L.; Vorley, B.; Blackmore, E.; Dallinger, J. *Sustainable Sector Transformation How to Drive Sustainability Performance in Smallholder-Dominated Agricultural Sectors?* Aidenvironment, New Foresight, IIED, Commissioned by IFC: Amsterdam, The Netherlands, 2015.

56. Nelson, V.; Phillips, D. Sector, landscape or rural transformations? Exploring the limits and potential of agricultural sustainability initiatives through a cocoa case study. *Bus. Strategy Environ.* **2018**, *27*, 252–262. [CrossRef]

57. Ionova, A. Mars aims to tackle "broken" cocoa model with new sustainability scheme. *Reuters*, 19 September 2018.

58. WCFO. The First Global Cocoa Farmers Conference Accra Declaration. In Proceedings of the First edition Global Cocoa Farmers Conference (GCFC1), Accra, Ghana, 27–28 September 2018.

59. World Cocoa Foundation World Cocoa Foundation. Vision & Mission. Available online: https://www.worldcocoafoundation.org/about-wcf/vision-mission/ (accessed on 1 September 2018).
60. Waarts, Y.; Ingram, V.; Linderhof, V.; Puister-Jansen, L.; Rijn, F.V.; Aryeetey, R. *Impact of UTZ Certification on Cocoa Producers in Ghana, 2011 to 2014*; LEI Wageningen UR: Den Haag, The Netherlands, 2015; p. 50.
61. Waarts, Y.; Ge, L.; Ton, G.; Mheen, J.V.D. *A Touch of Cocoa, Baseline Study of Six UTZ-Solidaridad Cocoa Projects in Ghana*; LEI Wageningen UR: Wageningen, The Netherlands, 2013.

Article

Biodiversity Protection through Networks of Voluntary Sustainability Standard Organizations?

Luc Fransen [1,*]**, Jelmer Schalk** [2]**, Marcel Kok** [3]**, Vivek Voora** [4]**, Jason Potts** [4,†]**, Max Joosten** [5]**, Philip Schleifer** [1] **and Graeme Auld** [6]

[1] Department Political Science, University of Amsterdam, P.O. Box 15578, 1001 NB Amsterdam,
    The Netherlands; p.schleifer@uva.nl
[2] Institute of Public Administration, Leiden University, 2511 DP The Hague, The Netherlands;
    j.schalk@fgga.leidenuniv.nl
[3] The Netherlands Environmental Assessment Agency (*Planbureau voor de Leefomgeving*), P.O. Box 30315,
    2500 GH The Hague, The Netherlands; Marcel.Kok@pbl.nl
[4] International Institute for Sustainable Development, International Environment House 29 Chemin de
    Balexert, 1219 Châtelaine, Geneva, Switzerland; vivek.voora@iisd.net
[5] Department of Political Science & International Relations, University of Geneva, 24 rue du Général-Dufour,
    1211 Genève, Switzerland; max.a.joosten@gmail.com
[6] School of Public Policy and Administration, Carleton University, 1125 Colonel by Drive, Ottawa,
    ON K1S 5B6, Canada; graeme.auld@carleton.ca
*   Correspondence: l.w.fransen@uva.nl
†   Deceased.

Received: 17 September 2018; Accepted: 19 November 2018; Published: 23 November 2018

Abstract: This paper explores the potential for voluntary sustainability standards (VSS) organizations to contribute to policy-making on biodiversity protection by examining their biodiversity policies, total standard compliant area, proximity to biodiversity hotspots, and the networks and partnerships they have in place that can support policy-making on biodiversity protection. The analysis undertaken is based on Social Network Analysis data, in combination with information from the International Institute for Sustainable Development (IISD) Standards and Biodiversity Review and the International Trade Centre (ITC) Standards Map on the focus and operation of VSS organizations. The significance of agriculture-focused private governance for global biodiversity policy and their relationship towards other forms of nongovernmental, governmental, and inter-governmental biodiversity policy are examined and described. We argue that, at present, a number of key agriculture-focused VSS organizations are important policy actors to address biodiversity because of their elaborate biodiversity policies, total compliant areas, and proximity to biodiversity hotspots. However, at present, most of these VSS organizations have relatively few ties with relevant governmental and inter-governmental biodiversity policymakers. The actor composition of their inter-organizational networks currently reflects a focus on nongovernmental rather than governmental organizations while substantively they focus more on development than on environmental protection issues.

Keywords: biodiversity; standards; sustainability; networks; hotspots; agriculture

---

1. Introduction

Policymakers and academics alike are interested in the degree to which Voluntary Sustainability Standard (VSS) policies can contribute positively to biodiversity and/or prevent harm to biodiversity [1]. Issues for discussion include halting deforestation, protecting particular animal and plant species, and preventing soil erosion and its consequences. This interest, at least in part, can be explained by the perceived stalemate in the development of inter-governmental policy-making on biodiversity [2]. VSS organizations, as policy actors developing and governing sustainability-standards, are among a variety of actors and institutions believed to potentially be more active in promoting cross-border advances in biodiversity. VSS organizations may, therefore, potentially be a more dynamic and effective hands-on global biodiversity protection and promotion practice than inter-governmental decision-making has achieved.

Conversely, studies on contemporary agricultural VSS organization efforts to protect biodiversity signals that they are limited to what they can achieve. VSS organization interventions are limited to the agricultural land supporting standard compliant production [3]. VSS organization biodiversity policy, therefore, is constrained in its scale and its contribution to protection [4]. This implies that VSS policymakers cannot go it alone when it comes to addressing biodiversity. VSS organization policy-making efforts to protect biodiversity should therefore be assessed by their potential for collective action and ability to engage with other governance organizations and institutions.

This study takes inspiration from a burgeoning literature studying VSS organization interactions and public-private interactions in the sustainability standard-setting [5–9], and examines the degree to which VSS organizations' current connections with one another, with other non-governmental parties, and with (inter-)governmental treaties, laws, and organizations allow for collectively advancing biodiversity goals. Using policy document and social network analysis [10], the paper assesses the stringency of current VSS biodiversity criteria, compliant land areas and their proximity to biodiversity hotspots, and the degree to which VSS organizations are embedded in networks that allow for collective action in tackling barriers to scaling up and strengthening biodiversity protection.

The study first draws from datasets from Fransen et al. [5], which focused on VSS organizations governing global agro-commodity chains, such as coffee, tea, cocoa, sugar, palm oil, cotton, soy, and flowers. Information from these datasets is then complemented by data on these commodities from the International Institute for Sustainable Development Sustainability Standards Initiative report on standards and biodiversity [1], the International Trade Centre's Standards Map data, and the recent groundbreaking study by Tayleur et al. [11] on the location of agriculture-focused VSS organization standard-compliant areas. As is the convention in academic and grey literature on VSS [1,5,11], we focus on multiple crops, given how many VSS organizations themselves focus on various crops and are therefore expected to affect policy-making on various crops. Combining these four data sources allows us to analyze 11 relevant VSS focused on agro-commodities. To our knowledge, this is the first time that large-N network, geographic data, and VSS organization performance data are combined in this way to make sense of VSS organizations' collaborative potential and potential to cross-fertilize with (inter-)governmental organizations and other actors on an issue area, such as biodiversity.

We argue that a few key agriculture-focused VSS organizations are important policy actors to address biodiversity because of their elaborate biodiversity policies, total compliant areas, and proximity to biodiversity hotspots. However, at present, most of these VSS organizations have relatively few ties with relevant governmental and inter-governmental biodiversity policymakers. Currently, their policy networks, in terms of actors, reflect an orientation towards nongovernmental rather than governmental organizations, and, substantively, an orientation towards developmental rather than environmental protection issues.

The following section examines the literature on VSS organizations and biodiversity. Section 3 presents the datasets and methodological approach that were used for the analysis. Section 4 discusses VSS organization biodiversity policies, coverage, and their networks while Section 5 provides some concluding thoughts.

2. Transnational Private Sustainability Governance Organizations and Biodiversity Policy

2.1. The Emergence of Agro-Commodity Focused VSS

The first wave of agricultural VSS organizations arose via individuals concerned with the impacts of industrialized and intensive forms of agriculture [12,13]. In the US, many individuals were connected via their readership of The Rodale Institute's magazine, Organic Farming and Gardening [14]. In 1972, national organizations working on organic agriculture launched the International Federation of Organic Agriculture Movements (IFOAM) to facilitate information exchange on organic practices and the development of common principles [15]. Fairtrade certification is similarly rooted in diffuse communities interested in alternative trade organizations in Europe and North America since the 1950s. The European Fair Trade Association was formed in 1987 to help national fair trade initiatives share experiences and ideas [16]. By 1997, the Fairtrade Labeling Organizations International (now Fairtrade International or FLO) was established, which now coordinates the standards and labeling work of over a dozen national initiatives [17].

Following a different process, more recent VSS have included dominant actors (e.g., certain Non-Governmental Organizations (NGOs) and retailers) that decide to establish a VSS alone or with a small group of partners and because of multi-stakeholder platforms that have emerged in specific agro-commodities. The WWF has been prominent in this role; it has played a role in establishing initiatives for palm oil (the Roundtable for Sustainable Palm Oil, RSPO) [18], soy (the Roundtable for Responsible Soy) [19]), sugar, and cotton (Bonsucro and Better Cotton Initiative, BCI) [20,21]. Retailers, government development agencies, and philanthropic foundations have helped launch VSS organizations, such as Utz Certified and Cotton made in Africa [20,22].

Recently, scholars have turned their attention to the degree to which VSS organization interactions with other VSS organizations may shape the effects of VSS on sustainable production, rather than studying the effects of VSS on production in isolation [23].

Scholars emphasize that the proliferation of VSS has led to coordination problems, making collective action more complicated. First, competitive interactions may arise when VSS organizations have a similar policy focus and address similar sectors. Competition among VSS organizations may stimulate standard revisions that could benefit effective governance [24], but competition may also lead to implementation challenges, rising costs, and stakeholder confusion [25,26]. Second, VSS organizations that have different policy foci may be less productive in addressing issues that surpass their respective sustainability scope [3]. Authors argue that embedding VSS organizations in networks may help foster more collaborative responses to these challenges [27].

In contemporary VSS policymaking, understanding interactions among organizations descriptively may help us assess the potential for VSS organization's collaboration with other relevant governance actors to address complex sustainability challenges [5]. This is also in line with an evolving research agenda looking at the interactions between VSS organizations and (inter-)governmental policymakers. Interactions studied include partnering among public actors and VSS organization's representatives [28], delegation of or orchestration of (inter-)governmental rules towards VSS [6,9], meta-governance of VSS by governments and international organizations [29], and lobbying by VSS organization representatives towards governmental organizations and vice versa [8].

2.2. VSS and Biodiversity

Collective action among VSS organizations, and interactions between VSS organizations and inter-governmental policy-making, is of special concern in light of their potential for contributing to biodiversity protection. VSS are viewed by policy makers and analysts as a relatively flexible approach to biodiversity protection with some promise. Decades of inter-governmental policy-making have left the world with a set of treaty texts on biodiversity that are mutually inconsistent, lacking in enforcement mechanisms, and prone to varied interpretation by signatory states [2]. Moreover, because of the successful institutional development of international trade governance through the World Trade Organization, and particularly the judicialization of trade dispute resolution among member states, environmental concerns politically tend to lose out relative to the efforts at governing the free flow of goods across borders [30]. Non-state actors, such as VSS organizations, working towards biodiversity protection are perceived as more meaningful, hands-on, and a vehicle for implementing treaties.

VSS organizations focused on agro-commodities are especially relevant given how the agricultural sector, operating on large tracts of land, impacts biodiversity.

Recent studies have therefore sought to gain insight into the potential for VSS to protect biodiversity. Studies focused on VSS organizations operating in the forestry, fisheries, and agro-commodity sectors offer slightly different results regarding biodiversity policy focus and impact. The literature identifies biodiversity protection in the policies and criteria of agricultural VSS organizations [31,32]. In terms of observed impacts, there is evidence that standard compliant farms are more biodiversity-friendly than non-standard compliant farms. However, this claim is not tested for the selection-effect: Farmers that are in a better position to advance biodiversity may opt for certification more than farmers that are less able to do so [33,34]. Observed positive effects include less deforestation, higher species richness, and healthier riparian zones [35,36].

The literature also signals limits to the biodiversity protection policies of VSS organizations, related to the main purpose of VSS as market actor-dependent-instruments. VSS generally are more focused on and better at promoting practices of conservation at the farm than beyond [33], and do a better job of preventing biodiversity harm than promoting biodiversity benefits [34]. They can struggle to offer direct economic benefits to farmers, which may reduce farmer enthusiasm for biodiversity protection [31]. As largeholders have more resources to become certified compared to smallholders, VSS policies are less likely to impact smallholder farms. Moreover, standard-compliant largeholder farms contributing to forest conservation often cannot contribute to habitat conservation [32,37]. Finally, VSS organizations' stakeholders' focus on expanding economic activities that transform natural resources limits the ability to implement policies that limit these transformations [38].

The International Institute for Sustainable Development (IISD) published a report [1] comprehensively dealing with VSS potential to impact biodiversity. To examine how VSS criteria are enabling biodiversity protection on agricultural landscapes, it uses the Biological Impact Indicators for Commodity Production (BIICP) developed by the Secretariat of the Convention on Biological Diversity and its partners. The report finds, first, that at present pace, the VSS examined will represent 10% of production volumes in eight markets (bananas, coffee, cocoa, tea, sugar, palm oil, soybean, and cotton) by 2020, but the agricultural area dedicated to these commodity sectors constitute less than 12% of the global agricultural land area. This means that significant presence in other crops is needed for VSS organizations to have a more meaningful impact on biodiversity protection; second, while most VSS analyzed have a clear emphasis on habitat conversation, only a few focus on climate change, another important driver of biodiversity loss; third, most standards prescribe practices rather than performance outcomes when it comes to biodiversity protection; fourth, it would appear that VSS organizations may not be operating in zones where there are the greatest threats to biodiversity and the absence or proprietary nature of geographic information system data on standard compliant farms prevents a more accurate assessment.

For this reason, many studies propose that the VSS approach to biodiversity protection should be complemented by other policy instruments that ensure that a broader set of biodiversity criteria is addressed, other lands are targeted, or biodiversity is addressed at the landscape rather than the farm level, enabling a more holistic approach to biological protection [32,39]. Complementary interactions should be sought with domestic law and enforcement and other government initiatives in producing countries, as well as with ecosystem service payment initiatives, public-private partnerships, and development assistance policies [40].

2.3. The Importance of Ties among VSS

Academics and policymakers focused on VSS organizations' biodiversity policy stress the relevance of VSS organizations' connections with each other and with other biodiversity-relevant governance organizations [1,5]. Similarly, the IISD report recommends a collaborative approach among various actors for the proper implementation of developing VSS biodiversity criteria, sharing data, researching impacts, and assuring VSS organizations' credibility to protect biodiversity.

For this reason, it is relevant to examine how VSS organizations develop ties with each other and with other policy-relevant organizations. VSS organization interactions with each other are important to reduce certification costs and to encourage policy learning that can result in more effective biodiversity protection policies. Moreover, VSS organizations' interactions with other institutions and actors may contribute to improved biodiversity protection, and biodiversity impacts on larger scales [1]. While recent studies systematically look at linkages among VSS policy-makers and other institutions [5,6,9,28,41], so far, none of these studies have assessed policy networks focused on biodiversity protection in particular. Moreover, so far, none of the studies have viewed the significance of linkages among VSS organizations and other organizations from the perspective of VSS organizations' potential to contribute to biodiversity protection policy-making given its policies and performance.

3. Materials, Analytical Approach, and Methods

3.1. Sample

The agricultural transnational VSS organizations examined were selected based on the availability of data from Fransen et al. [5,41], the IISD Standards and Biodiversity Review [1], and the ITC Standards Map providing data on VSS organizational network structures, policies, and operations. The Fransen et al. dataset sample is based on previous studies, interviews with VSS organization and business professionals conducted between 2010 and 2012. The sampling process led to a final selection of the 11 VSS organizations shown in Table 1 for which we have available data. Because many VSS organizations focus on various crops, and their policy impact is therefore expected to extend beyond single crops, we follow both academic [5,41] and policy-maker studies [1] in casting the net widely and analyzing many crops that have a variety of possible consequences for biodiversity protection. Our sample involves both VSS focused on single crops and VSS focused on many crops and there is overlap in crop focus across many of the VSS organizations.

Table 1. Key Voluntary Sustainability Standard (VSS) organization characteristics. Data from Fransen/Schalk/Auld [41] and Potts et al. [1].

VSS	Sustainability Problem Definition	Product Focus	Development History	Year of Development	Country of Head Offices
IFOAM	Environmental farming practices	Food consumer products	Consumer-local producer movement	1972	Germany
Utz	Farm-level comprehensive standard	Food consumer products	Multinational brand/retail with international NGO	1997	The Netherlands
Rainforest Alliance	Conservation/Biodiversity	Food consumer products	Environmentalists/Science	1987	USA
Better Cotton	Farm-level comprehensive standard	Cotton	Multinational brand/retail with international NGO	2005	Switzerland
Global Coffee Program (4C)	Farm-level baseline standard	Food consumer products	Multinational brand/retail with international NGO	2002	Germany
FLO (present with two standards for hired labor and smallholders)	Equitable development	Food consumer products	Consumer-local producer movement	1997	Germany
CmiA	Equitable development	Cotton	Multinational brand/retail	2005	Germany
Round Table Responsible Soy	Farm-level baseline standard	Food ingredients	Multinational brand/retail with international NGO	2005	Argentina
RSPO	Farm-level baseline standard	Food ingredients	Multinational brand/retail with international NGO	2002	Malaysia
RSB	Farm-level comprehensive standard	Energy	Multinational brand/retail with international NGO	2006	Switzerland
Bonsucro	Farm-level comprehensive standard	Food ingredients	Multinational brand/retail with International NGO	2005	UK

3.2. Analyzing Biodiversity Criteria and Geographic Operations

To gauge their significance, we rank VSS organizations according to three criteria: The amount of hectares covered by a VSS in terms of standard-compliant areas; the proximity of standard-compliant areas to so-called biodiversity hotspots, i.e., regions with significant biodiversity under threat of destruction; and the stringency of biodiversity criteria in the implementation of a given VSS. By doing so, we continue in a tradition of policy research that compares environmental and labor criteria quantitatively [42–45].

For stringency, we create an average stringency score for each VSS organization based on the IISD measure. The IISD report measures the breadth of standards in terms of biodiversity issue coverage, in combination with the degree of obligation associated with requirements on biodiversity in the standard ([1], p. 27). The focus is on so-called critical requirements, i.e., requirements that producers need to meet before being deemed compliant with the standard (as opposed to other requirements that may be met after certification). For this paper, we, in turn, create an aggregate score for this biodiversity stringency per VSS. Both the IISD measures and the aggregate measure have been created in a process using inter-coder reliability and tests with alternative measurements. For the aggregate measure, we report on this below. For IISD operationalization and checks on reliability, we refer to their report [1].

Table 2 shows stringency measures and ranks the VSS organizations according to the average score across the biodiversity indicators. Note that the sample is larger than in the main analysis of the paper because it includes some organizations not covered by ITC data or the data by Fransen et al., and because Fairtrade uses two different standards. The indicator-level ranking is based on the 9 indicators of biodiversity identified by IISD. This is based on 61 sub-indicators, where the organizations can score from 0–5. This means that an organization can score a total of 305 'points'. To robustly see if measuring it based on sub-indicators would have different implications, the sub-indicator level ranking is based on sub-indicators (RSB, for example, scores only 40% on indicator 5 that only has 5 sub-indicators, but scores 100% on indicator 3, which has 11 indicators).

Table 2. Stringency scores of VSS on biodiversity.

Organization	Indicator Level (Ranked)	Sub-Indicator Level (Ranked)	Difference
RSB	85.30% (1)	89.51% (1)	+4.21%
IFOAM	83.05% (2)	77.05% (4)	−6.00%
Proterra	79.72% (3)	80.00% (2)	+0.28%
RSPO	77.03% (4)	79.02% (3)	+1.98%
Utz	70.50% (5)	68.52% (6)	−1.98%
Fairtrade Hired Labor	69.81% (6)	68.13% (7)	−1.68%
Ethical Tea Partnership	69.37% (7)	67.21% (9)	−2.16%
Bonsucro	69.06% (8)	68.85% (5)	−0.21%
Rainforest Alliance	67.29% (9)	67.87% (8)	+0.57%
Global GAP	66.85% (10)	60.00% (10)	−6.85%
RTRS	61.11% (11)	60.00% (11)	−1.11%
BCI	56.48% (12)	50.16% (12)	−6.31%
Fairtrade Smallholders	50.30% (13)	49.84% (13)	−0.46%
Cotton Made in Africa	35.34% (14)	34.43% (14)	−0.91%
Global Coffee Platform	32.00% (15)	32.00% (15)	0.00%

Measuring on the sub indicator level versus on the indicator level does not change the results considerably. The ranking mostly remains in the same order too, only in the middle-part, there are some slight alterations. These changes are caused by organizations scoring high on indicators with not so many sub-indicators or vice versa.

VSS organization coverage is captured in terms of hectares of standard compliant area, based on Standardsmap data.

Biodiversity hotspot data is obtained from the Ecosystem Partnership Fund. To qualify as a biodiversity hotspot, a region must meet two strict criteria: Contain at least 1500 species of vascular plants (>0.5% of the world's total) as endemics (species found nowhere else on Earth) and have lost at least 70% of its original habitat (Critical Ecosystem Partnership Fund). Together, the VSS organizations in our sample certified 430,864,233 hectares, of which 36.3% (156,452,483 hectares) are in countries that contain biodiversity hotspots and 63.7% (274,411,750 hectares) in other countries.

For robustness purposes, we cross-check our estimation of VSS organization compliant areas proximate to hotspots with Tayleur et al. [11]. Their study, due to use of geo-positioning data, offers more precise measurement of proximity to hotspots, but cannot distinguish among different VSS, instead emphasizing commodities being certified by aggregate VSS data. We therefore check whether there is a match between reported compliant areas for a particular VSS organization, the commodity focus of this VSS organization, and the areas detected by Tayleur et al. as being used for farming such a commodity near a hotspot. This matching shows that generally our proxy for biodiversity relevance by using country-level data is good as it, in almost all cases, signals standard-compliant areas near hotspots in these countries. Below, we also report on particular insights from the Tayleur et al. studies where these have important implications for our network analysis findings.

Like the IISD authors, we hold that rankings in terms of stringency, coverage, and hotspot proximity are not a signal of VSS quality or success. A lower amount of hectares covered may, for instance, mean that a VSS organization has chosen to focus on a particular crop, region, or producer type. A lower degree of stringency may mean that a standard has deliberately chosen a narrow set of sustainability requirements for which it considers its intervention meaningful, or that a VSS organization is seeking to offer baseline certification to poor producers that may otherwise not enter certification processes. A VSS organization with many standard-compliant areas near biodiversity hotspots similarly may reflect VSS organization strength in focusing on particular geographic areas without interventions in such hotspots as the VSS organization's core mission.

Nevertheless, a higher or lower position in such rankings indicates a VSS organization's importance in a network of organizations and professionals that could be meaningful in promoting collaboration on biodiversity policy. This is because a VSS organization-node with a high amount of hectares covered may represent a lot of influence on farmers and their environment, as well as many governance activities pertinent to biodiversity; because a VSS organization with strict biodiversity requirements may provide expertise on a wide array of biodiversity-related issues and interventions; and because a VSS organization with relatively more activities close to hotspots can offer both knowledge of activities and conditions in these hotspots as well as potentially meaningful impact on the ground at these hotspots.

Moreover, we are interested to know whether ranking high in terms of stringency, total standard-compliant areas, and proximity to biodiversity hotspots are in any way related. A positive relationship between these three variables would mean that there are VSS organizations with exceptional relevance for biodiversity policy for which we need to closely examine their ties to other organizations. We are therefore interested to learn if higher scores in one ranking leads to higher or lower scores in another (see Figure 1). Are more stringent VSS biodiversity criteria conducive to uptake leading to a higher level of standard compliant hectares for a given VSS organization? Does more standard compliant area translate into greater coverage near or within hotspots? Additionally, do more stringent VSS criteria imply that VSS organizations operate close to or within hotspots?

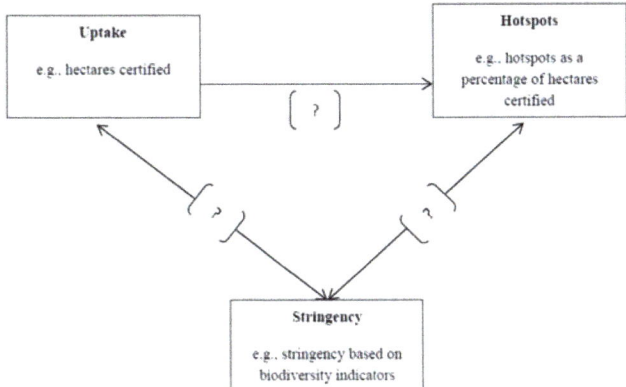

Figure 1. Stringency-uptake-hotspots' relations diagram.

3.3. Gathering Network Data

We examine three different relationship types between the 11 VSS organizations, which we all derive from Fransen, Schalk, and Auld [5,41] in terms of their definition, sample, and operationalization, but nevertheless update so that we can analyze the relationships of VSS organizations in the year, 2017. Social ties can be defined in numerous ways [10,46]. In our methodology, we do not use name generators or a snowball procedure, but rather let the data speak for itself, i.e., network membership is defined based on the appearance of organizations in secondary data obtained from multiple sources that were generated by VSS and other stakeholders, as described below. The main reason for this is that our focus is global, i.e., it transcends individual projects and a single VSS. Most studies on stakeholder management and social networks in biodiversity conservation have a project focus, often a specific region with a specific problem (see e.g., Cohen et al. [47] about Coral reef types targeted in the prioritization of marine areas for the Solomon Islands, or Prell et al. [48]). For such individual projects and case studies, it makes sense to depart from a researcher-defined core network, and ask this smaller subset of key actors, who are important in day-to-day operations.

In our network boundary definition, by contrast, we do not place restrictions on who is a member of the network based on our, or respondents', perceptions of the salience of actors/organizations for the policy at hand. This is because our main interest is not in identifying who is crucial in biodiversity conservation, but in what the overall global patterns of interdependence between VSS and associated organizations look like, and what they may mean for hotspots, stringency, and uptake. In this overall network structure, actors that are unimportant at face value can play a critical (structural) role. In mapping social networks, exhaustiveness and completeness is thus important for our analysis to be meaningful. This is also the reason that we analyze multiple types of relationships rather than a single one. Our approach, however, does come at the cost of losing the more fine-grained information of specific policy issues and actor positions for specific biodiversity projects. Our analysis should be seen as exploratory: We connect the overall VSS network structure to variations in stringency, hotspots, and uptake, without making strong causal claims on network effects.

The first relationship, the existence of actual partnerships and collaborations, we examine by searching across all available online VSS organization documentation in 2017, such as policy documents, annual reports, and newsfeeds, to identify links between VSS organizations and other sustainable agriculture organizations, including NGOs, governments, international organizations, businesses, and academic institutions [25]. Like Fransen et al., we code all these ties as belonging to the same category of partnerships and collaborations, while acknowledging that it is difficult to separate loose one-off partnerships from more institutionalized longer term relationships. It was too time-consuming to track and research each and every partnership individually, and the assumption is that if the VSS themselves find a partnership or collaboration important enough to mention in key documents, like their year reports as an organization, it is significant, and comparable in this sense. Moreover, in hand-coding the documents, multiple coders were involved who discussed projects and collaborations if doubts were raised about their significance. The resulting partnerships and collaborations network thus conveys the existence of collaborative relationships between VSS organizations and other organizations.

Second, using information from 2017 provided by the ISEAL Alliance, the Global Social Compliance Programme, the Ethical Tea Partnership, the Dutch Sustainable Trade Initiative (IDH), the Global Food Safety Initiative (GFSI), and the World Cocoa Foundation, we constructed meta-governance networks, which indicate participation of VSS organizations, NGOs, governments, intergovernmental organizations, academic institutes, and businesses in these seven meta-governance initiatives. Ties examined here include membership and governance roles in meta-governance, as well as voluntarily subjecting standards and policies to equivalence processes, so that standards become comparable. The meta-governance network thus consists of VSS organizations and other organizations, in which a relationship between two actors represents the number of shared memberships across the different initiatives (maximum of six).

Third, like Fransen et al., we analyze VSS policy documents from 2017 for references to other organizations as the basis of standard policies. We structurally compare documents detailing prevailing standard-setting policies. This includes the following categories of documents that are available online and that are comprehensive in their coverage of VSS organization operations (and functionally similar across the sample) in verifying compliance with sustainability requirements: Substantive requirements for businesses and how these should be weighted, auditing policies, policies assuring the origin of a product, and policies regarding the VSS organization's internal governance activities.

Fransen et al. [41] also apply network analysis to employment ties, forming a network of VSS organizations and their affiliated organizations, in which a relationship between a VSS organization and another organization is based on the number of employees who were, or still are, affiliated with both organizations, based on an analysis of the online resumes of the VSS organization employees (in the period of 2002–2012). We find these resumes too dated (2012) to include in the present study. Results are available on request, but do not upset the patterns described here on the basis of the other investigated ties.

We report on measures of these cross-references per organization (including all mentioned VSS policy documents). We code references to different policies and ideas for organizational sub-units within the same organization as it occurred in a VSS policy-document set (specifically the United Nations (UN), International Labor Organization (ILO), International Organization for Standardization (ISO), and the European Union (EU)). For the UN, we differentiated for example between UNDP, UNCTAD or UNHRC. The resulting references' network consists of VSS organizations and other organizations, in which a relationship constitutes the existence of a reference between two actors.

Finally, we use organization profiles from their websites to divide the organizations with ties to agro-commodity-focused VSS organizations into four generic groups: Government and Politics, Non-profit, Business, and VSS. Our analysis may include references to VSS organizations that are not part of our initial selection if the 11 VSS organizations analyzed have ties with them via, for instance, the partnerships or policy references.

4. Results

4.1. Biodiversity Criteria, Coverage, and Proximity to Biodiversity Hotspots

Table 3 shows descriptive statistics of the stringency scores (the average, the highest, and the lowest score per indicator) based on data from the SSI report. RSB is ranked highest most often, while the Global Coffee Platform (4C) and Cotton Made in Africa are ranked lower. As noted, we do not treat this as an indicator of success. Indeed, GCP's score mirrors its ambition to be a baseline standard, and CmiA's score is consistent with its ambition to be focused on social and developmental issues. Across the issue areas, RSB and IFOAM have the most aligned and have the most stringent biodiversity criteria for biodiversity protection.

Table 3. Stringency scores for VSS.

Indicator	Average Score	Highest Score	Lowest Score
1. Percent Farm Area in Land Classes of Different Habitat Quality	65.8%	RSB (100%)	Global Coffee Platform (34%)
2. Conversion/loss of natural habitat cover (land use change over time)	76.67%	RSB and RSPO (100%)	GG (36.67%)
3. Area-based conservation management	64.24%	RSB (100%)	BCI (41.82%)
4. Water Use per Unit Product	81.87%	BCI, Bonsucro, IFOAM, and RSB (100%)	Global Coffee Platform (44%)
5. Synthetic Pesticides and Fertilizer Use per Unit Area or Product	54.67%	IFOAM (100%)	Global Coffee Platform and CMA (24%)
6. Biological Oxygen Demand at Sampling Sites	60.95%	RSB (100%)	CMA (8.57%)
7. Soil Organic Matter	57.67%	IFOAM (100%)	Global Coffee Platform (0%)
8. Fossil Fuel Use per Unit Area or Product	72.80%	Bonsucro and IFOAM (100%)	CMiA (33.33%)
9. Carbon Footprint of Product and Land Use	49.20%	RSB (86%)	CMiA (10%)
Total	64.87% (average)	RSB IFOAM, Bonsucro, RSPO, BCI	Global Coffee Platform and CMiA, BCI

Table 4 reports the average stringency scores for all VSS organizations across the nine BIICPs in Table 3. Table 4 presents the descriptive statistics for standard-compliant area and proximity to biodiversity hotspots and network relationships. The VSS organizations for which we miss network indicators are ranked for other indicators.

Table 4. Descriptive statistics of the IISD, ITC, and network indicators of the VSS organizations.

Organisation	Stringency	Hectares	Hotspots Hectares	Partnership (Degree)	References (Degree)	Meta-Governance (Degree, Weighted)
4C	32.00% (11)	1,424,838 (6)	1,424,838 (6)	24 (1)	20 (5)	123 (2)
BCI	56.48% (9)	1,612,000 (4)	1,612,000 (4)	21 (2)	16 (6)	123 (2)
Cotton Made in Africa	35.34% (10)	585,339 (9)	585,339 (8)	18 (3)	12 (8)	123 (2)
FLO (hired labor)	69.81% (5)	1,295,379 (7)	1,295,379 (7)	7 (7)	26 (2)	123 (2)
IFOAM	83.05% (2)	31,536,885 (1)	28,691,726 (1)	5 (8)	11 (9)	123 (2)
Rainforest Alliance	67.29% (7)	1,431,383 (5)	1,431,383 (5)	12 (6)	23 (4)	251 (1)
Roundtable on Sustainable Palm Oil	77.03% (3)	2,619,436 (2)	2,619,436 (2)	16 (4)	31 (1)	123 (2)
Roundtable on Responsible Soy	61.11% (8)	483,934 (10)	480,204 (9)	0 (9)	16 (6)	251 (1)
Utz Certified	70.50% (4)	1,690,604 (3)	1,690,604 (3)	15 (5)	14 (7)	251 (1)
Bonsucro	69.06% (6)	963,990 (8)	n.a.	18 (3)	25 (3)	123 (2)
RSB	85.30% (1)	n.a.	n.a.	18 (3)	12 (8)	123 (2)
Global Gap	66.85%	1,849,086	1,551,725	n.a.	n.a.	n.a.
ProTerra	79.72%	1,215,349	1,212,849	n.a.	n.a.	n.a.

Overall, VSS organizations with a higher standard compliant area are most active in countries with biodiversity hotspots. We can therefore assume that VSS organizations with a larger coverage in terms of hectares will also matter for biodiversity.

Comparing the scores for standard stringency and standard-compliant areas in biodiversity hotspots suggests that some of the VSS organizations with more stringent standards are also active near biodiversity hotspots, in particular the members of IFOAM, as well as RSPO and Utz. In network terms, we would expect these VSS organizations to prove interesting organizations to link up to, offering both potential impacts as well as varied expertise and experience in terms of promoting biodiversity. An interesting outlier on this list is BCI, with a relatively less stringent standard, but a high proximity to hotspots.

Throughout this study, we must critically ask ourselves whether IFOAM, as the head organization of the organics movement, has a similar status as a transnational organization as the other VSS, in terms of its governing capacity relative to its national chapter organizations. We have reason to believe that much of the politically significant "action" when it comes to organics may take place elsewhere, in comparison to the head organizations of Utz, Rainforest Alliance, and RSPO.

The data by Tayleur et al. [11] confirm this, but add interesting commodity-specific insights. Palm oil certified data (including RSPO's), for instance, position certified areas concentrated in Indonesia and Malaysia, particularly in areas closer to towns and with lower levels of poverty. In biodiversity terms, these areas, compared to non-certified areas, have higher levels of tree loss, and lower coverages of IBAs and protected areas. Coffee and cocoa (the core commodities for Utz, and significant commodities for IFOAM), are certified across Asia, Africa, and Latin Americas in areas relevant for birds, more than in areas that are not certified. For coffee, in particular, areas also included high conservation areas for birds and mammals, more than non-certified areas. Certified tea (also a commodity certified by Utz and covered by IFOAM) production may occur in Asia, Africa, and Latin America in areas with amphibians, and in the study, is more associated with greater protected area coverage than areas without certification. In sum, geographic data shows that VSS organizations with stringent biodiversity policies have certified practices relevant for protected areas, high conservation value areas, birds, mammals, and amphibians. Their policies and activities are therefore geared towards impact on these issues.

4.2. Network Analysis Results

We proceed to describe the VSS organization networks for the four different types of relationships (see Section 3.3). We do so in a non-technical way. For a more elaborate description of the data manipulation and social network techniques applied, we refer the reader to Fransen, Schalk, and Auld [5,41], because the data structure for the networks is the same.

The networks are shown in Figure 2. In all three networks, each node represents an organization. Nodes with more ties are proportionately larger. The type of organization (VSS organization, Non-profit Private, Business, or Government and Politics) is represented by a specific color, according to the legend. When the edge weight is higher—meaning that a tie between two organizations has a higher value—the tie is proportionately thicker in Figure 2b Variation in edge weights only exists for the meta-governance networks. Recall that a link in the meta-governance network constitutes the number of shared memberships. Thus, organizations can have a stronger weighted tie if they share memberships of more meta-governance institutions. In contrast, because of our coding strategy (see Section 3.3), a partnership or a reference either exists or it does not, and thus has no weight. Compared to the other two networks, the meta-governance network is relatively dense (many of the ties between actors that could theoretically exist, actually do exist). This is because a tie between all pairs of organizations is created that are a member of a single meta-governance institution. With a substantial number of member organizations in each institution, the network shows a high level of density overall (in Figure 2b, roughly represented by the different clusters or 'clouds'). Apart from Figure 2, Table 3 provides the number of ties each of the 11 VSS organizations in our sample has in each of the networks, or their 'degree centrality' ([10], p. 178). For the meta-governance network, degree centrality is computed as the sum over all tie values, thus taking into account the edge weights. For all three networks, the higher an organization's centrality, the higher its structural prominence.

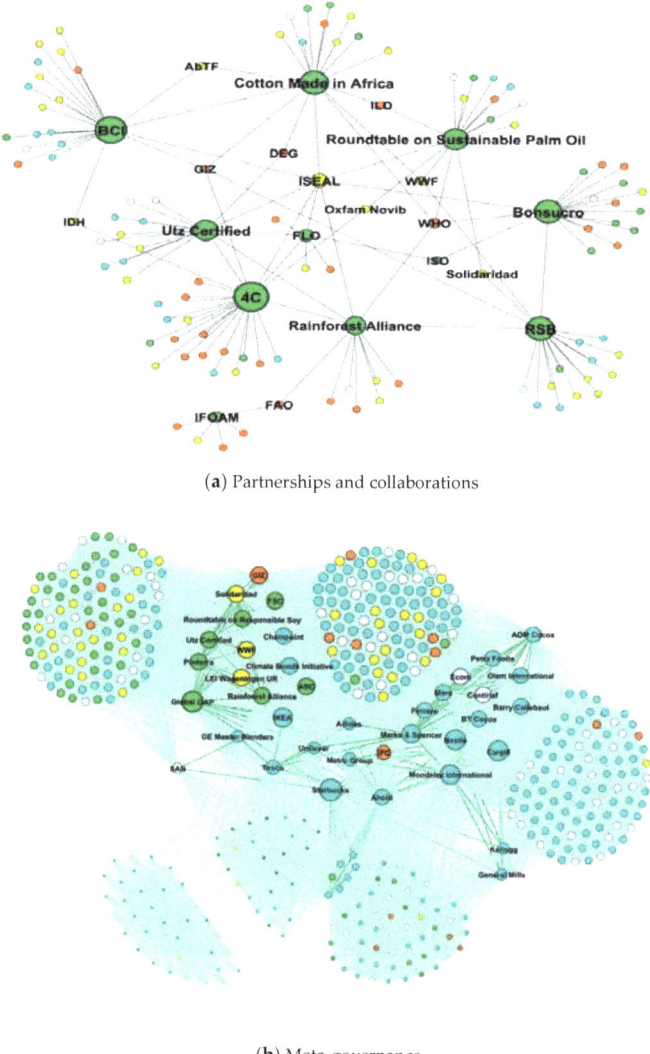

(**a**) Partnerships and collaborations

(**b**) Meta-governance

Figure 2. *Cont.*

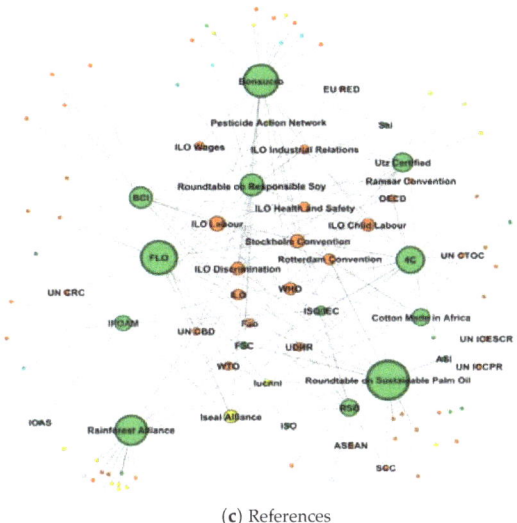

(**c**) References

Figure 2. The VSS networks for partnerships and collaborations, meta-governance, and references. Legend. Node size represents degree centrality. Color represents type of organization: Green = VSS, yellow = non-profit private, blue = business, red = government and politics, light-blue = missing. Edge weight represents the number of shared memberships (meta-governance). Node labels only shown for more central organizations.

A number of tentative interpretations can be derived from Figure 2. First of all, the different networks show different levels of activity, and specific central organizations. The partnership network is relatively sparse, which is most likely a consequence of the effort required: VSS organizations must choose their partners strategically because, due to resources' constraints, it is likely that VSS organizations can only establish a limited number of partnerships. We assume that partnering among VSS organizations can be substantively meaningful, assuring information exchange and building trust, which could be used for collective action purposes [5]. Table 3 shows that GCP and BCI have the most partnerships.

The meta-governance network is relatively dense, but one can question to what extent information exchange actively takes place within each dyad (i.e., pair of organizations). After all, among many of the meta-governance initiatives we studied, substantive exchange and coordination among policy-makers is expected, but not required. Policy-makers from VSS organizations and other governance organizations may not meet [5]. In this network, Rainforest Alliance, Utz, and Roundtable on Responsible Soy have most shared memberships with other organizations. At the same time, a number of VSS organizations not in the core sample of 11 are central in this network, namely Global Gap, ProTerra, and FSC. Finally, the most active 'referencers' are FLO and RSPO.

Second, it appears that more stringent and active VSS organizations are not necessarily more central in the three networks. Recall that IFOAM, RSPO, and Utz are, overall, the most stringent and active (in the stringency percentage, hectares, and activity near biodiversity hotspots). When we look at IFOAM, we observe in Table 3 that it is not central in any of the three networks, compared to the other VSS. This is notable, and signals that the organics movement is in terms of its policy ideas, partners, and employment pool, in a class of its own relative to the other, more mainstream business focused VSS. It also signals that collective action among VSS that includes the organics movement may be harder, also with regard to biodiversity objectives.

RSPO is most central in the reference network, but ranks lower in the other three. Utz is perhaps the most noticeable VSS organizations: Although it ranks lower than IFOAM and RSPO on the biodiversity indicators overall, it is very central in the meta-governance network, and moderately central in the partnership network. A possible contender for Utz in this sense is BCI, which is an interesting outlier in terms of stringency and activity—with a relatively less stringent standard, but a high proximity to hotspots and a dominant role in terms of centrality in the employment ties and partnerships and collaboration networks. The Tayleur et al. data does not cover cotton, which is why we are not able to provide more context on geography here regarding BCI.

Next, we explore the network positions of IFOAM, RSPO, and Utz for the significance of their ties to other organizations claiming to specifically address biodiversity protection in their policies. We then see that IFOAM does have a set of partnerships with international organizations relevant for biodiversity, most notably the Food and Agriculture Organization (FAO), unlike RSPO and Utz.

Furthermore, the three networks are characterized by quite different compositions when it comes to the types of organizations. Most evidently, VSS organizations tend to predominantly refer to government and policy organizations. Among these, the various sub units of the ILO, the Stockholm Convention, and the World Health Organization (WHO) are most popular. The dominance of government and policy partners in this network is most likely indicative of the desire of VSS organizations to legitimate their organization, and to be perceived as a reliable VSS organization regardless of their private nature. Alternatively, it could reflect an effort to be aligned with internationally recognized directives from UN agencies to leverage existing governance efforts from these agencies. Relevant for our purposes here, the links to governmental actors and international organizations within this network signal more of a "developmental" focus of the VSS, rather than a "biodiversity"-focus. Safe for the Stockholm, Rotterdam, and Ramsar convention, most IO treaties referenced seem to focus on social and economic issues reflecting more development despite their potential for biodiversity protection.

The meta-governance network is dominated by business organizations. The most important among these are IKEA, Starbucks, Unilever, Marks & Spencer, Cargill, and Mondelez International. These are significant actors for addressing biodiversity protection in global supply chains, but their linkage to VSS organizations does not imply collective biodiversity protection activities. Solidaridad, IUCN, and the WWF are relevant organizations for VSS organizations across the networks, and, especially the latter two, may prove useful partners in developing biodiversity activities.

In sum, networks of relevant actors in biodiversity protection are relatively sparse. Within the partnership network, deemed most relevant for biodiversity protection, the ties are sparser and not focused on relevant biodiversity policy-makers. Despite being the most significant VSS organization in terms of policies and standard compliant areas, IFOAM does not play a central role across these networks, but does have some relevant partnerships with the inter-governmental biodiversity policy-making world, while Utz and RSPO have mostly links to nongovernmental actors. Overall, the ties between VSS organizations and other types of organizations across the networks seem to exhibit a focus on development rather than on biodiversity protection.

Utz has recently announced a merger with Rainforest Alliance, another important VSS organization in our sample. It remains speculation what consequences this will have for Utz's relevance for biodiversity policies, but if the present links that Rainforest Alliance has in our network analyses remain intact, then this would mean that Utz would reduce its distance towards relevant biodiversity-related organizations, such as FAO.

5. Discussion

With increasing interest in the potential of VSS organizations to contribute to biodiversity protection and policy-making on biodiversity, we have investigated VSS organization standards, operations, locations of certified areas, and network ties. Based on analysis of standard stringency, coverage, and proximity to biodiversity hotspots, we first tentatively conclude that a few VSS organizations are in a promising position to potentially contribute through their policy-making to biodiversity protection goals. At the same time, based on analysis of network positions, VSS organization links to relevant biodiversity actors and institutions are still quite scarce, signaling that their ability to engage in collaborative policy-making and policy exchange with relevant biodiversity policymakers is, at present, limited. Possibly as a heritage of their initial policy focus, VSS organization links to the developmental policy world and to private parties are more prevalent than to the most well-known and relevant public biodiversity policymakers and policies. So, while VSS organizations, such as Utz, the organics movement, and RSPO, should be reckoned with as biodiversity actors, our results still reveal a gap between their activities and policies and the (inter-)governmental biodiversity policy world.

Previous research [48,49] has demonstrated that centrality is important in networks of organizations that seek to steer environmental policy and resource management. We suggest, based on 11 cases, that those in a promising position with regard to their biodiversity criteria, their proximity to hotspots, and total compliant areas are not necessarily the best-connected ones. Further research must (a) substantiate these empirical associations and (b) look at causal effects of network position and stakeholder strategy for project/organization success (e.g., targeting specific actors that were previously unknown in the network). Ours is a first step in the challenging task to 'collate, integrate, and analyse the large amounts of fragmented and diverse biodiversity data to determine the current status and trends of biodiversity in order to inform the relevant decision makers' ([50], p. 50).

While our insights pertain to the agriculture-focused VSS organizations and their relationship to biodiversity, scholars of public-private interactions and policy communities in environmental policy-making may draw broader lessons from our study. First, substantively, our findings suggest that the strategic perspective of agricultural VSS organizations is still developmental focused, despite VSS policymakers engaging with issues, such as climate change and water use. Second, analytically, our paper demonstrates that it may be useful to combine policy document analysis with geo-positioning and social network analysis when discussing the relevance of policy interactions. Arguably, these approaches reinforce each other, and enable us to pinpoint the relevance of actors and policies on a range of different dimensions.

Further research could investigate our observations in more detail. Our approach has limits in terms of its ability to develop social network analysis only for indicators where data gathering can be close to exhaustive. This means that avenues of exchange among biodiversity-relevant actors that are harder to describe completely and reliably (including informal meetings among policy actors, individual presence at conferences, and so on) are hard or impossible to analyze with our methods, and yet may be important for the exchange of ideas and points of view on biodiversity protection. Moreover, the particulars of the combination of datasets forced us to exclude some standards and organizations that are relevant to enrich our understanding of VSS organizations' potential in biodiversity policymaking. New studies may look at the characteristics of these. Next to this, our research offers only a view from the "VSS organization cockpits" when it comes to relevant strategic links to other organizations in the networks. Conversely, we are at present not able to see what links non-VSS organizations, such as the Convention on Biological Diversity (CBD) secretariat, develop by themselves, next to their affiliations to VSS. A further, very relevant avenue for research is therefore to create a more complete picture of the public and private policy network on biodiversity. Obviously, we also encourage much further research on how exchange, collaboration, and coordination efforts at biodiversity protection may or may not have effects on the ground in farms, at plantations, and their environments. We are interested in studies that examine the degree to which interactions among biodiversity-relevant actors and VSS organizations may or may not have the expected positive impacts on biodiversity protection. While the present study cannot directly engage with this issue, it does provide empirical insights that describe the potential for such impacts in the near future.

Author Contributions: Conceptualization: M.K., L.F., J.S.; Data curation: M.J., J.S., L.F., V.V., J.P.; Formal analysis: J.S., M.J., V.V., J.P.; Funding acquisition: M.K., L.F., J.S.; Investigation: L.F., J.S., V.V., J.P., G.A.; Methodology: M.K., J.S., L.F., V.V., J.P., G.A.; Project administration: L.F.; Resources: P.S., V.V., J.P.; Software: M.J., J.S.; Supervision: M.K., L.F.; Validation: P.S.; Visualization: M.J., J.S.; Writing—original draft: L.F., J.S., G.A.; Writing—Review & editing: L.F., J.S., V.V., P.S., M.K.

Funding: This research was funded by the Netherlands Environmental Assessment Agency (PBL).

Acknowledgments: Research for this paper was funded by the Netherlands Environmental Assessment Agency (PBL). We thank Mark van Oorschot, Philipp Pattberg, Oscar Widerberg, and Bas Arts for comments to an early draft of this paper.

Conflicts of Interest: The authors declare no conflicts of interest

References

1. Potts, J.; Voora, V.; Lynch, M.; Mammadova, A. Standards and Biodiversity. State of Sustainability Initiatives. 2017. Available online: https://www.iisd.org/ssi/standards-and-biodiversity/ (accessed on 16 December 2017).
2. Harrop, S. Biodiversity and conservation. In *Handbook of Climate and Environmental*; Falkner, R., Ed.; Wiley & Sons: London, UK, 2016; pp. 37–51.
3. Auld, G. Confronting Trade-Offs and Interactive Effects in the Choice of Policy Focus: Specialized Versus Comprehensive Private Governance. *Regul. Gov.* **2014**, *8*, 126–148. [CrossRef]
4. Van Oorschot, M.; Kok, M.; Brons, J.; Van der Esch, S.; Janse, J.; Rood, T.; Vixseboxse, E.; Wilting, H.; Vermeulen, W.J.V. *Sustainability of International Dutch Supply Chains: Progress, Effects and Perspectives*; PBL Publication No. 1289; PBL Netherlands Environmental Assessment Agency: The Hague, The Netherlands, 2014.
5. Fransen, L.; Schalk, J.; Auld, G. Community structure and the behavior of transnational sustainability governors: Toward a multi-relational approach. *Regul. Gov.* **2018**. [CrossRef]
6. Green, J.F. Blurred Lines: Public-Private Interactions in Carbon Regulations. *Inter. Interact.* **2017**, *2017 43*, 103–128. [CrossRef]
7. D'Hollander, D.; Marx, A. Strengthening private certification systems through public regulation: The case of sustainable public procurement. *Sustain. Account. Manag. Policy J.* **2014**, *5*, 2–21. [CrossRef]
8. Renckens, S. The Basel Convention, US politics, and the emergence of non-state e-waste recycling certification. *Int. Environ. Agreem. Polit. Law Econ.* **2015**, *15*, 141–158. [CrossRef]
9. Henriksen, L.F.; Ponte, S. Public orchestration, social networks, and transnational environmental governance: Lessons from the aviation industry. *Regul. Gov.* **2018**, *12*, 23–45. [CrossRef]
10. Wasserman, S.; Faust, K. *Social Network Analysis: Methods and Applications*; Cambridge University Press: Cambridge, UK, 1994.
11. Tayleur, C.; Balmford, A.; Buchanan, G.M.; Butchart, S.H.; Walker, C.C.; Ducharme, H.; Tracewski, L. Where are commodity crops certified, and what does it mean for conservation and poverty alleviation? *Boil. Conserv.* **2018**, *217*, 36–46. [CrossRef]
12. Dankers, C.; Liu, P. *Environmental and Social Standards, Certification and Labelling for Cash Crops*; Food and Agriculture Organization of the United Nations: Rome, Italy, 2003.
13. Guthman, J. *Agrarian Dreams: The Paradox of Organic Farming in California*; University of California Press: Berkeley, CA, USA, 2004.
14. Haedicke, M.A. *Organizing Organic: Conflict and Compromise in an Emerging Market*; Stanford University Press: Stanford, CA, USA, 2016.
15. Langman, M. Memories and Notes on the Beginning and Early History of IFOAM. 1992. Available online: http://infohub.ifoam.org/sites/default/files/page/files/early_history_ifoam.pdf (accessed on 30 October 2005).
16. Bird, K.; Hughes, D.R. Ethical Consumerism: The Case of "Fairly Traded" Coffee. *Bus. Ethics* **1997**, *6*, 159–168. [CrossRef]
17. Raynolds, L.T. Re-Embedding Global Agriculture: The International Organic and Fair Trade Movements. *Agric. Hum. Values* **2000**, *17*, 297–309. [CrossRef]
18. Schouten, G.; Glasbergen, P. Creating Legitimacy in Global Private Governance: The Case of the Roundtable on Sustainable Palm Oil. *Ecol. Econ.* **2011**, *70*, 1891–1899. [CrossRef]
19. Elgert, L. Certified Discourse? The Politics of Developing Soy Certification Standards. *Geoforum* **2012**, *43*, 295–304. [CrossRef]

20. Sneyd, A. When Governance Gets Going: Certifying 'Better Cotton' and 'Better Sugarcane'. *Dev. Chang.* **2014**, *45*, 231–256. [CrossRef]

21. Schleifer, P. Private regulation and global economic change: The drivers of sustainable agriculture in Brazil. *Governance* **2017**, *30*, 687–703. [CrossRef]

22. Ponte, S. 'Roundtabling' sustainability: Lessons from the Biofuel Industry. *Geoforum* **2014**, *54*, 261–271. [CrossRef]

23. Eberlein, B.; Abbott, K.W.; Black, J.; Meidinger, E.; Wood, S. Transnational Business Governance Interactions: Conceptualization and Framework for Analysis. *Regul. Gov.* **2014**, *8*, 1–21. [CrossRef]

24. Overdevest, C. Comparing Forest Certification Schemes: The Case of Ratcheting Standards in the Forest Sector. *Socio-Econ. Rev.* **2010**, *8*, 47–76. [CrossRef]

25. Marx, A.; Wouters, J. Competition and Cooperation in the Market of Voluntary Sustainability Standards. 2014. Available online: https://papers.ssrn.com/sol3/papers.cfm?abstract_id=2431191 (accessed on 19 November 2018).

26. Fransen, L. The Politics of Meta-Governance in Transnational Private Sustainability Governance. *Policy Sci.* **2015**, *48*, 293–317. [CrossRef]

27. Bernstein, S.; Cashore, B. Can Non-State Global Governance Be Legitimate? An Analytical Framework. *Regul. Gov.* **2007**, *1*, 347–371. [CrossRef]

28. Bitzer, V.; Glasbergen, P.; Leroy, P. Partnerships of a feather flock together? An analysis of the emergence of networks of partnerships in the global cocoa sector. *Glob. Netw.* **2012**, *12*, 355–374. [CrossRef]

29. Derkx, B.; Glasbergen, P. Elaborating global private meta-governance: An inventory in the realm of voluntary sustainability standards. *Glob. Environ. Chang.* **2014**, *27*, 41–50. [CrossRef]

30. Clapp, J.; Dauvergne, P. *Paths to a Green World: The Political Economy of the Global Environment*; MIT Press: Cambridge, MA, USA, 2005.

31. Blackman, A.; Naranjo, M.A. Does eco-certification have environmental benefits? Organic coffee in Costa Rica. *Ecol. Econ.* **2012**, *83*, 58–66. [CrossRef]

32. Rueda, X.; Lambin, E.F. Responding to globalization: Impacts of certification on Colombian small-scale coffee growers. *Ecol. Soc.* **2013**, *18*, 21. [CrossRef]

33. Tscharntke, T.; Milder, J.C.; Schroth, G.; Clough, Y.; DeClerck, F.; Waldron, A.; Ghazoul, J. Conserving biodiversity through certification of tropical agroforestry crops at local and landscape scales. *Conserv. Lett.* **2015**, *8*, 14–23. [CrossRef]

34. Milder, J.C.; Newsom, D.; Lambin, E.; Rueda, X. Measuring impacts of certification on biodiversity at multiple scales: Experience from the SAN/Rainforest Alliance system and priorities for the future. *Policy Matters* **2016**, *21*, 14.

35. Hughell, D.; Newsom, D. *Impacts of Rainforest Alliance Certification on Coffee Farms in Colombia*; Rainforest Alliance: New York, NY, USA, 2013.

36. Takahashi, R.; Todo, Y. The impact of a shade coffee certification program on forest conservation: A case study from a wild coffee forest in Ethiopia. *J. Environ. Manag.* **2013**, *130*, 48–54. [CrossRef] [PubMed]

37. Ruysschaert, D. The Impact of Global Palm Oil Certification on Transnational Governance, Human Livelihoods, and Biodiversity Conservation. *Policy Matters* **2016**, *21*, 45–58.

38. MacDonald, K.I. The devil is in the (bio) diversity: Private sector "engagement" and the restructuring of biodiversity conservation. *Antipode* **2010**, *42*, 513–550. [CrossRef]

39. Visseren-Hamakers, I.J.; Arts, B.; Glasbergen, P. *Partnership as Governance Mechanism in Development Cooperation: Intersectoral North-South Partnerships for Marine Biodiversity*; Edward Elgar: Northampton, MA, USA, 2007.

40. D'Hollander, D.; Tregurtha, N. Exploring the potential of government and voluntary standards collaborations to scale up sustainable production and supply. *Policy Matters* **2016**, *59*, 60–72.

41. Fransen, L.; Schalk, J.; Auld, G. Work ties beget community? Assessing interactions among transnational private governance organizations in sustainable agriculture. *Glob. Netw.* **2016**, *16*, 45–67. [CrossRef]

42. Dietz, T.; Auffenberg, J.; Chong, A.E.; Grabs, J.; Kilian, B. The Voluntary Coffee Standard Index (VOCSI). Developing a Composite Index to Assess and Compare the Strength of Mainstream Voluntary Sustainability Standards in the Global Coffee Industry. *Ecol. Econ.* **2018**, *150*, 72–87. [CrossRef]

43. Fuchs, D. Business and governance. In *Globalization*; Schirm, S., Ed.; Taylor & Francis: London, UK, 2006.

44. McDermott, C.L.; Noah, E.; Cashore, B. Differences that 'matter'? *A framework for comparing environmental certification standards and government policies. J. Environ. Policy Plan.* **2008**, *10*, 47–70.

45. Fransen, L. *Corporate Social Responsibility and Global Labor Standards: Firms and Activists in the Making of Private Regulation;* Routledge: New York, NY, USA, 2012.

46. Scott, J. *Social Network Analysis*, 4th ed.; Sage: London, UK, 2017.

47. Cohen, P.J.; Evans, L.S.; Mills, M. Social networks supporting governance of coastal ecosystems in Solomon Islands. *Conserv. Lett.* **2012**, *5*, 376–386. [CrossRef]

48. Prell, C.; Hubacek, K.; Reed, M. Stakeholder Analysis and Social Network Analysis in Natural Resource Management. *Soc. Nat. Resour.* **2009**, *22*, 501–518. [CrossRef]

49. Mills, M.; Álvarez-Romero, J.G.; Vance-Borland, K.; Cohen, P.; Pressey, R.L.; Guerrero, A.M.; Ernstson, H. Linking regional planning and local action: Towards using social network analysis in systematic conservation planning. *Biol. Conserv.* **2014**, *169*, 6–13. [CrossRef]

50. Hoffmann, A.; Penner, J.; Vohland, K.; Cramer, W.; Doubleday, R.; Henle, K.; Penev, L. Improved access to integrated biodiversity data for science, practice and policy—The European Biodiversity Observation Network (EU BON). *Nat. Conserv.* **2016**, *6*, 49–65. [CrossRef]

MDPI

St. Alban-Anlage 66

4052 Basel

Switzerland

Tel. +41 61 683 77 34

Fax +41 61 302 89 18

www.mdpi.com

Sustainability Editorial Office

E-mail: sustainability@mdpi.com

www.mdpi.com/journal/sustainability

Lightning Source UK Ltd.
Milton Keynes UK
UKHW050814150221
378796UK00003B/29